Images of an American Land

Images of an

Vernacular Architecture

American Land

in the Western United States

Edited by Thomas Carter

University of New Mexico Press
Albuquerque

First Edition

Library of Congress
Cataloging-in-Publication Data

Images of an American land : vernacular architecture studies in the Western United States / edited by Thomas Carter.— 1st ed.
p. cm.
Includes bibliographical references and index.
ISBN 0-8263-1729-4 (cloth).
ISBN 0-8263-1730-8 (pbk.)
1. Vernacular architecture—West (U.S.)
2. Ethnic architecture—West (U.S.)
I. Carter, Thomas.
NA725.I42 1997
720'.978—dc20
95-41803
CIP

Contents

List of Illustrations vii
Preface xiii

Places and Processes

1 Introduction: A Theory for Western Vernacular Architecture
Thomas Carter 3

Transplanting Traditions

2 False-Front Architecture on Montana's Urban Frontier
Kingston Heath 21

3 Folk Design in Utah Architecture, 1849–1890
Thomas Carter 41

Adaptations and Innovations

4 The Calef's Farm in Oregon: A Vermont Vernacular Comes West
Philip Dole 63

5 Dry Creek: Central Nevada's Damele Ranch
Blanton Owen 91

Cultural Convergences

6 When a Room Is the Hall: The Houses of West Las Vegas, New Mexico
Chris Wilson 113

7 Russian Churches, American Houses, Aleut People: Converging Cultures in the Pribilof Islands, Alaska
Alison K. Hoagland 129

Cultural Diversity

8 A Chinatown of Gold Mountain: The Chinese in Locke, California
Christopher L. Yip 153

9 Keeping House: Women, Domesticity, and the Use of Domestic Space in Nineteenth-Century Nevada
Margaret Purser 173

Urbanization

10 The Real Estate Associates: A Land and Housing Developer of the 1870s in San Francisco
Anne Bloomfield 201

11 Innovation without Paradigm: The Many Creators of the Drive-in Market
Richard Longstreth 231

Exploiting Resources

12 The Historic Industrial Landscape of Butte and Anaconda, Montana
Fredric L. Quivik 267

13 American Modernism in the West: Hoover Dam
Richard Guy Wilson 291

Contributors 321

Credits 324

Index 325

Illustrations

1.1 Movement of ideas 4
1.2 Major nuclei and regions of the West 7
1.3 The West as a cultural region of the United States 12
2.1 Bannack, Montana, ca. 1905 20
2.2 Sketch of Bannack by an English visitor, 1863 24
2.3 Miner's cabin, Nevada City, Montana 25
2.4 Antecedents to the false front 26
2.5 St. Paul Saloon, Unionville, Montana 27
2.6 Bannack's main street in the 1860s 28
2.7 Sod-roof store/house with later false front nailed to existing log facade 30
2.8 Gable-ended log store/house with appended sawn board facade 30
2.9 Massing and styling techniques for false fronts in Montana 32
2.10 Bannack's Skinner Saloon 34
2.11 Detail of Hudson Bay, or *piece sur piece,* framing technique 35
2.12 Labeau's Jewelry (Colorado Store), Virginia City, Montana, ca. 1863–70 36
2.13 Granite, Montana, 4 July 1894 37
3.1 Stone house in Harrisburg, Utah, with Pine Valley Mountains in background 42
3.2 Aerial photograph of Ephraim, Utah 46
3.3 Log house, Spring City, Utah 48
3.4 Rough ashlar wall of oolite limestone with scored mortar joints 48
3.5 An example of "bricking" 48
3.6 Brigham Young's house, Salt Lake City 49
3.7 Principal vernacular house types found in the Mormon West, 1849–90 50
3.8 Allred House, Spring City, Utah, mid-1870s 52
3.9 Mason House, Willard, Utah, mid-1860s 53
3.10 Judd House, St. George, Utah, ca. 1870 54
3.11 Gardner House, Mendon, Utah, 1880s 55

3.12 Jonathan Platts House, Salt Lake City, 1850s 55
3.13 Facade variations in Spring City, Utah, hall-parlor houses 56
3.14 Design diversity in one-and-a-half-story, dormered houses in the nineteenth-century Mormon West 57
4.1 View of the prairie from the Calef farm buildings 62
4.2 Map of the Calef property and neighboring farms 64
4.3 House and typical barn of the 1850s 66
4.4 Armitage barn (1877) and house (1856) 66
4.5 Ira Calef House and connected barn in Vermont, ca. 1870 68
4.6 Principal elevation of the Elmer Calef House 68
4.7 First-floor plan of the Elmer Calef House 69
4.8 Floor plan of the Robert Campbell House, Willamette Forks, Oregon 72
4.9 The A. V. Peters House, Eugene City, Oregon 73
4.10 Elmer Calef House, with four daughters on porch, ca. 1900 75
4.11 Elmer Calef barn, end elevation seen from the house 77
4.12 Plan of the Elmer Calef barn 79
4.13 Elmer Calef barn, section looking north 81
4.14 Details of braced purlin and tie girt at eave 81
4.15 Plan of Economy's barn, Seattle, Washington 82
4.16 Barn and attached shed, Mount Hope, Connecticut 84
4.17 Site plan of the Elmer Calef farm buildings 85
4.18 Ira Calef House and neighbors, 1900 86
5.1 Link Eddy and Benny Damele at Dry Creek Ranch 92
5.2 Entrance to Dry Creek Ranch 93
5.3 Aerial view of Dry Creek Ranch 93
5.4 Mud-and-willow cabin at Dry Creek Ranch 97
5.5 Mud-and-willow cabin at Dry Creek Ranch 97
5.6 Mud-and-willow wall construction of the Bates cabin 97
5.7 Bunkhouse on Dry Creek Ranch 99
5.8 Stockade fencing at Dry Creek Ranch 99
5.9 Mud-and-willow loafing shed at Dry Creek Ranch 100
5.10 Mud-and-willow loafing shed at Dry Creek Ranch 101
5.11 Dry Creek Ranch buildings 102
5.12 Blacksmith shop at Dry Creek Ranch 103
5.13 Open-fronted stone stable at Dry Creek Ranch 104
5.14 Open-fronted stone stable at Dry Creek Ranch 104
5.15 Chicken house at Dry Creek Ranch 105
5.16 Hay derrick at Dry Creek Ranch 105
5.17 Bunkhouse at Dry Creek Ranch 106
5.18 Main house at Dry Creek Ranch 107

5.19 Main house at Dry Creek Ranch 107
6.1 Sena-Silva House, stages of a changing tradition 114
6.2 Manuel Romero House (Casa Redonda), ca. 1875–1900 116
6.3 Julianita Romero de Baca House, ca. 1870 119
6.4 Julianita Romero de Baca House 119
6.5 1501 South Pacific Avenue, ca. 1879–82 120
6.6 324 Perez Road, ca. 1902 122
6.7 Rivera-Huie House, ca. 1865–90 122
6.8 Rivera-Huie House 123
6.9 Tafoya–C. de Baca House, ca. 1875–1925 124
6.10 Tafoya–C. de Baca House 124
6.11 Blanchard-Gallegos House, ca. 1875 126
6.12 Blanchard-Gallegos House 126
7.1 Aleut barabaras, St. Paul, Pribilof Islands, 1888 131
7.2 First church (1821) constructed on St. Paul, Pribilof Islands 132
7.3 St. Paul, Pribilof Islands, as drawn by I. G. Voznesenskii, ca. 1843 132
7.4 Aleuts in stylish clothes in front of their wood-framed house 135
7.5 St. Paul, Pribilof Islands, 1891 135
7.6 Second church (1873–75) constructed on St. Paul, Pribilof Islands 137
7.7 St. George church and village, from the water, Pribilof Islands 139
7.8 Houses built by U.S. government for Aleuts on St. Paul, Pribilof Islands 141
7.9 Houses built by U.S. government for whites on St. Paul, Pribilof Islands 141
7.10 Saints Peter and Paul Russian Orthodox Church, Pribilof Islands 142
7.11 Saints Peter and Paul Russian Orthodox Church, Pribilof Islands 143
7.12 Interior of Saints Peter and Paul Russian Orthodox Church, Pribilof Islands 144
7.13 St. George the Great Martyr Russian Orthodox Church, Pribilof Islands 145
7.14 St. George the Great Martyr Russian Orthodox Church, Pribilof Islands 145
7.15 St. George the Great Martyr Russian Orthodox Church, Pribilof Islands 146
7.16 Interior of St. George the Great Martyr Russian Orthodox Church, Pribilof Islands 146
7.17 Fog-enshrouded village of St. George, Pribilof Islands 148
8.1 Main Street, Locke, California 154
8.2 Levee Street, Locke, California 154
8.3 HABS Drawing, Dai Loy Gambling Museum, plans 158
8.4 HABS Drawing, Dai Loy Gambling Museum, elevations 159
8.5 HABS Drawing, Dai Loy Gambling Museum, section 159
8.6 HABS Drawing, Locke, California, site plan 161
8.7 Alley, Locke, California 162
8.8 Alley, Locke, California 163
8.9 Alley, Locke, California 163
8.10 Levee Street, Locke, California 164

8.11 HABS drawing, Main Street, east elevation, Locke, California 165
8.12 13936 Main Street, elevation, Locke, California 165
8.13 Vegetable gardens, Locke, California 166
8.14 HABS Drawing, Main Street, west elevation, Locke, California 168
8.15 Key Street, Locke, California 171
9.1 Wash-day in the backyard, ca. 1875 174
9.2 Main Street, Paradise Valley, ca. 1890 177
9.3 Floor plan types, town houses 180
9.4 Plat map, Paradise Valley, 1879 182
9.5 Plat map, residential property, Paradise Valley, ca. 1900 183
9.6 Meyer-Echeverria House plan, ca. 1881–1910 184
9.7 Freemont-Gastenaga House plan, ca. 1900–1910 184
9.8 Read-Case House, ca. 1895–1920 185
9.9 Read-Case House plan, ca. 1895–1920 185
9.10 Byrnes House plan, ca. 1915–20 186
9.11 Ugaldea House, ca. 1917–30 187
9.12 Ugaldea House plan, ca. 1917–30 187
9.13 Taylor-Riley House plan, ca. 1900–1920 188
9.14 O'Neal-Harvey House, ca. 1885–90 189
9.15 O'Neal-Harvey House plan, ca. 1885–90 189
9.16 Riley House plan, ca. 1910–18 190
9.17 Ritchie-Harvey House, ca. 1890–1905 191
9.18 Ritchie-Harvey House plan, ca. 1890–1905 191
9.19 Morey-Liotard House plan, ca. 1885 193
9.20 Liotard family beside their newly clapboarded home, ca. 1910 193
10.1 2643–2667 Clay Street, San Francisco, 1874–75 200
10.2 San Francisco, northeast portion, showing improvements through 1867–68 203
10.3 Number of buildings erected in San Francisco, 1860–80, 1890 204
10.4 Map of San Francisco, northeast portion, with locations of lots with houses built and sold by T.R.E.A. 206
10.5 920–945 Valencia Street, San Francisco, 1876–77 207
10.6 330–342 Lexington Street, San Francisco, 1876–77 208
10.7 San Francisco, block bounded by Mission, Valencia, Twentieth, and Twenty-first Streets, as subdivided by T.R.E.A. 1875–76 209
10.8 Doorway, 1689 Sutter Street, San Francisco, 1875 210
10.9 2315–2319 Webster Street, San Francisco, 1878 210
10.10 1712 and 1710 Bush Street, San Francisco, 1875 212
10.11 Villa 2373 California Street, San Francisco, 1876 212
10.12 Northeast corner of Twenty-first and Bartlett Streets, San Francisco, 1876 213
10.13 Stairs, 1513 Golden Gate Avenue, San Francisco 214

10.14 T.R.E.A. Building, 230 Montgomery Street, San Francisco, 1876–77 215

10.15 2564 Sacramento Street, San Francisco, 1871 216

10.16 William Hollis, *San Francisco Call,* 30 June 1895 218

10.17 Retaining wall, 1848 and 1836 Pine Street, San Francisco, 1875 220

10.18 T.R.E.A. advertisement, *San Francisco Chronicle,* 9 May 1875 221

11.1 Wilshire at Fourteenth Drive-In Market, Wilshire Boulevard, Santa Monica, California 233

11.2 Wilshire and Harvard Market, Wilshire Boulevard, Los Angeles 234

11.3 Mesa-Vernon Market, Crenshaw Boulevard, Los Angeles 235

11.4 Taxpayer block, South Vermont Avenue, Los Angeles, ca. 1925 237

11.5 Commercial buildings, including Mac Marr food store, South Vermont Avenue, Los Angeles, mid- to late 1920s 238

11.6 Sunset-Western Market, Sunset Boulevard, Los Angeles 242

11.7 Wilshire Boulevard, Los Angeles 245

11.8 Beverly Boulevard at La Cienega, Los Angeles 245

11.9 Von's Grocery unit of Palm Market, Wilshire Boulevard, Beverly Hills 247

11.10 Alpha Beta Market No. 28, Philadelphia Street, Whittier, California 247

11.11 Beverl'y Open Air Market, Beverly Boulevard, Los Angeles, 1925 249

11.12 Unidentified design for a drive-in market, ca. 1929 250

11.13 Plaza Market, Pico Boulevard, Los Angeles 252

11.14 Chapman Park Market, West Sixth Street, Los Angeles 253

11.15 Leess Drive-In Market, North Vine Street, Los Angeles 253

11.16 Mission Motor-In Market, Sunset Boulevard, Los Angeles 254

11.17 Clock Market, Wilshire Boulevard, Beverly Hills 256

11.18 Mesa-Vernon Market 256

12.1 Location map of Butte and Anaconda 268

12.2 Foundation ruins and waste dumps from silver-mining activity west of Butte 270

12.3 Map of Anaconda showing locations of major industrial facilities 273

12.4 Roundhouse and shops at the BA&P's West Anaconda Yards 274

12.5 Tuttle Manufacturing and Supply Company 275

12.6 Ruins of the Upper Works 276

12.7 Site plan of the Washoe smelter 277

12.8 The Washoe stack 279

12.9 Surviving steel headframes on the Butte Hill 280

12.10 Site plan of the Anselmo mineyard 281

12.11 Anselmo mineyard 282

12.12 Hoist house at the Anselmo mine 283

12.13 Rainbow Falls Dam 284

12.14 Rainbow Falls powerhouse 285

12.15 Steel transmission towers from 1910, Elk Park, east of the Continental Divide 286

12.16 Steward mine 286

13.1 Hoover Dam, downstream face with water overflow test 295
13.2 Hoover Dam, plan and section 296
13.3 Hoover Dam, highliners at work on canyon wall 298
13.4 Hoover Dam, placing concrete in column forms 299
13.5 Hoover Dam, construction of dam and intake towers 300
13.6 Los Angeles Times Building, Los Angeles 301
13.7 Hoover Dam, artist's conception of dam, power plant, and Arizona outlet works 303
13.8 Hoover Dam, Gordon B. Kaufmann's conception of dam, power plant, and Arizona outlet works as approved 304
13.9 Hoover Dam, downstream face and powerhouse as completed 305
13.10 Hoover Dam, Nevada entrance tower with sculpture by Oskar J. W. Hansen 306
13.11 Hoover Dam intake towers at night and Lake Mead 307
13.12 Hoover Dam, Arizona spillway 308
13.13 Hoover Dam, Nevada wing of powerplant 309
13.14 Hoover Dam, *Winged Figures of the Republic* by Oskar J. W. Hansen 311
13.15 Hoover Dam, Nevada spillway 313
13.16 Hoover Dam, aerial view with Lake Mead 314

Preface

One of the principal changes in American architectural historiography during the last decade has been the increased attention scholars have given vernacular architecture. Vernacular architecture is an admittedly awkward term that has come over time to refer to the numerically common and therefore representative buildings of a particular community, region, or area. That such ordinary buildings are being considered at all is surprising since architectural history has customarily been written from the standpoint of a few exceptional achievements—the Parthenons and Taj Mahals of the world—divorced from their less spectacular and often seemingly disreputable surroundings. Times change, however, and such narrow, elitist thinking has become untenable as older Western European, male, capitalist hegemonies have failed.

The so-called new social historians of the 1960s led the way toward the vernacular revolution by producing strange histories that talked about people rather than events, about common people rather than the elite, and about culture rather than chronology. Minorities and the marginalized, the poor and the disenfranchised, the everyday and mundane found their way into the new history, and it was a democratic approach to the past that eventually came to have an equivalent in architectural studies. By the 1980s a new type of architectural history emerged where scholars recognized, really for the first time, the existence of economic, racial, and gender distinctions in the built environment.

The discovery of vernacular architecture began in the East. There the new architectural historians were first concerned with reinterpreting preindustrial building traditions of the original colonies, but slowly the vision expanded to embrace all kinds of everyday buildings placed in their everyday contexts. Vernacular architecture as a field of inquiry now includes buildings from all historical periods and from all parts of the country, including the West, although it should be admitted that the study of vernacular architecture in the western United States has barely begun. This collection of essays was created as a kind of exploratory first step in the process of rewriting the history of architecture in the West. It is intended to call attention to the region's rich though generally overlooked architectural resources while at the same time proposing a general method for studying them.

The central notion in this book is that the study of western architectural history, if it is to be useful at all, must be divorced from the romantic tradition that so clearly dominates the field today. The West means many things to many people: Cowboys and Indians come to mind, as do sagebrush deserts, expansive blue skies, rushing clear rivers, and (at least to me) endless slopes of untracked powder snow for skiing. It is all these things and more, but I would bet that for most Americans in the late 20th century, it remains primarily what it was from the start, and this is a place of refuge. The West is now often called "The Last Best Place," but this is not a new idea. From the beginning of western settlement, the frontier country lying beyond the hundredth meridian was popularly viewed as a place where people could escape the all too civilized world knowingly and willingly being created in the East (a designation which from a westerner's perspective curiously includes regions as diverse as the North, the South, and the Midwest). By the end of the Civil War, the East was becoming increasingly urban and industrial, its people living more and more in suburbs and worrying about crime in the nearby cities. Days were marked off by time clocks that left little time for freedom and adventure, and as the rich got richer, opportunities for economic advancement became fewer and fewer. Horace Greeley said it first, but his words echo for succeeding generations of Americans: "Go west," and if it's not fortune you seek, it may be just some clean air, or fewer cars, or a new start, or some open space. The West remains, as it was, the Last Best Place.

The image of the West as refuge is a romantic one because it is full of longing for something loved and lost. What is gone is the presumed innocence and dignity of preindustrial life, and we look for it, expecting to find it "out West." The fascination with the cowboy—generally but simplistically perceived as a rugged man acting alone in nature—is not surprising if you think about it, for through him countless generations of Americans have touched, albeit mostly vicariously, the world we think we have lost. We need this West—the romantic West—for all the right reasons. Just knowing it is there, or at least some of it is still there, is comforting for people who lead hectic urban lives. The romance of the West is anything but silly. Like millions of others, I never get tired of watching the buffalo in Yellowstone National Park.

We should not be embarrassed about this slightly perverted western love affair, nor should we deny its existence. For more than anything else, it tells us a lot about who we are as Americans, of our abiding need for refuge. At the same time, it is important to admit, frankly and openly, that this romanticized version of the West is only part of the story. While pining away for a lost love it is easy to ignore blemishes and forget realities. The West has both. The story of western settlement certainly has its romantic side. For example, there was open land and the promise of a new life for my own great grandparents, Joe Billy and Julia Smith, who came to Ruby Valley, Nevada during the 1860s. But there were hardships too. The valley's severe winters, it's cultural isolation, and general lack of medical and school facilities are elements that turn up repeatedly in family stories. And there were other realities. Access to the last best place was and continues to be available to a select few. As in the West generally, opportunities in Ruby Valley were there for people who had some capital to begin with, and paradoxically, ones who could quickly connect with Eastern markets. The Smiths and their descendants survived and prospered in Nevada by hauling foodstuffs and supplies, first by ox team and then by truck, to early urban centers of the region like Ely, Eureka, and Pioche, and later to places like Salt Lake City, Las Vegas, and Los Angeles. The point here is simply that the western story is a complicated one. The true West is one of both romance and reality, of refuge and opportunity, of stewardship and exploitation.

From all this it appears that the history of the western United States is best told from the perspective of Americanization. Up to about 1820, the part of North America that was to become the West was one place. After the opening of the Santa Fe Trail, the Oregon Trail, and all the other trails, railroads, and highways, it was quite another. What happened was simply that the land was opened up for settlement and people came. They came for many reasons—some romantic and benign, others probably quite pragmatic and ruthless—but underlying the whole drama was a general reconfiguration of the place into an *American Place.* The values, beliefs, and practices of American capitalism guided settlement here as it had in other regions of the country. The main difference maybe was that in the West the country was so dry and so vast that it could not be developed by traditional agricultural methods, nor could it be completely occupied. Nevertheless, the signs of Americanization are all there. As much as possible the land was used (to make money from timber, minerals, cattle, fish, and grain), the wilderness tamed (and made safe for human consumption), its life ordered (cowboys are after all only wage-laborers in the larger corporate system), and its resources plundered (in the 1890s Eureka Nevada was one of the most polluted cities in the country).

One hundred and fifty years of American occupation have left their mark on the land, the people, and the buildings. Western architecture is more than anything else American architecture, and while the easy thing to do would be to confine ourselves to studying buildings that fit the romantic notion of the West, concentrating on such things as settler cabins built of stone, lonely log ranch houses, and red tile roofed adobe haciendas, it would be dishonest. We have to make it all much harder and more truthful by complicating the architectural portrait with such things as suburban track houses, factories and smelters, and steel-and-glass office towers.

Together, all these kinds of buildings constitute the architecture of the American West, and they are all *Images of an American Land.*

This book presents ten essays intended to start people thinking in new ways about western architectural history. We as authors have conspired jointly in this endeavor, but must acknowledge certain debts. First and foremost we thank Carl Inoway, Dean of the University of Utah's Graduate School of Architecture. Carl believed in us from the start and provided the money that brought together in April of 1989 a group of scholars to discuss the question of just what western architecture was all about. Dell Upton (University of California–Berkeley), Paul Groth (University of California–Berkeley), Blanton Owen (Nevada State Commission on the Arts), Chris Wilson (University of New Mexico), Robert McCarl (Idaho Arts Commission), and John Vlach (George Washington University) were there, as were Peter Goss and Dean May (University of Utah). The idea of the "West as America" emerged strongly from this meeting and led me to work further with western historians like Donald Worster, Patricia Limerick, and particularly, my (one-time) colleague at the University of Utah, Richard White. These historians at the time were engaged in rewriting western history from a regional standpoint and their influence is evident throughout the volume.

The work has also been aided by a research grant from the National Endowment for the Humanities (NEH). The NEH money was for another, larger project, but the grant application provided the introduction and the initial incentive for gathering together these essays. The work of compiling, editing, and producing the volume has taken longer than anticipated, but the authors have remained patient, and I thank them for that. The University of Utah provided funds for graduate students Susan Anderson and Alan Barnett to prepare drawings and Holly Horten, the Graduate School of Architecture secretary, helped me juggle all the pieces so they landed in the right places. For all these people, I hope that seeing the final product helps make it all seem worthwhile.

Finally, the process of working through this material helped me get to know my own parents, Bob and Beth Carter. This book is for them, children of the West, actual westerners.

Thomas Carter

Places and Processes

CHAPTER ONE

Introduction

A Theory for Western Vernacular Architecture

THOMAS CARTER

Images of an American Land introduces a method for looking at and thinking about the vernacular architecture of the western United States. Defined generally as the buildings common to a particular region or community, vernacular architecture has proven itself a worthy addition to the larger discipline of architectural history. On one hand, the interest in ordinary buildings has significantly broadened the scope of traditional architectural history, pushing it beyond the architect-designed monuments that have been its normal domain. And on the other, because the major emphasis in vernacular architecture research has been on cultural history, tendencies toward connoisseurship—treating the artifact removed from its social and cultural context—have been tempered with a new concern for understanding the powerful relationships between people and their material world.

The authors in this volume follow an increasingly familiar path in using the term vernacular architecture to denote not a particular type of building but rather an approach to architectural history that has several distinctive components.[1] First, vernacular architecture research encompasses the widest possible range of buildings. While the tendency has been for architectural historians to study either the high-style creations of the elite or the common buildings of the masses, vernacular architectural research, with its emphasis on entire architectural communities, aspires to look at both ends of the economic spectrum, and everything in between. After all, it is the connections between these buildings that helps us understand better the particular cultural conditions that produced them.

A second aspect of vernacular architecture research is that the approach assumes the cultural historian's objective of studying human behavior in past time. The principal driving force in vernacular architecture research is a fundamental belief in the artifact as historical evidence. Buildings and building landscapes encode in tangible form deeply held and often otherwise unstated cultural, social, and eco-

Figure 1.1. Movement of ideas. The arrows in Professor Glassie's map indicate "the directions in which folk cultures were carried out of the source areas by diffusion and migration." (Reprinted, by permission, from Glassie, *Pattern in the Material Folk Culture of the Eastern United States,* 38)

nomic values. Students of vernacular architecture have as their goal the task of moving, in the words of folklorist Henry Glassie, "away from a concern for the [building's] fabric itself toward the ideas that were the cause of the fabric's existence."[2]

The strongest push in vernacular architecture research has occurred along the Atlantic seaboard where studies of colonial building traditions have aided historians in piecing together a portrait of early American life. Midwestern research has dutifully charted the extension of eastern building practices into the Heartland and described the emergence of a national vernacular building style during the early nineteenth century. Vernacular architecture studies in the West, however, with "the West" defined here as that part of the United States lying west of the ninety-eighth meridian, have lagged behind, with notable exceptions in the Hispanic Southwest and the Mormon-settled Great Basin. Fieldwork throughout the region has increased, aided to a great extent by the survey efforts of the various state historic preservation offices, but the kind of theoretical sophistication that typifies most recent vernacular architecture research in the East is missing. This failing is best explained by the absence of an effective model for organizing and interpreting the abundant architectural resources of the West. In short, what we lack is theory.[3]

Students of vernacular architecture in the eastern United States rely on a cultural diffusion paradigm established during the 1960s by cultural geographers and folklorists (fig. 1.1). According to this view, distinctive American architectural traditions emerged in response to the specific environmental, economic, and social conditions of the New World. During initial settlement, English, Dutch, German, and Swedish colonists held tenaciously to familiar Old World practices, but as regional economies developed during the colonial period, local modifications to the imported building traditions occurred, yielding distinctive regional vernacular architectures in New England, the Hudson River Valley, the Delaware River Valley, and the Chesapeake Bay. From these colonial "hearth" areas, building ideas and practices spread inward with the advancing frontier, where they further fused into the regional traditions of the upland South and Midwest. While diffusion studies are no longer viewed as legitimate ends in themselves, they have been extremely useful in bringing the vernacular architecture of the East and Midwest into better focus by tying it to a specific settlement process.[4]

However beneficial it may be, the diffusion model breaks down in the West precisely because there the steadily east-west moving frontier upon which the theory is based also breaks down. In both the popular mind and the scholarly literature the West stands as the last American frontier, but it has defied facile regional synthesis for several reasons.[5] First, Americans settled it at a time when the United States as a whole was already in the throes of industrialization. From the beginning of American occupation the region exhibited a combination of agricultural, commercial, and industrial exploitation that inextricably tied it to the markets and power centers of the East. Second, the West never experienced the kind of steady and sustained growth associated with other American frontiers. The movement of people and resources into the region was intermittent, often came from various points in both the East *and* the West, and invariably followed the vagaries of the national economy.

The legacy of such a complex settlement history is a diverse architectural mosaic reflecting the various ethnic, religious, and occupational backgrounds of the people, all tempered by the often harsh realities of the environment itself. But the vernacular architectural landscape of the western United States is not the kind of isolated, preindustrial landscape that vernacular architecture researchers are accustomed to finding in a frontier context. Nor is it one that fits neatly into the existing pattern of American settlement geography. Noted geographer Donald Meinig tackled the western cultural landscape by proposing an alternative pattern of development. Rather than a continuous westward-moving line of settlement, the West, according to Meinig, is composed of various subregions separated by a vast and inhospitable territory, each developing separately and having their own spheres of influences (fig.1.2). Meinig writes:

> Although folk colonization is always selective and uneven in area, in the East the general tide of settlement was relatively comprehensive, and local nuclei and salients in the vanguard were soon engulfed and integrated into a generally contiguous pattern. Obviously such a description rests upon a particular scale of observation, but holding to the same scale, the pattern in the West is a marked contrast: several distinctive major nuclei so widely separated from one another and so far removed from the advancing front of the East that each expands as a kind of discrete unit for several decades, only gradually becoming linked together and more closely integrated into the main functional systems of the nation.[6]

Meinig's model is useful in describing the West's subregions, but it ignores certain factors that work to unite the area into a single region rather than to further divide it. There are, that is, architectural and cultural similarities in the subregions that cannot be denied. Ungainly as it may appear, this landscape—spectacularly beautiful and often ruthlessly exploited—is the American West and it is the landscape that begs exegesis. Any attempt to explore its distinctive regional qualities must begin with an understanding of the special circumstances of western history itself.

But what of western history? What are its main precepts and theories? Until recently, western history has been synonymous with frontier history, and "frontier" in this sense has a definite meaning. In the 1890s the distinguished historian Frederick Jackson Turner introduced his now famous frontier thesis, describing the frontier, that ever-present, contiguous body of free land that lay along the advancing line of settlement, as the principal factor in shaping American democratic institutions. Turner defined the frontier largely in terms of *process;* on the frontier, constant renewal occurred as Americans, and European immigrants being turned into Americans, were forced to retrace their steps from a primitive, preindustrial social condition to a civilized and industrial one. The continual settling of successive belts of unoccupied land allowed all generations of Americans to relive the agricultural past of their ancestors and thereby participate in what Turner saw as the "perennial rebirth" of the nation. The Turner Thesis is essentially a tale of modernization, a vehicle for charting the inevitable and inherently progressive march of American communities toward their place in the modern world.[7]

For all its persuasiveness the Turnerian model has had an enervating effect on western historiography. By stressing the modernization process, frontier-oriented

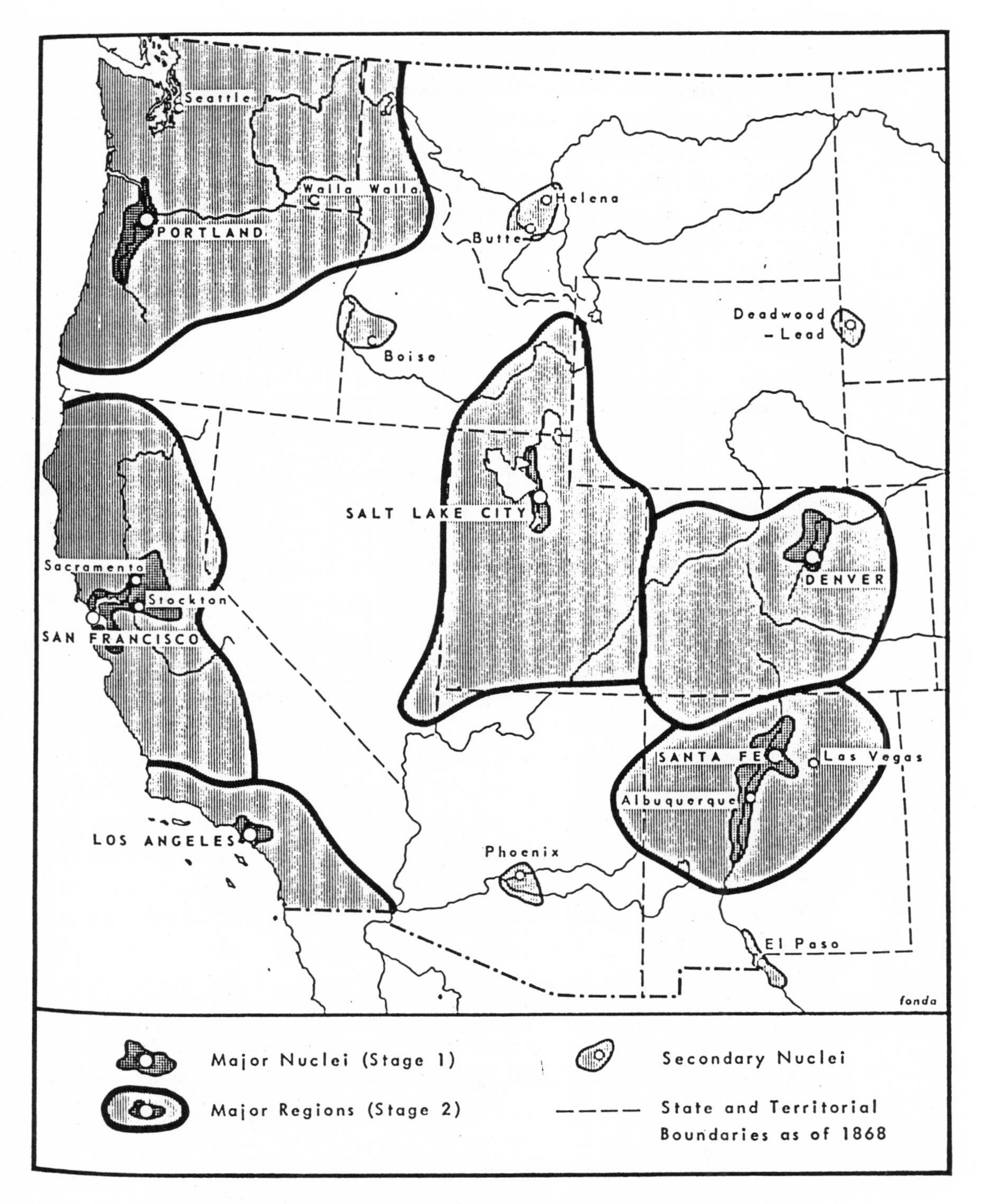

Figure 1.2. Major nuclei and regions of the West in stages 1 and 2. Initial settlement areas are located by stage-1 nuclei. During stage 2 growth and development, subregional areas sprang up around these cultural hearths. (Reprinted, by permission, from Meinig, "American Wests," 169)

historians have helped undermine the West's already fragile psyche by carving it up into various themes, or frontiers, which are treated separately in a diachronic or chronological manner. These frontiers can be geographically constituted, as for instance the Spanish Borderlands Frontier or the Mormon Frontier; they can represent widely dispersed occupational frontiers like those associated with farmers, miners, and ranchers; they can highlight the evolution of some kind of technology, as in the case of the transportation frontier; and they can even showcase architecture, as in Harold Kirker's *California's Architectural Frontier.*[8] Most published state architectural surveys and guidebooks are in fact Turnerian in the sense that they trace the linear development of building ideas from the simplest ("frontier vernacular") to the most complex ("modernism").[9]

Turnerian theory as a model for western architectural research is therefore problematic on several counts. First, it lacks regional continuity. Encountering the West through a series of isolated "frontiers" obscures the fundamental connections that exist between western people, people who more often than not participated in more than one of the various frontiers at the same time. Mormons, for example, were undoubtedly devoted to their religion, but they were also farmers and soon became miners as well. Western miners were often deeply religious, as were the Hispanic farmers of the Southwest. To top it all off, cowboys become farmers when it comes time to put up the annual crop of hay.

Second, an emphasis on the modernization process assumes a neat evolutionary pattern that never existed. The western economy, again, experienced an early and rapid industrialization; there were indeed family farms and ranches, but these small-scale enterprises coexisted with an equal if not greater number of corporate operations. Almost from the beginning, for example, what opportunities there were in western mining beyond the short-lived placer phase were open only to those with sufficient capital to initiate industrial-level methods and procedures. Finally, the Turnerian West is largely a rural, nineteenth-century West. When there is no more available land, the frontier closes and western history ends. It is no coincidence that most histories of the West deal with nineteenth-century subjects; the story is over when you get to the urban and industrial present, even though it has been demonstrated that certain behavior patterns set in motion during the initial settlement of the West are very much alive today.[10] To circumvent the lingering preoccupation with the rural and preindustrial West, a research model must be flexible enough to accommodate the present as well as the past.

A more promising path toward the objective at hand lies in what might be called the New Western History. By the 1980s a group of western historians, dismayed by the strong antiquarian bias in the Turnerian camp, began to seriously question the relevance and even the substance of the Frontier Thesis. Shifting their attention away from *process,* at least from the kind of rejuvenation process Turner described, "new" western historians like Donald Worster, Patricia Limerick, Richard White, and Michael Malone have discovered the West as *place* and have adopted a regionalist posture. While they might disagree on the specific boundaries of the place, these scholars find common ground in the belief that the West constitutes one of the principal regions of the United States, with its own history. "Like all regions of all nations," Malone wrote in the introduction to his *Historians and the American West,* "the western United States has produced a history which is in part an aspect of the larger national mosaic and is in part a singular entity. Regional history is a composite of local, national, and even global factors that have merged, diverged, and recombined over time to form a distinctive, yet also a familiar pattern."[11]

Adopting a regional stance, however, is not the same as developing a powerful regional theory, and many of the New Western Historians wonder aloud about the direction their field is heading. Donald Worster asks, "What strategies should we employ for analyzing this West as region, as opposed to the West as frontier?" In a similar vein, Michael Malone poses the question, "Aside from the classical interpretation of [Frederick Jackson] Turner and [Walter Prescott] Webb, are there other established models that might hold the key to a new regional approach?" While Limerick warns that Turner will not be replaced by a "simple, unitary model," she, along with many of her colleagues, would agree with Worster's general call for "understanding the specific processes that went on in the specific region." But what are these specific processes? What qualities contribute to a western identity? What makes western things western? There are seemingly as many answers to these questions as there are historians.[12]

For Donald Worster, the "core history of the West" may be found in human ecology. "A region emerges," he writes, "as people try to make a living from a particular part of the earth, as they adapt themselves to its limits and possibilities." Others have chosen to view the West as a "plundered province," or as the product of an attempt at human and environmental conquest. While still others offer environmental determinism as the key concept. These and other approaches are useful for the study of western vernacular architecture but lack the overarching capabilities necessary for a unified theory of western culture. Regionalism certainly involves modes of production, environmental adaptation, external exploitation, and human conquest, but it also implies connection: shared relationships among people within the region and with those in the country or nation in which the region exists. Writing in the influential volume *Regionalism in America,* Rupert Vance pointed out that a "region gains its significance only from its relation to a total structure. The relation that regionalism presumes to study is that of parts to wholes." In an effort to devise a regional perspective, it is tempting to focus on certain essential qualities of the West—its lack of water, for instance. However, following Vance's advice, perhaps a more meaningful approach lies in recognizing and delineating the region's connection to the larger nation, for despite the lingering frontier mythology, it never really left.[13]

What is it that binds the seemingly disparate areas of the West into a discernable whole? To find an answer we must look, as many historians already have, for lessons in other frontier experiences. We must adopt, that is, a comparative approach to the problem. Particularly useful in this regard is historian Bernard Bailyn's study of the outward expansion of Britain in the sixteenth and seventeenth centuries. Bailyn notes that a prime characteristic of modern historiography is the recognition of international communications and connections. Early in the modern period there was a breakdown of isolation that embraced the entire western world, creating a global capitalist culture—what economist Immanuel Wallerstein calls the "modern world system."[14] "Large-scale orbits developing through time have become visible," Bailyn writes, "and within them patterns of filiation and derivation." Applying the concept of global connections to his own study of British colonial history, Bailyn found that "what was involved was an expansion of the English, later British, world from its core in southeastern England out into a series of expanding alien peripheries—Wales, the north country of England in the sixteenth century, Scotland, Ireland, and North America in the seventeenth centuries." The bond between parent community—the *core*—and its offspring—the *periphery*—was largely intangible and cultural:

> This arc was nothing so simple as the trade route of an empire in the traditional sense, commercial or territorial. Nor was it merely an expanding frontier line. It was not a line, an edge, comprehensible in Turnerian terms as such, but a ring of territories, or marchlands, separated in important ways from the territories on either side of it. In these linked territories a central culture encountered a variety of different human and physical environments and formed a variety of subcultures, all of which were contained within a single overall system that might be designated "British."[15]

Bailyn's basic *core-periphery* theory is not itself new, for it has strong parallels in global economic theory, but its use here to illuminate "orbits of cultural affiliation and derivation" is noteworthy. The idea that developing communities may be physically separated both from each other and the core culture, but nevertheless continue to be linked through a similar peripheral relationship to the core, suggests comparisons and applications to the seemingly disparate and isolated communities in the American West.[16]

Western communities, whether filled with Native, Hispanic-, or Anglo-Americans, Mormons or miners, farmers or ranchers, were American communities (either by choice or by force) and as such fell within the orbit of the American core culture, which for most of the nineteenth and twentieth centuries lay in the northeastern United States. The core values were essentially those of American industrial capitalism—free markets, individualism, private enterprise, technological progress, and Anglo-American virtues—and they exerted a powerful influence over the western peripheries.[17] These peripheries were not cultural backwaters. Rather, they were places where the core values were adapted and changed to meet the exigencies of a new environmental and social context—*and* places where the original inhabitants and later non-Anglo-American immigrants were forced to conform and adjust to the omnipresence of the core culture. In the West, the core culture encountered, to use Bailyn's words, "a variety of different human and physical environments" and "formed a variety of subcultures." For all their distinctiveness, however, these subcultures displayed and continue to display an affiliation with the core, and it is through this affiliation that a viable regional theory for the study of western vernacular architecture may be fashioned.

The underlying premise of this book is that the various and seemingly disparate vernacular building traditions of the western United States may be bound together through a shared peripheral relationship to an increasingly industrialized and urban American core culture. The book's goal, from this perspective, lies in describing the dynamic process by which distant impulses combined with such local factors as environment, ethnicity, occupation, religion, and race to create the distinctive vernacular architectural subcultures of the American West. It should be emphasized that the focus of these essays is on the *American* West, and not the northern extension of New Spain or the eastern reaches of the Russian Empire. The time frame for the project begins in the 1820s, with the first major American intrusion into that part of the United States lying west of the ninety-eighth meridian, and extends into the present.

A cautionary word is necessary in using the core-periphery model: it describes a series of external (etic) rather than internal (emic) relationships. Western vernacular architecture is defined here largely in terms of the region's ongoing association with the core culture—with the eastern United States—but it does not mean that certain internal conditions that give western architectural landscapes what folklorist Gary Stanton calls "collateral connections" must be ignored. Some connections are formed simply through a shared attachment with the East, for example, the widespread occurrence of certain balloon-frame house types that may have originated in a central warehouse in Chicago. Other collateral connections are formed through the widespread application of particular adaptive strategies: irrigation is one that comes readily to mind. Lack of water necessitates irrigation, so we find irrigation systems throughout the region yielding a distinctively western element to the landscape. There are other occupational practices—for instance, working cattle on horseback—which are uniquely western and produce regional likenesses, with subtle differences of course. And we must not forget the essential fact of space. The

Figure 1.3. The West as a cultural region of the United States. In this map, the eastern boundary of the region is demarcated by the hundredth meridian. (Map by Alan Barnett)

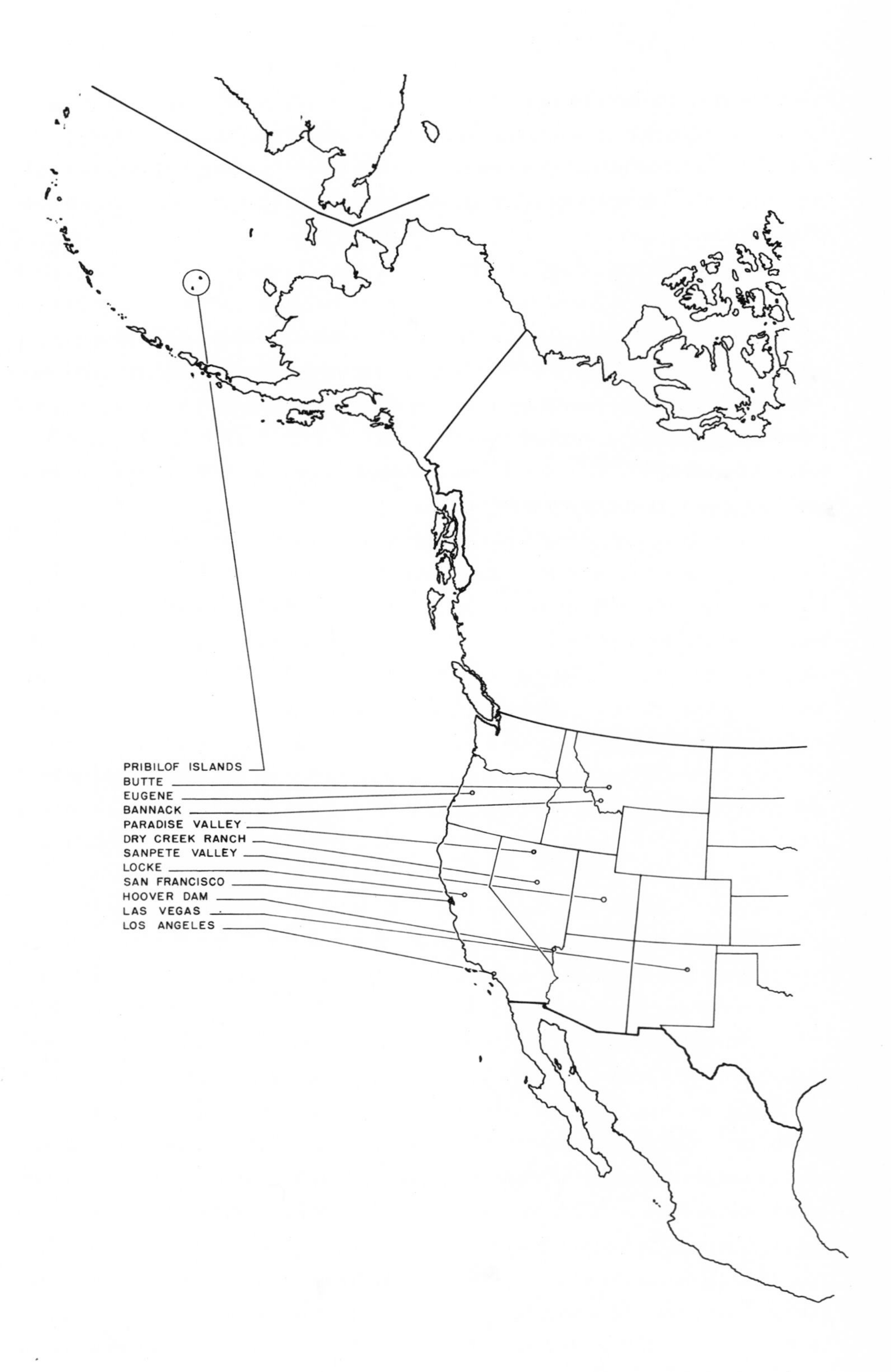

overpowering presence of open country, what writers of the west call "that awesome space" has left its mark, and continues to leave its mark, on western people. Such things are the threads holding the regional fabric together, but the basic pattern, the cultural template of the West, remains embedded in the values of industrializing America.[18]

So we find ourselves describing an approach to vernacular architecture that should sound familiar, for it is one that centers upon the process of change, or change process. As anthropologist Robert Bee describes it: "the interaction of causal factors so as to produce a transformation of one condition into another."[19] The condition we begin with is what people knew when the came west; they arrived in their new homes with definite ideas about how their environment should look and function. This imported condition changed in response to a new set of social and environmental circumstances into another condition—a western condition. Change process lies at the heart of both regional and vernacular architecture studies, for in the end they are one and the same thing. Vernacular architecture is for all intents and purposes regional community architecture. In vernacular architecture studies we are looking for the connections between people and place, between people and *their* place; and it is this dynamic, the adaptation of broadly American forms to a western context that underlies the core-periphery model outlined here. The move to a regionally based theory turns us back to historian Donald Worster's call for "understanding the specific processes that go on in a specific region." Place and process. The place is the American West; the process is not Turner's, but one that focuses on the intersection of East and West, of core values being played out in peripheral settings.

The essays in *Images of an American Land* have been selected to demonstrate the applicability of the core-periphery approach to western architectural history. They cover representative building communities in the region and are organized in sequence according to central themes in the history of the West (fig. 1.3). The collection begins with two essays describing the close cultural connections between East and West during the second half of the nineteenth century. Kingston Heath's study of false-front commercial buildings in Montana points out the real human need for familiar surroundings. As miners pushed into the rugged mountain country of the West, they re-created, albeit cosmetically, the urban atmosphere of eastern cities and towns. Likewise, the Mormons, when confronted with the prospect of designing an architecture for the Kingdom of God, fell back on what was a well-known, essentially American Neoclassical style. The essay by Thomas Carter suggests that perhaps the most distinctive thing about the Mormon western landscape is how quickly the Latter-day Saints fashioned for themselves an eastern-midwestern, middle-class, architectural environment.

The second set of essays, Philip Dole's study of the Calef Farm in Oregon and

Blanton Owen's on the Damele Ranch in Nevada, set American building forms in their western context, emphasizing the distinctive regional qualities of the buildings and the lifeways they represent. The Calefs adapted a building tradition from Vermont to the exigencies of farming in the West, and the Dameles, Italian-immigrants-turned-Nevada-buckaroos, found the specific needs of their new occupation and environment dictating an architectural response. Both these essays point out the "westernness" of western vernacular architecture.

The West of course is only "the west" if you are coming from the east. For the natives, the land later-Americans called the West had always been home, the center of their existence; for the Spanish moving in from Mexico, the West was "the north," and for the Russian imperialists it was "the east." The third pair of essays call attention to the simple but often (conveniently) overlooked fact that in settling the West, Americans had to brush aside existing populations, often with serious ramifications for the displaced. Chris Wilson's essay, "When a Room Is the Hall," explores the architectural results of the convergence of cultures—Hispanic and Anglo—in central New Mexico. In a similar vein, Alison Hoagland offers a sensitive portrait of the plight of the Aleut people on the remote Pribilof Islands of Alaska. The Aleuts, as Hoagland points out, were "buffeted by two major cultural influences, first Russian, then American." The resulting landscape, one of Russian churches and American tract housing, tells of a kind of cultural subjugation that is typical of European efforts to "civilize" the natives.

The next couplet focuses on segments of the western population often left out of the traditional historical narrative: ethnics and women. It is unfortunate that we must continually remind ourselves that, despite the popular image of the West as a male domain, there were women here, lots of them, and that the West was and continues to be a destination for people of many races and nationalities. Architecture, as Christopher Yip shows in his study of the Chinese inhabitants of Locke, California, helped one group of these newcomers survive the intense hostility and racism that greeted them in the American West. Margaret Purser's work in Paradise Valley, Nevada, stresses the active role women played in shaping the architectural landscape. By placing women within Paradise's social and economic system, Purser provides a useful model for introducing gender into the vernacular building process.

The next two essays—Anne Bloomfield's "The Real Estate Associates: A Land and Housing Developer of the 1870s in San Francisco" and Richard Longstreth's "Innovation without Paradigm: The Many Creators of the Drive-in Market"—have several purposes. First, these studies move us out of the rural West and make us recognize the city as an important and essential feature of the western regional environment. Bloomfield's Real Estate Associates could be found in any American city and that is precisely the point—the West, like America generally, provided a fertile field for developers of all kinds. A second theme here is found in Longstreth's piece: while the east-to-west, core-periphery model holds true for much of the nineteenth and early twentieth centuries, after 1920, southern California, and particularly Los Angeles, begins to assert itself as another cultural core area in America. As the automobile gained in popularity, Americans began to look toward the area of the country where the new car-culture reigned supreme. New buildings types associated with the car, as Richard Longstreth demonstrates in his research on the drive-in market, developed in the West and spread eastward, becoming in the process American institutions.

The final set of essays touches upon the management and exploitation of resources as a significant facet of western architectural development. Fred Quivik's study of the mining landscape around Butte and Anaconda, Montana, should make us all aware not only of the pivotal role technological systems played in settling the West, but also the effect that this industrial system, a system laden with cultural meaning, had on the western landscape. And finally there is Richard Guy Wilson's powerful treatment of Hoover Dam as cultural symbol. Perhaps more than any other image, it is the one of Hoover Dam that embodies a nation's belief in itself, a belief in our ability to harness nature's energy for human good, whatever the cost to the environment.

If there is a unifying theme or message in this collection, it may be found in a passage from one of David Weber's publications. Weber, a thoughtful historian of the American Southwest, wrote that one of the main obstacles we face in doing western history (and architectural history) is provincialism. "Specialists in the history of English colonial Virginia or colonial New York are understood to write *American* history; specialists in Spanish colonial Florida or California write *regional* history."[20] Weber is talking about Spanish history generally, but he has also touched upon a problem in western history and architectural history. A book on the early buildings of colonial Virginia is considered to be a book in American studies, while a study of similar buildings in the West is something less, being relegated to the category of "regional" studies. Quite simply, the West—whether as a frontier or a region—is somehow considered to lie outside the mainstream of American life and culture. The problem we face, as we attempt to build a strong regional paradigm, is one of overcoming a powerful exclusionary bias.

The West is one of the main regions of the United States. Western studies is a branch of American studies. Mormon churches in Utah are as much American churches as those built by Anglicans in Virginia. By adopting a unified regional approach to the region's architecture, one built around both place and process, we can finally begin to understand how the West became the American West.

Notes

1. Useful definitions of vernacular architecture may be found in Eric Mercer, *English Vernacular Houses: A Study of Traditional Farmhouses and Cottages* (London: Her Majesty's Stationery Office, 1975), 1–3; Dell Upton and John Michael Vlach, *Common Places: Readings in American Vernacular Architecture* (Athens: University of Georgia Press, 1986), xiii–xxiv; Camille Wells, "Old Claims and New Demands: Vernacular Architecture Studies Today," in *Perspectives in Vernacular Architecture,* ed. Camille Wells (Columbia: University of Missouri Press, 1986), 2:1–11; Thomas Carter and Bernard L. Herman, "Toward a New Architectural History," in *Perspectives,* ed. Carter and Herman (1991), 4:1–10. See also, Dell Upton, "Architectural History or Landscape History?" Journal of Architectural Education 44 (August 1991): 195–99.

2. Henry Glassie, "Eighteenth-Century Cultural Process in Delaware Valley Folk Building," *Winterthur Portfolio* 7 (1972): 29–57.

3. On New England, see Abbott Lowell Cummings, *The Framed Houses of Massachusetts Bay* (Cambridge: Harvard University Press, 1979); Robert Blair St. George, "'Set Thine House in Order': The Domestication of the Yeomanry in Seventeenth-Century New England," in *New England Begins: The Seventeenth Century,* ed. Jonathan L. Fairbanks and Robert F. Trent (Boston: Museum of Fine Arts, 1982): 159–351; St. George, "Artifacts of Regional Consciousness in the Connecticut River Valley, 1700–1780," in *The Great River: Art and Society of the Connecticut Valley, 1635–1820,* ed. Gerald W. R. Ward and William N. Hosley Jr.(Hartford, Conn.: Wadsworth Athenaeum, 1985): 29–40; and Thomas C. Hubka, *Big House, Little House, Back House, Barn: The Connected Farm Buildings of New England* (Hanover, N.H.: University Press of New England, 1984). For the Midatlantic region, see Alan Gowans, "The Mansions of Alloways Creek," in *Common Places: Readings in Vernacular Architecture,* ed. Dell Upton and John Michael Vlach (Athens: University of Georgia Press, 1985): 367-93; Glassie, "Eighteenth-Century Cultural Process," 29–58; Scott T. Swank, "The Architectural Landscape," in *Arts of the Pennsylvania Germans,* ed. Scott T. Swank (New York: W. W. Norton, 1983): 20–34; and Bernard L. Herman, *Architecture and Life in Central Delaware* (Knoxville: University of Tennessee Press, 1988). For southern studies of vernacular architecture, see Henry Glassie, *Folk Housing in Middle Virginia: A Structural Analysis of Historic Artifacts* (Knoxville: University of Tennessee Press, 1975); Cary Carson et al., "Impermanent Architecture," *Winterthur Portfolio* 16 (summer–autumn 1981): 135–96; and Dell Upton, *Holy Things and Profane: Anglican Parish Churches in Colonial Virginia* (Cambridge: MIT Press, 1988).

On the Midwest, see James Patrick, *Architecture in Tennessee, 1768–1897* (Knoxville: University of Tennessee Press, 1981); Howard W. Marshall, *Folk Architecture in Little Dixie: A Regional Culture in Missouri* (Columbia: University of Missouri Press, 1981); Wilbur D. Peat, *Indiana Houses of the Nineteenth Century* (Indianapolis: Indiana Historical Society, 1962); Betty I. Madden, *Arts, Crafts, and Architecture in Early Illinois* (Urbana: University of Illinois Press, 1974); Richard N. Campen, *Architecture of the Western Reserve* (Cleveland: Press of Case Western Reserve University, 1971); Sally McMurry, *Families and Farmhouses* (New York: Oxford University Press, 1987); and John M. Coggeshall and Jo Anne Nast, *Vernacular Architecture in Southern Illinois* (Carbondale: Southern Illinois University Press, 1989).

On the definition of "the West," see Donald Worster, "New West, True West: Interpreting the Region's History," *Western Historical Quarterly* 18 (April 1987): 141–56; and Rodman W. Paul and Michael P. Malone, "Tradition and Challenge in Western Historiography," *Western Historical Quarterly* 16 (January 1985): 24–54.

On the Southwest, see Bainbridge Bunting, *Architecture of New Mexico* (Albuquerque: University of New Mexico Press, 1974); Agnesa Lufkin Reeve, *From Hacienda to Bungalow: Northern New Mexico Houses, 1850–1912* (Albuquerque: University of New Mexico Press, 1988); Beverly Spears, *Rural Houses of Northern New Mexico* (Albuquerque: University of New Mexico Press, 1986); and Janet Ann Stewart, *Arizona Ranch Houses: Southern Territorial Styles, 1867–1900* (1974; reprint, Tucson: University of Arizona Press, 1987). Mormon studies include Laurel B. Andrew, *The Early Temples of the Mormons* (Albany: State University of New York Press, 1978); and Richard Francaviglia, *The Mormon Landscape* (New York: AMS Press, 1982).

For exceptions to vernacular research in the East, see Paul Groth, "'Marketplace' Vernacular Design: The Case for Downtown Rooming Houses," in *Perspectives,* ed. Wells, 2:179-91; Margaret Purser, "All Roads Lead to Winnemucca: Local Road Systems and Community Material Culture in Nineteenth-Century Nevada," in *Perspectives,* ed. Carter and Herman (1989), 3:120-34; and Kingston Heath, "False Front Architecture on Montana's Urban Frontier," in *Perspectives,* 3:199–213.

Allen Noble's attempt to create an all-encompassing text for vernacular architecture falls short, particularly in the West. See Noble, *Wood, Brick, and Stone: The North American Settlement Landscape* (Amherst: University of Massachusetts Press, 1984): 67–86.

4. On the cultural diffusion paradigm, see Fred Kniffen, "Folk Housing: Key to Diffusion," *Annals of the Association of American Geographers* 55 (December 1965): 549–77; Henry Glassie, *Pattern in the Material Folk Culture of the Eastern United States* (Philadelphia: University of Pennsylvania Press, 1968); and Fred Kniffen and Henry Glassie, "Building in Wood in the Eastern United States: A Time-Place Perspective," *Geographical Review* 56 (January 1966): 40–66.

The regional process in New England is discussed in James Deetz, *In Small Things Forgotten: The Archaeological of Early American Life* (New York: Anchor Books, 1977). For the Chesapeake Bay, see Dell Upton, "Vernacular Domestic Architecture in Eighteenth-Century Virginia," *Winterthur Portfolio* 17 (summer–autumn 1982): 95–119; and for the Delaware River Valley see Glassie, "Eighteenth-Century Cultural Process," 29–57.

On the spread of building ideas and practices, see Pierce Lewis, "Common Houses, Cultural Spoor," *Landscape* 19 (March 1979): 1–22.

Current theories in vernacular architecture are outlined in Dell Upton, "The Power of Things," in *Material Culture: A Research Guide,* ed. Thomas J. Schlereth (Lawrence: University of Kansas Press, 1985): 57–78.

5. The following analysis follows Patricia Nelson Limerick, *The Legacy of Conquest: The Unbroken Past of the American West* (New York: W. W. Norton, 1988).

6. D. W. Meinig, "American Wests: Preface to a Geographical Introduction," *Annals of the Association of American Geographers* 62 (June 1972): 159–84.

7. Frederick Jackson Turner, *The Frontier in American History* (1920; reprint, Tucson: University of Arizona Press, 1986). A good example of the Turnerian model is found in Martin Ridge and Ray Allen Billington, *America's Frontier Story: A Documentary History of Westward Expansion* (New York: Holt, Rinehart and Winston, 1969). For modernization theory, see Richard D. Brown, *Modernization: The Transformation of American Life, 1600–1865* (New York: Hill and Wang, 1976: 3–22.

8. See John Francis Bannon, *The Spanish Borderlands Frontier, 1531–1821* (New York: Holt, Rinehart and Winston, 1970); W. J. Eccles, *The Canadian Frontier, 1534–1760* (Albuquerque: University of New Mexico Press, 1969); and Eccles, "The Mormon Frontier," in *America's Frontier Story,* 509–29.

Gilbert C. Fite, *The Farmer's Frontier, 1865–1900* (New York: Holt Rinehart and Winston, 1966); Rodman Wilson Paul, *The Mining Frontiers of the Far West, 1848–1880* (New York: Holt, Rinehart and Winston, 1963); and Paul "The Rancher's Frontier, 1865–1890," in *America's Frontier Story,* 592–612.

Oscar Osburn Winther, *The Transportation Frontier: Trans-Mississippi West, 1865–1890* (New York: Holt, Rinehart and Winston, 1964).

Harold Kirker, *California's Architectural Frontier: Style and Tradition in the Nineteenth Century* (Salt Lake City: Peregrine Smith, 1973).

9. For examples of this progressive approach to architectural history see Sally B. Woodbridge, *California Architecture: Historic American Buildings Survey* (San Francisco: Chronicle Books, 1988), 15–103; Pamela S. Mediell, ed., *Architecture Oregon Style* (Portland: Professional Book Center, 1983); Thomas Carter and Peter Goss, *Utah's Historic Architecture, 1847–1940: A Guide* (Salt Lake City: University of Utah Press, 1988); Drury Blakeley Alexander, *Texas Homes of the Nineteenth Century* (Austin: University of Texas Press, 1966).

10. Limerick, *Legacy of Conquest,* 97–133, 23–26.

11. See Worster, "New West, True West," 141–56; Limerick, *Legacy of Conquest,* 25–27; Gerald Thompson, "Frontier West: Process or Place?" *Journal of the Southwest* 29 (winter 1987): 364–73; Howard R. Lamar, "Much to Celebrate: The Western History Association's Twenty-Fifth

Birthday," *Western Historical Quarterly* 17 (October 1986): 398–416; Paul and Malone, "Tradition and Challenge in Western Historiography," 27–53; Roger L. Nichols, ed., *American Frontier and Western Issues: A Historiographical Review* (New York: Greenwood Press, 1986); Michael P. Malone, ed., *Historians and the American West* (Lincoln: University of Nebraska Press, 1983); and Richard White, *"It's Your Misfortune and None of My Own": A New History of the American West* (Norman: University of Oklahoma Press, 1991). The quotation is from Malone, *Historians and the American West,* 1.

12. Worster, "New West, True West," 146; Malone, "Beyond the Last Frontier: Toward a New Approach to Western American History," *Western Historical Quarterly,* 20 (1989): 409–27; Limerick, *Legacy of Conquest,* 25; Worster, "New West, True West," 144.

13. Worster, "New West, True West," 149. On the West as a "plundered province," see Bernard DeVoto, "The West: Plundered Province," *Harper's Magazine,* August 1934, 1–13; and Richard D. Lamm and Michael McCarthy, *The Angry West: A Vulnerable Land and Its Future* (Boston: Houghton Mifflin, 1982); as the product of conquest, see Limerick, *Legacy of Conquest;* on environmental determinism, see Walter Prescott Webb, *The Great Plains* (New York: Grosset and Dunlap, 1931).

Rupert B. Vance, "The Regional Concept as a Tool for Social Research," in *Regionalism in America,* ed. Merrill Jensen (Madison: University of Wisconsin Press, 1965): 119.

14. Bernard Bailyn, "The Challenge of Modern Historiography," *American Historical Review,* 87 (February 1982): 1–24; Bailyn, *The Peopling of British America: An Introduction* (New York: Random House, 1986); Immanuel Wallerstein, *The Modern World-System: Capitalist Agriculture and the Origins of the European World-Economy in the Sixteenth Century* (New York: Academic Press, 1974). See also, Anthony D. King, *Urbanism, Colonialism, and the World-Economy: Cultural and Spatial Foundations of the World Urban System* (London: Routledge, 1990).

15. Bailyn, "The Challenge of Modern Historiography," 14–15.

16. Dell Upton, "Reading the Vernacular Landscape," paper delivered at the Graduate School of Architecture, University of Utah, 25 April 1989. The core-periphery nature of the American West is also noted in Malone, "Beyond the Last Frontier."

17. Gilded Age culture is the subject of a number of studies, including Daniel Walker Howe, ed., *Victorian America* (Philadelphia: University of Pennsylvania Press, 1976); H. Wayne Morgan, ed., *The Gilded Age* (Syracuse: Syracuse University Press, 1963); Vincent P. DeSantis, ed., *The Gilded Age: 1877–1896* (Northbrook, Ill.: AHM Publishing, 1973); Karen Halttunen, *Confidence Men and Painted Women: A Study of Middle-class Culture in America, 1830–1870* (New Haven: Yale University Press, 1982); and Daniel Horowitz, *The Morality of Spending: Attitudes toward the Consumer Society in America, 1875–1940* (Baltimore: Johns Hopkins University Press, 1985).

18. Stanton, personal correspondence, November 1988; Donald Worster, *Rivers of Empire: Water, Aridity, and the Growth of the American West* (New York: Pantheon, 1985); Terry G. Jordan, *North American Cattle-Ranching Frontiers: Origins, Diffusion, and Differentiation* (Albuquerque: University of New Mexico Press, 1993); E. Richard Hart, *That Awesome Space: Human Interaction with the Intermountain Landscape* (Salt Lake City: Westwater Press, 1981).

19. Robert L. Bee, *Patterns and Processes: An Introduction to Anthropological Strategies for the Study of Sociocultural Change* (New York: Free Press, 1974), 4.

20. David J. Weber, "John Francis Bannon and the Historiography of the Spanish Borderlands," *Journal of the Southwest* 29 (winter 1987): 354.

Transplanting Traditions

Figure 2.1. Bannack, Montana, ca. 1905. (Courtesy Montana Department of Fish, Wildlife, and Parks)

CHAPTER TWO

False-Front Architecture on Montana's Urban Frontier

KINGSTON HEATH

> Virginia City [Montana]. Good Lord! . . . A street of straggling shanties, a bank, a blacksmith's shop, a few dry goods stores, and barrooms, constitute the main attractions of the "city." A gentleman has informed me that Virginia *City* contained brownstone front houses and paved streets, equal he guessed to any eastern *town*. How that man did lie in his Wellingtons! The whole place was a delusion and a snare.
>
> Earl of Dunraven, *Hunting in the Yellowstone*

The focus of this investigation is the identification, analysis, and interpretation of a significant western frontier building type that served as a critical indicator of social change: the commercial false front. Bannack, southwestern Montana's earliest mining community, provides the principal setting for the investigation. The earliest period of settlement is crucial because it was during the frontier period—marked by struggle and uncertainty—that the commercial false front evolved as a central factor in the development of community life on the "urban" frontier.

Given the appearance of Bannack at the turn of the century (fig. 2.1), we must ask if it is even appropriate to refer to such humble, understated, and even hopelessly underscaled buildings (given the enormity of the natural context) as part of a legitimate urban fabric. However, the mining camps of Montana self-consciously re-created—out of memory and necessity—an urban experience amid a rugged human and natural landscape that approximated, in its concentrated human activity, life in distant cities "back in the States."[1]

During the 1860s in Montana, compact groups of buildings huddled together along the lifeline of main street traffic constituted the only urban context for hundreds of miles. In such settings, seemingly, whole cities were created overnight. In the year 1862–63, for example, Bannack's population went from zero to four thousand, while approximately five hundred thousand dollars in gold was taken out in the first six months of 1862 alone. The linear progression of tightly packed false-front buildings that were hurriedly constructed to accommodate the miners was at once the pretense and the reality of the "city." The buildings were false in material pretense (wood feigning masonry), structural pretense (log party walls supporting a balloon-frame front wall for greater light and display area), and formal pretense (a rectilinear facade hiding a gable or shed roof). In the early stages of camp life, expediently built structures that housed schools, saloons, banks, and brothels were grouped together on the same block of the burgeoning town center. Little distinguished the buildings where these varied activities took place except the lettering painted on the front. In essence, these buildings were little more than planar surfaces for the distribution of signage. To be sure, the residents were not deluded; all one had to do was venture behind these buildings. The effort to make the "town" look more mature than it was was a forced one, and the visitor to the camp (like the one quoted above) often sensed the hoax.

What *was* real was the striving for legitimacy and permanence through architectural expression. The prosperity of the mines was immediately evident in the visual well-being of the town as it evolved from tents and wagons, to log structures, to frame buildings, and finally, to iron and masonry buildings. The rapid swelling of population during the boomtown phase brought instant urbanization to the western frontier and with it the need for law, order, education, sanitation, housing, entertainment, banking, and so on. Basically, the psychic and social conditions at Bannack (just as in any mining camp) differed from other entrepreneurial ventures of nineteenth-century town life in the degree of intensity with which they were experienced. Hence, while many of the building forms that appear in the camp are similar to those found elsewhere in urban American environments during the same period, their appearance on the mining frontier and their role in signaling social, economic, and technological change give them added significance. The sooner the young mining camp grappled with the sudden urban realities and provided the facilities necessary to manage or exploit the moment, the better were its chances for survival. The wooden commercial front, then, reflects the first attempt at stability on the western frontier.

The presence of a commercial front in a mining camp summoned concepts of a hopeful beginning. Its purpose in the larger destiny of the town was not only to address the immediate needs of the miner but also to serve as a catalyst for further growth. Ironically, like the western salmon that struggles to spawn upstream and sacrifices its own life to ensure the continuance of the species, the false front as the germ of a potential city was often an expendable but necessary step in a town's rite of passage. If the town flourished, the humble, wooden structures would soon be superseded by buildings of grander scale and more precious materials; if the mining venture failed, the abandoned buildings remained like a banner of defeat.

Bannack is acknowledged as the site of the first major gold claim in Montana.[2] The first miners into the area on 18 July 1862, panned on creek banks choked with sage, and remarked that "clouds of grasshoppers filled the air and swarmed on the hills and valley," thus giving the place its first name, Grasshopper Creek. In a matter of weeks, hundreds of prospectors invaded the area of Grasshopper Creek, setting up a camp known as the Beaver Head Mines and later renamed Bannack. The settlement soon proved to be one of "the noisy, crude, and isolated little camps that existed solely to supply and entertain miners."[3] No pretense marked the camp's first temporary shelters. Structures like those found on the mining frontiers of California, Colorado, and Idaho also appeared in Bannack. One common type utilized green timbers as a log frame for a canvas roof. Less substantial was the bush house, which consisted simply of a blanket over some bushes. Sometimes, in the absence of a blanket, the natural mat of branches overhead served for a roof. Frequently used at Bannack was the "wickiup," a crude hut of brush and poles.[4] Other miners simply made a dugout by tunneling into the earth or built a shelter from a natural cave outcropping.

Emigrant Emily Meredith arrived in Bannack on a wagon train consisting of forty Murphy wagons that were immediately converted into housing for the camp. The wickiup—the make-do shelter of the hardcore miner—and the Murphy wagon—the mobile unit of the hopeful emigrant—were products of a life of impermanence. The improvised shelters served to underscore the impermanence of the miners' existence: "Already the pleasant fall weather was passing; [these were] truly golden hours, since they could be transmitted into that metal; [time] could not be spared for buildings which they might not remain to occupy, so it was a town of wagons and tents."[5]

In the fall of 1862 miners cared little about personal comfort, knowing that their future depended on the amount of gold they could extract before winter. Nevertheless, the great success witnessed at Grasshopper Creek during the first few months convinced the miners to stay through the winter to avoid the risk of abandoning their claims. (Mining district law required the miner to work the claim every day water was available or lose the claim after three days). By early October, wickiups, wagons, and tents had begun to be replaced by more permanent forms of dwellings as materials changed from canvas and shrubs to logs on the outskirts of the emerging town center (fig. 2.2). Gable-ended, dirt-floored log structures (some with riverstone fireplaces) were common among the miners. Generally, a cantilevered roof protected the entry from snow and gave shelter to firewood and butchered meat (fig. 2.3). The interior often had untreated cow skins for rugs, bunk beds to conserve space, and an assortment of furniture pieced together from saplings and shipping crates. Items were often hung from pegs on the wall to safeguard them from water damage from the sod or canvas roof. Empty tin cans were often pounded flat and

Figure 2.2. Sketch of Bannack by an English visitor, Robert Holladay, 1863. Note single-pen rental cabins for miners in the bottom left, wickiups in the foreground, and shed-roof stores in between the two. (Courtesy Montana Historical Society)

used for flashing, while newspapers, rags, and wood from crates served as backing for mud chinking between the log walls in this supply-dependent mining camp hundreds of miles from civilization. Log single-pen cabins also served as rental lodging closer to "town."

The merchant, on the other hand, knew he could profit greatly by supplying the commercial and outfitting needs of the new settlement throughout the long winter; therefore, the enterprising merchant immediately focused his energies on acquiring teams and wagons for freighting supplies, preferring to pay to have someone build his house and store so they would be ready for business when he returned with his goods. Often, the builder incorporated the house and the store in one structure, producing the store/house. In this chain of interdependence, the builders produced cabins and stores for the merchants, while the merchants gathered inexpensive or

Figure 2.3. Miner's cabin, Nevada City, Montana. (Photo by Thomas Carter)

nonperishable goods such as canned beans, flour, tobacco, and liquor, which would command high prices in the isolated camps. As Maj. John Owen noted, "Captain deLacy [the author of the first map of the Montana Territory] arrived at Fort Owen, December 17, 1862 from Beaver Head via Big Hole, Montana and reported . . . news from the Beaver Head mines [at Bannack] favorable. Clothing, blankets, tobacco and groceries in great demand and bring enormous prices."[6]

Initially, small businesses operated from log, shed-roof shops among the dwellings on Yankee Flat and along the creek beds. Others chose to build across Grasshopper Creek in what would become the established commercial district; here, shed-roof central-door structures and gable-oriented, double-cell forms predominated (fig. 2.4). Both types are pictured in large numbers in figure 2.2. Parallel rows of log, gable-ended store/houses faced what would become the main street of the town

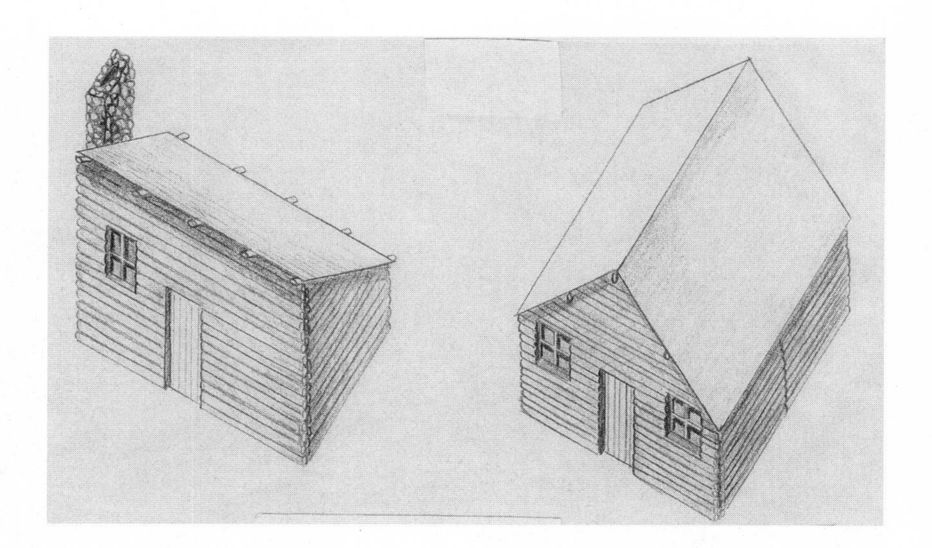

Figure 2.4. Antecedents to the false front: (*left*) shed roof, log-facade store form; (*right*) gable-ended log store/house form. (Drawing by Michael Ludovico and author)

center. These gable-ended commercial structures had little to characterize them as business establishments, however, for their facades lacked the distinctive framed false fronts that would later provide a rhythm of rectilinear facades strung along the main street (fig. 2.4b). Until the appearance of the false fronts, shopkeepers conducted business through the front doors of these simple, gable-ended, domestic-looking forms, while seeking domestic seclusion inside the rear entrance.[7]

This functional dichotomy of a home and a commercial enterprise under one roof was not found in the horizontally oriented shed-roof form (fig. 2.4a).Instead, the attraction of the shed-roof type lay in its suitability for commercial display. The chinked, rough-hewn, log-front wall offered an ideal space for signage that could be seen by miners as they passed along the street. This form appears to be an early example of a rectilinear false front, only at this stage the rectilinear facade was structurally integral. Builders of these rectangular and square forms generally employed the traditional grammar of a centered door flanked by one or two windows and surmounted by a flat roofline. This window-door-window arrangement would be retained as part of the "pattern language" of the later false fronts, just as the broad expanse of the rectangular facade alone would signal "store." The shed-roof format had the advantage of providing more visual accessibility to interior display space and a broader facade for signs. The high cost of sawn lumber, nails, and glass (a sheet of glass measuring eight by ten inches cost $2.50, nails cost $1.40 a pound, and whip-sawn lumber cost $400 per thousand eighteen-foot lengths) likely precluded the use of framed fronts early in Bannack's development.[8] Instead, as the costs of materials fell (there were no fewer than three sawmills in Bannack at the end of the first year), many of the owners of these log, shed-roofed, and gable-ended stores merely nailed planed sheathing over the log facade in an attempt to upgrade their facilities (fig. 2.5). Within the framework of frontier awareness, the mere use of sawn

Figure 2.5. St. Paul Saloon, shed-roof log saloon in Unionville, Montana. Note clapboard covering over log load-bearing front wall. (Courtesy Montana Historical Society)

and planed lumber was viewed as an expression of progressiveness that was part of the physical evolution from camp to town.

As in most mining camps, saloons made an early appearance. During the first year at least five were available to the Bannack population.[9] Most likely the saloons, with their large volume of trade and keen competition, were the first establishments to be upgraded. Saloon owners would have been able to afford expensive sawn boards, planed sheathing, nails, and glass long before other shopkeepers, and even before they were found on schools and churches. An 1864 letter written from Bannack by Mary Edgerton explains why: "The men washed fifteen hundred dollars in one day, a thousand dollars another day, and six hundred dollars another day; but that is all the good the money will do them, for as soon as they get any, they gamble and drink it all up."[10]

Figure 2.6. Bannack's main street in the 1860s. (Courtesy Montana Historical Society)

The growing camp was depicted in the fall of 1863 by Capt. James L. Fisk as consisting of one long and several short, irregular streets lined with log and frame shanties and stores; bakeries and restaurants abounded for the floating population. Shoemakers, tailors, blacksmiths, and wheelwrights were represented in the trades. Saloons, gambling houses, and houses of ill repute were numerous.[11] Bannack was coming of age (fig. 2.6).

Bannack made its rapid transition from tent town to boomtown in just one year. Rapid growth between 1862 and 1863 provided the nurturing ground for the appearance of the commercial false front, a characteristic building form found in most western towns. It was during the boomtown cycle on the mining frontier that the false front made its debut, for the prospect of large economic returns pushed shopkeepers into building structures that exhibited architectural ambitions. Where bartenders had sold shots of whiskey over flour sacks in tents or log-and-canvas structures, drinks were now being poured in log-and-frame structures (some two stories tall) with sawn-board facades reflecting a new level of camp maturity. Speed of construction and the minimization of financial investment continued to be emphasized, but the physical evolution of the commercial structures suggested that a degree of order and stability had arrived.[12]

The better the quality of materials, it was now assumed, the better the quality of the merchandise. The goal was to appear legitimate by approximating in sawn lumber and plate glass the kinds of buildings being built of cast iron or brick in more established cities. As Elliott West, author of *The Saloon on the Rocky Mountain Mining Frontier* notes, "Whether building a town or a saloon, men strove to re-create patterns of an older, 'settled' society, but they did so within the needs and limitations of an isolated frontier."[13]

For the four thousand people who inhabited Bannack in the fall of 1863, growing pains were evident. Crowds jostled for more room down the long, irregular main street, incongruously located in the midst of miles and miles of open space. Following the precocious example of Goodrich's saloon constructed during the winter of 1862–63 with a "neatly finished front," framed false-front facades began to be seen with increasing regularity on Main Street. Representative of this transitional stage in the town's architectural history is what is referred to in Bannack as the "sod roof building" (figs. 2.7, 2.8). The building began as a gable-ended, double-cell, log store/house, with a sod roof placed over saplings. Later it received a shingled roof and a rectangular frame facade that defined it visually as a "store." It now had a flat, projecting cornice line and a central door flanked by two-over-two double-hung windows; a touch of formality was added by studding and sheathing over the existing gable-ended log facade with expensive nailed drop-siding and corner boards. Such early false fronts evolved by combining the basic vocabulary of their two commercial progenitors, the log gable-ended store/house and the shed-roofed commercial block. The broad facade of the shed-roofed store was translated from log to frame and grafted onto the gable end of the store/house type.

A common misassumption about western boomtown architecture is that it is stylistically uninformed. In fact, the false fronts of Bannack and other early southwestern Montana settlements are wooden manifestations of masonry and iron commercial buildings found in other mid-nineteenth-century urban areas. After all, the miners and merchants were mostly new arrivals on the isolated urban frontier and can hardly be thought of as being cut off from current trends that defined progress. They had come from established jumping-off points in Omaha, St. Paul, St. Joseph, St. Louis, Denver, or Salt Lake, and they carried with them, in diluted form, a clear understanding of stylistic formulas that defined urban prosperity. Cut off from quarrying facilities, skilled craftsmen, and railroad lines, the builders of stores in Bannack turned to their only abundant resource: wood. Masonry details may have lost something in their new wooden guises, but the stylistic features applied to the wooden false fronts were appropriate for the popular tastes of the day. On first inspection the stylistic attributions are elusive because the features are minimally expressed: a row of Tuscan pilasters on an otherwise nondescript wooden false front may be all that attests to a Greek Revival heritage; a row of lancet arches or wooden crenelation represents the Gothic Revival; and round-headed arches (with or without modillions) are all that establish the Renaissance Revival (fig. 2.9a–i). Yet, these details reflect mental templates of masonry commercial structures translated into wood on the Rocky Mountain mining frontier in the form of the ubiquitous western false front.

From the outset the "formula" applied to shaping these new urban landscapes aimed at transforming the wilderness into settings familiar to the recent arrivals from the industrialized East. This common desire for cultural persistence was demonstrated in the various attempts to resist the forces of the new landscape (rather

Figure 2.7. *(Below)* Bannack's sod-roof store/house with later false front nailed to the existing log facade. (Courtesy Montana Department of Fish and Game)

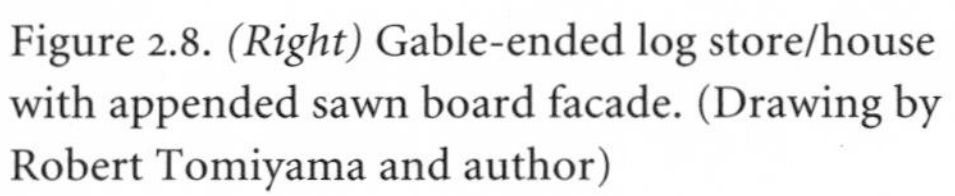

Figure 2.8. *(Right)* Gable-ended log store/house with appended sawn board facade. (Drawing by Robert Tomiyama and author)

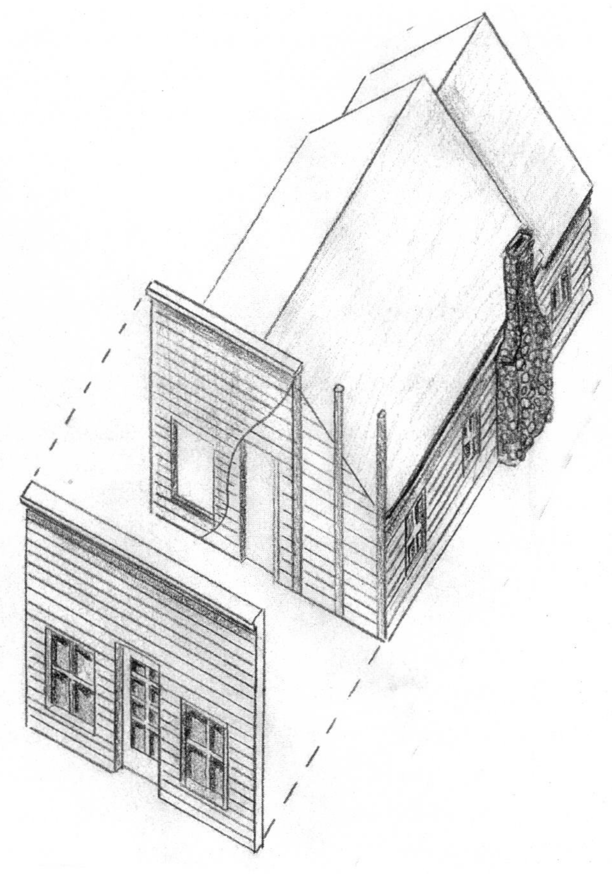

than adapt to them) by manipulating the built environment to conform to recollected urban images of the immediate past. The strategies, both conscious and unselfconscious, ranged from reconstructing basic commercial building types out of locally available materials that reflected national popular styles of the day, to designing entire communities from preexisting plans. Town planner and real estate developer Nathan W. Burris, for example, drew up plans in 1863 for Gallatin City, Montana, to serve the gold towns of Bannack and Virginia City. This urban plan was similar to the three-prong scheme of towns tied to a major transportation network that Burris had applied earlier in the mid-1850s for his development at Burris City, Iowa.[14] Hence, even the conceptual framework for establishing a new urban fabric on the Montana frontier was based, in the earliest efforts, on transplanted patterns.

Paralleling the improvements in materials and the addition of stylistic embellishments to the fronts of these boomtown commercial establishments was a more daring and informed response to the structural system *behind* the facade. Unlike the earlier structurally integral log facades, independent (nonload-bearing) balloon-frame fronts appeared on these buildings, often as an alteration to extant log structure. The original log-front wall was removed and the "new" false front affixed to the remaining log party walls either by nails or by tenon connections that fit into open-mortised corner posts. By these means the log party walls were attached to new upright corner posts that partially supported the nonload-bearing balloon-frame facade (fig. 2.10). Tenoned logs that fit into full-length mortised posts were common in Hudson Bay Company's *piece sur piece* construction in early Montana (fig. 2.11).[15] These vertical corner members would likely be reinforced by horizontal tying members (probably a log sill and an end girt) to make the gable end square (forming a structural bay) as well as to serve as nailers for the parallel rows of upright studs. The studs, in turn, received the sheathing. The spanning members lent lateral support to the log party walls in addition to the diaphragm action of the sheathing. Unlike the so-called sod-roof building in Bannack, where the presence of a front load-bearing log wall behind the applied false front limited the number of openings, the new structural system of the balloon-frame facade offered the store owner a facade almost entirely of glass for displaying his goods and illuminating his shop. The frontier merchant now had a "modern" storefront.

The false front, then, is worthy of its name: the building type was essentially false in materials, structural integrity, and stated formal configuration. Later, wooden false fronts did away with the log/balloon-frame scheme and relied on either a full balloon-framing system (fig. 2.12) or a masonry superstructure with a cast-iron single-story shop front. The massing formulas, however, remained basically the same since they were derived from masonry prototypes initially. At this point, the false front became structurally less deceitful but nevertheless retained the basic premise of feigning better materials and a three-dimensional rectilinear massing it seldom possessed.

While Victorian architectural critics such as A. W. Pugin and John Ruskin could rant against the "paper Gothic" and the deceitful use of materials, the wooden and later cast-iron false fronts were nevertheless "true" and appropriately urbane expressions of the mining frontier. Their existence was a result of economic and social symbiosis. The commercial false front was constructed by the merchant to meet the most basic needs of the miner; and the merchant, in turn, profited. Indirectly, the merchant had also begun to establish a firm economy, something that was of utmost importance if the camp was to mature into a stable town. These stores provided an urban context that resisted the more primitive aspects of the wilderness that loomed just outside town, and the architectural presence of the stores provided a catalyst for further growth. The social environments they created inside their log

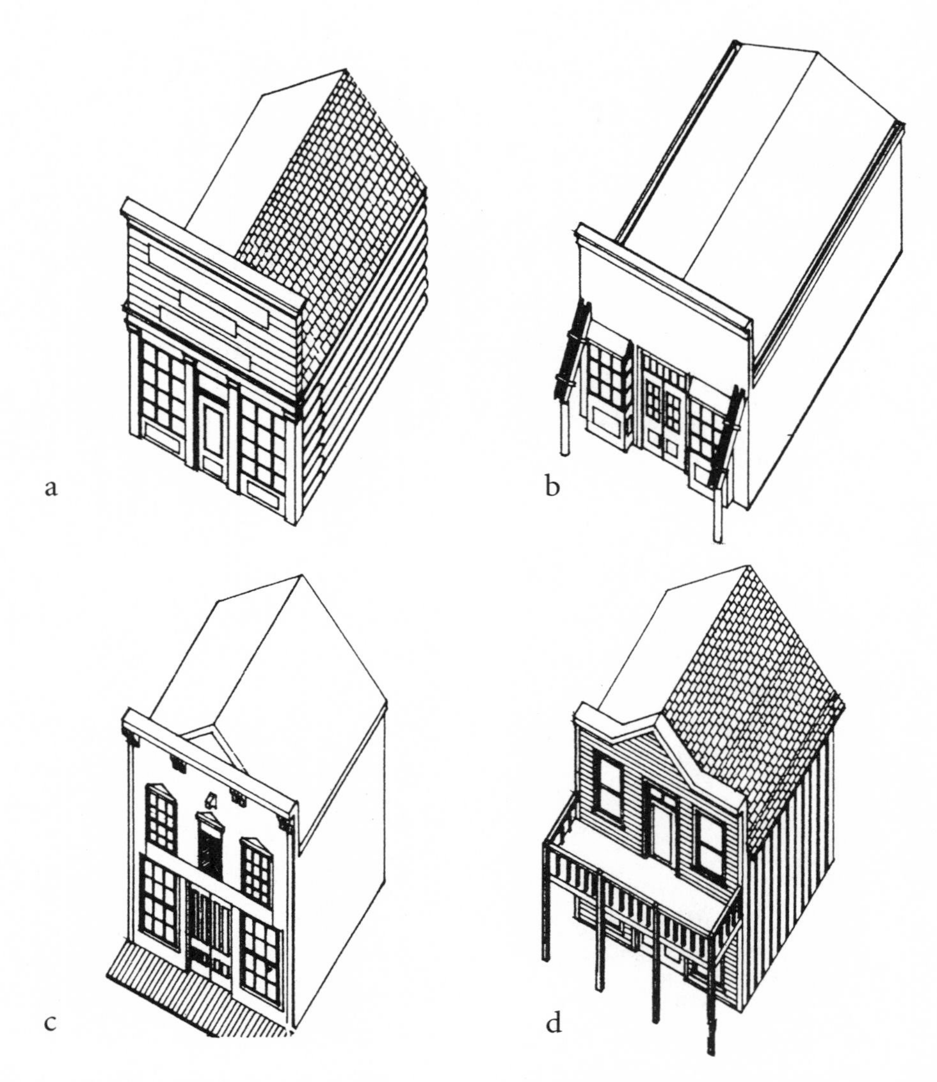

Figure 2.9. Massing and styling techniques for false fronts in Montana: *a.* flat cornice, hidden gable format; Greek Revival example of pilaster treatment; *b.* variation, extended rain gutters off hidden roof eave ends and projecting window bays; *c.* flat cornice, protruding gable format with pedimented Greek Revival hood moldings over windows; *d.* broken cornice, integrated gable treatment; *e.* integrated cornice, gable feature as appliqué or symbol; *f.* projecting cornice and half-round, Queen Anne centering device; *g.* Gothic stepped-gable format; *h.* Renaissance/ Gothic hybrid cornice and arch treatment; *i.* castellated Gothic cornice embellishment with wooden lancet-arch frieze and arched projecting oriel. (Drawings by Robert Tomiyama and author)

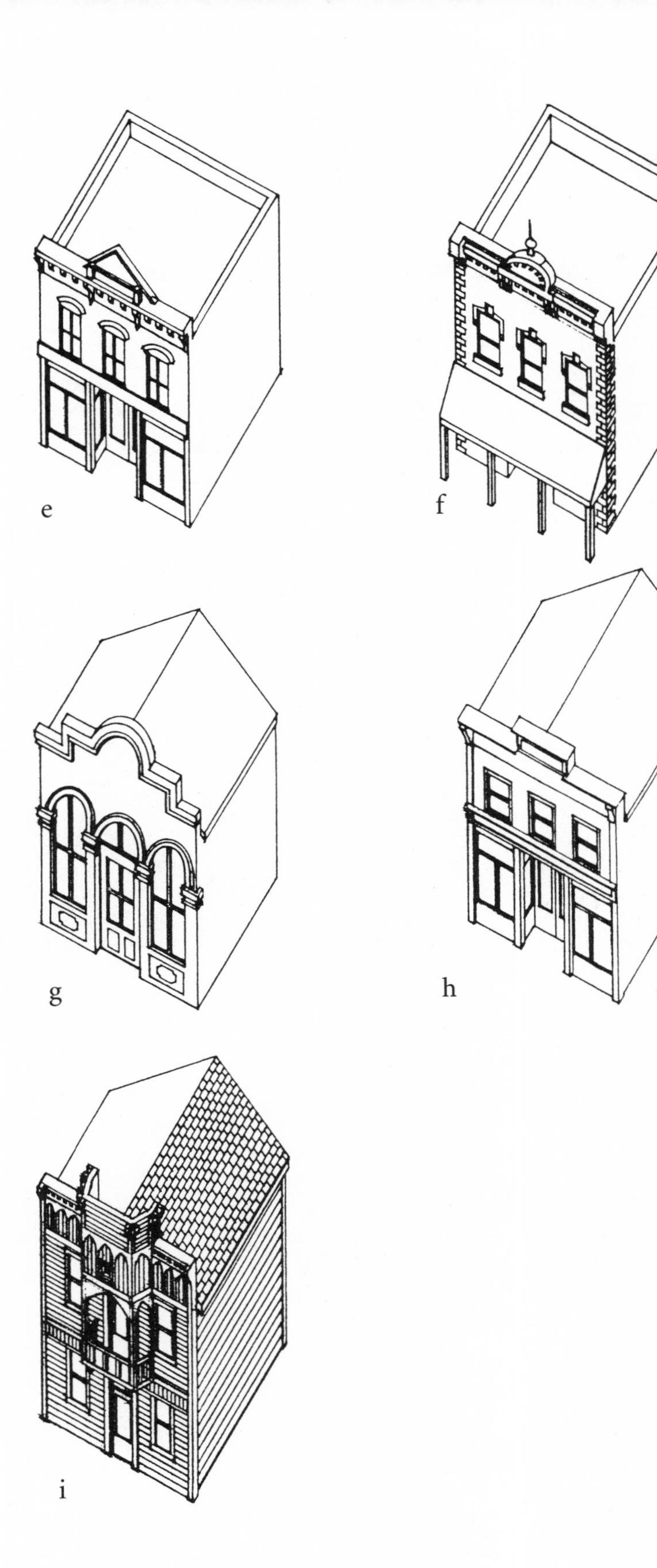
e
f
g
h
i

walls and sometimes pretentious facades often offered more important contributions to the community than the goods sold over the counter. For the townspeople the general store provided one of the few respectable gathering places. Governor Edgerton's nephew Wilbur Fisk Sanders described George Crisman's store (which opened for business in the early boomtown days of 1863 and was one of the most popular places in Bannack) as "the news bureau, the university, the social settlement of the hamlet to which intelligent genial companionship and a wide fireplace gave cheerful welcome." It should be pointed out that such socializing was restricted to males. Edgerton's daughter, Martha, lamented that "men did most of the shopping and nearly all the gossiping," while women "led secluded lives—almost cloistered in their lack of contact with the world outside."[16]

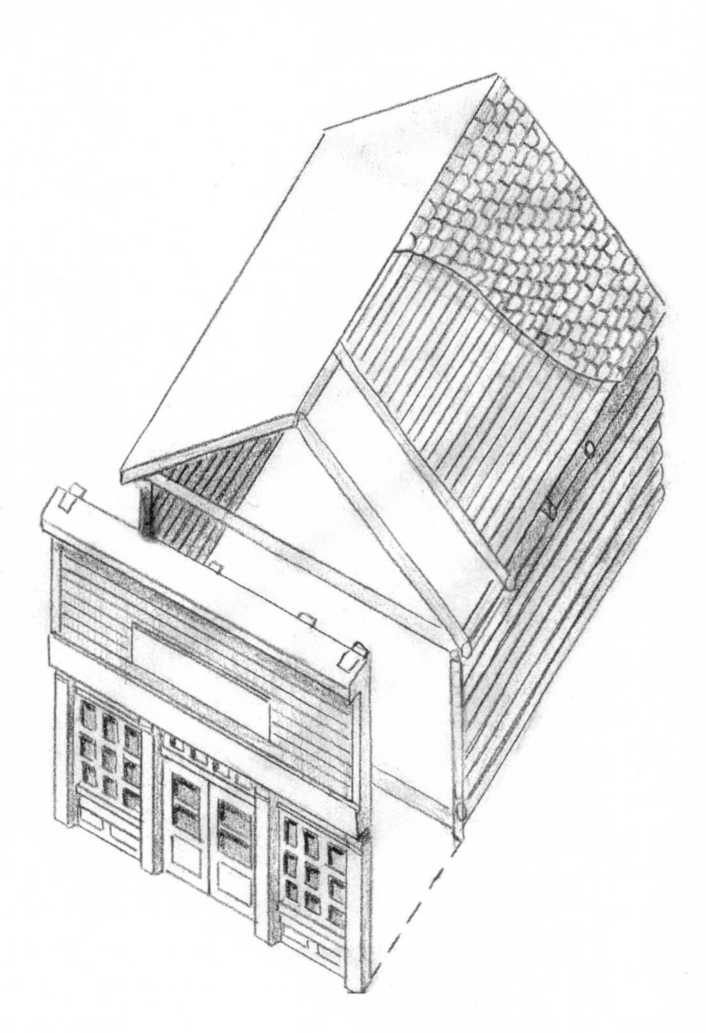

Figure 2.10. Bannack's Skinner Saloon, balloon-frame false front hung on log load-bearing party walls. (Drawing by Robert Tomiyama and author)

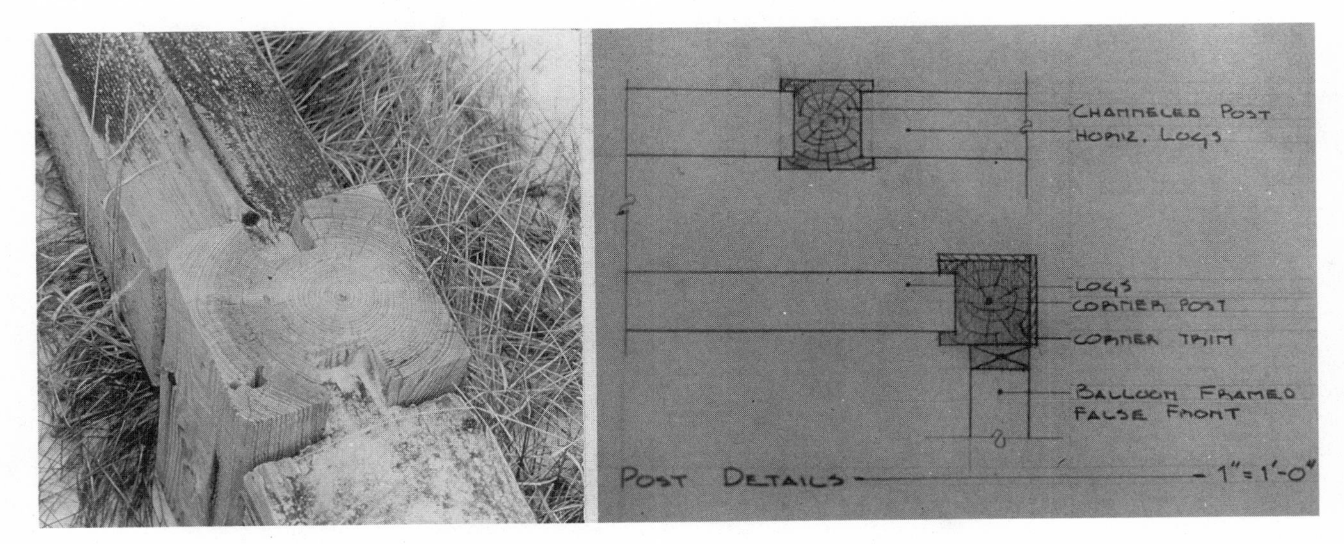

Figure 2.11. Detail of Hudson Bay, or *piece sur piece,* framing technique popular during Montana's frontier settlement period. Tenons were slipped into full-length open H-channel mortises for lateral stability. (Photo by author)

During winter snowstorms or during spring thaws when the supply and mail routes were impassable, prices soared in the mining camps. Shopkeepers could practically hold a town at ransom during times such as these. Mary Edgerton wrote home from Bannack on 21 May 1865:

> The snow has been so deep and the roads so bad between Salt Lake and this place that those who had flour on the road could not get over the "divide" with wagons, but had to pack everything over. At one time there was not a pound of flour to be bought in this town and many families lived on meat and dried fruit (if they had any). The first flour that was brought in sold for one dollar a pound [almost 40 times the cost in the States].[17]

Optimism, tempered by caution, marked all the mining camps and lent some justification to the inordinate prices placed on everything. The shopkeepers, after all, were no different from anyone else who was attempting to exploit the mining venture and make as much money as possible as quickly as possible.

To attract the business of those new to the camp, the flat facades that lined both sides of Main Street were generally used for signage. These commercial structures often succinctly stated their purpose on large, prominent signs on the upper half of the false front, denoting them as "drug store," "laundry," or "hotel." In effect, the built facade *was* the sign.

Early photographs of Bannack and other early Montana mining towns depict very little pedestrian space other than what might be offered under an extended porch. As Elliott West has noted, "The streets, pounded continuously by feet, hooves, and the wheels of heavy ore wagons, became quagmires of oozing mud in which pack animals foundered and occasionally drowned. Into these thoroughfares resi-

Figure 2.12. Labeau's Jewelry (Colorado Store) ca. 1863–70, Virginia City, Montana. The original facade was load-bearing log in 1863, but was replaced in 1870 with the balloon-frame front shown here. (Photo by Thomas Carter)

dents threw dirt from cellars, garbage, manure, and even dead animals, which in turn attracted large numbers of swine as scavengers."[18] People afoot and in wagons, then, traveled the muddy, litter-ridden centers of the street, observing the shops from a fair distance. Hence, planar wall signage was appropriate and practical before a town matured.

Until courthouses, schools, and churches were constructed to meet specialized institutional needs, church services, school classes, or lodge meetings were held in private homes or behind commercial false fronts. However, it may well be that these urban Americans, like other urbanites in increasing numbers after 1850, spent far more time in retail and commercial environments than in schools or churches or houses of any kind. In Bannack, for example, more retail business and saloon trade took place on Sunday than any other day of the week.

Figure 2.13. Granite, Montana, 4 July 1894. A zone of compressed activity was created by the tightness of the urban fabric defined by the false fronts. Often, behind this false sense of order and urban density existed rambling miner's cabins, as the organizational element of the main street yielded to the remote expanse of the frontier. (Courtesy Montana Historical Society)

Placed increasingly closer together because of rising property costs and a need to locate new businesses near the center of town, the rectilinear fronts began to enclose and define the linear progression of Main Street. By reproducing the rhythms of urban row buildings, the false fronts represented an attempt to establish an urban scale that would help to retaliate against the vastness of the country and extreme isolation. Low, outstretched awnings attached to the wooden fronts served a similar purpose. The awnings provided a type of protective shroud against the elements, and perhaps against the grand western panoramas as well, giving the mining town dweller a psychologically comforting sense of "enclosure" (fig. 2.13). Further, the incremental repetition of parallel facades created a vista down the length of Main Street that pointed to the all-important supply lines upon which the town's survival depended. In addition, the concentration of the false fronts forced a vertical expression to offset the inordinately wide expanse of Main Street, which was designed to allow room for ox-drawn wagons to turn around (since oxen refuse to back up). The result was a tightly defined space approaching the quality of a large city in terms of motion, density, and activity. Within this compact and narrowly defined urban space, all the activity of the town was concentrated.

The sense of enclosure offered by Main Street did not extend far, however, for the rest of the town outside the business district assumed the amorphous grouping of structures characteristic of its predecessor—the camp. Nevertheless, the brief disengagement from the vast spatial surroundings created by the breadth, height, and expanse of the business block spoke clearly of an environment specially created and controlled by humans. People had established their presence in the wilderness and intended to stay—at least for the moment. The appearance of false-front buildings, replacing as they did the impermanent camp structures, signaled to western mining town residents that a significant hurdle had been passed in the process of urbanization. For many mining camps, of course, further maturation never occurred; claims "played out" or miners moved on to other diggings. For such camps, their highest point of urban attainment was embodied in the form of the abandoned false front.

Notes

For an expanded version of this study, see Kingston Heath, "Striving for Permanence on the Western Frontier: Vernacular Architecture as Cultural Informant in Southwestern Montana" (Ph.D. diss., Brown University, 1985). Special thanks to John Strobel, whose 1978 term paper "The False Fronts in Montana Mining Communities: 1863–1894" began to establish basic concepts of alignment and meaning from which I would expand years later.

1. For more on western mining communities as part of the "urban frontier," see Duane A. Smith, *Rocky Mountain Mining Camps* (Lincoln: University of Nebraska Press, 1974).

2. The first pay dirt was discovered in Montana ca. 1852 by François Finlay at Gold Creek, located on the branch of the Hellgate River off Mullan's Pass. Although Finlay found only small quantities of gold, word spread about the ore deposits in that area. Throughout the late fifties and until the strike at Grasshopper Creek, parties from California (spring 1858) and "Pike's Peakers" continued to pan Gold Creek and its tributaries. Montana's first major placer diggings were discovered by John White and his party on 28 July 1862. Grasshopper Creek had been named Willard Creek by Lewis and Clark. For more on the first gold claims, see Oran Sassman, "Metal Mining in Historic Beaverhead" (master's thesis, Montana State University, 1941), 52.

3. Smith, *Rocky Mountain Mining Camps*, 4.

4. Ken Karsmizski, "Bannack, Montana: Frontier Mining Town, 1862–1863," paper prepared for K. Heath, Montana State University, School of Architecture, 1980, p. 6.

5. Clyde McLemore, ed., "Bannack and

Gallatin City in 1862–1863: A Letter by Mrs. Emily R. Meredith," *Sources of Northwest History*, no. 24 (summer 1937): 4 n. 12.

6. Seymour Dunbar, ed., *The Journals and Letters of Major John Owen*, 2 vols. (New York: E. Eberstadt, 1927), 1:263–66.

7. Such forms as the gable-ended store/house were not exclusive to mining camps; because of similar conditions in the cost and availability of materials, this commercial format found its way to Bozeman in its first year (1864–65) and probably to other communities as well.

8. The Pioneer Milling Company was located on Godfrey's Canyon. It offered boards for mining rockers for $400 per thousand. By 18 November 1862, however, lumber prices had been reduced to $150 per thousand (probably because of competition by other mills). See Muriel Walle, *Montana Pay Dirt* (Chicago: Swallow Press, 1971), 53.

9. The saloons were operated by Durant, Perie, Jack Ganns, Bill Goodrich, and Cyrus Skinner. Indicating the waning popularity of Yankee Flat for the growing commercial interests, Goodrich and Skinner moved their "whiskey shops" from Yankee Flat, where they had located in the fall of 1862, to the other side of the creek by February 1863. Karsmizski, "Bannack, Montana," 14.

10. James L. Thane Jr., ed., *A Governor's Wife on the Mining Frontier* (Salt Lake City: University of Utah Library, 1976), 84. The same pattern of saloons being among the most pretentious of the early settlement structures is true as well of the distribution center and agricultural community of Bozeman, whose first brick structures (1872) were the Laclede Hotel and the Dunvian Saloon–Billiard Hall facing it.

11. Capt. James L. Fisk, *Expedition from Fort Abercrombie to Fort Benton*, 37th Cong., 3d sess., Ex. Doc. no. 80 (Washington, D.C.: Government Printing Office, 1863), 27.

12. For more on how the physical evolution of the "drinking house," or saloon, parallels the growth and maturation of a mining town, see Elliott West, *The Saloon on the Rocky Mountain Mining Frontier* (Lincoln: University of Nebraska Press, 1979), esp. chap. 2.

13. Ibid., 28.

14. Kingston Heath and Mikel Kallestad, "Gallatin City: Its Significance in Montana's History" (Helena: Montana State Historic Preservation Office, January 1986),

15. During my tenure as the state architectural historian in the Montana State Historic Preservation Office, I located several examples of this construction technique in western Montana that dated from between 1840 and 1870. For more of this earlier tradition, see T. Richie, "Plankwall Framing: A Modern Wall Construction with an Ancient History," *Journal of the Society of Architectural Historians* 30:1 (March 1971): 66–70. See also Richard W. Hale Jr., "The French Side of the 'Log Cabin Myth,'" *Proceedings of the Massachusetts Historical Society* 72 (October 1957–December 1960): 118–25; for how this framing technique fits into the broader timber-framing tradition, see Fred B. Kniffen and Henry Glassie, "Building in Wood in the Eastern United States: A Time-Place Perspective," *Geographical Review* (January 1966).

16. Augustus Welby Pugin's *Contrasts, or a Parallel between the Architecture of the Fifteenth and Nineteenth Centuries* (1836) and *The True Principles of Pointed or Christian Architecture* (1841), John Ruskin's *Seven Lamps of Architecture* (1849) and *The Stones of Venice* (1851), and the later theories of William Morris all purported that architecture had a mission to reform society through "honest" craftsmanship, "truthful" use of materials, and forthright applications of structural systems. Hence, the stated dread of "falseness" in architecture during the Victorian era was part of the popular consciousness.

Wilbur Fisk Sanders, "Early History of Montana," Montana Historical Society manuscript no. 217, quoted in Thane, *A Governor's Wife*, 40; Martha Edgerton Plassman, "Excerpts from Letters of Mary Edgerton, 1863–1865," Montana Historical Society typescripts, quoted in Thane, *A Governor's Wife*, 48.

17. Quoted in Clyde McLemore, "Bannack and Gallatin City in 1862–1863," 124. Flour was short everywhere in Montana during the winter of 1864–65. In April 1865 speculators bought up local supplies in Nevada City, Montana (not far from Bannack), and forced prices up. On 2 and 3 April, a mob of five hundred men in Nevada City and nearby Virginia City confiscated all flour, rationed it to the citizens on the basis of need, sold it at standard price, and returned the adjusted profit to the merchant. See *Montana Post*, 8, 15, 22 April 1865.

18. West, *The Saloon on the Rocky Mountain Frontier*, 33.

CHAPTER THREE

Folk Design in Utah Architecture, 1849–1890

THOMAS CARTER

Silhouetted against the rugged Great Basin landscape, folk architecture in Utah is highly visible (fig. 3.1). The old adobe, stone, and brick houses of the Mormon pioneers have captured the attention of scholars and the general public alike with their stately affirmation of historical continuity.[1] As visible signs from the past, these old buildings are comforting yet at the same time aloof and mysterious, for while such houses have the potential to tell us much about early Utah history, our inability to comprehend the architectural vocabulary remains frustrating. For a variety of reasons, old houses have proved to be elusive historical documents.

For one thing, the precise intentions of people working in the 1860s are impossible to know directly. Builders' diaries and record books are uncovered only rarely, and the people who could answer our questions about architectural motives are long dead. Deprived of the irretrievable initial context, the historian logically turns back to the buildings themselves. Yet even here, standing before the real and touchable artifact, complicated methodological problems remain. The majority of nineteenth-century houses, mostly the average or smaller ones, are gone. Of those that do remain, many have been altered to the point that they retain little of their original appearance and personality. Utahans approach them and speak of their "architectural heritage," expecting vague recollections of pioneer forefathers to suffice for explanation and meaning. The term *heritage* implies something acquired from predecessors—architecture, in this case. Our task as historians is to discover the nature of that inheritance.

Dismayed by the scarcity of primary sources, intimidated by the size of the state, and confounded by the complexity of the extant architectural record, students of Utah folk housing have consistently turned from the analysis of actual buildings to seek answers elsewhere. Often the labels popularly attached to such buildings have served as the basis for scholarly interpretation. In Utah, houses from the period

Figure 3.1. Stone house in Harrisburg, Utah, with the Pine Valley Mountains in the background. (Photo by author)

between 1849 and 1890 are typically "Mormon" or "Pioneer" houses and are identified with the folk (or vernacular) phase of architectural development. "Pioneer" suggests sacrifice and hardship, "folk" connotes the plain and unsophisticated, and the fact that Utah folk housing is overwhelmingly Mormon furnishes the emerging image with the saintly qualities of purpose and order. From this perspective, the houses may be viewed as practical adaptations to the frontier environment, they are primitive and simple in their design, and ultimately they are the solid and humorless manifestations of Mormon religious kingdom-building in the Great Basin.[2] Accordingly, the unknown has been rendered understandable through an informal partnership with concepts that are locally well known.

Such an interpretation of folk architecture, while convenient, remains problematic, for it is necessarily built on stereotypes of both folk culture and Mormon society and deals only marginally with actual buildings. Houses become what they should be, rather than what they are. If the study of folk housing is to be used effectively to tell us something new about nineteenth-century Utah and thus transcend a nostalgic antiquarianism, thorough description must replace broad generalization. While this essay cannot be exhaustive, it does highlight several of the key aesthetic principles operative within the folk building tradition. By questioning the design assumptions of the pioneer builders we can begin to solve the architectural and historical puzzle.

A Folk Aesthetic

Folk objects have consistently been denied artistic merit. In a 1952 study of Utah architecture, David Winburn voiced a widely held opinion that early Mormon houses were "in most cases so simple and unostentatious that it may be, in speaking of most of them, 'architecture' is too dignified a term to employ, since the term implies a conscious attempt toward artistic expression." The recognition of a particular folk aesthetic is impeded by the feeling, deeply rooted in Western consciousness, that artistic expression is confined to the progressive and elite segments of society. We are uncomfortable with the idea that the university-trained architect and the folk builder grapple with similar design problems. Of course, their solutions may be different—one striving for innovation, the other inherently conservative—but both are united by the common desire to produce an attractive and workable finished product. No builder consciously rejects the right to artistic expression. All artifacts—pioneer dwellings included—are shaped with an eye for their appearance.[3]

If folk buildings today appear starkly utilitarian, they are nevertheless ill served by being relegated to a rigid craft category. Eulogies to good craftsmanship ("they don't build them like that anymore"), however well-intended, inherently circle back to an exaltation of the pragmatic at the expense of the artistic. In such a scheme, craftsmen become insensitive machines, blindly cranking out useful and well-made objects with no thought to appearance. In one study of Mormon architecture, Cindy Rice points to the apparent incompatibility between folk and style when she writes that "the Mormon style house, with its austere lines, symmetry, and primarily brick or rock construction imparts a feeling of permanence and purpose but not frivolity."[4]

While durability is admittedly a factor influencing any builder, this preoccupation with the practical implies that folk objects can have no beauty save in economy. A house, however, is more than any scholar's set of "juxtaposed rectangles,"[5] and in life it is imbued with a variety of specific functions.[6] The roof keeps out the rain and the windows let in light, but the house is also meant to be visually pleasing to the builder and others in the community. Most contemporary examples of architecture are considered successful if they demonstrate singularity (or effectively emulate popular elements of an original idea). Folk builders, on the other hand, achieve their goal if their design resembles the familiar. We know that building a house is an important event. Time and money are expended on a structure that confers status upon its occupant. Decisions affecting house design therefore cannot be frivolous in a careless sense. Designs can be playful, but only so long as they remain sensitive to prevailing ideas about what is beautiful. The realization that both progressive and conservative designs are expressive gestures makes possible a meaningful synthesis of the concepts of folk, architecture, and art.

A folk house can be studied as art because it is the material articulation of a specific designing process. By concentrating on the more inclusive concept of design, the exclusive and prescriptively elitist meanings of the word art can be avoided. Art historian Kenneth Ames has suggested "that it is time to admit that art is not an eternal truth but a time-linked and locally variable concept, its definition being altered in response to complex patterns of social interaction." In shifting away from the study of art to the study of the "designed world," the realm of aesthetic experience is opened up to all people. The mansion on Salt Lake City's South Temple Street and the stone farm house in rural Willard *both* comply with the visual requirements of their respective Utah audiences. Neither design is inherently better than the other, nor is one considered "art" and the other something less. A house is not folk because it is plainly utilitarian, but because its design is considered traditional within the culture that produced it. *Folk* describes the process of building, not the absence of style.[7] The likes, dislikes, and persistent needs of Utah's pioneer builders are thus expressed in the controlling decisions that shaped their houses. Design preferences can be discerned in three main areas: construction, decoration, and composition.

Construction

Driven from Illinois into the desert wilderness of Utah, the Mormon pioneers were well aware of the biblical precedent of their exodus. They were also aware of the symbolic importance of wilderness. The formidable Great Basin landscape became a place where the Saints would be tested. From pulpits across the territory echoed a familiar message: A kingdom of God would be built on Earth and the desert would give way to earthly paradise. The individual Mormon undoubtedly saw the task in a more immediate and dramatic way. The rugged mountains, endless skies, and semiarid valley must have struck these dislodged easterners as awesome indeed, and from that first day in the summer of 1847 when the creeks of Salt Lake Valley were diverted for irrigation water, the struggle against the wilderness was joined. The village townscape, which became ubiquitous in Utah, with its geometrically defined streets and overstated visual order, comforted the settlers by effectively drawing a boundary between humans and nature (fig. 3.2).[8] Domestication was the watchword of the day. LDS church president Brigham Young instructed his followers not to ravage and despoil the land, but rather to subdue it and make it beautiful: "There is a great work for the Saints to do; progress and improve upon and make beautiful everything around you. Cultivate the earth and cultivate your minds. Build cities, adorn your habitations, make gardens, orchards and vineyards, and render the earth so pleasant that when you look upon your labors you may do so with pleasure, and that angels may delight to come and visit your beautiful locations."[9] The Edenic garden envisioned by the Utah Mormons would become the blueprint for the future. Following the Parousia, the Millennium would be ushered in according to the plan that the Saints had established in Utah. In their efforts to realize the prophecy, the kingdom builders of the Great Basin sent nature reeling before them. The rejection of nature constitutes the first tenet of the folk architectural aesthetic.

The conflict between garden and wilderness is peculiar neither to Utah nor to the Mormons. It is a simple opposition found deeply embedded in the American psyche. Early colonists reached the shores of this continent confident that a true paradise awaited. To the uninitiated, America was a land of "fabulous riches, a temperate climate, longevity, and garden-like natural beauty."[10] The reality was different. Surrounded by what many described as a "howling wilderness," the newcomers of the seventeenth century struggled valiantly to transform wild reality back into Edenic dream. Untamed land threatened people on several levels. First, the untouched forest darkness harbored ferocious beasts, savage men, and demons of the imagination. On a second and deeper level, wilderness was believed to be an area where civil and moral laws became inoperative and behavioral restraints broke down. However one viewed it, wilderness presented an affront to human sensibilities.

The story of the domestication of our continent is well known. The forest was cleared, crops planted, and the land transformed into an orderly arrangement of farms, roads, and cities. The "pioneer tradition" that conquered the land had little sympathy for nature. The French historian Alexis de Tocqueville visited America in 1831 and rightly observed that "living in the wilds, [the pioneer] only prizes the works of man."[11] Plow and ax would effectively control the natural world. When Brigham Young spoke of "beautiful houses," his concept of beauty was consistent with that of his fellow frontier travelers: he was looking for a beauty based on artificiality. The western European folk design aesthetic is built around the square, not the circle; it favors the smooth over the roughness of texture; and it glorifies the balanced over the irregular. The organic is stifled by the synthetic, and in building up Zion the

Figure 3.2. Aerial photograph of Ephraim, Utah, showing the town grid within its surrounding fields. (Courtesy Utah State Historical Society)

Utah Mormons followed a well worked-out American tradition of "turning nature into culture."[12]

The Mormon landscape is self-consciously controlled and fundamentally synthetic. While the first settlers were forced out of necessity to live in dugouts, the experience only intensified their antipathy to nature. If compelled to utilize native materials like adobe, stone, and logs in building permanent structures, the settlers used their technological prowess to shape these materials into the geometry of civilization. The various construction techniques employed in Utah demonstrate the settlers' willingness to devote considerable time and expense to differentiate the human from the natural landscape.[13]

Logs for dwellings were sawed or hewn square and thus deprived of their identity as trees. Often the logs were further disguised by the application of lumber siding or plaster (fig. 3.3). The organic irregularities of stone were chiseled into a smooth regularity of pattern pleasing to the settler's eye. The process of quarrying the stone, hauling it to the building site, shaping it into blocks, and placing the mortar in evenly coursed lines transcended pioneer expediency (fig. 3.4). Clay was extracted from the ground, mixed with sand, and molded into the adobe bricks that became the most commonly used of all Mormon building materials. To help protect the soft, sun-dried bricks from the weather, builders often plastered walls to present a smooth exterior finish. Plastering helped to preserve the fragile bricks; it also made the house more attractive. In many parts of the state a plaster veneer resembling brick or stone was applied over the adobe (fig. 3.5).[14]

In shaping the house exterior, the Utah builders made their meaning clear: gold camps and railroad towns might come and go, but the Mormon communities would stay as permanent fixtures on the land. The West might indeed be wild and woolly, but the civilized world of middle-class America reigned in Utah. The house goes beyond the practicality of shelter in affirming Mormonism as a "correct, wholesome, and successful way of life." As folklorist Austin Fife reminds us, "their [the Saints' houses] every line bespeaks the will to survive with dignity and the rationale of a well ordered household in a well ordered world."[15]

Decoration

Driven by the desire for permanence and decency in a hostile environment, the early Utah settlers moved quickly away from the level of simple subsistence. By the 1850s and 1860s houses that displayed an ever-increasing concern for the comforts and fashions left behind in the East began to appear. Brigham Young's first Salt Lake City residence (fig. 3.6) and later the Beehive House and the Lion House (1857–58) exhibited features of architectural design well above the minimal requirements

Figure 3.3. The log walls of this Spring City, Utah, house have been covered with willow lathe and plaster. (Photo by author)

Figure 3.4. Rough ashlar wall of oolite limestone with scored mortar joints, Spring City, Utah. (Photo by author)

Figure 3.5. "Bricking," a plaster technique in which a painted surface veneer is placed over adobe to resemble red kiln-fired brick, Spring City, Utah. (Photo by author)

of shelter.[16] The Saints, following Brigham's concern for beauty, demonstrated a remarkable capability for building substantial dwellings and for keeping their designs abreast of current architectural fashion.

Mormon society has never known the stark, self-imposed asceticism found in some American religious sects. Although Utah's pioneer buildings have often been characterized as austere and spartan, the architectural evidence indicates that the Mormon people took Brigham Young's admonition to "build beautiful houses" to heart and whenever possible chose the adorned over the plain. Traditional houses like the single-cell, hall-parlor, double-cell, temple form, and central-passage dominated much of nineteenth-century Utah building (fig. 3.7a–e), but these basic types were more often than not decorated with features from the latest architectural fashion.[17] Architectural historian Peter Goss has identified five major styles surfacing in Utah during the 1847–90 period—Federal, Greek Revival, Gothic Revival, Second

Figure 3.6. Brigham Young built this house, called the "White House," between 1850 and 1851 in Salt Lake City for his first wife, Mary Ann Angell. Despite its early date, the house (now demolished) had stylistic pretensions, including Greek Revival cornice returns, cantilevered balcony, and plastered adobe walls. (Courtesy Utah State Historical Society)

Empire, and the various eclectic styles associated with the Victorian period—and all appear regularly within the folk idiom as decoration applied to specific areas on the building's outer fabric.[18] On the gables, eaves, dormers, and entrances, builders could experiment with the frivolities of fashion without jeopardizing the successful appearance of the house.

Folk housing in the United States generally adheres to a formal arrangement and symmetrical composition traceable to the dramatic influence of the Neoclassical architectural style on Colonial America. Directed by the Palladian-derived preference for visual order and rhythmical balance, Utah folk builders, like their counterparts in other sections of the country, manipulated decorative elements in such a way as to make them compatible with the discipline exerted by these structuring principles. As new architectural fashions emerged from the architect's sketchbook, they were quickly inspected for decorative features appropriate to the folk reper-

Figure 3.7. The principal vernacular house types found in the Mormon West, 1849–90: *a. single-cell,* with rear kitchen, ca. 1880, Fairview, Utah; *b. hall-parlor,* with rear kitchen, ca. 1880, Manti, Utah; *c. double-cell,* ca. 1875, Fountain Green, Utah; *d. temple-form,* with side kitchen wing, ca. 1870, Manti, Utah; *e. central-passage,* with rear kitchen wing, ca. 1890, Manti, Utah. (Drawings by Alan Barnett)

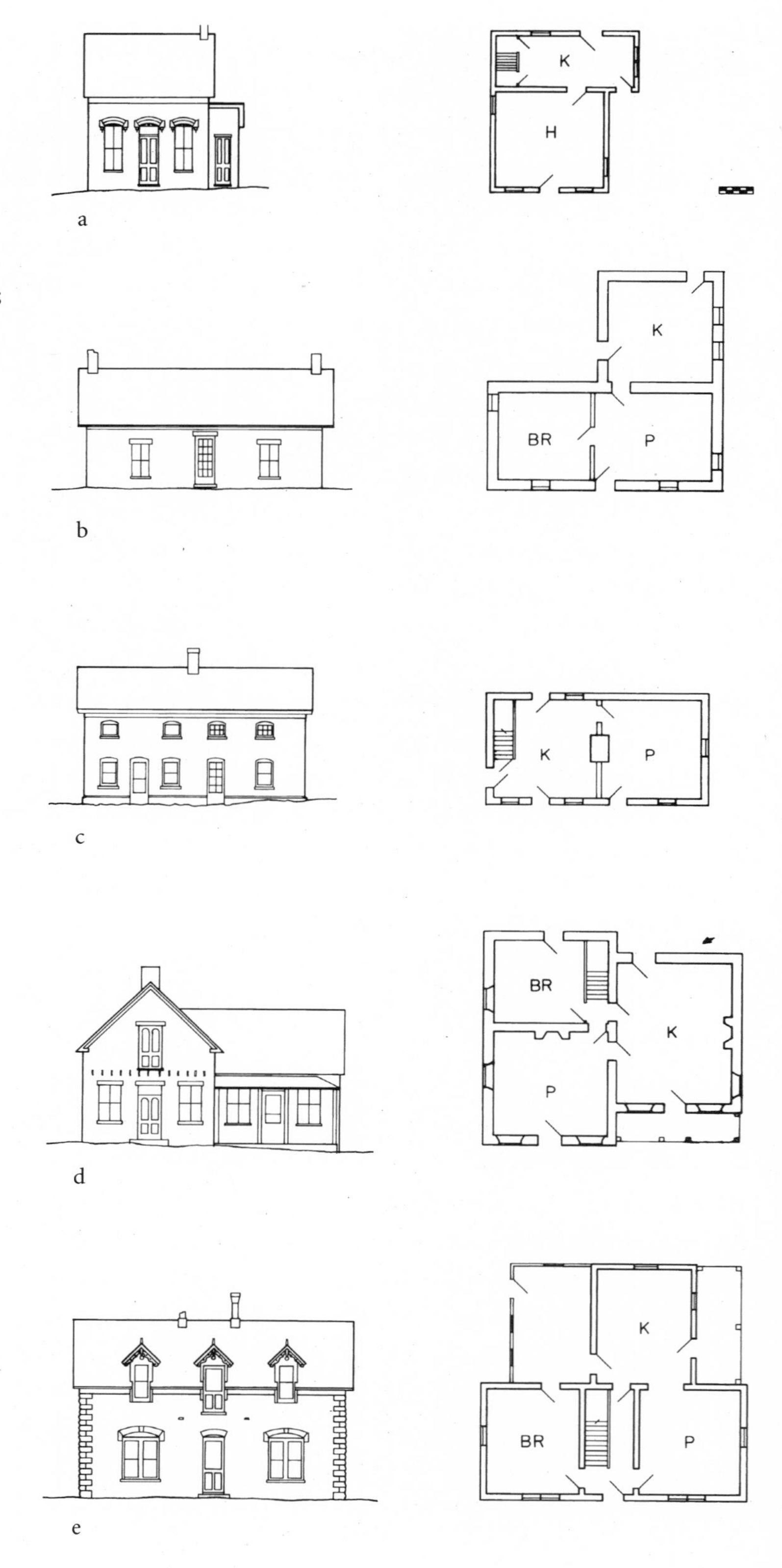

toire. The Federal style lent a shallow, low-pitched roof to the builder's book, but did not change the shape of the house (fig. 3.8). The colossal columns and pedimented gables of the Greek Revival were rejected at the folk level, but a scaled-down version of the Greek house became a part of the Mormon New England tradition and can be found in Utah, often with Greek Revival–inspired entablature, pediment-shaped window heads, and plain cornice returns (fig. 3.9). The visual complexity associated with the picturesque Gothic Revival style was translated by folk carpenters into a simple center facade gable, symmetrically incorporated into the older house plan. Such houses often had spired finials and intricately cut bargeboards (fig. 3.10). Later nineteenth-century styles, often lumped together rather casually under the term *Victorian,* are also found in the folk builder's repertoire, surfacing primarily in such things as wall shingling, clipped gables, and an occasional turret (fig. 3.11).[19]

Most of the ideas for decorative work were disseminated in the countryside through popularly oriented house pattern books. Such books, really builder's manuals, contained house plans, decorative ideas, and landscaping suggestions. If the builder was attracted by a particular geegaw or filigree found in these catalogs, it could be ordered from a local mill specializing in such materials. Folk architecture does not exist in a cultural vacuum. People in early Utah were exposed to progressive ideas in architecture through a wide variety of books and newspapers, not to mention firsthand accounts of travelers to Salt Lake City and the East. Yet the willingness to accept the new was tempered by its reconciliation with the old.[20] Innovation was tolerated, but only to the extent that the line of tradition remained unbroken. It is important to remember that folk buildings encountered in Utah that have some, but not all, of the characteristics of certain recognized architectural styles are not incomplete and naive renderings of the high-style designs, but result instead from a vigorous dialogue between the old and the new, the conservative and the innovative.[21]

Composition

How a house is decorated is but one part of a larger, more complex system of house design or composition. Beginning from a base concept—in this case, the floor plan—the house rises to completion as a series of decisions the builder makes about size, height, roof orientation, window placement, and decoration.[22] The choices are made through the application of a series of designing rules—rules that gain authority by their compatibility with the prevailing traditional aesthetic.[23] The rules work to narrow the field of choice and ensure that the house, when finished, will look "right." Within the system there is a degree of freedom, but at the same time limits are placed on the number and types of selections a builder may make. For example,

Figure 3.8. Allred House, Spring City, Utah, mid-1870s. (Photo by author)

assume that a family in St. George, a city in southwestern Utah, wanted a new house. After choosing the basic floor plan, their next step would be to decide the orientation of the roof. Within the Utah tradition, the ridge of the roof may be placed either parallel or perpendicular to the public space (usually the street), but never at an angle. Once the orientation of the house has been determined, the family proceeds to questions about height. The folk repertoire contains rules for one-, one-and-a-half, two-, and two-and-a-half-story buildings. Depending upon their resources and needs, they decide how tall their house will be. Similar decisions determine the placement of chimneys, the arrangement of the front door and windows, and the application of decorative elements.

Obviously there is no set order for the consideration of the designing rules, but all are brought into action before the house is completed. The rules bring order to chaos and make the builder's task practicable. How many choices the builder will

Figure 3.9. Mason House, Willard, Utah, mid-1860s. (Photo by author)

have within a given rule set is determined by the restrictions the culture places upon acceptable variation. In some areas of the United States folk builders labored under a severely circumscribed rule set. In Utah, however, the compositional options appear remarkably open, a condition that probably reflects both the secure nature of the compact Latter-day Saints' religious communities and the heterogeneous convert population.[24] The rules pertaining to the fenestration of the facade are particularly illustrative of the latitude available within the Utah folk building style.

On the whole, folk housing in Utah reflects the continued influence of eighteenth-century Neoclassicism. The overriding preference in the early settlement period was for a bilaterally symmetrical and tripartite house.[25] An object is bilaterally symmetrical if it can be divided visually into two identical parts. Inserting a third element between these two halves leads to a construction that is tripartite (containing three distinct components) and yet is still bilaterally symmetrical (dividing the object down

Figure 3.10. Judd House, St. George, Utah, ca. 1870. (Photo by author)

the middle continues to yield two identical halves). The house Jonathan Platts built in Salt Lake City is a good example of bilateral, tripartite symmetry (fig. 3.12). Piercing the facade of the house—that is, making openings for the doors and windows—usually follows the controlling guidelines of symmetrical balance. Upstairs windows (and occasionally doors) are located directly over the lower openings to achieve a facade that is in perfect equilibrium. Utah folk houses generally reflect this desire for order, and the placement of second-story openings over first-floor openings was the first and most obvious choice for piercing the house facade.

Within the Utah tradition, however, other rules exist that deviate from this rigidly balanced pattern. The houses pictured in figure 3.13 were all constructed in Spring City, a town in Central Utah, between 1870 and 1880. Although the houses all have the same hall-parlor floorplan, they display a high degree of compositional diversity. Spring City residents achieved visual complexity by effectively playing off the upper against the lower openings. Figures 3.13a and 3.13b are unusual and in-

Figure 3.11. Gardner House, Mendon, Utah, 1880s. (Photo by author)

Figure 3.12. Platts House, Salt Lake City, 1850s. (Drawing by Lee Udall Bennion)

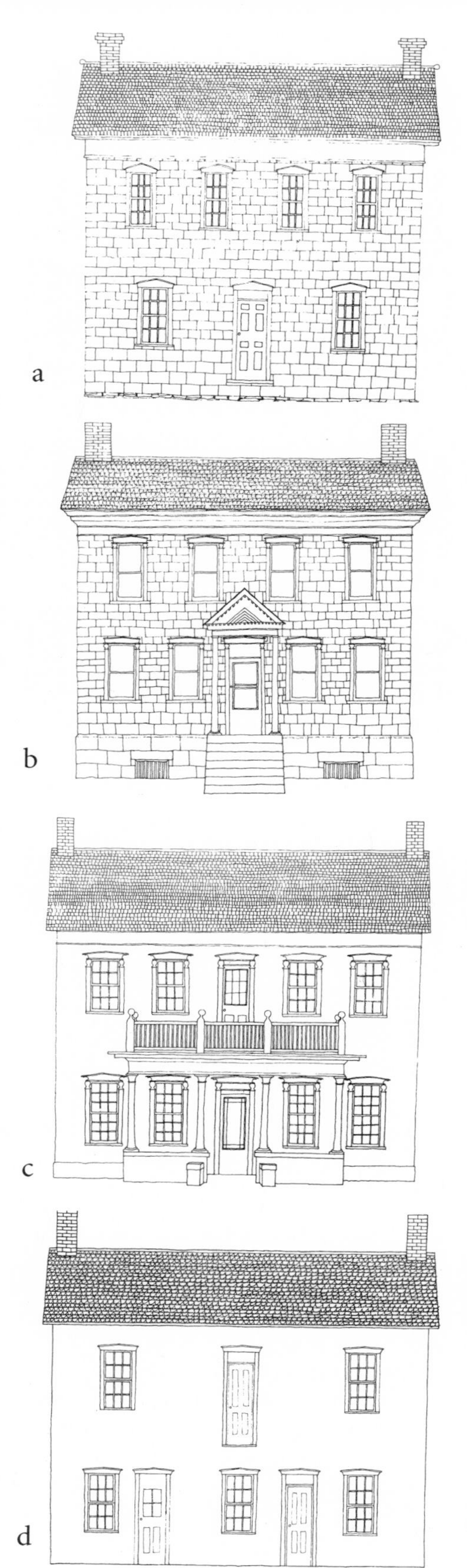

Figure 3.13. Facade variations in Spring City, Utah, hall-parlor houses: *a.* Crawforth House, four bays over three, early 1880s; *b.* Hyde House, four bays over five, mid-1860s; *c.* Crisp House and Hotel, five bays over five, mid-1870s; *d.* Borresen House, asymmetrical facade arrangement, mid-1860s. (Drawings by Lee Udall Bennion)

triguing variations on the theme of bilateral symmetry, playing off rows of odd- and even-numbered openings on the first and second floors. Figure 3.13c brings the house back into perfect harmony, although there are five rather than three bays. Symmetry breaks down completely in 3.13d, the finished house remaining successful only because of a tolerance within the designing system itself. The mismatching of the facade openings cannot be attributed to naivete or incompetence. On the contrary, such diversity indicates that the rules for facade piercing have been extended to compensate for a deeper confusion within the tradition itself, a confusion resulting from conflicting internal and external priorities.

A perfectly balanced house would have a symmetrical principal facade and a symmetrical floorplan. Such balance is achievable in a design that has an even number of bays—usually four or six—and a double-cell plan with two equal-size rooms (fig. 3.7c). Three- and five-bay facades adhere most closely to the tripartite ideal, yet their unequally divided hall-parlor plans sacrifice the symmetrical division of internal space (fig. 3.7b). The houses pictured in figures 3.13a and 3.13b reflect a conflict in the builder's mind between external and internal priorities. Each of these houses has a hall-parlor first-floor plan and a double-cell second-level room arrangement—hence the odd-numbered opening pattern downstairs and the even-numbered on top. The lack of control on the facade suggests that the conflict between inside and outside concerns was never fully resolved and that a compromise solution was never totally effected. The insertion of a central passage between two equal-size rooms is one solution to the problem of internal-external symmetry (fig. 3.7e). Yet Utah's experience with the central-hall house has been overstated.[26] Rather than adding a new room, many builders chose instead to work out their spatial problems on the facade of the hall-parlor house type itself.

The selection of one particular house type with one predictable facade pattern would point to the consolidation of design principles and the contraction of the rule set. In Utah, despite the theocratic organization of the society, such a selection and contraction did not occur. The hall-parlor houses in figure 3.14 effectively demonstrate the openness of the design tradition on a statewide level. The three-over-three, four-over-four, and five-over-five bay houses are the most commonly encountered forms in Utah, and the attention given here to the unusual houses has not been to highlight the exotic but rather to illustrate the flexibility of the tradition to accommodate a wide range of facade designs. The rules could be stretched to cover an astonishing range of actual designs, with builders manipulating ideas of order and symmetry up to and beyond the breaking point.

Most writers, probably out of a desire to find the closed system viewed as intrinsic to the orderly, authoritarian world of Zion, have ignored this diversity in Mormon folk architecture. Yet design

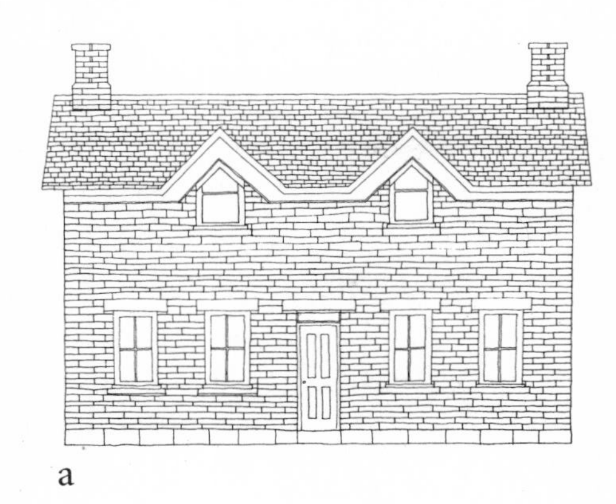
a

b

c

d

e

Figure 3.14. Design diversity in one-and-a-half-story, dormered houses found in the Mormon West during the nineteenth century: *a.* Fairview, two bays over five, hall-parlor plan, mid-1870s; *b.* Panguitch, three bays over five, hall-parlor plan, late 1870s; *c.* Fillmore, five bays over five, hall-parlor plan, ca. 1870; *d.* Paragoonah, three bays over four, double-cell plan on the ground floor, mid-1860s; *e.* Manti, four bays over four, double-cell plan, ca. 1875.

eclecticism was a reality in early Utah.[27] As John Taylor, Brigham Young's successor to the church presidency, told a group of Saints in Malad, Idaho: "You have a beautiful location, and I would like to see you make the most of it. I would like to see at least a hundred times more apple, pear, and cherry trees planted out; and all of your streets lined with shade trees. And improve your dwelling houses. If you cannot find the style of a house to suit you, go off to other places until you do find one, and then come back and build a better one."[28]

This short essay only begins to suggest the richness of Utah's early architecture. The size of the state and the great number of nineteenth-century buildings available for study makes these observations inescapably cursory. The pressing need remains for detailed community studies that will elevate this subject, overly simplified to date, back to its true complexity. A Mormon landscape has been discerned in the Mountain West, but its identity is still masked by an overriding concern for its form rather than its content. By trying to see the artistic basis for the design of pioneer buildings, we have shifted our gaze toward aspects of construction that transcend the practical; we have found that the solid and durable can also be decorative; and we have discovered that these old buildings are far from simple in their design. Folk houses are an important tool for understanding the everyday events and for getting to know the average people of the past. The task is to move beyond the Brigham-Young-slept-here-so-the-house-is-historic stage to the full realization of the potential all old buildings have in helping us construct a more complete historical record—a history that includes the unheralded many in addition to the glorified few. In the process, as the historian Davis Bitton has pointed out, we can begin to see the "Saints as human beings."[29] And, we can add, as Americans.

Notes

The obvious debt here is to the teaching and published works of Henry Glassie. Glassie's intriguing model for folk-housing analysis has provided an excellent framework for revising our perception of the Mormon architectural landscape. Thanks also to Peter Goss and Jan Shipps for valuable comments concerning the content of this essay.

1. A listing of works dealing with the material folk culture of Utah can be found in William A. Wilson's "Bibliography of Studies in Mormon Folklore," *Utah Historical Quarterly* 44 (fall 1976): 393–94. See also Thomas Carter, "Studies in Utah Vernacular Architecture: An Overview," *Utah Folklife Newsletter* 24 (spring 1990): 2–4.

2. One folklorist has written that Mormon houses "embody the same virtues of solidity, simplicity, and practicality that characterized the Saints themselves." See Jan Harold Brunvand, "The Architecture of Zion," *The American West* 13 (March–April 1976): 29.

3. David Winburn, "The Early Houses of Utah: A Study of Techniques and Materials" (master's thesis, University of Utah, 1952), 1–2; see Henry Glassie, "Artifacts: Folk, Popular, Imaginary, and Real," in *Icons of Popular Culture*, ed. Marshall Fishwick and Ray B. Browne (Bowling Green, Ohio: Bowling Green University Popular Press, 1970), 110–11; and John A. Kouwenhoven, *The Arts in Modern American Civilization* (1948; reprint, New York: W. W. Norton, 1967), 3.

4. Cindy Rice, "Spring City: A Look at a Nineteenth-Century Mormon Village," *Utah Historical Quarterly* 43 (summer 1975): 271.

5. Leon S. Pitman, "A Survey of Nineteenth-Century Folk Housing in the Mormon Culture Region" (Ph.D. diss., Louisiana State University, 1973), 191.

6. Henry Glassie, "Folk Art," in *Folklore and Folklife: An Introduction*, ed. Richard M. Dorson (Chicago: University of Chicago Press, 1973), 253; and Glassie, "Structure and Function: Folklore and the Artifact," *Semiotica* 7 (1973): 339.

7. Kenneth L. Ames, *Beyond Necessity: Art in the Folk Tradition* (New York: W. W. Norton, 1977), 16; Glassie, "Folk Art," 257–58.

8. For a discussion of the American concept of wilderness, see Roderick Nash, *Wilderness and the American Mind* (New Haven: Yale University Press, 1967), 8–43. Specific analogies in Mormon thinking are detailed in George H. Williams, *Wilderness and Paradise in Christian Thought* (New York: Harper and Bros., 1962), 117–20. The rationale of the village is outlined in Lowry Nelson, *The Mormon Village* (Salt Lake City: University of Utah Press, 1952); Leonard J. Arrington, Feramorz Y. Fox, and Dean May, *Building the City of God* (Salt Lake City: Deseret Book, 1976); and Charles S. Peterson, "A Mormon Town: One Man's West," *Journal of Mormon History* 3 (1976): 3–12.

9. Hugh W. Nibley, "Brigham Young on the Environment," in *To the Glory of God*, ed. Truman G. Madsen and Charles D. Tate Jr. (Salt Lake City: Deseret Book, 1972), 8.

10. Nash, *Wilderness and the American Mind*, 25.

11. Quoted in ibid., 23.

12. See Henry Glassie, *Folk Housing in Middle Virginia* (Knoxville: University of Tennessee Press, 1975), 122–36.

13. The most complete description of early folk construction techniques in Utah is found in Pitman, "A Survey of Nineteenth-Century Folk Housing," 17–109.

14. See Harley J. McKee, *Introduction to Early American Masonry*, National Trust–Columbia University Series on Technology of Early American Building, no. 1 (Washington, D.C.: National Trust for Historic Preservation, 1973), 86. The Mormon temple at Kirtland, Ohio, was covered with a similar "bricking" technique. See Laurel B. Andrew, *The Early Temples of the Mormons*, (Albany: State University of New York Press, 1978), 38–39.

15. Pitman, "A Survey of Nineteenth-Century Folk Housing," 59; Austin E. Fife, "Stone Houses of Northern Utah," *Utah Historical Quarterly* 40 (winter 1972): 19.

16. G. Y. Cannon, "Some Early Domestic Architecture in and around Salt Lake City, Utah," *American Architecture* 125 (May 1924), 473.

17. These house types are described in Henry Glassie, *Pattern in the Material Folk Culture of the Eastern United States* (Philadelphia: University of Pennsylvania Press, 1968). Austin Fife's work with stone house types remains the best early attempt to classify Utah folk architecture;

a more recent taxonomy is found in Thomas Carter and Peter Goss, *Utah's Historic Architecture, 1847–1940: A Guide,* (Salt Lake City: University of Utah Press, 1988).

18. Peter L. Goss, "The Architectural History of Utah," *Utah Historical Quarterly* 43 (summer 1975): 208–39.

19. On Neoclassical influence, see James Deetz, *In Small Things Forgotten: The Archaeology of Early American Life* (Garden City, N.Y.: Anchor, 1977), 98–117; Glassie, *Folk Housing in Middle Virginia,* 88–113; on Federal style, see Carter and Goss, *Utah's Historic Architecture,* 97–98; on Greek Revival, see Pitman, "A Survey of Nineteenth-Century Folk Housing," 207–8; on Gothic Revival, see Glassie, *Folk Housing in Middle Virginia,* 158; on Victorian, see Carter and Goss, *Utah's Historic Architecture,* 110–35.

20. The work of one particular architect also served to introduce popular eastern styles into Utah; see Paul L. Anderson, "William Harrison Folsom: Pioneer Architect," *Utah Historical Quarterly* 43, (summer 1975): 240–59; Glassie, "Folk Art," 260; Ames, *Beyond Necessity,* 78.

21. See Goss, "Architectural History," 215–16.

22. Glassie, "Structure and Function," 238–331. See also Milton B. Newton Jr. and Linda Puliam-Di Napoli, "Log Houses as Public Occasions: A Historical Theory," *Annals of the Association of American Geographers* 67 (September 1977): 360–66.

23. Glassie, "Folk Art," 259.

24. Glassie, *Folk Housing in Middle Virginia,* 19–40; see Thomas Carter, "Building Zion: Folk Architecture in the Mormon Settlements of Utah's Sanpete Valley, 1849–1890" (Ph.D. diss., Indiana University, 1984).

25. Pitman, "A Survey of Nineteenth-Century Folk Housing," 191–97; Glassie, "Folk Art," 272–74.

26. The internal-external symmetry issue is discussed in Glassie, *Folk Housing in Middle Virginia,* 68, and by Gary Stanton, "German-American Log Building in Franklin and Dubois Counties, Indiana," paper read at the Hoosier Folklore Society Annual Meeting, Connor's Prairie, Indiana, 11 March 1976.

The presence of the central-hall house has been vastly overestimated in Utah because of the general acceptance of Richard V. Francaviglia's early work, "Mormon Central-Hall Houses in the American West," *Annals of the Association of American Geographers* 61 (1979): 65–71. Compare Pitman, "A Survey of Nineteenth-Century Folk Housing," 167.

27. Dolores Hayden, *Seven American Utopias* (Cambridge: MIT Press, 1976), 142.

28. Quoted in Francaviglia, *The Mormon Landscape* (New York: AMS Press, 1978), 85.

29. For an overview of material dealing with the definition of the Mormon landscape see Wayne L. Wahlquist, "A Review of Mormon Settlement Literature," *Utah Historical Quarterly* 45 (winter 1977): 4–21; Davis Bitton, "Early Mormon Lifestyles; or the Saints as Human Beings," in *The Restoration Movement: Essays in Mormon History,* ed. F. Mark McKiernan, Alma Blair, and Paul Edwards (Lawrence, Kans.: Coronado Press, 1973), 306.

Adaptations and Innovations

Figure 4.1. View across the prairie toward the Calef farm buildings. (From Walling, *Illustrated History of Lane County*)

CHAPTER FOUR

The Calef's Farm in Oregon

A Vermont Vernacular Comes West

PHILIP DOLE

The farmhouse Elmer Norton Calef built in Oregon's Willamette Valley in 1872–73 deliberately copied a New England house.[1] Further New England characteristics are seen in the barn and in the farmstead complex. But the Calef buildings in Oregon were placed in a settlement pattern, landscape, and climate strongly in contrast to those of the Vermont original. A lithograph of 1884 shows the Calef farm buildings in the distance, to the left center (fig. 4.1). In the background, rising above the McKenzie River, are the Coburg Hills. Although modeling and artistic foreshortening have modified the real appearance of extensive prairie surrounding the Calef structures for a mile and sometimes more in every direction, the illustration nevertheless dramatizes the solitary position of the farmstead in the Oregon landscape, its very isolation reinforcing traditions, while simultaneously demanding their adaptation to western conditions. The lithograph was taken from the cemetery on top of Gillespie Butte. There, a marble monument capped with a shrouded urn is inscribed "Elmer N. Calef born in Orange Co., Vt., July 25, 1834, died near Eugene, Feb. 2, 1890."

The Elmer Calef farm lies at the center of a locality consisting of some twenty square miles of prairie defined by the confluence of the McKenzie and Willamette Rivers. The property lines of the farms in the area demonstrate how the first settlers marked out their claims to relate desirable land holdings, established by the diagonal drainage-ways of the rivers (south-east to north-west), to the rectangularity of the townships and mile-square section lines that were the legal basis for land distribution (fig. 4.2).[2] First claimants, such as the Stevens family (1847) and Armitages (1851), sought proximity to the river, which furnished scrub timber along its banks and, in particular, a variation in soil types. To this end, both low bottom land, for vegetable gardens, and, further from the river, the more elevated prairie land, for grain crops, were acquired.[3] Later arrivals like the Calefs had to settle for a less attractive location and a smaller farm, for after 1851 donation land laws granted less

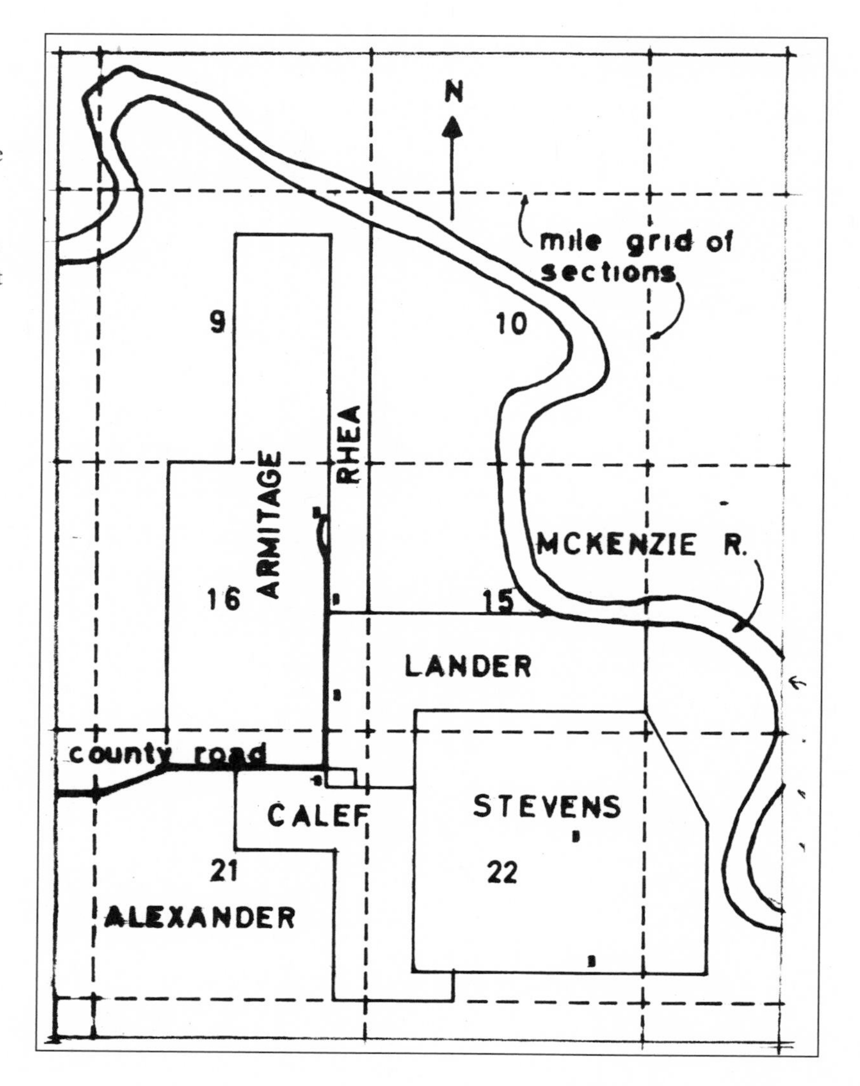

Figure 4.2. Map of the Calef property and neighboring farms. (Adapted from a map in Lane County Court House)

than the 640-acre parcels of the first land acquisitions.[4] The specific site for the Calef farm buildings was determined by their relationship to the road that led north to the nearby Armitage farm and that turned to form a sharp right angle at the center of the Calef purchase, thus providing a spot that commanded long views toward both directions of approach. A previous owner had begun development here with a cabin and a well.

Many pioneers crossed the continent by such slow stages that they had had residence in several states before arriving in Oregon, a factor to be noted in a detailed study of regional style. Elmer Calef's father-in-law, Mahlon Harlow, had moved in two stages. Born in 1811 in Barren County, Kentucky, he spent fifteen years there and twenty-five in Missouri before coming west with his family and several members of his wife's family to Lane County, Oregon. Here, about 1852, "for five dollars and a pistol" he took up a claim of 320 acres along the Willamette River.[5] On the

Harlow farm the settler's usual cabin, of board or log construction, gave way to a permanent house in the early 1850s. An account of Harlow's house indicates that it was a "saddlebag" type associated with the southern United States, having a central chimney dividing the house into two equal and completely separate parts.[6] The long, low, one-story, symmetrical building provided a loft on either end, "one with three double beds to sleep the boys, the other with two double beds for the girls" of the family. On the main floor the separation was emphatic for "it was necessary to go outside to get from one half of the house to the other." An open, recessed porch furnished the only communication between the two halves of the house.[7]

Mahlon Harlow's house in Oregon is representative of the "colonial" compulsion pioneers everywhere feel to reproduce the architecture of their earlier homes. The first Oregon settlers of the 1840s and 1850s had been born between the end of the Revolutionary War and the first quarter of the nineteenth century. Their birthplaces were along the eastern seaboard or in that first tier of inland states: Ohio, Kentucky, and Tennessee. It is from these areas that most of the ideas for the Pacific Northwest's first period Anglo-American architecture came. Ideas for early buildings sometimes came from the popular literature, too, but this source provided detail more often than either plan or form.

The Jacob Spores farm of 1847, located two and a half miles north of the Calef place, contained a typical barn and a prevalent type of house (fig. 4.3). The house is contemporary with and similar to the Harlow house in its double-cell, two-door form, but has end chimneys and interior connections between all rooms. The side elevation of the Spores house displays the Greek Revival eave moldings in fashion during the 1850s; the front elevation, featuring two main entrances, indicates direct derivation from a long-used type of house found in many eastern states, including New York State—where, in Montgomery County, Jacob Spores was born in 1795.

Just to the north of the Calef's sat the two-story house built by George Armitage about 1856 using materials from his own sawmill, a simple operation destroyed by a flood in 1862 (fig. 4.4). The house recalls, through its symmetrical pedimented Neoclassical front, the established character of farmhouses found in New York State. George Armitage was born there in 1824; in his twenties, he moved to Missouri, Illinois, Iowa, and Louisiana before arriving in the Oregon Territory at age twenty-nine. The Calef farmhouse is derivative, too, but it also is indicative of a more universal stylistic expression current after 1865 throughout the Willamette Valley, a vernacular version of the Gothic Revival. These Oregon houses—the Harlow house, the Spores house, the Armitage house, and the Calef house—in their stylistic and formal disparity and in their physical proximity to each other, offer a fair sample of Oregon's rural, domestic architecture during the third quarter of the nineteenth century.

Twenty-one-year-old Elmer Calef arrived in Lane County, Oregon, in 1855, hav-

Figure 4.3. The Spores buildings, house and typical barn of the 1850s. (From Walling, *Illustrated History of Lane County*)

Figure 4.4. Armitage barn (1877) and house (1856). (From Walling, *Illustrated History of Lane County*)

ing left his native Vermont earlier that same year. Although he came via the "Isthamus" and stopped off to visit the California gold fields, his trip west is simple and direct compared with the prolonged progression of other pioneers. Sarah Naomi Harlow and Elmer Calef were married in 1863.[8] In 1869 the couple bought from Walker Young, its second owner, the farm of 160 acres located on the northern boundaries of the Harlow place, measuring out the boundaries with a rope. Neither the maples that Mrs. Walker Young had set out the year before nor a fall of ten feet in the mile, diagonally across the site, were sufficient to modify the impression of a level, open landscape.

The presence of the maple trees must have pleased the Calefs. Such road or yard plantings had been a New England tradition since the eighteenth century.[9] A renewed interest in tree plantings around 1870 left its mark across New England, the Pacific Northwest, and elsewhere. Rows of planted trees added significantly to the towns and roads of the West. The public pursuit of that interest was described in the *Willamette Farmer,* 16 March 1872 under "Plant Out Maples": "Latterly the public taste has been improving and we see, especially . . . in the larger towns, a large annual increase in the planting of native trees, especially maples for shade and ornament. . . . Every farm will look better and appear to be more thrifty and prosperous if the public highway through it is lined with ornamental trees. It is no trouble to get small maples."[10] The size of Elmer Calef's farm in Oregon was similar to the size of many farms in Vermont; such characteristics as the uses of stock and a degree of diversified farming were similar, too. By 1880, exclusive of pasture and buildings, Elmer Calef's land was designated as three "fields," or "forties"—the East field, South field, and West field, each containing about forty acres. The Calef's crops were typical of the vicinity: half the acreage was placed in wheat, about another twenty each in oats and barley, plus a few acres to corn and hops and for the orchard that stood on both sides of the house. Another twenty acres, back of the barn, was enclosed as pasture for a small number of stock.[11] From 1870 to 1880 some similarities relate the farming in Vermont and the farming in the Willamette Valley in Oregon,[12] although the railroad, for example, which had reached Vermont in the 1850s, arrived at Eugene only in 1873, about the same time as the Calef buildings. Accessibility to railroad shipments had accelerated dairy production in Vermont; proximity to a city gave a farm such as the Calefs' similar advantage—as his butter production, though modest, may indicate. But for the most part dairy production in Oregon was for home use, and for Elmer Calef, like his neighbors, dairying was an agricultural venture not developed in a major way until the 1890s. Elmer Calef's agricultural experience and interests were largely transferable across the continent, usable in the development of his land and his buildings.

In 1872 Elmer Calef traveled the three thousand miles back to Washington, Vermont, where "all the surviving eleven sons and daughters assembled on the 10th of

Figure 4.5. Ira Calef House and connected barn in Vermont, ca. 1870. (Courtesy Miss Olive P. Calef)

Figure 4.6. Principal elevation of the Elmer Calef House in Oregon, with detached barn shown to the rear. (Photo by author)

June" for the family reunion at the home of their mother, Martha Paine Calef. Martha lived in the house her unmarried son Ira had built six years before (fig. 4.5). The house impressed Elmer to such an extent that by 1873, within a year of his return, the Ira Calef house had been copied "exactly" on the Oregon farm. In part the Oregon house is a replica of that in Vermont. However, major differences occur in its relationship to the site and the relationship between the house and the barn. The three-thousand-mile displacement had in fact produced changes.[13]

Ira Calef had constructed all his farm buildings at the same time, attached to each other in a single line, with the house on one end, the barn on the other, and the kitchen and woodshed filling the space between them. For reasons related to climate, efficiency, and aesthetics, this tightly connected building pattern had become prevalent in Vermont by the 1860s. But in contrast to Vermont's severe winters, Oregon's are so mild that

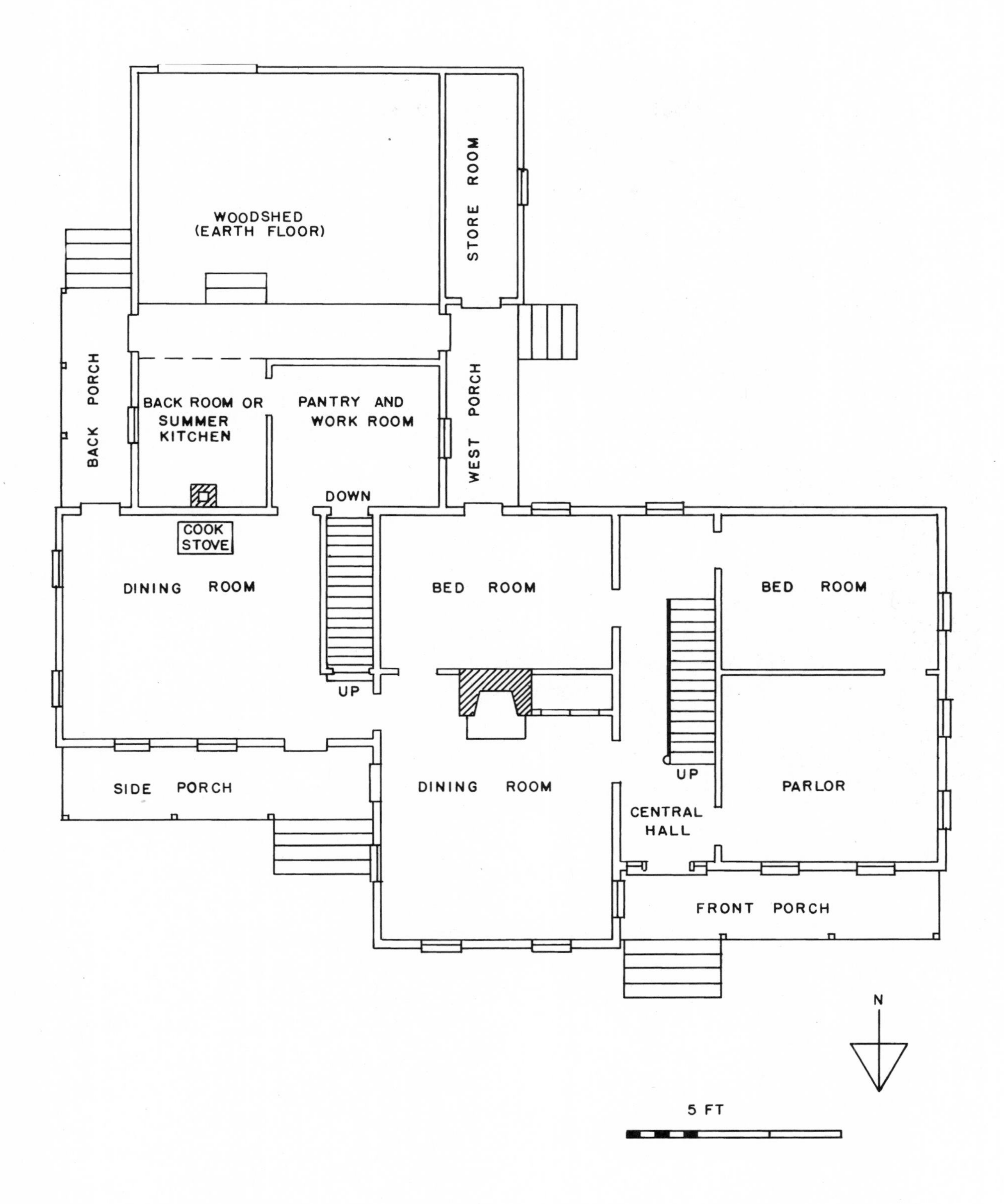

Figure 4.7. First-floor plan of the Elmer Calef House. (Drawing by author)

"the grass is green all winter." In Oregon, climate, as well as concerns about fire and barnyard odors, encouraged the separation of barns from houses, usually by more than one hundred feet. This separation had been the earlier practice in grouping farm buildings in New England. And, unlike his brother, Elmer Calef did not build his permanent farm buildings at the same time: first he built the house; a year or two later, the barn. Although the barn was placed a little more than one hundred feet behind the house, the barn and the house were directly related, and both were placed at a joint of the Z-shaped piece of property, a central position on the Elmer Calef farm (fig. 4.6)

Another deliberate difference was the placement of the woodshed in a second ell behind the kitchen wing, rather than as a linear extension of it, as would have been the practice in Washington, Vermont (fig. 4.7).[14] This located the woodshed along the driveway and near the work areas by the barn. Elmer's decision to have the main rooms of his house (parlor, living room, and kitchen) placed parallel to the road in Oregon also contrasted with the prevailing style in Vermont, which placed the kitchen to the rear, facing south.[15] In this, Elmer and his wife, Sarah Naomi, chose the strong relationship to the public road inevitably favored by the newer farmhouses in their Oregon neighborhood, an important social connection for all in this developing, rather dispersed, rural community. The parallel alignment of the Calef house to the road also capitalized on existing amenities. The presence of the two-room log cabin and of a well were primary determinants in locating the house, for the new building was placed behind the cabin, so that the existing maple trees were located in front parallel to the road. That one could "step from the cabin right into the kitchen" of the new house indicates the transitions in living arrangements before and during the construction period on a pioneer site. An open space on the front lawn still marks the cabin site.

Calefs east and west agree as to the story of the houses and are in some agreement that the cost of the Oregon house was defrayed from the East either by contributions of the Vermont brothers or with a savings of seven hundred dollars that Elmer Calef had collected on his return to Vermont, a reasonable cost for such a plain house in 1873. The money may have been inherited, for at the family reunion the final settlement of their father's estate was made as the youngest brother, John, had just reached twenty-one.[16] These stories, although sketchy, illustrate the ties, especially strong for Elmer and his children, maintained between the East Coast and the West Coast Calef families through periodic letters and visits for more than a hundred years. Other pioneer families in Oregon record similar family attachments, which are of interest in considering the building forms they employed.

Neighbors on the nearby farms would have seen the Elmer Calef house as large and fashionable, for stylistically it is like the homes they, too, were building in the 1870s. These vernacular expressions of the Gothic Revival style in the Pacific Northwest combined a selective, literal use of some Andrew Jackson Downing principles with other, pragmatic non-Downing modifications. The popularity gained for the Gothic Revival style in domestic architecture after 1840 is largely attributed to Downing, whose published articles and books were widely read.[17] To literal copying are ascribed the incorporation in vernacular Gothic Revival houses of porches and extensive verandas below a composition of steep roofs marked by tall chimneys, sometimes with a lancet window in the front gable. The pragmatic modifications of Downing designs resulted in the vernacular Gothic's penchant for plain features. In contrast to Downing's passionate preference for vertical siding, for example, horizontal siding was usually selected. And despite Downing's equally passionate plea for earth colors and his expressed repugnance toward white paint, white was the color most favored by the vernacular Gothic builders in Oregon, as well as such colors as yellow trimmed in brown, red, or a dark green.

The existence, both east and west, of a Calef house in the vernacular Gothic style suggests its popularity and the national extent of its use. Throughout the 1870s numerous examples of the style were constructed in the Pacific Northwest including all four of the other new Willamette Forks farmhouses built within a radius of a mile to a mile and a half of the new Calef house—houses for the Robert Campbell family (1873); for the Jimmy Stevens family (1875); for Delia Harlow Day, a sister of Mrs. Calef (about 1870); and for the family of Andrew Jackson Harlow, a brother of Mrs. Calef (1874). Although all the houses share similar T- or L-shaped cross-wing forms, there are differences. For example, the Delia Harlow Day house (now modified) was organized as a southern saddlebag into two separate parts, the kitchen wing and the front rooms. As in the house of her father, Mahlon Harlow, who built a saddlebag there twenty years earlier, the only connection between the two parts of Delia's house was through an open porch. Like the Calef house, these neighboring houses are arranged with their major rooms looking out at the road. In each, the parlor, dining room, and kitchen share that exposure. In contrast to the Calef house, the other houses have shallow floor plans dominated by one-room-deep spaces (fig. 4.8). They also have proportions and elements that more strongly accent verticality, height, and narrowness, and they have a more decorative character than the Calef house through jigsaw work on their porches and, usually, a lancet window above the front doors.

A version of Gothic Revival architecture very different from any of the Willamette Forks farmhouses was built at the same time three miles to the southeast in the small but urban county seat, Eugene City. This new house, constructed for the merchant A. V. Peters in 1872, represents an elegant and academically correct Gothic Revival house, a true high style building (fig. 4.9). The design appears to have been lifted from a popular architectural book by Cleaveland and Backus, *Village and Farm Cottages.* Cleaveland was a devotee of Andrew Jackson Downing, as the book's text

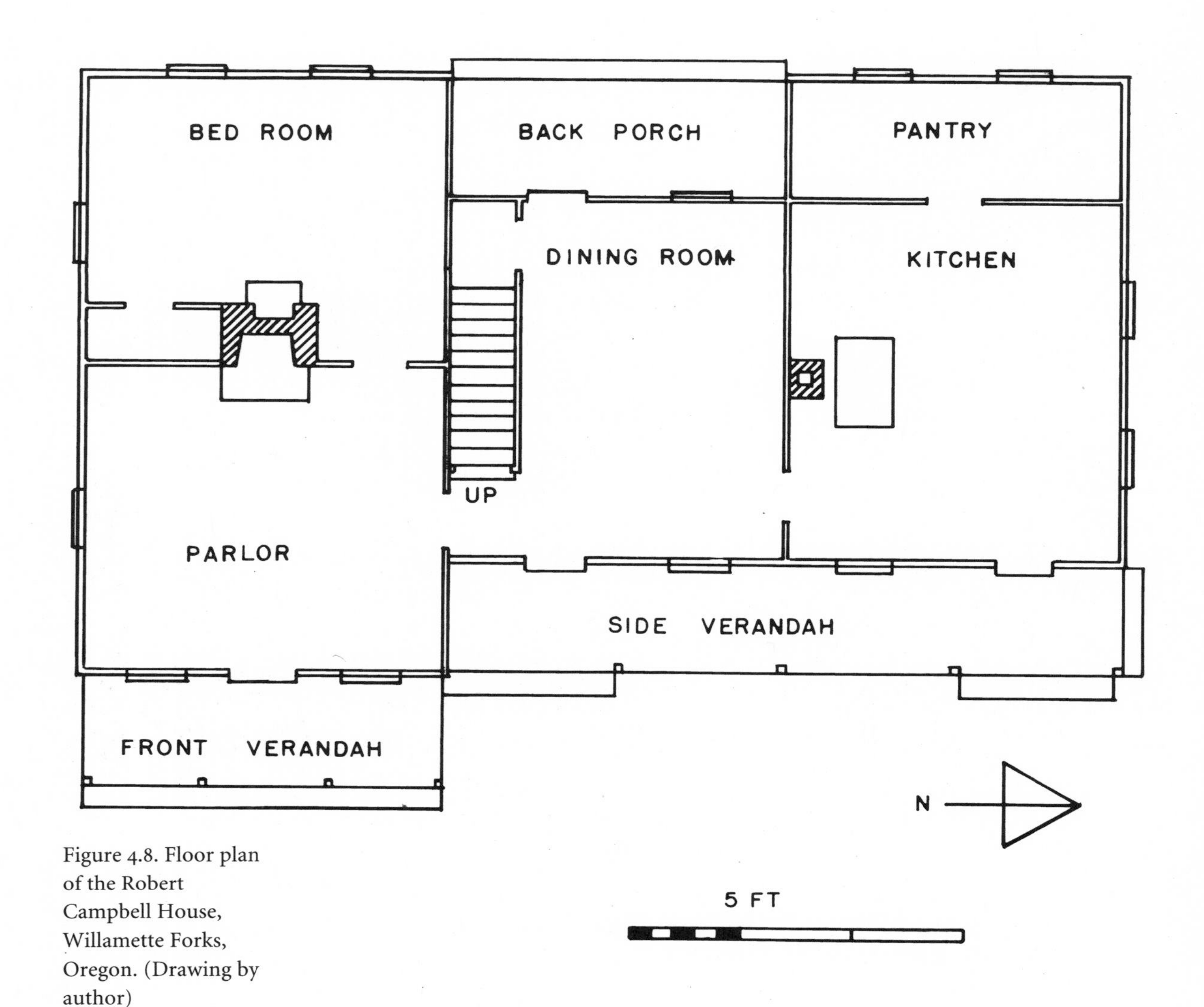

Figure 4.8. Floor plan of the Robert Campbell House, Willamette Forks, Oregon. (Drawing by author)

and plates make clear, and the Cleaveland plan used in the Peters house seems, in its turn, to have been lifted from A. J. Downing.[18] Except that a plain modern chimney has replaced the Gothic one, which had a base, shaft, and cap, most of the original detail on the Peters house has survived. The rather perfect A. J. Downing presentation made by the A. V. Peters house with its vertical board and batten siding over a balloon-frame wall, bracketed eaves, and earth-toned, gum-colored paint contrasts with the five new Willamette Forks farmhouses.

The Peters house demonstrates that the ingredients necessary to build an academically correct, high style, Gothic Revival house—popular literature, standing models, appropriate materials, skilled carpenters—were available and close at hand. But, in its use of materials, special millwork and detailing, building in high style Gothic was comparatively expensive, and it was more demanding aesthetically. While building in a vernacular Gothic Revival mode not only made use of commonly avail-

Figure 4.9. The A. V. Peters House, Eugene City, Oregon. (Photo by author)

able materials and standard millwork and detailing but also more easily accommodated traditional interests, including spatial ones. This may explain why Elmer Calef and his neighbors did not choose high style Gothic homes.

While akin to its vernacular Gothic neighbors in its emphasis on verticality, the Calef house contrasts with them in its thick, bulky proportions. The main block of the Calef house is composed of two units, each two rooms deep, flanking the entrance hall (fig. 4.7). This arrangement, with a central chimney for each pair of rooms, had been a commonplace plan in New England for more than a hundred years, fixed as a type in the 1770s.[19] The Calefs' four rooms were a parlor to the right and a living room with fireplace to the left of the central stairhall, with two bedrooms behind. The asymmetrical appearance achieved by projecting two gables out from the main roof increased the cubic content of the living room but did not seriously alter the basic symmetrical sense of the plan. The mildly gothicized roofs added nothing critical to a conventional building form, for the high, sharp gables are only appliques to a simple, gabled building (fig. 4.10). The plan, symmetry, massiveness, and the broad pitch of the main roof indicate a New England background.

The room opening off the living room, sometimes referred to by the Calefs as the kitchen, was also called the dining room and "had the cookstove in it." (The Calefs made quite a bit of the fact that the cookstove was in the dining room.) Here the backstairs led to the room above for hired help. A pantry, or scullery, behind the dining room took many of a kitchen's functions—"the work and cleaning up," which must have been considerable in threshing season when they "always planned to cook for twenty-one or twenty-two men." The cookstove could be "taken down" and "set up" again in the back room or back kitchen, a summer kitchen.[20] This was a plastered alcove off the woodshed, a somewhat cooler place for cooking in hot weather, keeping the dining room much cooler for the threshing crew. Cellars were rare in Oregon, but as in New England houses, the Calef house has a small cellar, walled in stone and floored with stones standing on edge. This was under the dining room and served as a coolroom—an essential element in Oregon, but on more typical farms found as a small separate building in which to store perishable foods, milk, and butter. In 1880 the Calef house slept the parents and ten children (two more were born later); Sarah McGee, who "works in the kitchen"; and N. C. Taylor, boarder and teacher. At times during the year there were more hired help, but each of the three eldest sons, Cutting, 16, Charles, 15 and Otis, 13, "works on the farm."[21] Eight bedrooms would not have been excessive.

From the 1840s to the 1870s building materials had evolved, principally due to improvements in lumber manufacture, but the Oregon houses of the 1870s employed structural systems in use since the first permanent buildings there. These buildings employed either the box system (vertical planking without studding) or the balloon-frame—both systems stressed dimensional standardization and simple volumes;[22] both were equally popular among the Calef's neighbors. Box and balloon-framing were widely publicized in contemporary magazines and books.[23] Where older eastern building forms were emulated, they were compatible with these systems or readily adaptable to them. The Calef house structure is typical of balloon-frame construction of the region at that time. The only large members and the only hewn, mortised, tenoned, and pegged assemblies are in the ten-inch-square girders and sills that support the ground floor. The hewn work at the sills indicates a stand of large timber in this rural area and that using it was less expensive and more convenient than purchasing and hauling lumber from a distant mill. (In contrast, the balloon-frame of the Peters house in Eugene City sits on eight-by-nine-inch sills that are rough sawn.) On this ground-floor platform the balloon-frame walls were erected. These are of full-size two-by-four studs with each piece running the full height of the building. A one-by-six board, known as a ribbon or ledger, was cut

Figure 4.10. Elmer Calef House, with four daughters at the side of the house, ca. 1900. (Courtesy Miss Ora Calef)

into the studs to provide a horizontal seat for second-floor joists. Then the exterior shiplap siding was nailed directly to the studs. This combination of light and heavy pieces is in line with the earlier instructions on balloon-frame construction published from the Midwest and the eastern seaboard.

The interiors of the Calef house are lathed and plastered, indicating "finer" construction, while the interiors of the new houses nearby were of horizontal boards covered with wallpaper over muslin sheeting. Wainscot in the Calef's living room is of shiplap siding set vertically, then grained to appear as oak.

Smaller outbuildings on a farm such as the Calef's might also use balloon construction. But for barns, heavier construction was recommended with mortised, tenoned, and pegged frames, often of hewn work rather than sawn.[24] In the pursuit of good, suitable accommodations, pioneer builders sometimes turned to very conservative practices, even practices now obsolete in the region where they remembered having seen them. That degree of extreme conservatism is found in the barn that Elmer Calef built and also in the arrangement of his building group. While these cultural associations with his family and his past must have given Elmer Calef great satisfaction, including some nostalgic pleasure, his choices for the most part were logical and thrifty.

The history of Vermont's earliest barn type, a rectangular, eaves-front building, about thirty-by-forty, is divided into two successive phases.[25] A major distinction between the two is that the first was generally utilitarian in character; the second was more finished and architectural in character. Much of Elmer Calef's scheme came from phase one, the Vermont barn of 1780 to 1840. In reference to that earlier period, in the Calef barn are exterior walls of rough sawn unpainted vertical boarding with the only daylight in the dark windowless building coming through the long transom sash above the wagon doors, and one sash window put in to light the work bench (fig. 4.11). But structurally, Elmer Calef's barn falls within both phases. Its heaviness, as in its twelve-by-twelve hewn sills, is of the pre-1840 technology; its lightness, as in the use of a single set of roof rafters, is of the post-1840 technology. The Calef barn used sawn pieces for smaller members, for instance the rafters. But a few sawn posts, placed at random, are sized, detailed, and pegged to match the hewn members. The general provisions of Elmer Calef's barn are traditional, but the larger amount of grain storage, and perhaps the double wagonways, respond to the increased discussions of efficiency found in the periodicals and in improved methods and machinery for grain production.

In fact, Elmer Calef's Oregon barn is in appearance older than that of his brother Ira's in Washington, Vermont. Ira Calef's barn has the finished detail and architectural appearance suited to the fashionable Vermont type of the 1860s, the period when it was built. This detail includes cupola and weather vane; interiors lighted with six-over-six double-hung windows, ornamented on the outside with blinds; and an exterior paint scheme matching the house. Architecturally Elmer Calef's barn was conservative, even in Oregon, but the functions it contained were those for which Oregon barns were providing.

The critical invention or development to which Elmer Calef did not respond was the "horse power pitchfork."[26] By 1875 a few neighboring farms had begun to exploit the forklift in building barns with a higher and more commodious volume. Before the invention, hay had been pitched by hand from the loaded wagon for storage in the mow, using relays of men for higher storage. The new invention, using pulleys, ropes, and horse power, could lift a mechanical fork loaded with hay to great heights and carry it across space before dumping it. Beginning in the mid-nineteenth century, the development of the fork lift went through steady improvements into the early twentieth century. It also took many years to develop barns with an open structural system compatible with the fork lift, and the frustrating conflict between the dangling mechanical fork and the post-and-beam frame's tie girts must have discouraged many from installing the labor-saving device. At the same time, the fashion in Oregon barn designs from the late 1860s had been for higher roofs, steeply pitched at forty-five degrees. As a fashion, the bolder forms were very effective on prairie landscapes, pronouncing a farm's prosperity, increasing storage capacity and efficiency, and depending to some extent upon detail, relating well to the new houses built in such revival styles as the Gothic Revival.

Figure 4.11. Elmer Calef barn, end elevation seen from the house. (Photo by author)

An example of this fashion and of these problems is the large hewn post-and-beam frame barn George Armitage built only a few years after construction of the Calef barn (fig. 4.4). Until 1877 the Armitage barn had been one of the earlier type found in the region. In making the change George Armitage also shifted from a side opening to an end opening barn, capturing in form, function, and detail the current fashion in New England barn design, but also giving a sense of the shape and including some characteristics of the traditional New York State Dutch barn.[27] The construction of the new building responded to the increase in the farm's size, which almost doubled from 640 acres to about 1,000. The twenty-five-year-old barn, the first barn, was demolished and some of its hewn members incorporated in the new structure. The new barn was a sixty-by-seventy-five-foot building, forty-four feet high at the ridge, dramatically increasing space for hay, grain, and work horses. Although the Armitage barn contained a fork lift, it may have been introduced later, about 1900. The interior space is hardly compatible with the use of a fork, for it is filled with fourteen-foot-square bays of the post-and-beam structural system, and vertically is divided by three tiers of tie beams. Getting the hay fork to pass each of these structural impediments must have been a maddening frustration. Yellow paint dramatized the great bulk, calling attention to the exterior's finished architectural character. Its walls were beautifully developed. Boxed-in eaves, shiplap siding, symmetrically placed openings, including double-hung sash windows, accented the barn front, which faced the driveway and the house. The board and batten side walls were constructed, with equal care, of standard twelve-inch-wide vertical boards and milled, shaped battens. Many years later, recalling the new building, Miss Mira Calef said, "It was quite a barn. It was so big! And the color . . . it was *yellow!*"[28]

Most of the major barns in western Oregon at this time were horse barns with bays for wagons and for the haymow. Some had large, roomlike bins for grains, as did the Calef barn, both for stock and for seed (fig. 4.12). Here the Calef stalls, later rebuilt, had stabled from five to eight horses, a ratio suitable to the acreage. In 1880 it was six horses, and 143 acres tilled; the Armitage farm had seventeen horses, 600 acres tilled. A few cows, "just for our needs," sufficed to supply the Calef family milk and butter.[29] In 1879 the four milch cows produced three hundred pounds of butter; the Armitage four, two hundred.[30] Not until the 1890s did dairy farming introduce major changes, and perhaps it was then that the Calef horse stalls were replaced by stanchions for cows. Until then, cows were given minimum shelter, without stalls or stanchions, probably in the "strawhouse" used also for milking. This hewn-framed building, perhaps the only one on the farm that could be called "typically western," was a type in use on many western farms. The strawhouse was an open structure, associated with mild winters, for sheltering and feeding loose stock; the Calefs also referred to it as the cowshed. No illustration is included of the Calefs' strawhouse, as it was too ruinous to record in detail. Usually, a strawhouse was three bays in width with both ends open, and two bays or more in depth, producing a very broad roof. A loft above held the straw saved from threshing, or hay, to be pitched down to two lines of feeding racks below. Agricultural periodicals recommended this handsome, earth-floored, building type as an economical collection device for manure.[31]

A small hop barn, built in the later 1870s, stood northwest of the big barn. It, another machine shed, a windmill, water trough, and hoghouse have disappeared. In the 1880s or 1890s, with money from the Vermont family, a white picket fence was built around the house and "fenced out the barn." A picket fence set off most Oregon farmhouses from the activities around them. With this construction, the Calef building group could be considered complete—until at least the next change in the farm's agricultural interest.[32]

Family tradition has the Calef barn built shortly after the house, perhaps in 1872 or 1873, although on many Oregon farms the barn was built first. There were barns in the neighborhood very like the Calef in form, but they belonged to an earlier Oregon period—for example the Spores barn of about 1850 (fig. 4.3) and the first George Armitage barn (ca. 1855) demolished as outmoded in 1877, were similar to many.[33] These side-opening barns, like the Calef barn, contained a combined threshing floor and wagonway, or drive, with grain bins along one side of the wagonway

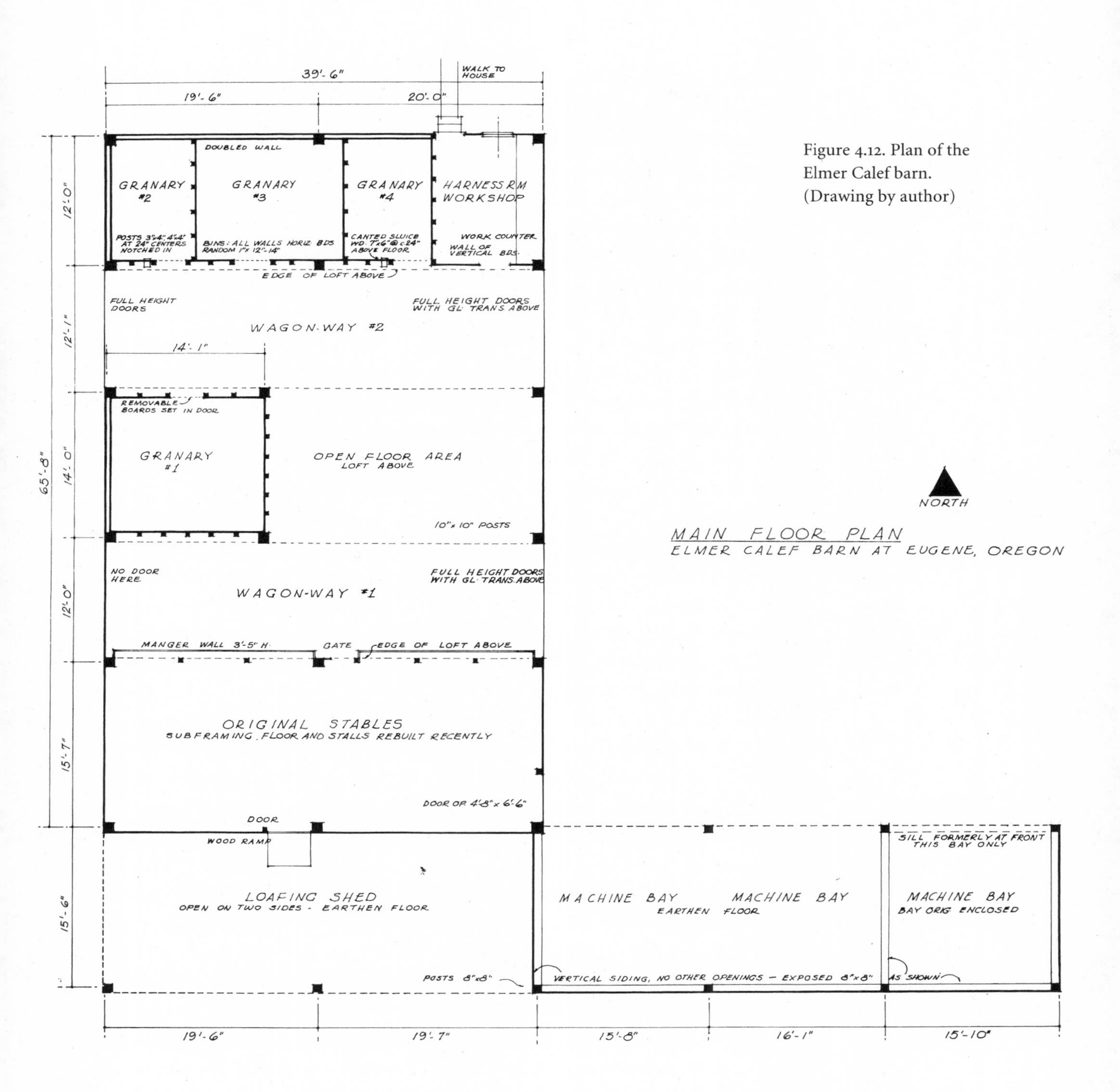

Figure 4.12. Plan of the Elmer Calef barn. (Drawing by author)

and a haymow at the other. However, by 1870 Oregon farmers were ordinarily building barns of a radically different sort, using from three to five bays in both width and length to support an extensive roof pitched at nearly forty-five degrees and carried down to rather *low* eaves. An example is the Armitage barn of 1877. The Calef barn has *high* walls at the eaves; a short, moderate pitch, about thirty-five degrees; and is two bays by five.

These characteristics are standard in much of New England, and other photographs of Washington, Vermont, show barns that are similar. Although the Calef barn has these features, several other attributes distinguish it from any other known Oregon structures. Differences found in Elmer Calef's barn—the use of extended tie beams, discontinuous plates at the roof structure, and the presence of a shed attached as an ell—are distinctively related to New England practice. In the Calef barn the roof rafters at midspan are carried on purlins. A system of braced struts supports the purlin from each tie beam (fig. 4.13). The latter were set at plate height, not dropped as is usual, so the plates end in each bay, mortised and tenoned into a tie beam. The ties cap the posts and extend exposed beyond the face of the building to the eave line, which just covers them (fig. 4.14). A variety of extended ties were used in New England.[34] They project out under the eaves in Connecticut, New Hampshire, and eastern Massachusetts, neatly detailed and encased; their ends also form the support for the eaves.

The *American Agriculturist* in 1863 described a barn in "Cheap and Convenient Barns for New Countries," an article sent from Seattle, Washington Territory where the barn had "just been built." The author, writing under the name Economy, recommended a construction of poles set into the ground (pole construction), a method which had some use in the Pacific Northwest. But it is not that aspect that is of interest here nor the fact that it also had two wagonways. Of interest to the Calef building are the tie beams, for Economy said "let the ties project eight inches beyond each outside post, (i.e. let the ties be one foot and 4 inches longer than the width of the barn)."[35] This matches the Calef eave detail. Nevertheless, similarities between Economy's barn and the Calef barn are probably coincidental, for certainly the concept of the Calef barn was derived directly from Vermont and Economy's barn also owed much to New England. However, as early as 1850, Oregon farmers did respond to the instructions in various agricultural publications. The style and design recommendations of specific periodicals are demonstrated in buildings on several Willamette Valley farms. The impact of literary sources is most often seen just in detail, for in plan and mass these examples also owe much to a provincial and conventional eastern source. And often, as in the article on Economy's barn, publication served to share or reinforce the continuation of cherished design traditions.

While two parallel wagonways or threshing floors are found in a few other Oregon barns other than Elmer Calef's, Economy's plan is of further documentary

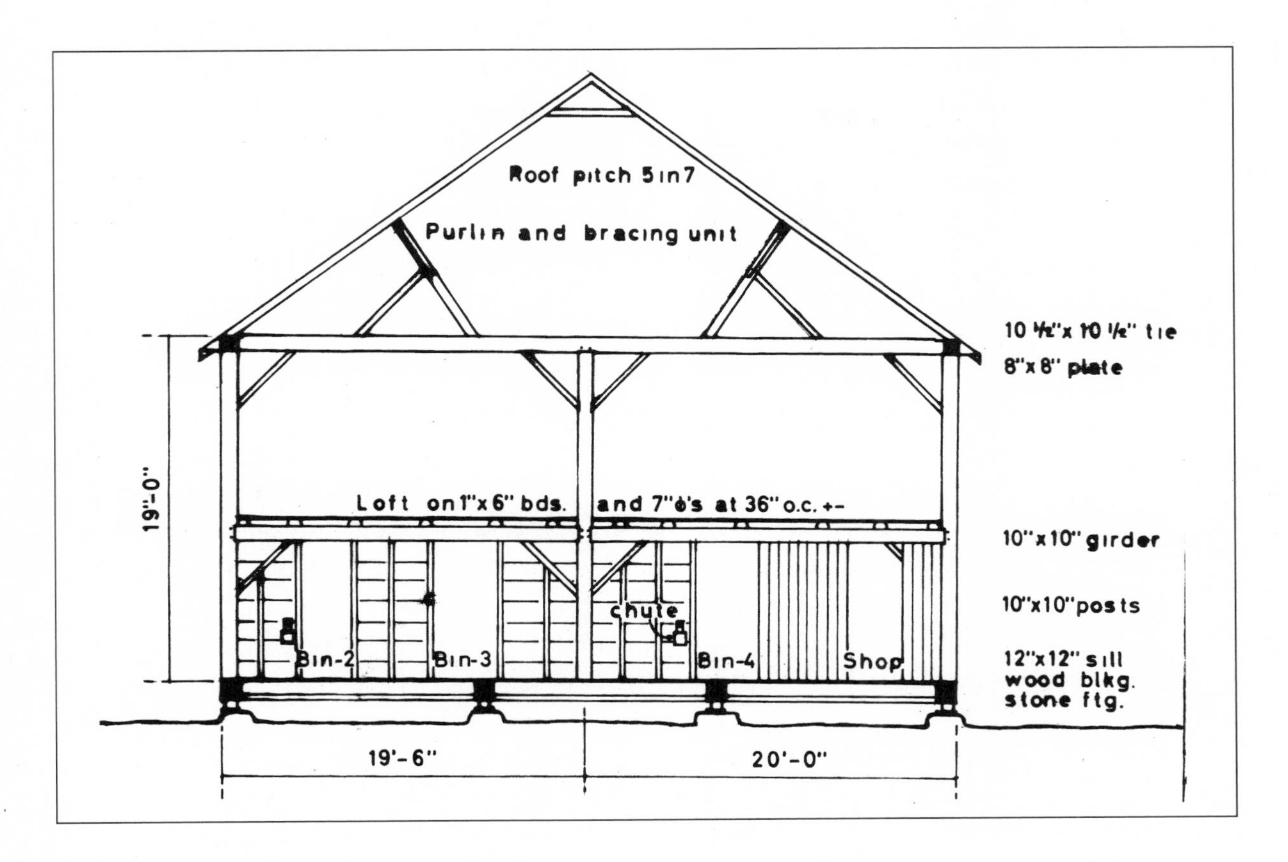

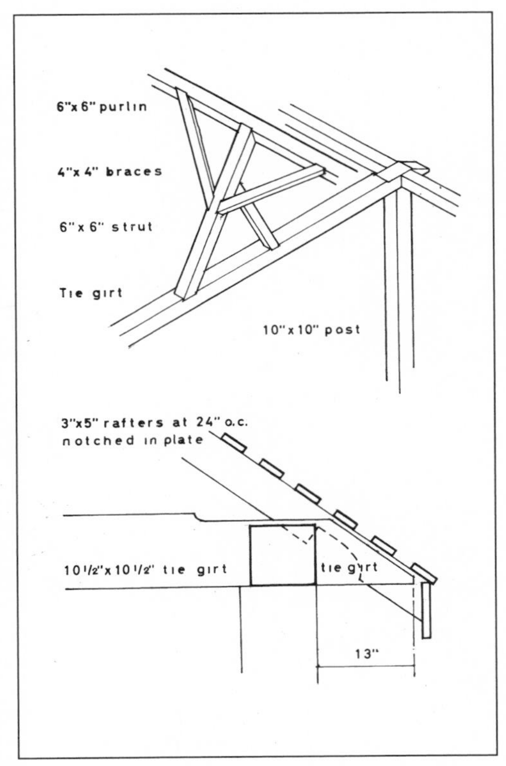

Figure 4.13. Elmer Calef barn, section looking north. (Drawing by author)

Figure 4.14. Details of braced purlin and tie girt at eave. (Drawing by author)

interest (fig. 4.15). Such abbreviated drawings must have been typical, sufficient to indicate the specific form of the building and the major construction details necessary to achieve it. Such drawings would be supplemented with certain written instructions (such as that bays *a, b, c, d* were stable, wagonway, wagonway, and hay bays). From this, the whole fabric and its components would have been envisioned by the nineteenth-century building crew. This is impressive when one realizes what a sizable list of details, joints, and members even a simple barn commands. It may be surmised that on such scraps of paper as these the ideas for the Calef barn and house were carried from Vermont to Oregon. During construction, Elmer Calef must have left much to local builders, with the expectation that their vocabulary was relatively national. Obviously, his own involvement was continuous and major.

The conservative characteristics of Elmer Calef's architecture cannot be explained by limitations in local technology or a shortage of skilled and knowledgeable local carpenters. The farmer, immediately to the north, George Armitage, had run sawmills in Iowa and Oregon, been a ship's carpenter, and in Oregon, a general carpenter. He had built his own house, as well as others. A great deal of family discussion, advice, and assistance must have been exchanged between the Calefs and Elmer's father-in-law, the neighbor to the immediate south. While Mahlon Harlow farmed on the side, he had "worked at the carpenter's trade [in the locality] since 1852," constructing a number of important buildings.[36] About 1855, following a design and specifications furnished by the county commissioners, he built the Lane County courthouse, a Neoclassical temple type building in Eugene City. And there were many experienced builders about. Four years after the construction of the Calef barn, for his twenty-man crew and two-day barn raising in 1877, George Armitage found the skills required among nearby farming families and among the people living in Eugene City:

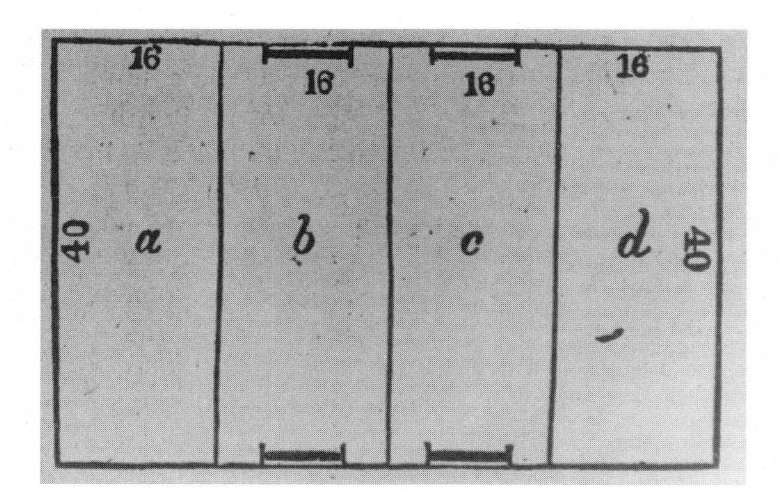

Figure 4.15. Plan of Economy's barn, Seattle, Washington. (From the *American Agriculturist*)

> There was no special barn builder or designer. . . . Had one or two good carpenters including Dave Rice who also ran a saloon in Eugene. Could possibly be some one like that who did the drawing. . . . The main raising had about twenty men. Elliot King was one of the main ones; he kept saying "depend on your pike pole boys, thars [there's] danger lies ahead." . . . The Bonnet boys were at the raising, they were good climbers—Perry, Cephas and Martin. One of them fell from the top [at least forty-five feet], fell all the way but a beam broke his fall, he broke it, went right through it, but was back at work the next day.[37]

To put up his house in 1873 and to raise his barn in 1873 or 1874, Elmer Calef may have brought together many of the same people. With such experts available or involved, it is amazing that Vermont detail survived and was so thoroughly incorporated in the construction of Elmer Calef's Oregon farm buildings.

Building technology presented few, if any, problems in the transfer of these designs across the continent. Vermont and Oregon had reached a comparable state of sophistication, although Oregon had reached it more recently. Similar technological advances, for the most part, were used by Elmer in his house as had been used by Ira in both his buildings. Milled materials found in Elmer Calef's house, such as standardized full-size studding, shiplap siding, and moldings to cap windows, could have been procured at the W. H. Abrams and Brothers' Sash and Door Factory in Eugene, a planing mill opened in 1870.[38] There Elmer Calef also could have gotten the contemporary, popular, double-hung windows with four-light (or even those with two-light) sash, which his neighbors used. Instead, the anachronistic double-hung, six-light sash—perhaps especially made for Elmer Calef—were installed for the Calef windows as they had been in Vermont. Elmer's barn was kept to simpler materials than his house, and its very conventional detailing was utilitarian.

In New England barns the upper gable wall often projected. This slight pediment, and its shadow line, standardized vertical siding to the one-eave-high-length on all faces of the building. Oregonians preferred flush-end elevations. But a more typical, certainly more significant, feature of New England barns is the projecting shed often accompanying them (fig. 4.16). This form provided an external space sheltered from the wind, incidentally setting the asymmetrical note recurrent in New England farm groupings. Elmer Calef's machine shed, integral with the barn although attached as an ell, is an unusual relationship in Oregon; I have not seen another example. In contrast to the Calef barn's two parts, used as a means of gaining more space, barns in the Willamette Valley ordinarily favored enlargement by increasing the perimeter of the original rectangle so that the complete plan was a larger rectangle. Otherwise, where several buildings are constructed, they stand as completely separate structures. Twenty years before Elmer Calef built his barn and shed, traditional New England barns had been described by Solon Robinson in an

Figure 4.16. Barn and attached shed, Mount Hope, Connecticut. (Photo by author)

article entitled "An Old Fashioned New England Farmhouse": "A New England Barn. —Now let us look into the most important building on every farm. It is 40 feet x 60 feet and 18 feet high." The foreyard of the Calef barn was unwalled, but this further quotation is also pertinent: "Two sides of the yard are fenced with a very high stone wall, and the other two by the barn and long shed."[39] A barn type and a spatial configuration were imported by Elmer Calef from New England, a combination that had been a convention there for generations.

For weather protection and efficiency, one long connected line of buildings—house, kitchen, shed, barn—was built by the Calefs in Washington, Vermont. This was the practice there. "New England style, when a place had but one barn, it used to be attached, an ell being the kitchen."[40] Ira Calef's buildings appear to be almost a single block. Ira Calef's house sought protection from the north; on the long sheltered south wall are all three entrances and the many windows that open out upon the extensive, landscaped slope. Critical to the Oregon house, however, are the prevailing winter winds with rains that hit the exposed site from the southwest, and to the southwest the walls of the Elmer Calef house are almost blank. All but two of its eleven rooms, most of the windows, five of the six entrance doors, and three of its four porches open east to the side yard or north to the lawn and road. Numerous porches and outside doors were characteristic of Oregon farmhouses. The section system was set by the compass, and although the Calef buildings, like all in the locality, are aligned with cardinal points, awareness of the diagonal storm direction had a clear impact on the Calef farmstead (fig. 4.17). In a southwest wind, a fire in the barn would not be directed toward the house; nor would a fire in the house be directed toward the barn. To arrange his buildings, Elmer did refer to common New England methods, but not to the equally common system employed by his brother Ira.

The view taken about 1900 (fig. 4.18) in Washington, Vermont, shows to the left the Ira Calef house, roof raised and a bay window added in 1889. The proximity to the road and, particularly, to other houses is a survival of the New England village tradition of long lots that implied a constriction that subsequent subdivision often had made a fact. These New England groupings and their lots were part and parcel of a European tradition. The constricted building group that existed in villages was frequently carried over to solitary New England farms as well.[41] The Elmer Calef farm in Oregon demonstrates, in the size and shape of the area occupied by buildings, that same tradition carried across the continent. Timothy Dwight's New England description, taken from his travels made between 1796 and 1817, could almost fit the Calef farm in Oregon: "In a convenient spot, on each of these [lots], a house is erected at the bottom of the courtyard (often neatly enclosed); and it is furnished universally with a barn, and other convenient outbuildings."[42]

In the Willamette Valley a usual length for a farmstead including the barn on one end and the house on the other was 500 feet. (A few of 700 feet are found). The long dimension would cover one simple row of separate buildings usually arranged perpendicular to a driveway, but both perpendicular and parallel farmstead groups are found. Elmer Calef's buildings extend over 300 feet parallel to the driveway, while the Vermont farm is about 120 feet long, parallel to its driveway. The arrangement of the Elmer Calef farm, however, has very little relationship to neighbors, for his

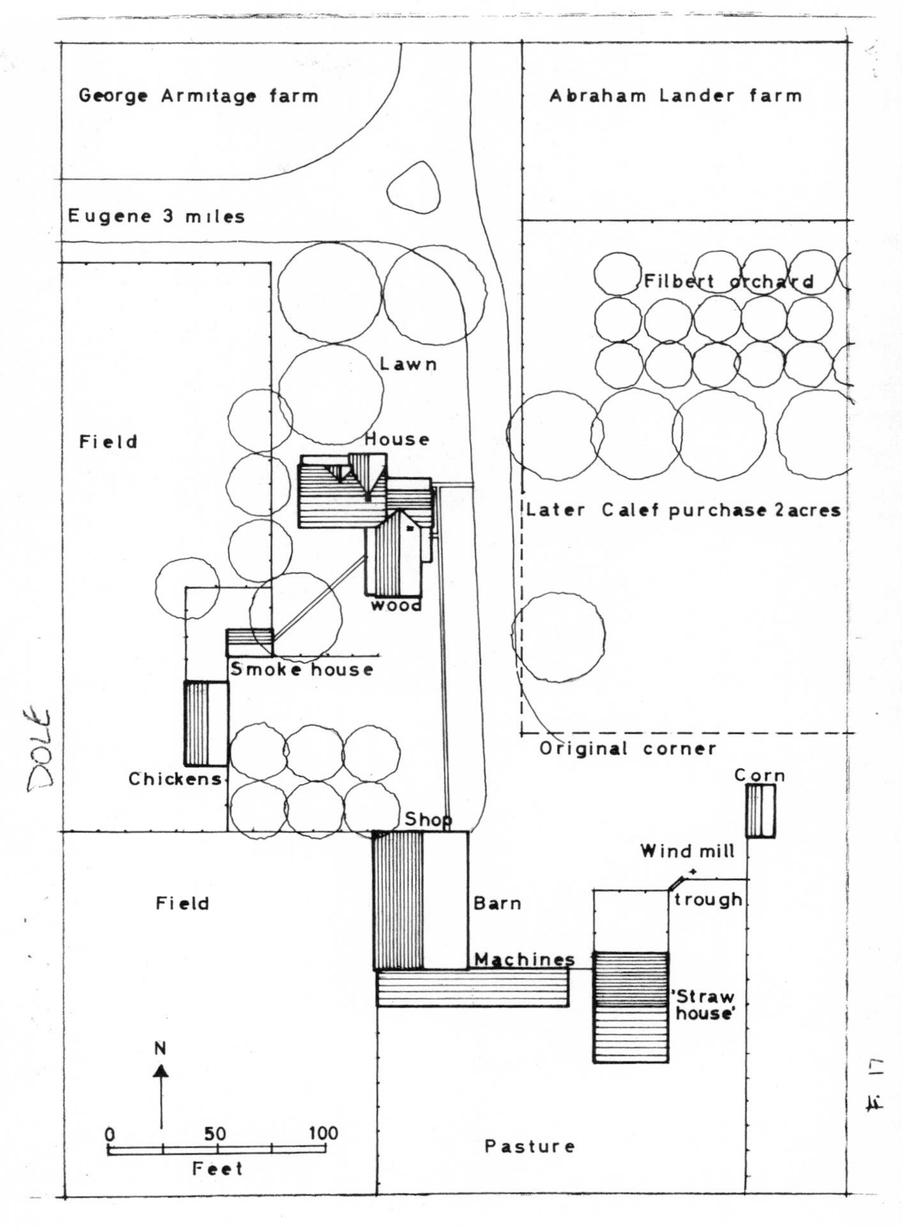

Figure 4.17. Site plan of the Elmer Calef farm buildings. (Drawing by author)

Figure 4.18. Ira Calef House and neighbors, 1900. (Courtesy Miss Olive P. Calef)

nearest one was half a mile away. There were another six or seven neighbors, each at a radius of a mile or more. He could not, like his brother in Vermont, step across the road to several neighbors and to the house of another Calef.

The house facing the road symbolizes social and hospitable considerations, as well as critical functional concerns. In terms of aesthetics, this was a placement the landscape architect Andrew Jackson Downing and others of the period had criticized. D. H. Lawrence, the English novelist, saw the farmhouse and the farm from a different perspective, relating the farmstead's organization intimately to the interests and the aspirations of the farmer and the farmer's wife: "Her house faced out from the farm-buildings and fields, looked out to the road and the village with church and Hall and the world beyond . . . the magic land to her . . . whilst her husband looked out to the back at sky and harvest and beast and land." Each Oregon farmstead inevitably acquired the role of a distinctive landmark with strong social and physical significance, known within miles of rural landscape. Formal considerations could reinforce that role, an affinity seen in the distinction made between the house part and the barn part of Elmer Calef's farm buildings. A. J. Downing may be recalled by the farmhouse itself in the porches, chimneys, and in his words, "the broad . . . high roof, . . . as essentially a handsome feature in a farm house as the . . . broad shoulders of the farmer himself." If the emphasis given the house in family recollections and the architectural emphasis given the building itself carry a faint hint of the showplace concept (felt even more of the Vermont house), it is also clear that the house took a traditional, relative, and functional position among the farm buildings as one of two pivotal points.[43]

It is necessary to reject "eclecticism" as an issue here, and "anachronism" has only limited application. This is country building, and associated with the farmer's deliberations as to function and economy were the assurances that precedent and practical building traditions guaranteed him. Farm buildings, taken singly, usually earn only moderate acclaim. On the Calef farm the impact of the several building forms is related to their importance and position in one of two subgroupings: the house group with its trees and the barn group with its yards are balanced about an axis, and since that axis is the major service route, most circulation, vehicular and pedestrian, follows its path.[44] The house, momentarily diverting almost like a screen before the barn, performs as one control point; the barn acts as the other in a large, orderly, industrial composition. The farmstead must be regarded as a whole and as a considerable achievement in vernacular architecture.

Notes

1. This material first appeared as "The Calef Farm: Region and Style in Oregon," *Journal of the Society of Architectural Historians* 23, no. 4 (December 1964): 201–9. In this version other information has been incorporated, but the text remains in the "present tense."

2. Robert C. Clark, *History of the Willamette Valley, Oregon*, (Chicago: S. J. Clark, 1927), 1:407.

3. "The prairies and bottom lands, and especially those lands which were naturally moist . . . were the first occupied by the hardy pioneer." Albert G. Walling, *Illustrated History of Lane County, Oregon* (Portland, Ore.: A. G. Walling, 1884), 298.

4. The map of the Calef property and neighboring farms was adapted from an untitled, undated map in the Lane County Court House, Eugene, Oregon, probably descriptive of 1860–65. Section lines and house sites have been added. "Calef" has been substituted for E. Stewart, the first owner, shown on the original drawing.

5. Walling, *Illustrated History*, 483.

6. Henry Glassie, *Pattern in the Material Folk Culture of the Eastern United States* (Philadelphia: University of Pennsylvania Press, 1968), 78–79, 82–83.

7. The following children of pioneers have supplied information: Mr. Frank L. Armitage of Eugene, a son of George H. Armitage; Mrs. Frank L. Armitage (nee Ada Calef), Miss Mira Calef, and Miss Ora Calef of Eugene daughters of Elmer Calef and of Sarah Naomi Harlow

Calef. Correspondence with a cousin, Miss Olive P. Calef of Washington, Vermont, supplied other details and two photographs. Quotations throughout the chapter indicate statements made by one or more of the above.

8. Walling, *Illustrated History*, 494.

9. For example, in Woodstock, Vermont, from the late eighteenth century, it was usual to plant trees in front of private homes as well as on the Green. Rhoda Teagle, *Woodstock, Then and Now* (Woodstock, Vt.: Elm Tree Press, 1957), 7, 20.

10. A monthly publication, first published in 1869. Salem (Ore.) *Willamette Farmer*, 16 March 1872, p. 4.

11. Elmer Calef's farming was similar to his neighbors', although smaller in acreage than many. U.S. Census, Lane County, Oregon, Springfield Precinct, 1880.

12. *Oregon's Agricultural Development: A Historic Context, 1811–1940* (Salem: State Historic Preservation Office, 1989); *Vermont Historic Preservation Plan, Agricultural Theme* (Montpelier: Division for Historic Preservation, 1990).

13. "It [the Elmer Calef house] was patterned largely from the one here but had far more bedrooms." Letter, Miss Olive P. Calef (Washington, Vt.) to the author, 10 August 1963.

14. No examples of the connected farm buildings, house and barn joined, have been found in the Pacific Northwest. However, by the time the Calefs built their connected farm buildings in Vermont the form was practically ubiquitous in northern New England. For an excellent study, see Thomas C. Hubka, *Big House, Little House, Back House, Barn, the Connected Farm Buildings of New England* (Hanover, N.H.: University Press of New England, 1984).

15. Hubka, *Big House, Little House*, 114–15.

16. Letter, Miss Olive P. Calef (Washington, Vt.) to the author, 10 August 1963.

17. Andrew Jackson Downing's writings on horticulture, landscape architecture, and architecture were published in such widely read journals as the *American Agriculturist*. His books on architecture began with *Cottage Residences* (1842), which was republished in various editions for forty-five years. *The Architecture of Country Houses* (1850) was reissued until 1866. During the same period a number of other authors also wrote popular books on the Gothic Revival.

18. Downing's architectural concepts were emulated in this scheme as elsewhere in the book. Henry W. Cleaveland, William Backus, and Samuel D. Backus, *Village and Farm Cottages* (1856; reprint, Watkins Glen, N.Y.: American Life Foundation, 1912), 86–87.

19. "In the plan arrangement there now began a change which must be regarded as of extreme significance. This was the introduction of the central hallway, extending from the front to the rear of the house . . . and the consequent division of the chimney into two parts. . . .The central hall arrangement of plan did not make its appearance until about 1750, between which time and the Revolutionary Period . . . it became fixed as a type." J. Frederick Kelly, *Early Domestic Architecture of Connecticut* (New York: Dover Publications, 1963), 14–16.

20. Mira and Ora Calef, interviews 19 March and 17 May 1963. Summer kitchens had widespread usage on the eastern seaboard. The author's great grandmother had an arrangement similar to the Calefs' in her new home of 1865 in Centerville, Cape Cod, Massachusetts.

21. U.S. Census, Lane County, Oregon, Springfield Precinct, 1880.

22. Clark, *History of Willamette Valley*, 389.

23. The balloon frame was "thus designated on account of the extreme lightness . . . composing the frame . . . and as an economical substitute for the old style frame, by nailing pieces together instead of mortising and tenoning them together." Daniel T. Atwood, *Atwood's Country and Suburban Houses* (New York: Orange Judd, 1871), 76–77. But Elmer Calef chose to retain the earlier, large, hand-hewn sill, mortised and tenoned together; this sill had often been used with the balloon frames constructed in the 1850s.

24. Although sawn lumber was readily available, hewn members remained in use for the principal pieces in barn frames, partly because of difficulty in transporting long, heavy pieces distances. Continued usage also was promoted in publications, as by Atwood (the exponent of the balloon frame) for a "Farm Barn": "The frame is heavily timbered, taken from the forest and framed in the old style [mortised and tenoned] with 12 by 12 sills, . . . [and] braces" (Atwood, *Atwood's Country and Suburban Houses*, 201).

25. Exterior characteristics of the Calef barn in Oregon relate to the earliest Vermont barns, 1780–1840; exterior characteristics of Ira Calef's

barn in Vermont closely resemble the later, post-1840 Vermont barn—more apt to be clapboarded and trimmed. *Vermont Historic Preservation Plan,* 5, 18, 19.

26. "Improved Horse Power Pitchfork," *American Agriculturist* 29, no. 7 (1860): 201; and "Barns without Beams," *American Agriculturist* 37, no. 3 (1878): 98.

27. John Fitchen, *The New World Dutch Barn* (Syracuse: Syracuse University Press, 1968), 13–14. Fitchen suggests about 1680 to 1796 as dates encompassing the type called the New World Dutch barn. Perhaps George Armitage recalled similar New York state barns, along with other concerns, in developing the shape of his barn in 1877, for it has more than a sketchy resemblance: squarish plan; openings on the gable end; ridge (forty-four feet) more than twice as high as eaves (sixteen feet); and some interior similarities, too, but not the structure.

28. Mira and Ora Calef, interviews 19 March and 17 May 1963.

29. Ibid.

30. U.S. Census, Lane County, Oregon, Springfield Precinct, 1880.

31. Also called a summer feeding shed. See illustration, the *American Agriculturist* 23, no. 5 (May 1864): 141.

32. Philip Dole, *The Picket Fence in Oregon: An American Vernacular Comes West* (Eugene: University of Oregon, Historic Preservation Program, 1986).

33. Dole, "Farmhouse and Barn in Early Lane County," *Lane County Historian* 10, no. 2 (1965): 40.

34. Similar eave details were recorded by the author on the Currier-Foster barn built in 1843, Lower Warner, and in other barns in the town of Warner, New Hampshire, summer 1960.

35. Economy [pseud.], "Cheap and Convenient Barns for New Countries," *American Agriculturist* 22, no. 2 (1863): 45–46.

36. Walling, *Illustrated History,* 483.

37. Letter, F. L. Armitage to the author, 18 June 1963; Philip Dole, "Pioneer Days, Farmhouses, and Barns of the Willamette Valley," in *Space, Style, and Structure; Building in Northwest America,* ed. Thomas Vaughan and Virginia Guest Ferriday (Portland: Oregon Historical Society, 1974), 211.

38. Walling, *Illustrated History,* 439.

39. Solon Robinson, "An Old Fashioned New England Farmhouse," *American Agriculturist* 10, no. 12 (1851): 369.

40. In reference to the Ira Calef buildings and, across the street, those of John Calef. Letter, Miss Olive P. Calef (Washington, Vt.) to the author, 10 August 1963.

41. Henry Glassie, "The Wedderspoon Farm," *New York Folklore Quarterly,* 22, no. 3 (September 1966): 167, 183.

42. Timothy Dwight, *Travels in New England and New York,* 2d ed., 4 vols. (London: Barnes and Sons, 1823), 2:317.

43. D. H. Lawrence, *The Rainbow* (1915; reprint, New York: Viking, Penguin, 1979), 3; A. J. Downing, "Hints on the Construction of Farm Houses," *American Agriculturist* 5, no. 10 (1846): 248–50.

44. The maple trees, an old fruit tree or two, and brush now mark the site of the Elmer Calef farmstead. In the winter of 1974, ironically the farmstead's centennial, the house and barn were sold as salvage for one thousand dollars and demolished. At that time it was reported that salvage workers were getting three dollars a square foot for weathered barn siding. *Eugene Register Guard,* Eugene, Ore., 31 March 1974.

CHAPTER FIVE

Dry Creek

Central Nevada's Damele Ranch

BLANTON OWEN

The cedar stable posts, burnished for almost a hundred years by the rubbings of countless horses and people, shine orange in the setting sun. Benny Damele and his young helper, Link Eddy, put the finishing touches on a horsehair mecarty they twisted in the waning afternoon (fig. 5.1). The nearly finished rope is attached to a nail driven long ago into a post and bent just for this purpose. They are surrounded by a high stockade corral, its cedar uprights casting a ragged-edged shadow on the ground. The large homemade gate is latched shut with a hand-forged hook. Underneath the open-fronted stable, protected from the northwesterly weather, hang slick-fork saddles, tapaderos, headstalls, braided rawhide reins, silver mounted bits and spurs, mecarties, rows of horseshoes and shoeing tools, feed buckets, and myriad other paraphernalia associated with western ranch and horse work.[1]

The mountain ranges that cleave Nevada are creased with canyons, and natural hay meadows are often located in their wide mouths. The meadows drink profusely of the water that flows toward the valley floor, but that often disappears before it arrives there. The older ranchsteads are almost invariably located in or near the canyon mouths, where some protection from the elements is provided and water is most plentiful.

Dry Creek Ranch, at an elevation of sixty-five hundred feet, is located on Dry Creek in central Nevada's Lander County where the northern terminus of Monitor Valley bumps into the southern base of the Simpson Park Mountains. It has been there for over 130 years. The original cabin at this spot, built of mud-and-willow and log, still stands, though in ruin. The place was then known as Dry Creek Station and, as long-time owner Benny Damele says, "was started by the ponies"—the Pony Express—which had a supply and remount station there in 1860 and 1861.[2] The Overland Stage and Mail Company operated a way stop two miles southeast of the current ranchstead from 1861 until 1869.[3] The water supplies and natural meadows at Dry Creek made it an ideal stopover spot.

Figure 5.1. Link Eddy and Benny Damele twist a horsehair mecarty at the open-fronted stable. (Photo by author; NSCA Folklife Archive, P-88-16-19)

Dry Creek Ranch follows the layout pattern commonly seen in other ranches of the Great Basin. Given the option, ranch buildings are usually arranged parallel and perpendicular to one another, either in a rectilinear or linear plan. But when there are terrain features that make this arrangement difficult, the buildings ooze and flow according to the dictates of the topography. Such is the layout of the Dry Creek buildings (figs. 5.2, 5.3). There is the semblance of a courtyard, but none of the outbuildings except the new Quonset hut open onto it; the older buildings all face downhill, in a southerly direction.

The stable is the working heart of Dry Creek Ranch. It faces south, overlooking the hay meadows and long flat valley below. Above it is the main house, which overlooks the outbuildings spread out below it. The cattle corrals and original ranch cabin stretch around the hill, up the canyon and behind the main ranch buildings.

The Great Basin's heart is Nevada, described by John McPhee as the place where "austere new ranges begin to come in waves, range after range after north-south

Figure 5.2. The entrance to Dry Creek Ranch, looking northwest. The open-fronted stable is on the left, with the snow-capped Simpson Park range in the background. (Photo by author)

Figure 5.3. An aerial view of Dry Creek Ranch, looking northeast. Clockwise from the left are the stone stable, chicken house, Quonset hut, main house, bunkhouse, and blacksmith shop. The Bates cabin and cattle corrals are up the road that goes north behind the house. (Photo by author)

range, consistently in rhythm with wide flat valleys: basin, range; basin, range; a mile of height between basin and range." But, McPhee continues, "the Great Basin, which is centered in Utah and Nevada, [is] not to be confused with the Basin and Range, which is centered in Utah and Nevada. The Great Basin [is] topographical, and extraordinary in the world as a vastness of land that [has] no drainage to the sea. The Basin and Range [is] a realm of related mountains that coincide with the Great Basin."[4]

Rural vernacular architecture in Nevada reflects this bifocal view of place. Buildings sometimes harken back in form to older, well-understood models, but just as often do not. The environment of this semiarid place forces new twists and inventive solutions to basic building needs. Building forms, construction materials, and techniques are all strongly shaped by environmental concerns. Occupational practices, especially those involved with raising livestock, are also influenced by environmental matters, and buildings associated with these occupations follow accordingly. The Great Basin's environment and its occupational, craft, and building traditions are all interrelated, yet all are expressed individually. A buckaroo twisting a horsehair mecarty to use on his horse during weeks of gathering cows on the unfenced range is as closely tied to the land as is the open-fronted stable under which he works.

The annual cycle of work at Dry Creek is similar to that of the neighboring ranches, but remains uniquely old-fashioned in some ways. In the winter, hay is hauled to the cows and bulls, which are separated. Even though the cows are kept fairly close to the ranch, the twice-a-day feeding chore is cold, hard work. At one time, the ranch became dependent on tractors and trucks for moving hay to the cattle. One winter, however, temperatures of thirty to forty degrees below zero held for weeks. Tractors and trucks would not run. From that time on, the ranch has never been without a good team of horses and a feed sled.

Cattle are fed sometimes as late as the end of April, depending on the weather and snow cover. In March or April calves are branded and turned out onto the public range.[5] They usually stay fairly close until the grass comes in on the mountains, at which time they move off. In June, the cows are gathered in the mountains and the unbranded calves are worked at corrals scattered throughout the mountains. The gather circuit runs from south to north, finishing up at Ackerman Ranch fifteen miles east of Dry Creek. This work is usually finished by mid- to late June. During the summer months haying the meadows is the order of the day.

Feed on the mountain begins to dry up in August and the cows start to move down to the flats. They are then put in the hayed fields below the house and a number of yearlings are separated out to sell in September or October. Calves are weaned in November and generally shipped in December.

The first record of sale of what was then known as the Bates Ranch occurred on

26 October 1899; William Bates sold the ranch to John H. Spencer. The sale specified 160 acres, which included "one cabin, one stable, two corrals and fencing [plus] ranges adjacent."[6] Spencer then sold the property, apparently with no notable improvements, to Emil Bauman and Emil Steiner on 26 March 1900. Steiner relinquished his interest in the ranch to Bauman on 25 November 1904, and Bauman, in turn, sold the ranch to John Hickison on 6 August 1908. The property retained the name Bates Ranch throughout all these transactions.

The Pony Express and Overland Stage buildings were apparently demolished by the time Bates sold the ranch to Spencer, for the property listed in the deed book does not appear to be the old station buildings. According to notes referring to Dry Creek Station made by Sir Richard Burton on 11 October 1860, "we found this station on a grassy bend at the foot of low rolling hills. It was a mere shell, with a substantial stone corral behind." Other histories of the Pony Express that mention Dry Creek Station also refer to the stone corrals and "rock remains" of the station.[7] Virtually nothing of the stone remains or the corrals is visible today, although they were located a short distance below the current ranch headquarters.

It was probably during the time of Bauman's ownership that significant building improvements to the ranch were begun. Benny Damele recalls that Emil Bauman and his brother "Hoppy" were known as expert rock masons, and the first stone building constructed on the ranch where the current headquarters is was probably the stone structure that now serves as the chicken house. It is this building that Benny thinks was built first and lived in until the main stone house was completed a few years later; it still has whitewashed interior walls, an interior connecting door between the two main rooms, a stove flue hole through the roof, and a framed-in door with a hand-hewn lintel.

John Hickison kept the ranch until 27 September 1927, when he sold it to Juan (also referred to as "John") Yturbide. Hickison reacquired the place from Yturbide and another Basque man, Jose Zelayeta, on 16 October 1931. On 2 March 1943, Peter Damele bought what was now referred to as Dry Creek Ranch and the adjoining Ackerman Ranch from Hickison, and it has remained in the Damele family since.

Benny Damele is part of the third generation of Damele ranchers in central Nevada. His grandfather John came to Eureka in 1879 from northern Italy and worked as a *carbonari* for almost ten years. Carbonari, or charcoal burners, made charcoal for use in the silver and lead smelters located in Eureka, Nevada, during the boom years from 1869 through the 1880s. He arrived shortly after the Charcoal Burner's War of 1879, just as the mining industry was beginning to wane.[8]

The inevitable mining bust, or *borrasca,* began in Eureka in the mid-1880s, and the town of almost nine thousand people dwindled fast. Many of the people who worked in the mining industry, which included a large percentage of Italians, left, some returning to the old country or back East, others moving on to newer mining camps in the West. Still others left to seek their fortune in the fast-growing areas on the West Coast.

John Damele stayed. During the hard winter of 1889–90, he found work on a cattle and sheep ranch near Eureka and never returned to work as a carbonari. He sent back to Italy for his wife and three children and, upon their arrival, leased his own ranch. Two years later they bought Three Bar Ranch located about twenty miles east of Dry Creek. When Benny's grandfather John bought Three Bar before 1900, the ranch buildings were already there. The same is true of all the ranches subsequently bought by the Dameles, including Dry Creek.

John Damele's son, Peter, bought Dry Creek Ranch in 1943 and most of the buildings on the ranch were already built by then. Benny Damele recalls that when his father, Peter, then a young man, rode through the Bates Ranch in early 1907, there was nothing there but the original cabin, barn, and some cedar corrals located above the present ranchstead. Although there is some evidence to show that construction of the main house could have begun as early as 1907, it is generally conceded to have been built around 1910–12 by Matt Hickison, John Hickison's brother. Matt Hickison also built the large stone stable below the smaller stone barn probably built by the Baumans.[9]

Benny's father, with the help of sons Benny and Peter Jr., built the large stone addition to the original house in 1944. This addition now serves as the main living room. The cobblestone fireplace in the addition was built by a rock construction specialist, an Irishman named Bill Wholey (perhaps, Benny thinks, the proper way to spell the name is O'Holey). Wholey also helped Benny build the one-room stone bunkhouse a few years later.

Dry Creek Ranch is both architecturally significant and typical. The earliest extant structure, the Bates cabin, was probably built in the 1860s or 1870s perhaps as part of either the Pony Express or Overland Stage remount stations (figs. 5.4, 5.5, 5.6). The building is a combination of log and mud-and-willow construction. The log portion is 11' x 14' 5" with rough V-notch corners. Chinking is poles laid between the logs with mud packed around the poles. The entry door is off center; there is a window in the east and south walls; and there is no flooring.

The mud-and-willow portion measures 10' x 13' 10" and is constructed of cedar posts set in the ground between four and six feet apart, with willow saplings nailed horizontally inside and out between the uprights, and the space between filled with rock and mud. The entry door is off center, there are windows in the west and north walls, and there is no evidence of flooring.

Mud-and-willow buildings in the central Great Basin, where they are fairly common, are often referred to as "mud houses," "willow houses," or "Indian houses." The latter term refers to the fact that such houses were sometimes built by Paiute

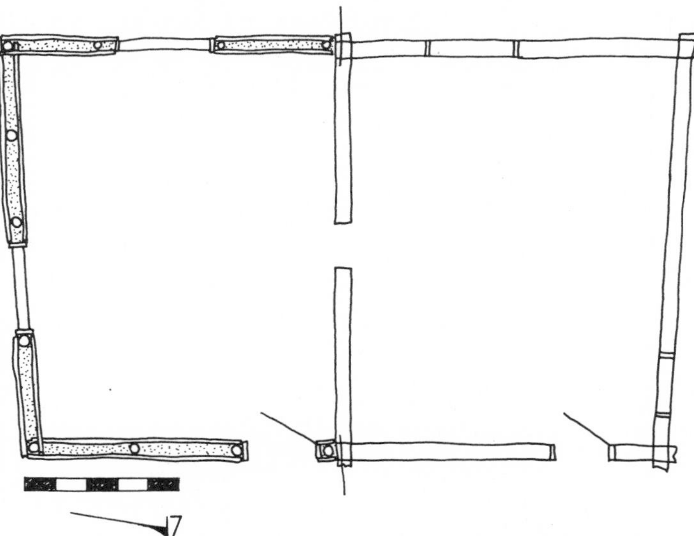

Figure 5.4. The Bates Cabin, looking northeast. The mud-and-willow section is built against the log cabin and both were covered with a single dirt roof with the gable on the long side. This is the oldest building at the Dry Creek Ranch complex. (Photo by author)

Figure 5.5. The small log and mud-and-willow Bates cabin, the oldest extant structure on Dry Creek Ranch, is noticeably wider across the rear than the front. The entire structure was covered with a single gable roof, now fallen in. The front door of the log portion is hung with leather hinges. (Drawing by author)

Figure 5.6. The mud-and-willow wall construction of the Bates cabin is slightly unusual in the large number and size of stones incorporated in it. (Photo by author)

and Shoshone Indian ranch employees, especially in the first quarter of the twentieth century.

The normal mud-and-willow construction method was to set cedar uprights into the ground and nail saplings, with about one to three inches between them, up a couple of feet from the bottom. This space was then filled from the top with a mud and stone mixture, occasionally with horsehair, twigs, or straw added as an additional binder. The mud used was very alkaline and dried extremely hard, providing a durable wall. The same sort of mud made excellent adobe bricks. The walls grew a foot or two at a time until they were the desired height, usually about six feet.[10]

The log portion of the Bates cabin was clearly built first, for the mud-and-willow section is actually a three-sided structure built directly against the log crib with access to it provided via a door through the logs. The shallow, gable roof spans both structures, but may have been rebuilt when the mud addition was added.

The log barn, 140 feet west of the Bates cabin, is probably the same building referred to as "one stable" in the early deed books. It has, however, been heavily modified over the years. The west and north walls are probably original, as is a portion of the roof structure, but the remainder appears to have been rebuilt. The west and north walls are a solid row of vertical cedar logs set into the ground, with a row of cedar posts placed in the ground two feet in from the solid wall, and the space between filled with horizontal logs and mud. The east wall was probably open on the original structure but is now covered with chain-sawn logs spiked to the uprights. Heavy double doors are on the south side. The quaking aspen pole rafters of the shed roof have been replaced on the western half, but the ones on the eastern half appear to be original. All rafters are spaced between eight and sixteen inches. Over the rafters, parallel to the purlins, is a thick mat of willow sprouts on top of which is about a foot of dirt.

Very flat-pitched dirt roofs are ubiquitous on ranch buildings in the Great Basin (fig. 5.7). They cover everything from multiroom houses to small dugout cellars. A dirt roof is not to be confused with one made of sod. Sod is turf and often has grass growing out of it. Highly alkaline desert dirt used for roofs and other adobe construction, however, dries very hard after it has been wet and rarely has anything growing out of it except rolls of rusting wire, old tires, and pieces of scrap iron. Water from the occasional rain shower runs off dirt roofs like water over flour, although a long, soaking rain will eventually leak through. Advantages of a dirt roof include its ease of construction, use of readily available materials, and insulating properties.

The stockade corrals connected to the Bates stable are also probably original, though somewhat modified to facilitate the handling of cattle as well as horses. There are two rectilinear pens, one around and to the east of the stable, the other on its north side with a round corral attached to its northwest corner. Two wings lead out

Figure 5.7. The bunkhouse, looking northeast. The very flat, purlin-supported dirt roof is typical of central Great Basin ranch buildings. The steer skull is a common decorative element. (Photo by author)

in northerly and northeasterly directions from the round corral. All of the fencing is of abutting cedar posts set into the ground with horizontal aspen stretchers wired to the uprights (fig. 5.8). Modifications to the original corral complex include a loading chute and home-built squeeze chute with its necessary runway.

Round corrals are located on any ranch where horses are broken for cow work. A young horse naturally goes to the outside of an enclosure looking for a way out. A round corral has no corners

Figure 5.8. Most of the Dry Creek corrals are of vertical cedar posts with cedar or aspen poles wired to them horizontally for strength. Such stockade fencing is common on Great Basin ranches. (Photo by author)

Figure 5.9. The large mud-and-willow loafing shed located south of ranch headquarters is ninety-six feet long. Shown are the back and southwest sides, looking northeast. It is open on the front (southeast) side and has a concrete water trough inside. (Photo by author)

and the horse moves around it, round and round. Such corrals sometimes have a snubbing post in the center. They are constructed of everything from cedar poles to railroad ties to stone.

Although the Bates cabin area is the original ranch locus, it serves today as "the corrals"; the place where cattle are worked. The Bates cabin is slowly turning back into earth and is not even maintained for storage. The conglomeration of mostly stone buildings around the corner of the hill, downstream to the south of the Bates place, is the main focal point for the ranch and most its activities.

As one approaches the ranch headquarters from the valley floor and passes through a galvanized pipe gate, a loading chute is seen. It is made of heavy, unhewn cedar timbers with aspen poles nailed horizontally to vertical cedar posts. The loading ramp is four feet high, twelve feet long and six feet wide. A complex of pole and wire fencing fans out behind the ramp and includes a round corral thirty-three feet in diameter.

Further along and off the road about a hundred yards to the left is a huge mud-and-willow "loafing shed" (figs. 5.9, 5.10). This three-sided structure is 96' 4" x 30' 10" and the open side faces southeast. There is a newer mud-and-willow addition, with split horizontal poles nailed to the uprights forming a wall on the east side, connected to the larger building by a covered passageway. The addition is 31' 6" x 29' 6". The entire ell-shaped structure is covered with a shallow gable dirt roof and is surrounded with miscellaneous machine, truck, and wagon parts. Loafing sheds provide shade and wind protection for cattle and horses, and this one has a twenty-five-foot-two-inch-long concrete water trough along the inside of the north wall. The scant remains of the stone Pony Express station buildings are found between the loafing shed and pipe entry gate.

Open-fronted stables, loafing sheds, and lambing sheds are common on Great

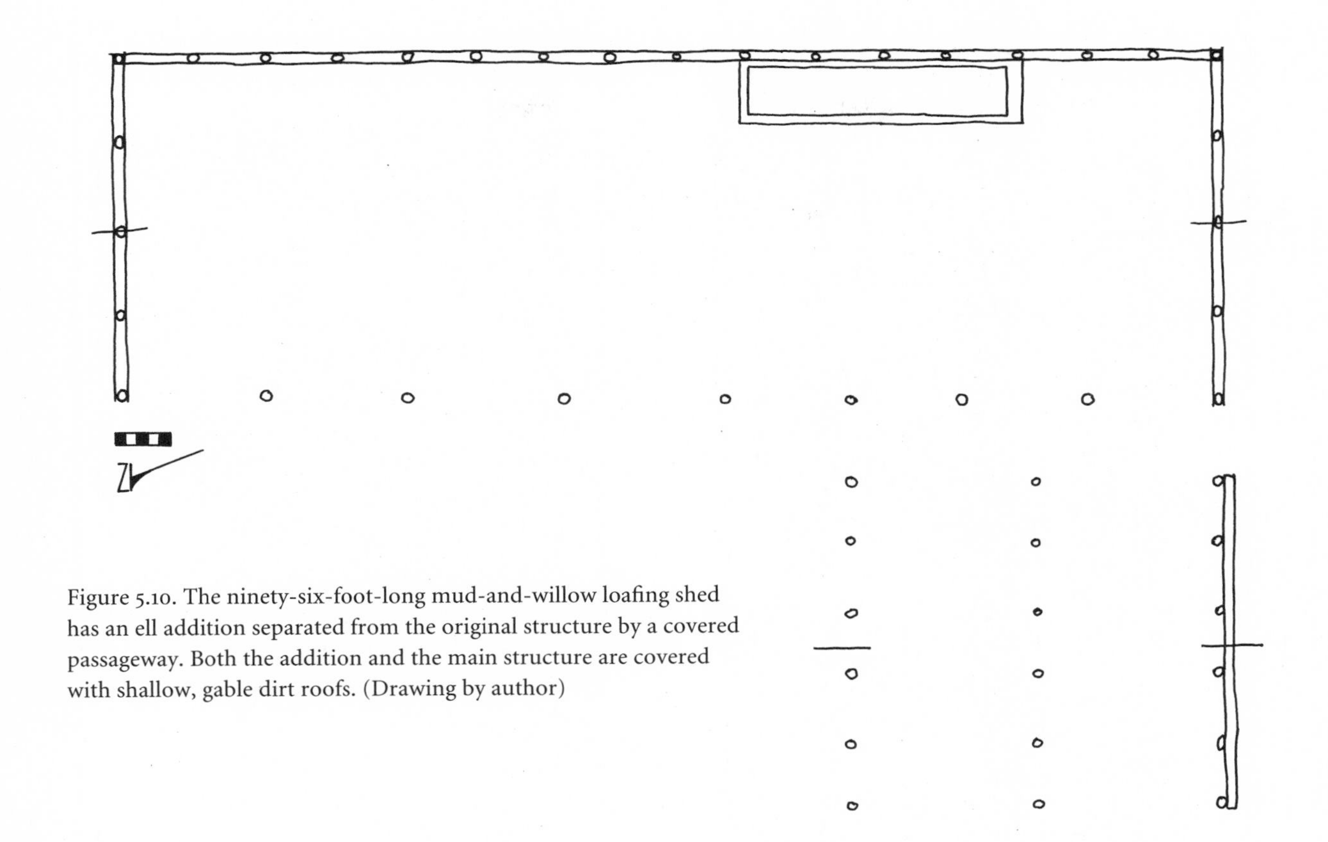

Figure 5.10. The ninety-six-foot-long mud-and-willow loafing shed has an ell addition separated from the original structure by a covered passageway. Both the addition and the main structure are covered with shallow, gable dirt roofs. (Drawing by author)

Basin ranches. Although not unique to the Great Basin, such animal shelters are, nonetheless, the most significant structures for identifying a ranch within the great American desert. They are commonly made of railroad ties, mud-and-willow, adobe bricks, rammed earth, sheet metal, and stone, often being partially set into a hill-side.

The ranch headquarters complex consists of a stone blacksmith shop; the long, open-fronted stone stable; another long stone building that is now the chicken house; a Quonset hut-shaped garage and machinery storage unit; the main house, also stone, with rambling railroad tie additions out the back and sides; and the stone, one-room bunkhouse (fig. 5.11). All the buildings on the ranch, except the metal Quonset hut, have dirt roofs. The main house has an additional, more steeply pitched tin roof built over the original dirt structure.

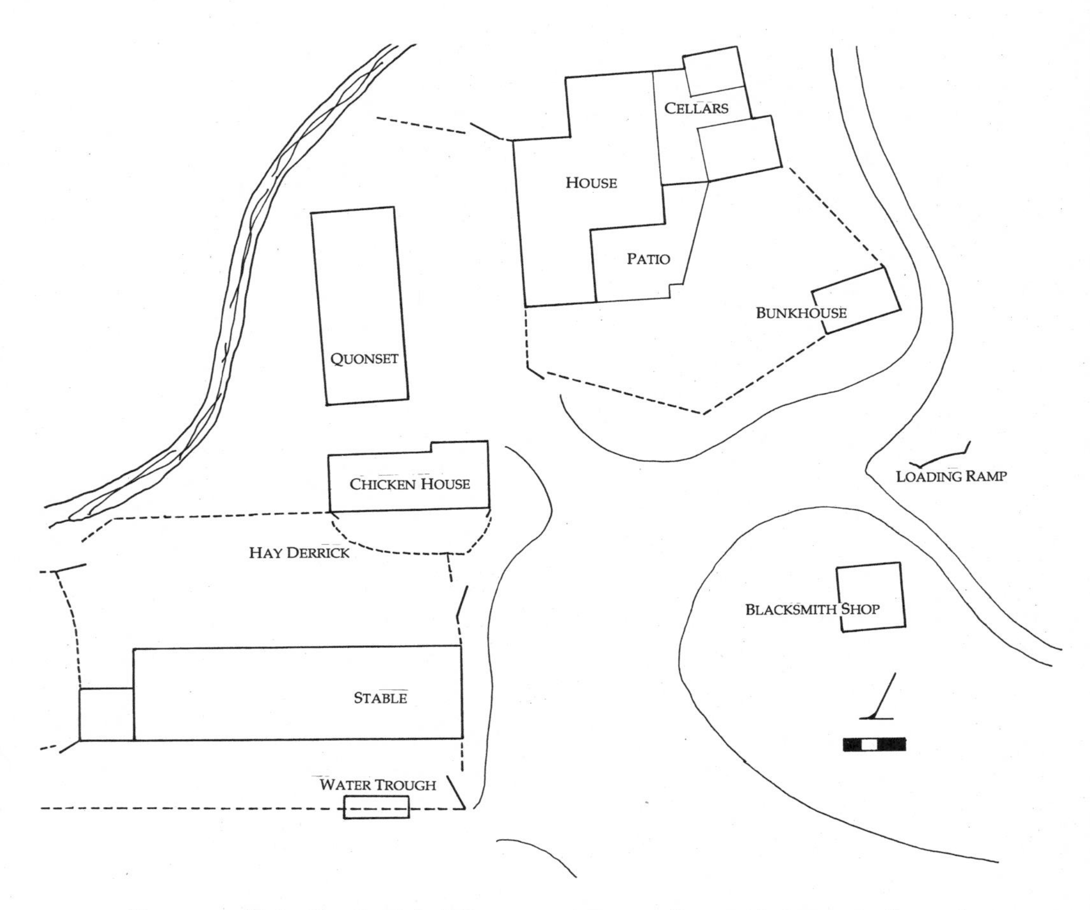

Figure 5.11. All the Dry Creek buildings, except the new Quonset hut, open to the south, downhill, facing the direction of entry into the ranch. Vehicles usually park on the slope in front of the house or between the house and the chicken house. (Drawing by author)

As the ranch headquarters is entered from the southeast, the first building seen is the blacksmith shop, surrounded by tons of iron scrap, machine and wagon parts, sled runners, barrels, and assorted other items no ranch can operate without. This uncoursed, rubble stone building is 19' 8" x 19' 4"; the large double door opening is in the southeast gable end and has a heavy wooden beam lintel set into the stone wall, with two-by-ten-foot framing for the door (fig. 5.12). It is evident the doors have not been closed for generations. There are two windows in the southwest wall and one in the northeast, now boarded over. The northwest wall is built into the slope of the hill and has horizontal logs stacked against the stone as an extra retainer between the dirt and the stone. The shallow dirt roof has a pitch of ten degrees with pole rafters supported by five purlins. The roof extends two feet past the walls. The height from the floor to the base of the center purlin is seven feet. A stone-and-brick forge is in the north corner, surrounded by an anvil, blower, and racks of forge

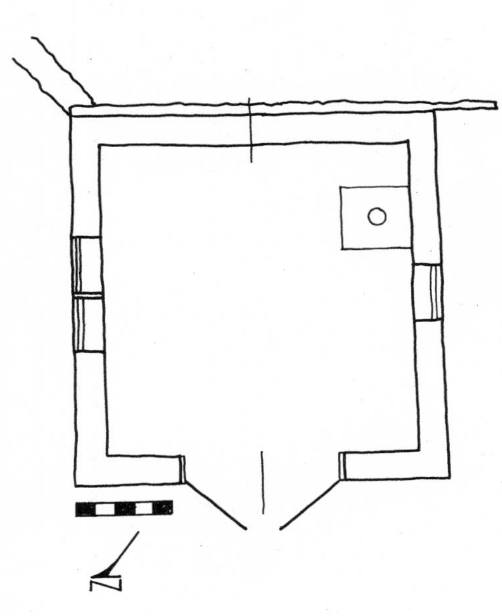

Figure 5.12. The almost square blacksmith shop is surrounded by tons of scrap iron and machine parts. It has a concrete floor, and smoke from the forge has stained the purlins, rafters, and willows of the dirt roof black. (Drawing by author)

tools. Benches and shelves line both side walls. The stone walls are one foot, eight inches thick; there is a concrete floor.

The open-fronted stable at Dry Creek is about a hundred feet west of the blacksmith shop and is constructed of uncoursed rubble with a shallow-pitched, gable dirt roof supported in the front with eight- to ten-foot cedar posts (figs. 5.13, 5.14). It is set into the south-sloping hill and has about four feet of wall extending above ground level. The immediate area in front is surrounded by a tall stockade fence, also cedar, with a stone-and-concrete water trough that is usable from both in- and outside the fenced enclosure. The area immediately under the open front is where saddle repairs are done, horses are shod, mecarties are twisted, and talk is conducted. Access to the stable and the common work area is through a twelve-foot-wide gate made of cedar poles hung on hand-forged hinges.

The Dry Creek stable incorporates enclosed stalls on the southwest end of the building, used to house draft horses, with a trap door in the roof above the feeding troughs through which hay is tossed down for the stock below. There is a draft horse harnessing area just outside the enclosed stalls and under the open front. The area under the open front is full of horse gear; saddles hang from forked sticks from the rafters; headstalls, bridles, reins, and bosals hang from pegs; and horseshoes are hooked over the side of the tool storage bin. A fenced-in room on the northeast side is for holding leppy (motherless) calves and sick animals that need to be kept protected and near.

The stone structure above and behind the stable is probably the first building constructed at the present headquarters site (fig. 5.15). It appears to have been built as a combination short-term dwelling and stable. The larger, open-fronted pen was built first, and the two-room addition built onto it. The western-most room, the one with the stove flue, is enclosed on the front with vertical planks, whereas the

Figure 5.13. The open-fronted stone stable with enclosed draft horse stalls, looking west. (Photo by author)

Figure 5.14. The stable is the working heart of the ranch. The stalls in the west end are for work horses and their gear. The area immediately outside the stalls is where the gear is put on. The two center vertical pole pens are for feed and gear storage; the plank-lined grain room adjoins them. The enclosure on the east side is for holding leppy (motherless) calves; the low south and west walls of this pen are of planks and wire. (Drawing by author)

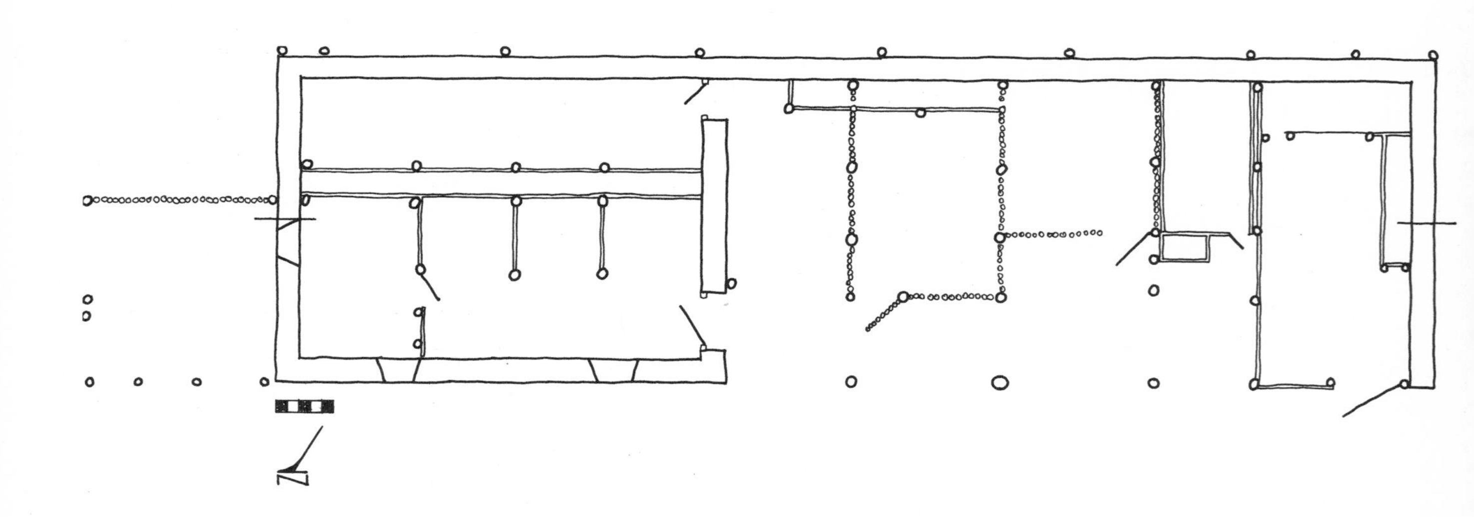

center room is stone fronted. It is the two-room section that was once lived in; the interior walls are whitewashed, and the door is nicely framed into the stone and has a hand-hewn lintel. A narrow, vertical log addition on the western side of the stone building was added sometime later. The rafters of this section are set on posts abutting the stone walls and wired to the protruding rafters of the original building. Chicken wire encloses the front of this addition, as well as a run along the south side of the entire building. Before the advent of baled hay, the area between the chicken house and the stable was used for hay storage. The trap door through the roof of the stable opens onto this area and is easily reached from ground level. A hay derrick, unusual in that it is immobile, stands here and was used to unload wagons of loose hay and stack it (fig. 5.16). A movable arm, an eight-by-eight-foot timber about thirty feet long, is attached to a thirty-foot vertical pole and can rotate around the pole and pivot up and down. Pulleys and wire cable are arranged to manipulate the arm and to lift and lower the load.

Large hay storage barns are rarely seen on older Great Basin ranches. Hay, either stacked loose or in bales, is stored outside. Large, open-sided shelters, however, under which hay bales are stacked, are seen more and more.

A corrugated metal Quonset-shape equipment storage building is behind and above the chicken house. It has a three-foot-high concrete wall around the perimeter, but a dirt floor. The metal uprights on either side of the sliding door

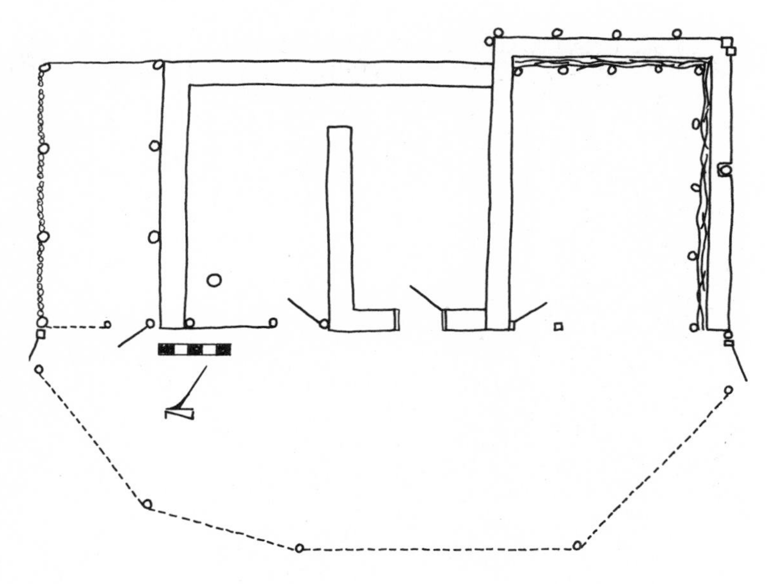

Figure 5.15. The chicken house was originally built as a combination dwelling and stable. The exterior walls of the stable unit are lined with thickly packed willows. The living portion has whitewashed walls, hewn door and window lintels, a stove flue, and dirt floors. (Drawing by author)

Figure 5.16. The hay derrick's operation is dependent on two cable systems; one raises and lowers the boom, the other the load. (Drawing by author)

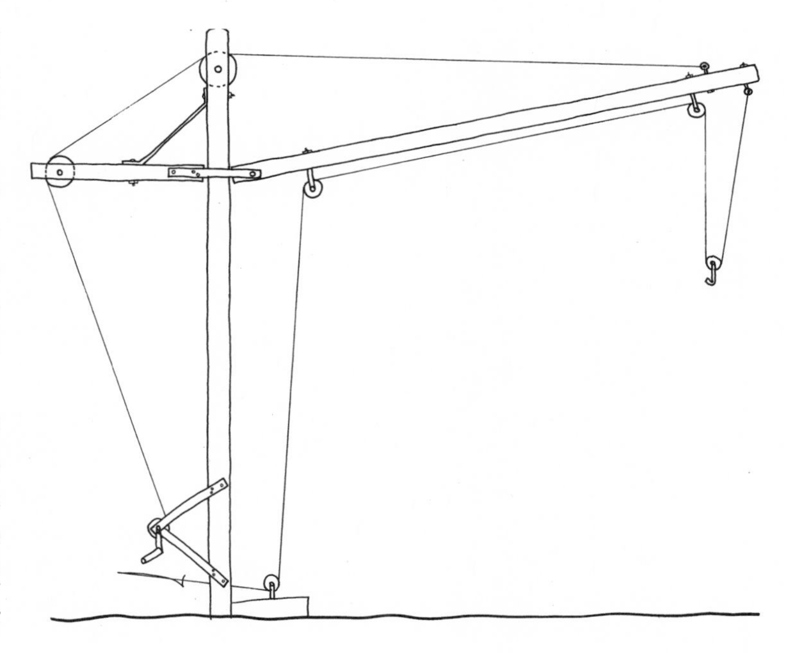

opening are set in concrete-filled fifty-five-gallon drums. This building measures 60' x 25' and is the largest on the headquarters site. It was built in the 1960s.

Just east of the main house is a one-room, uncoursed rubble bunkhouse built by Benny Damele and Bill Wholey in 1944 or 1945 (fig. 5.17). It is 23' 10" x 14' 10" and is, as are the other stone outbuildings, built into the hillside. The interior walls are covered with concrete stucco, and the floor is concrete. The southwest gable facade, which opens into the fenced yard of the main house, has a door and window, each with a stout, hand-hewn wooden lintel. The dirt roof is very shallow, an eight-degree pitch, and is supported by three purlins. The ceiling inside is of fiberboard. The original stove flue was in the east corner, but the stove is now in the west corner. There is one vertical post in the center, which helps support the ridge post.

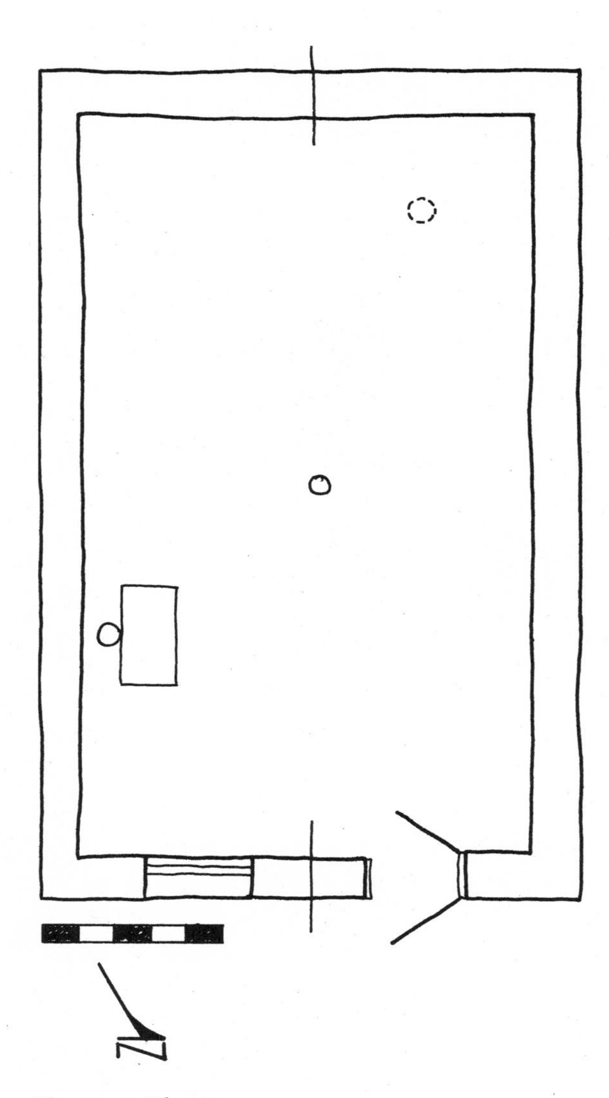

Figure 5.17. The stone bunkhouse was built in the mid-1940s. The stove, originally in the back corner, has been moved to the front. The floor and walls are concrete; there is one vertical support in the center. (Drawing by author)

The main house is an organic assemblage of disparate parts (figs. 5.18, 5.19). The original core, built between 1907 and 1911, is of uncoursed stone covered with a shallow-pitched dirt roof. Two stone, dugout cellars are about fifteen feet northeast of the house and were probably built around the same time as the original house. In 1944, a stone addition, with a cobblestone fireplace and chimney, was built out from the front of the house. Sometime around that same time, a two-room railroad tie addition was built out from the back, and the space between the house and the cellars was closed in with railroad tie and frame construction. New tin roofs were built over the old dirt ones covering the original house and the cellars, and the new railroad tie additions were also covered with tin roofing.

The original, rectangular stone house has uncoursed rubble walls two-feet-five-inches thick. The interior walls are stuccoed and covered with newspaper and wallpaper. The interior divider walls are vertical planks with no two-by-four-foot framing. The front of the house is one long, open room, with the kitchen and dining area

Figure 5.18. The main house at Dry Creek Ranch, looking northwest. The section with the gable projecting forward is the "new" addition built in 1944. The railroad tie passageway connecting the two cellars to the house is on the right. The hay bales are for the many dogs and cats to burrow in during the winter. (Photo by author)

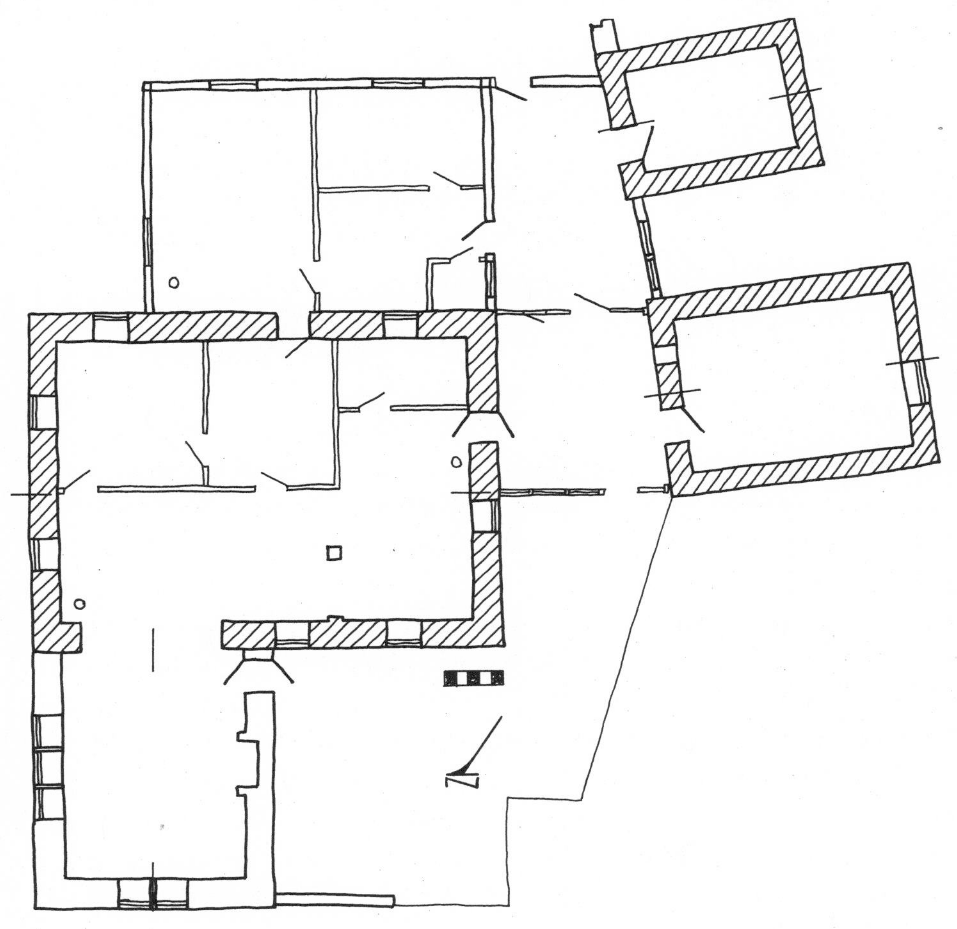

Figure 5.19. The original stone house and cellars were built around 1907–11. The rock addition out the front, railroad tie rooms in the rear, and closed in passageway between the house and the cellars were built in the mid-1940s. A concrete patio links the enclosed passageway and front addition. (Drawing by author)

at the northeast end, and the stove on the west. There is no stone chimney in the original house. A section of the front wall was removed when the stone addition was added to incorporate it with the older structure.

The railroad tie addition out the rear is reached through what was originally the back door of the house. Access to the enclosed passageway between the house and the cellars is through former exterior doors as well.

The two stone cellars, the larger with a concrete floor and small window, are built into the hill on the northeast side of the house. Both have purlin-supported, shallow gable roofs covered with dirt. The space between the cellars has a retaining wall of railroad ties, and the whole cellar-passageway complex is covered with a new, multisloped, gable, purlin-supported tin roof. The former eastern exterior wall of the house, now the interior wall of the passageway, has chicken wire attached to it, but has never been stuccoed.

A concrete patio extends around the east corner of the house, connecting the front door with the entry into the covered passageway between the house and the cellars. A woven wire fence surrounds a grassed yard. Branding irons, leather harness parts, and other miscellaneous items are stuck into the fence. The gate is made of a wooden wagon wheel and is self-closing, using a rope with weights as the motive force.

Around the corner of the hill, upstream toward the Bates cabin and about sixty feet from the main house, is a small spring house, about nine feet square and mostly covered with dirt. The arched concrete roof is supported by two railroad rail purlins, and in the front is a small wooden hatch held in place on the corners with turn latches. The hatch has a six-inch-square opening in it covered with screen wire. The spring house is about fifteen feet higher than the house below.

Great Basin ranches are working places. All of a ranch's structures—house, outbuildings, corrals, ditches, fences—are parts of a larger, working whole. Each structure can be examined separately, but cannot be understood as a living entity without an examination of the interrelated whole. Ranch structures must be viewed as organic, as coexisting beings. Corrals are connected to stables; water troughs are split between stable yard and field; loading chutes are connected to holding pens and roads; paths, roads, and fencing run like umbilical cords from place to place; houses are partially isolated by fencing, not only to keep animals out, but sometimes to keep them in. Structures are connected to one another physically and through work patterns and routes.

Ranch buildings adhere very closely to traditional forms and are invariably tied to function. Scarcity of building materials more abundant elsewhere, such as timber, has necessitated the development of construction techniques and building forms closely aligned with available materials. Buildings of stone, adobe, railroad tie, and mud-and-willow are all evident in the arid West. Dwellings with thick walls, dirt roofs, and high ceilings are partial responses to environmental concerns, and low-slung outbuildings, backed against and dug into hills, are the same.

Ranch architecture in the Great Basin, more so, perhaps, than rural architecture in most other parts of the country, is environmentally and occupationally determined rather than dictated by communal norms and aesthetics. Most ranch buildings show very little ethnic identity; few exhibit architectural fads of their day; and building alignments and grouping are determined by topography and use more than by road or compass point. Most areas outside mining towns (which are actually small, urban rather than agrarian settlements scattered throughout the sagebrush ocean) were not settled until the last quarter of the nineteenth century or later. Individual ranchsteads, whether family owned or part of a larger corporate entity, were usually family or small group affairs. They do not exhibit, for example, the communal settlement patterns more commonly seen in rural areas settled by members of the Church of Jesus Christ of Latter-day Saints. The Great Basin's rural architecture reflects the facts of geographic isolation and its incumbent self-sufficiency, and less of a communal aesthetic. Pressures to adhere to group norms and pressures, such as building alignments and architectural embellishments, were slight.

As darkness sets in, Benny Damele, who operates on daylight savings time year-round, sits down to an ample evening meal. The table is loaded with turkey, mashed potatoes and gravy, green beans, coleslaw, iced tea, coffee, and a large jug of red wine. Butter is taken from the gas-operated refrigerator. Conversation ranges from politics to American Bashkir Curly horses to the old timers and beyond. After supper, everyone congregates around the fireplace, sensing the dark as it grows. A kerosene lamp is lit if something needs to be read or seen more clearly, otherwise the light of the never-quenched fire suffices. The day's events are discussed, and tomorrow's very briefly touched on. The talk soon ranges toward the abstract. Life at Dry Creek seems as solid and enduring as the buildings themselves.

Notes

1. Field research for this essay was conducted between 1986 and 1991. For a brief look at central Nevada folk traditions, including ranching and ranch architecture, see Andrea Graham and Blanton Owen, *Lander County Line: Folklife in Central Nevada* (Reno: Nevada State Council on the Arts, 1988).

2. Benny Damele died 12 November 1991.

3. Dorothy Mason (Nevada BLM), *The Pony Express in Nevada* (Reno: Harrah's, n.d.), 30.

4. John McPhee, *Basin and Range* (New York: Farrar, Straus, Giroux, 1980), 18, 27.

5. Most ranches in the Great Basin include a combination of relatively small tracts of private, "deeded" land and larger areas of public range leased from the Bureau of Land Management, the U. S. Forest Service, or both according to the dictates of the Taylor Grazing Act of 1934.

6. Deed transfers for Dry Creek Ranch are recorded at the Lander County Courthouse, Battle Mountain, Nevada, and are located in the following deed books and pages: 49/354; 49/400; 50/174; 51/566; 57/235; 58/339; 61/469.

7. Burton quoted in Mason, *The Pony Express in Nevada*, 30; see, for example, John M. Townley, *The Pony Express Guidebook* (Reno: Great Basin Studies Center, n.d.), 44.

8. For accounts of Eureka's Italian *carbonari*, including the Charcoal Burner's War of 1979 and the important role played by Italian immigrants in the history of Nevada, see Philip I. Earl, "Nevada's Italian War," *Nevada Historical Quarterly* 3, no. 2 (summer 1969); and Franklin Grazeola, "The Charcoal Burner's War of 1879: A Case Study of the Italian Immigration in Nevada" (master's thesis, University of Nevada, 1969).

9. *Cedar* is the regional term for Utah juniper *(Juniperus osteosperma)*. Old growth cedars are especially resistant to rotting and make a durable building material. During rewallpapering in 1990, some of the newspapers uncovered were dated 1906.

10. This technique is obviously similar to wattle-and-daub, rammed earth, and *jacal* construction. Preliminary research about the mud-and-willow construction technique and building forms in the central Great Basin is found in Graham and Owen, *Lander County Line.* See also Owen's abstract "The Great Basin 'Mud' House: Preliminary Findings" in *Perspectives in Vernacular Architecture III,* ed. Thomas Carter and Bernard L. Herman (Columbia: University of Missouri Press, 1989), 245–46. Christopher Martin's "Skeleton of Settlement: Ukrainian Folk Building in Western North Dakota" in *Perspectives III,* shows identical mud-and-willow construction among western North Dakota's late nineteenth- and early twentieth-century Ukrainian settlers plus examples from the Ukraine (86-98). David Murphy's "Building in Clay on the Central Plains," also in *Perspectives III,* briefly mentions the same technique (81). A thorough examination of jacal construction is found in "The *Jacal* in South Texas: The Origins and Form of a Folk House" in *Hecho en Tejas: Texas-Mexican Folk Arts and Crafts,* ed. Joe Graham (Denton: University of North Texas Press, Publications of the Texas Folklore Society, 1991), 50:293–308.

Cultural Convergences

CHAPTER SIX

When a Room Is the Hall

The Houses of West Las Vegas, New Mexico

CHRIS WILSON

Living and traveling in northern New Mexico and southern Colorado, in the villages and old sections of our towns, we see thousands of small adobe houses. While we are vaguely aware of minor differences from one area to another, we tend to class them all together as a simple folk or vernacular type. A closer study, however, reveals a more complex and varied history. How these buildings are constructed, how their rooms are laid out and used, how we approach such a house or receive a visitor are all shaped by cultural values and attitudes. In one building we can see evidence of Pueblo Indian values; in another, Hispanic practices; in yet another, we find the two traditions mixed. If we are willing to put aside romantic preconceptions about the Spanish-Pueblo style, we even see that Anglo-American attitudes frequently play an important part.

Each area and each building is unique; each reveals the workings of a distinctive local tradition. A series of detailed studies of the folk houses of New Mexico would teach us much about the state's various cultures—their development, spread, and intermingling.[1] This article presents the findings of one such study. The exteriors of the approximately eight hundred houses of west Las Vegas, New Mexico, were photographed and described on New Mexico Historic Building Inventory forms. Twenty of these were selected as representative examples and studied in more detail, including the drawing and analysis of measured floor plans.

These buildings and related historical records indicate that a Spanish-Mexican style of building and the focus of a household's activities in a single multipurpose room provided the basis for local folk architecture. After the Civil War, Anglo-American buildings introduced new construction practices and house plans that separated public and private space. From 1870 to 1910 these new ideas were incorporated into the existing tradition. This hybrid tradition directed new construction up to 1940 and continues to affect house remodeling today (fig. 6.1a-f).

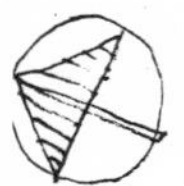

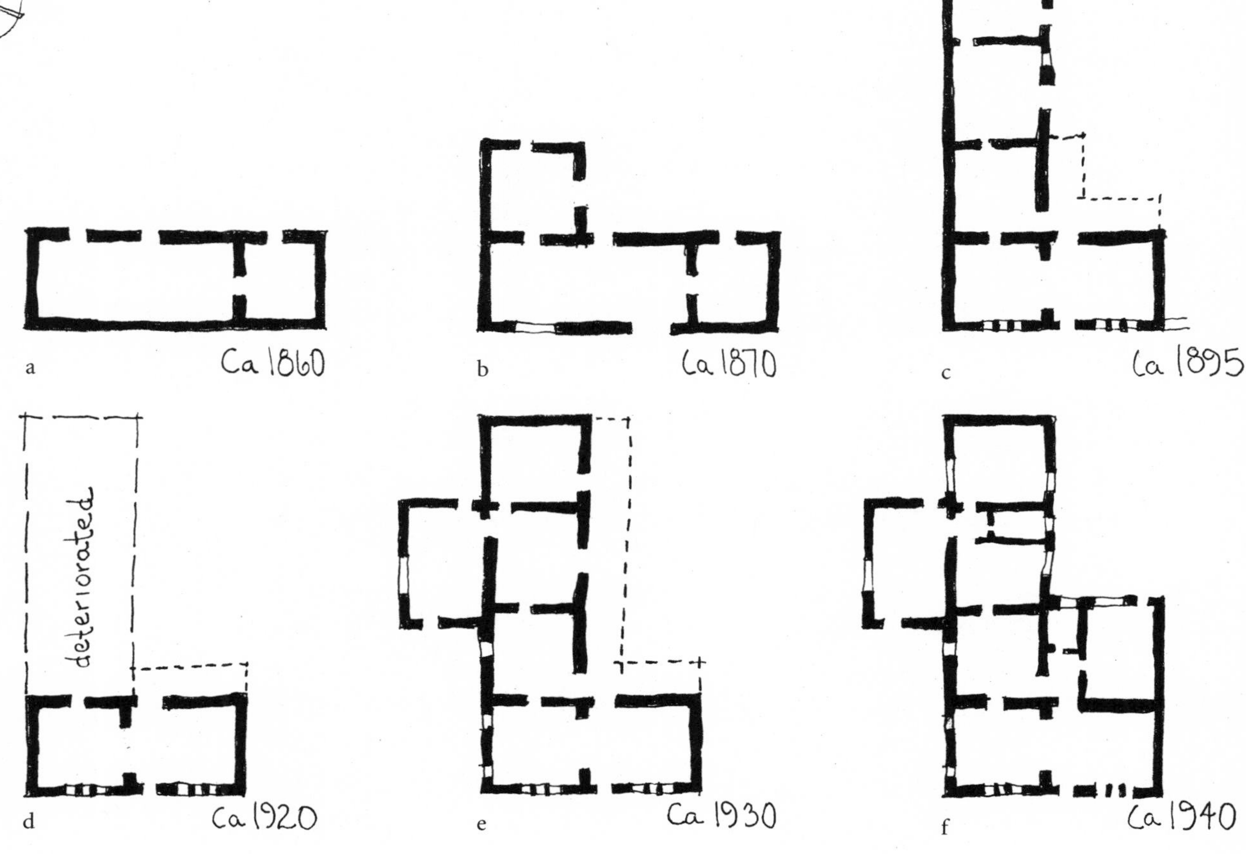

Figure 6.1. Sena-Silva House, 1906 North Gonzales. Stages of a changing tradition, 1860–1940: *a–b.* piecemeal additions in the linear, Hispanic manner; *c.* Anglo-introduced symmetrical window-door-window facade; *d.* contraction; *e.* second entrance allows traditional Hispanic division into two households; *f.* Anglo organization of kitchen, bathrooms, and first interior hallways. (Drawing by Sven Govaars)

There are two useful ways of interpreting Hispanic houses in New Mexico. One is to focus on the ideal—the fully realized courtyard house; the other is to emphasize the individual unit—the room. The keenest observer of New Mexico in the 1850s, U.S. attorney W. W. H. Davis, wrote in *El Gringo,* his popular account of the region, that all houses "whether in town or country, are built in the form of a square, with a courtyard in the center."[2] This is an exaggeration caused, perhaps, by Davis's familiarity with the homes of the wealthy. The 1846 "Gilmer Map of Santa Fe," for example, shows fifty-five complete courtyard houses, but also over a hundred U-shaped, L-shaped, and single-file buildings—the homes of common families. Of the 250 adobe residences on the 1882 "Bird's Eye View of Las Vegas" only two are courtyard houses. The more numerous L-shaped and single-file houses were generally extended by adobe walls and by connected houses to form family courtyards. In fact, New Mexican Spanish acknowledged this situation by calling a courtyard surrounded on all sides by rooms, a *placita,* and a courtyard finished in part by a wall, a *plazuela.* Placita is now often applied to the courtyard house type and not simply the courtyard.[3]

Both placitas and plazuelas lacked exterior windows and had only one large door or a pair of doors that led directly into the courtyard. Defense against nomadic Indian attack is the explanation commonly given for these unbroken exteriors. But in the cities, as well as in the heart of the settled area, where the threat of attack was small, the actual explanation is less romantic. As Davis remarked: "There is a great dread of robbers among the people, and they will not always admit you before you are known."[4] This comment is repeated by other early observers and seems to be the more plausible explanation.

In addition to guarding against thieves, this arrangement provided a spatial and temporal distance between the threshold facing the public way and the family's private quarters. If a visitor was unacquainted enough with local custom to arrive during the afternoon siesta, the family could take whatever time necessary to compose themselves. In a wealthy household a servant might be sent to the door to conduct the guests to a large room, the *sala.* Much more commonly, the host greeted the visitors at the exterior door, exchanged courtesies there, then conducted the party across the courtyard to the sala.

The flat-roofed house of adobe or stone, built around a courtyard, has its roots in Mediterranean and Middle Eastern antiquity. Colonists carried it from Spain to central Mexico where a similar, indigenous type already existed. Spanish explorer-settlers and their Tlaxcalan Indian auxiliaries probably share credit for bringing the courtyard house to New Mexico about 1600. (Robert West, in an article on folk dwellings in Mexico, emphasizes the Indian role, whereas others have traditionally given sole credit to the Spanish.[5]) The persistence of the type in New Mexico is remarkable; one example remaining in Las Vegas, the Manuel Romero House, was

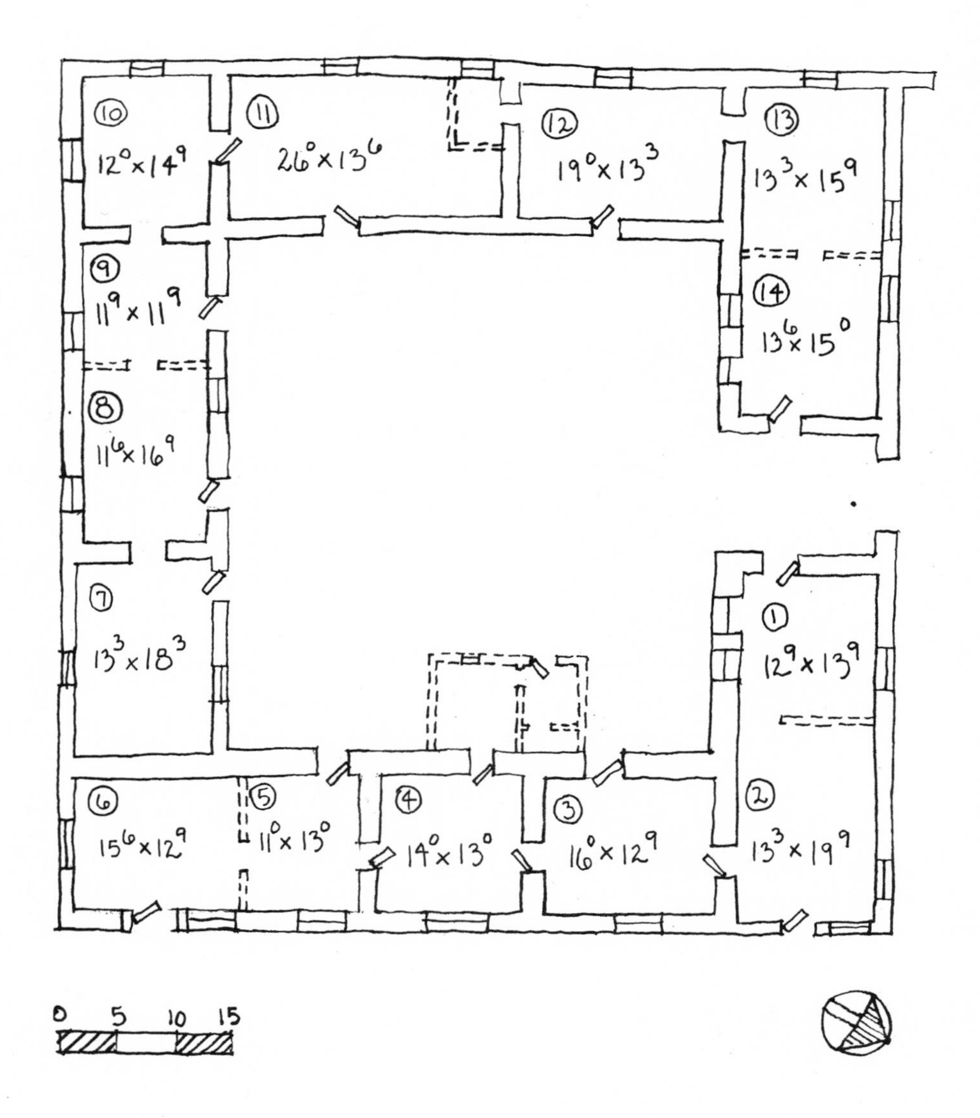

Figure 6.2. Manuel Romero House (Casa Redonda), South Pacific Avenue and Socorro Street, ca. 1875–1900. (Drawing by Sven Govaars)

not completed until about 1900 (fig. 6.2). In 1882 this house was a flat-roofed, L-shaped building of three rooms (rooms 1–4; the frame partition between 1 and 2 is recent.) Rooms were added in stages, which completed the courtyard by 1902. The characteristic features of the Hispanic tradition are here: a single file of rooms forming an enclosure, a covered passage, or *zaguan,* leading in from the street, and a door for each room opening onto the courtyard.

The second approach to the Hispanic house has been most perceptively advanced by J. B. Jackson who emphasizes the importance of the individual room. Observing the tradition along the upper Rio Grande in New Mexico, Jackson wrote in 1959:

> The house and the room are identical; the room is thought of and designed to be a completely self-sufficient unit with its own corner

Table 6.1 Cultural Patterns in the Adobe Houses of West Las Vegas

Spanish/Mexican-American *(1840–1900)*	Anglo-American *(1870–1900)*	Hybrid *(1870–1940)*
room-by-room accretions	built at one time	multiroom accretions
linear or courtyard design	central hall or picturesque cottage	linear/central hall fusion
unwritten tradition	blueprints, builders' handbooks	unwritten tradition
inward, rear facing	street frontality	street frontality
at street's edge	set back from street	set back from street
connected to other houses	isolated	isolated
informal symmetry of openings to each room	overall exterior symmetry of openings	isolated symmetrical groups of openings
additions at edges (sides or rear)	additions at rear (maintain facade composition)	additions at rear (narrow lots)
rooms step w/slope	single-level foundations	low to ground
on ground	raised foundations	single-level foundations
rectangular, some square rooms	square rooms	square or divided rectangles
13' to 15' room widths	15' to 16' room widths	12' to 13' room widths
one exterior door per room, facing rear	two entrances (front, rear)	one front door, many rear
one story	one and two story	one story
one room deep	two or more rooms deep	one room deep
flat roofed	gabled	gabled
courtyard and rooms for circulation	center hall organizes circulation	porch and rooms for circulation
one room for all uses	specialized rooms	specialized room
public/private combined	public/private separated	partial separation of public/private

> chimney (or flue), its own door, its own window; plenty of young Spanish-American working couples start married life in a one-room house standing by itself in a yard. They rapidly acquire a second room, it's true, and a third when they think they need it, but each of these additional rooms is pretty much of the same size, and built to be self-sufficient if necessary.[6]

One way to elaborate this idea of the self-sufficient room is to consider how it is used. Santa Fe Trail travelers of the 1840s and 1850s were invariably struck by the use of a single, large room for every household function except food storage. Few had a more interesting first day in a New Mexican house than Lewis Garrard who later recounted his travels in *Wah-to-Yah and the Taos Trail.* Arriving at the Mexican village of Taos, New Mexico, late one day in 1846, he dined on potatoes with his hosts in their large sala. He declined an invitation to attend a *fandango,* and a mattress was unrolled from the wall for him. Shortly after he laid down, though, the dance commenced in the very room in which he was to sleep. Exhausted, he nevertheless fell asleep "amid a delicious reverie." He continues his tale the next morning: "At a late hour for a mountain man, I dressed by a blazing fire, although Señora St. Vrain and sister—a handsome brunette of some sixteen years—were in the room; they probably being accustomed by the 'free and easy' manners of the Valley to this liberty which they themselves took an hour before."[7] In less than a day, Garrard had seen a single large sala used as a place for cooking, eating, entertaining, sleeping, bathing, and dressing. Other early travel accounts reinforce this picture of the multipurpose sala.

These same accounts hint at another pattern, however. At a wedding in a wealthy household, W. W. H. Davis noted the use of adjoining rooms. Arriving at the house, he was conducted across the courtyard and through the sala to an adjacent room. There, he received refreshments before being invited back into the sala for the ceremony. Davis' general comment that "all rooms open directly into the patio except some that communicate directly with the sala and with each other" implies that rooms sometimes functioned in tandem.[8] Additional evidence of this practice can be found in the original portions of several Las Vegas houses, which pair a large rectangular room with a smaller square one (figs. 6.1, 6.2, 6.8, 6.10).

But if one or at most two rooms served as the focus of family life, why were houses of up to twelve rooms built? Historically, some rooms stored food supplies. In a wealthy household, servants sometimes occupied a second set of rooms. Traveling the court circuit, Davis leased a room in a Socorro house: "The remainder of the building was inhabited by two families, one occupying the wing across the courtyard, while the other lived in the sala."[9] The generations of one extended family might organize and reorganize various households over the years and rent out unused portions of a courtyard house. The largest house in this study, the Romero

House (fig. 6.2), was occupied by six families (four of which were related) in 1919. Each family rented a pair of rooms from the absentee owner. Today, the building's owner occupies rooms one to six across the front. Her daughter's family lives in rooms twelve through fourteen. A pair of two-room apartments are currently used for storage.

Anglo-American influences on architecture in New Mexico were slight before 1846. After the American occupation, however, a permanent military force and resident merchants and officials quickly began a campaign of modernization. By the end of the forties, sawmills were providing the territory's first milled lumber, doors, and windows. New windows, doors, and porches were used to reorient existing houses to the street. (*Portals* on the streets of Spanish colonial cities were primarily for commercial, not residential, use and were concentrated on the plaza.) New construction in Las Vegas after the American occupation continued to use adobe as the major material, however, and to follow the courtyard or linear house type. Only after the Civil War was a new center-hall house plan introduced by major construction projects at Fort Union, twenty miles north, and at Fort Marcy in Santa Fe. About 1870 the builders of the Julianita Romero de Baca House in Las Vegas closely followed the blueprints used at Fort Marcy for officers' houses (figs. 6.3, 6.4). They altered the rigid symmetry of the original by moving one interior wall to enlarge the parlor (room 3) at the expense of the kitchen (room 5). Another concession to

Figure 6.3. Julianita Romero de Baca House, 2008 North Gonzales Road, ca. 1870. (Photo by author)

Figure 6.4. Julianita Romero de Baca House. (Drawing by Sven Govaars)

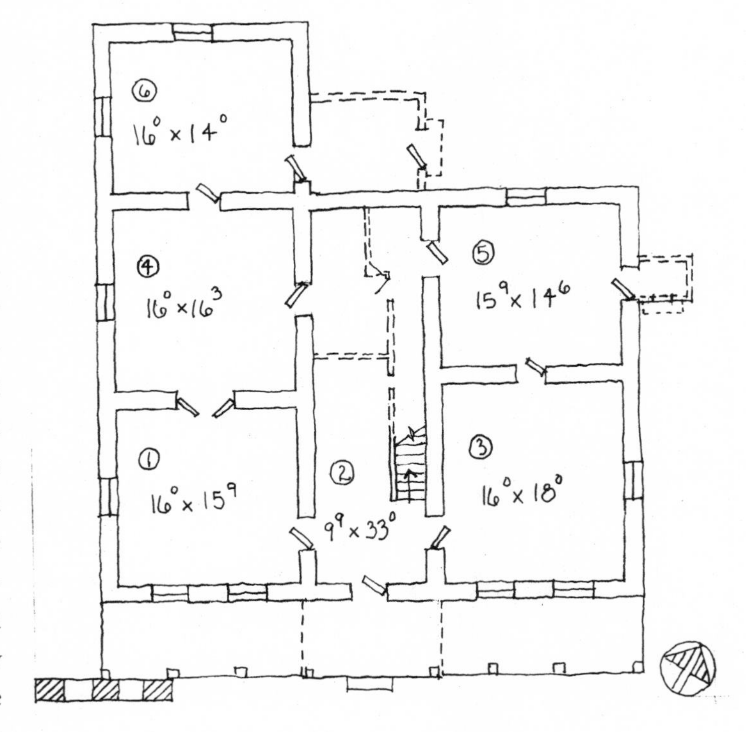

Figure 6.5. 1501 South Pacific Avenue, ca. 1879–82. (Photo by author)

the local tradition was to place the house low to the ground rather than on the two-foot-high foundation indicated on the blueprints.

Of the nineteenth-century floor plans brought to Las Vegas this center-hall plan was to have the greatest impact on the vernacular tradition. The picturesque cottage type, however, had some influence after the arrival of the railroad in 1879 (fig. 6.5). These houses have asymmetrical facades, often with a front-facing gable to one side balanced by a porch across the remainder of the facade. Inside, the plan is informal, with the parlor and dining room opening into each other through double doors. To the rear, a short hall often organizes communication with the kitchen and bedrooms.

In contrast to the earlier Hispanic tradition, these new house types—the center-hall plan and the picturesque cottage—consciously address the street with full porches and symmetrical facades or balanced asymmetry. They were built all at once as self-contained units, set back from the street and apart from their neighbors. Hallways internalize the social distancing provided in the Hispanic tradition by the courtyard. Rooms begin to have specialized uses. On the Fort Marcy plan, for example, room 3 is designated as an office, room 5 a kitchen, rooms 1 and 4 merely as rooms (presumably bedrooms), and room 6 a storeroom. The hall allows movement within the house without passing through other rooms. This specialization of rooms and introduction of hallways combined to separate public and private spaces and functions within the house—a significant change from the multipurpose sala.

In his groundbreaking social history of the family, *The Centuries of Childhood,* Phillipe Aries correlated similar developments in Europe to a reorientation of social structure from the medieval to the modern.[10] He described a density of social contact in the late Middle Ages, different from today but quite similar to New Mexico in the 1840s. The wealthy households, in which social changes first occurred, were composed of a married couple, their children, unmarried relatives, protégés, servants, and visitors, often numbering fifteen to twenty people. All households, whether wealthy or poor, dwelt in one general-purpose room, called in Middle English a *halle.* Here they ate and slept, danced and worked, entertained and cooked. As a new desire for isolation and a sense of individuality developed during the Renaissance, some wealthy families began to create a private realm, isolated from the incessant sociability of the wider public realm. The organization of houses began to change, yielding specialized rooms and open corridors; servants were separated from the family, public spaces from private. These changes occurred first in urban centers among the lower nobility and middle class. They spread only gradually to provincial and rural areas, and both up and down the social order.

We know, for example, that similar changes occurred in rural Virginia between 1750 and 1800. Henry Glassie, in his structuralist study *Folk Houses in Middle Virginia,* identifies them as evidence of a shift from an agrarian economy with a sense of communal and familial obligation to a money economy with the disintegration of the community into smaller groups and ultimately to the isolated individual. This change was accompanied by the telltale division and specialization of space and by the appearance of symmetrical facades, which he feels "suggested impersonal stability." Such changes in society and house design, Glassie notes, were often accompanied by overt signs of social upheaval: in Virginia by the Great Awakening and the American Revolution, in Ireland by the revolution of 1916, and, it can be added, in Las Vegas from 1889 to 1892 by the farmers' rebellion led by *Las Gorras Blancas,* the White Caps. This burst of overt resistance to the privatization and fencing of common lands around Las Vegas corresponds to the peak of experimentation and change in the local building tradition.[11]

As early as 1870, Hispanic builders had begun to incorporate elements from the Anglo-American house types in their work. Evidence of the new attitudes often first

Figure 6.6. 324 Perez Road, ca. 1902. (Photo by author)

Figure 6.7. Rivera-Huie House, 531 National Street, ca. 1865–90. (Photo by author)

appeared in small additions, alterations, or demolitions. The adobe walls forming the private courtyards of existing houses gradually disappeared. The addition of exterior porches completed the reorientation of once-private Las Vegas houses toward the street. Groups of connected buildings were likewise broken into separate units by the removal of connecting rooms. For new construction, the L-shaped house was a popular design during this transitional period and continued to be built at least until the Second World War (fig. 6.6). Constructed of adobe, with a linear organization of rooms, each with its own door to the porch, which served as a hallway, this type clearly had its roots in the Hispanic tradition. But these houses were built in one or, perhaps, two stages; they face the street with porches, stand apart from other houses, and often rest on raised foundations—all indications of Anglo-American influence. The asymmetrical massing of this design coincides with the picturesque house type—a convergence of influences.

Among the most interesting houses of this period of experimentation from 1870 to 1910 are those that began as traditional flat-roofed, two-room adobes and incorporated the new influences in later additions. When the original core of the Rivera-Huie House was remodeled in the 1880s, its new facade was modeled closely on the symmetrical window-door-window grouping and centered gable of the officer's house (figs. 6.7, 6.8 rooms 1–3). Inside, a hall was partitioned out of the original large room on the right, leaving it slightly smaller than the room to the left of the hall. Behind the symmetrical facade and beyond the centered entry hall, the builders continued to rely on Hispanic norms. Although the rear arm, like the second story, uses new frame stucco construction, it takes the traditional form of a string of rooms, which serve as their own corridor and which step with the slope of the site. (Steps indicating changes in level between rooms are noted in fig. 6.8).

The Tafoya–C. de Baca House began as a similar, flat-roofed, two-room adobe (figs. 6.9, 6.10 rooms 1, 2), but took a different direction as it developed. The original core was enlarged about 1890 by the addition of rooms 3 and 4 and of a wrap-around porch. The asymmetry of the facade and the wide opening between the new living room and parlor show the direct influence of the picturesque cottage. The use of a window-door-window grouping from the center-hall house type is an isolated bit of symmetry. The grouping is shifted slightly to the right to balance the front gable and to create a

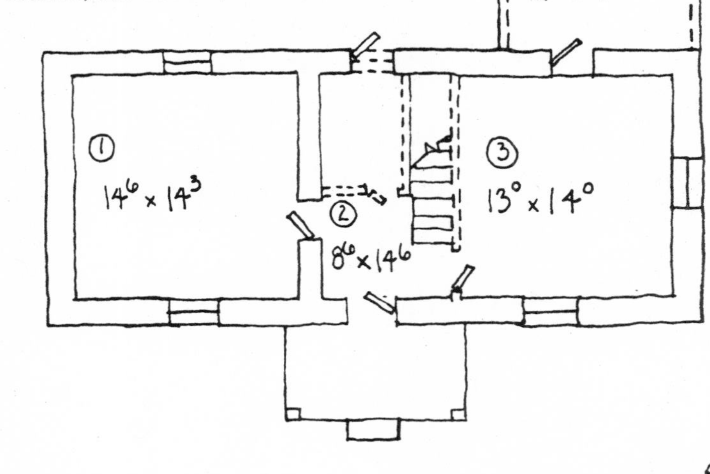

Figure 6.8. Rivera-Huie House. (Drawing by Sven Govaars)

Figure 6.9. Tafoya–C. de Baca House, 411 Santa Fe Avenue, ca. 1875–1925. (Photo by author)

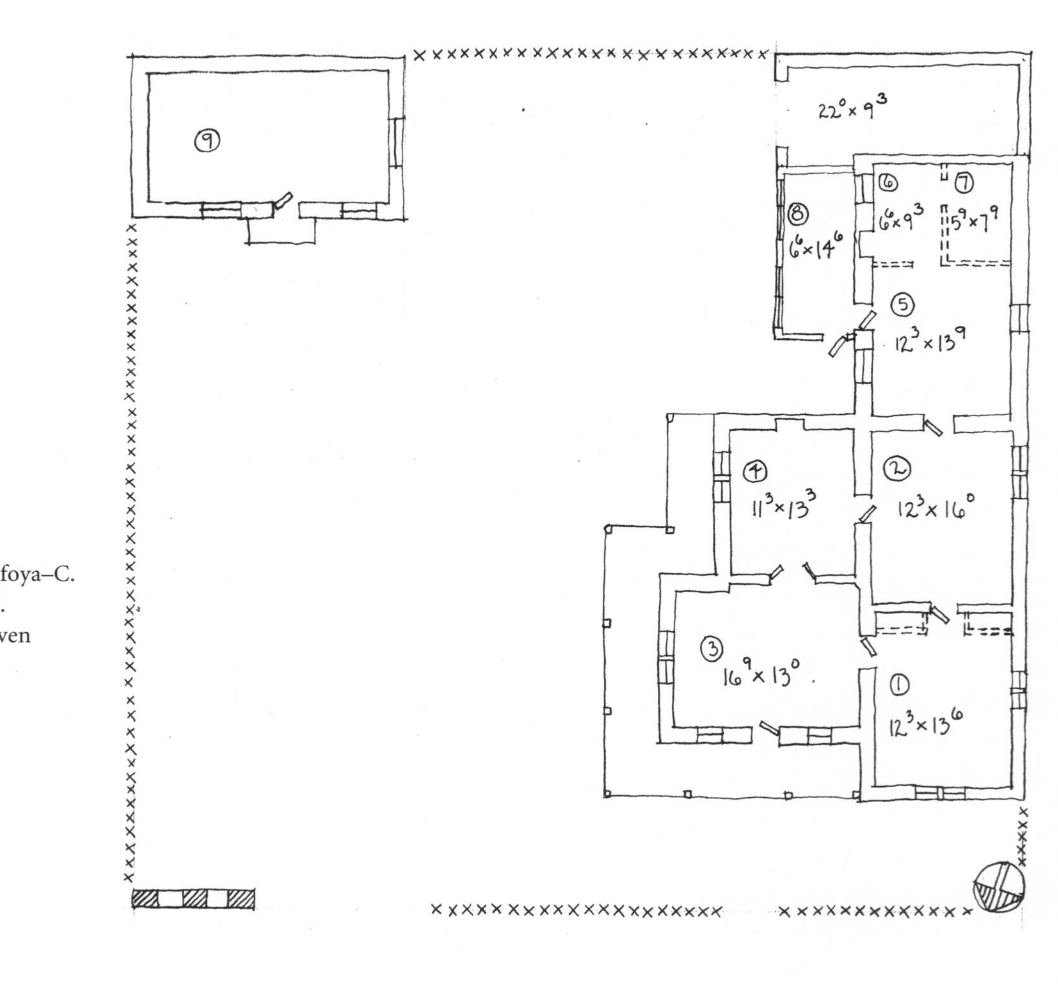

Figure 6.10. Tafoya–C. de Baca House. (Drawing by Sven Govaars)

symmetrical window placement inside. This subtle adjustment of the openings and the quality of the wood details reveal the hand of an inventive folk builder whose work is identifiable elsewhere in town. Subsequent additions show a less fashionable builder at work. Rooms 5 through 7 extend the original two-room portion in the traditional linear fashion. The separate newlyweds' house, built in the 1920s, reproduces room 3 of the large house—even repeating the off-center window-door-window grouping.

All of the houses studied have been remodeled inside to meet changing needs. (The wood frame walls of these remodelings are noted by dotted lines in the plan illustrations.) The most significant change has been the division of the large salas into smaller spaces. These subdivisions and additions to existing houses accommodated the new desire for specialized rooms. But because corridors generally were not also added, many rooms double as hallways. Although the earlier uses of the sala had been parceled out to separate rooms, the adoption of linear circulation patterns continues to blur the distinction between public and private space. The parents' bedroom was sometimes located at one end of the row, affording them a degree of privacy, although children's rooms typically doubled as a passageway.

Starting in the 1920s, the installation of utilities fixed the location of modern kitchens in existing rooms. The creation of interior bathrooms has been less straightforward. In some cases, the bathroom was added on the outside, connected to one of the many existing doors (fig. 6.2). More frequently, it is cramped into the corner of a bedroom or beside the kitchen. In the three houses with center halls, the bath has been placed at the rear of the hall (figs. 6.4, 6.8, 6.12). This solution closes the corridor and forces circulation through the rooms.

The implications of this development are clearest in the Blanchard-Gallegos House, because it was built by an Anglo-American family but remodeled by a Hispanic-American family (figs. 6.11, 6.12). An elaborate Territorial Style entrance marks the original hallway (room 3), which organized a hierarchy of spaces: kitchen and parlor to either side, private spaces further removed. Today, with the bathroom inserted in the hall, this entrance is not often used. A chain-link fence fronting the house directs the visitor instead to a door in the corner bedroom. The circulation pattern runs through the long file of rooms: from the bedroom, through the living room, across the hall, through the kitchen, and either to another bedroom or out to the back courtyard. This reassertion of linear circulation suggests the continuation of a close-knit family structure rooted in a local tradition that has different attitudes about privacy than one would find in the suburbs.

Given the choice, many families do move into new suburban tract houses north of town; but the old tradition lives on in the way the historic buildings are used and, here and there, in small building additions. It is difficult to know whether, in the

Figure 6.11. Blanchard-Gallegos House, 1315 Chavez Road, ca. 1875. (Photo by author)

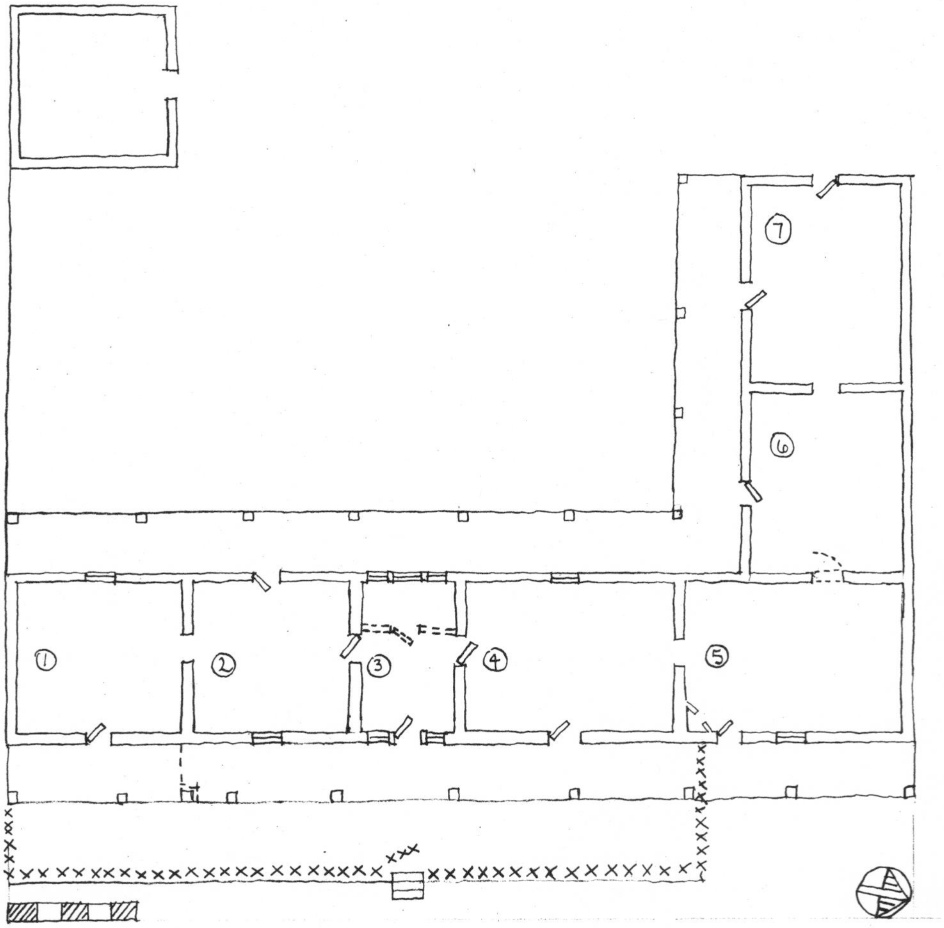

Figure 6.12. Blanchard-Gallegos House. (Drawing by Sven Govaars)

adobe houses of Las Vegas, we are seeing merely the remnants and vestiges of the Hispanic way of building or the signs of a modified but still vital tradition.

Architects, planners, and historians working in New Mexico should be aware of this question. We often claim to respect and support the continuation of New Mexico's cultural variety, but that sentiment too often goes no further than a romantic appreciation of folk architecture and the application of superficial Spanish-Pueblo styling to new buildings. A deeper response requires us to delve into the relationship between cultural values and architecture. Designers of low-income or senior citizen housing, city plans, or tract houses should consider the values of those who will inhabit their work. A handful of young Pueblo Indian architects and planners are working with their elders to infuse their work with their cultures's values. It is more difficult, however, for a person of one culture to fully understand and design for people of another culture. In addition, the Uniform Building Code, HUD and FHA standards for new construction make demands based on unarticulated cultural values that constrain the designer. These difficulties may best be circumvented by emphasizing the rehabilitation of historic houses and neighborhoods as a direct way to help sustain cultural variety.

Notes

This article is a shortened version of Chris Wilson, "The Adobe House of West Las Vegas," in *History and Preservation in Las Vegas*, vol. 3 (Las Vegas: Citizens' Committee for Historic Preservation, 1984). That work was funded in part by the New Mexico Historic Preservation Division. Field survey forms, measurements, photographs, and measured plans of the houses studied in detail are housed at their offices in Santa Fe. Sven Govaars produced the measured plans. Thanks to Eileen Devereax for her editorial assistance.

1. Studies that treat the regional variations in the Spanish-Mexican building tradition in northern New Mexico and southern Colorado include Bainbridge Bunting, *Taos Adobes: Spanish Colonial and Territorial Architecture of the Taos Valley* (Santa Fe: Museum of New Mexico Press, 1964); Beverly Spears, *American Adobes: Rural Houses of Northern New Mexico* (Albuquerque: University of New Mexico Press, 1986); Chris Wilson and David Kammer, *Community and Continuity: The History, Architecture, and Cultural Landscape of La Tierra Amarilla* (Santa Fe: Historic Preservation Division, 1989); Arnold Valdez, "The Hispanic Vernacular Architecture of the Culebra River Valley, Colorado: 1850–1990" (master's thesis, University of New Mexico, 1992).

2. William Davis, *El Gringo, or New Mexico and Her People* (1857; reprint Santa Fe: Rydal Press, 1938), 40.

3. Bainbridge Bunting, *Early Architecture in*

New Mexico (Albuquerque: University of New Mexico Press, 1976), 60.

4. Davis, *El Gringo,* 50.

5. Robert West, "The Flat Roofed Folk Dwelling in Rural Mexico," *Geoscience and Man* 5 (1974): 125–27. See also John Kantner, "A Study of Form and Space in Spanish Colonial Domestic Architecture in New Mexico" (senior thesis, Colorado College, 1989).

6. J. B. Jackson, "First Comes the House," *Landscape* 9, no. 2 (winter 1959–60): 28.

7. Lewis Garrard, *Wah-to-Yah and the Taos Trail* (1850; reprint, Norman: University of Oklahoma Press, 1955), 168–70, 172.

8. Davis, *El Gringo,* 52, 138–39.

9. Ibid., 205.

10. Phillipe Aries, *Centuries of Childhood: A Social History of the Family* (New York: Knopf, 1962), 390–400.

11. Henry Glassie, *Folk Housing in Middle Virginia* (Knoxville: University of Tennessee Press, 1975), 86–91, 190, 193; see also Robert Rosenbaum, *Mexican Resistance in the Southwest* (Austin: University of Texas Press, 1981), 99–154.

CHAPTER SEVEN

Russian Churches, American Houses, Aleut People

Converging Cultures in the Pribilof Islands, Alaska

ALISON K. HOAGLAND

Cold, wet, windy, and treeless, boasting some of the worst weather in the world, the Pribilof Islands in the Bering Sea lay barren, devoid of human settlement for centuries. Yet as home to about 85 percent of the world's population of northern fur seal, the Pribilofs offered nonetheless a certain attraction. After their discovery by Russian traders in 1786, the islands were plundered for seal pelts for the next two centuries. It was the Russians who brought natives from the Aleutian Islands to live on the Pribilofs and perform the seal harvest for them. In less than fifty years, the Russians and their native workers took over 3 million seal pelts from these islands.[1] Such bounty did not go unnoticed. After the United States purchased Alaska in 1867, the U.S. government kept tight control on the profitable Pribilofs.

The Aleuts, brought forcibly to these islands in the early nineteenth century, have been buffeted by two major cultural influences, first Russian, then American. The net effect of removal and isolation on the Aleuts is perhaps best illustrated in the architecture: Russians introduced Russian churches but left the Aleut dwellings alone, and Americans introduced American housing but ignored the Russian religious buildings. Using the buildings as evidence, this paper examines the Russian and American cultural traditions, how they interacted with each other and acted on a third, the Aleut. Today, the Aleut villages still reflect these influences, having standard-design gable-roofed houses arranged in a neat grid plan that forms a typical American community, at the heart of which is a Russian Orthodox church.

After Vitus Bering discovered Alaska for the Russians in 1741, Russian exploration was predicated on resource exploitation, not settlement and colonization. *Promyshlenniki,* or independent fur traders, obtained these resources—usually furs—by enslaving and brutalizing Aleuts to hunt for them. Particularly valued for its pelt was the sea otter, which was hunted in the ocean. In 1786 Gerasim Pribilof of the Lebedev-Lastochkin Fur Company, one of forty-two Russian fur-trading companies operating in Alaska, discovered four barren, seal-inhabited islands previously known only to the Aleuts. Located 300 miles west of the Alaska mainland, and 250 miles north of the Aleutian Chain, the Pribilofs were to become the richest source of fur seal pelts. Situated forty-five miles apart, St. Paul and St. George are small but habitable islands; they and two rock outcroppings known as Walrus and Otter Islands constitute the Pribilof Islands. The summers are wet and foggy; the winters have dry, windy weather—so windy that no trees grow in the volcanic soil. The islands' main attraction is their wildlife, especially the northern fur seal. Seal pelts were easily gathered, even easier than those of sea otters. Seals did not have to be hunted, since they come up on land in the summer to mate. Slow-moving on land, they were easily herded and clubbed to death. Initially the Russians slaughtered indiscriminately, but later they realized that harvesting only the bachelors—adolescent males too young to mate—would enable the species to survive. The seal flesh was used for food, the blubber for fuel, and the furs were processed in salt and exported.

In 1799 Tsar Paul I granted a monopoly on trading in Alaska to the Russian-American Company. Fur seals were just one of its many ventures, but the company undertook sealing with a vengeance. Between 1800 and 1802, nine hundred thousand fur seals were killed, more than could be effectively handled. The processing of the pelts was so poor that about one-third were destroyed as useless and the remainder brought poor prices. Moreover, the seal population had been reduced to one-tenth its former size. Consequently, the company suspended sealing for the next five years, although the ban was poorly enforced. By the 1860s, the harvest was up to seventy thousand furs a year on St. Paul, and six thousand on St. George.[2]

The Aleuts were paid about fifteen cents per seal skin for their work. They divided the pay communally, roughly according to work performed. In the beginning, the Russian-American Company brought Aleuts to the Pribilofs for a few years at a time, sending them back to their homes on Atka or Unalaska.[3] By 1820 it was apparent that the Aleuts were on the islands to stay. Permanent settlements were established on St. Paul and St. George and were named for their respective islands.

In these villages, the Aleuts built their traditional semisubterranean dwellings, called barabaras. Loosely framed with driftwood, barabaras were covered with sod and originally were reached through a hole in the roof. The house had a single room, and was so well insulated that body heat alone was enough to keep it warm. After contact with the Russians, barabaras underwent some transformations (fig. 7.1). Windows and doors were introduced and rooms were added, changes visible throughout the Aleutians as well as on the Pribilofs. The barabaras on St. Paul were described in 1871 as having three rooms: an outer room, where the cooking was done, using seal blubber for fuel; a middle room, part workshop, part outhouse;

Figure 7.1. Photographed on St. Paul in 1888, these traditional Aleut barabaras—semisubterranean sod-covered dwellings—have windows, doors, and stovepipes, showing the influence of Russian and American cultures. (Courtesy Alaska State Library, PCA 27)

and an inner room, used for living, usually lit by one window. Less than half the living rooms on the island had wooden floors and ceilings. The living room was crowded: ten to fifteen people lived in a 12' x 15' room, 6' high.[4]

Although the Russians in Alaska did little to alter the Aleuts' customs, they did introduce the Russian Orthodox religion. In the absence of a priest, lay members of the church were authorized to baptize new congregants, which the promyshlenniki did throughout Russian Alaska in the eighteenth century. (For this reason, most Aleuts—and most residents of the Pribilofs—have Russian surnames.) It is likely that most of the Aleuts brought to the Pribilofs had previously been converted to the Russian Orthodox faith.

In 1821, Ignatii Cherkashenin, a Russian, and Kassian Shayashnikov, a creole (of mixed Russian and native heritage), built the first Russian Orthodox church on St.

Figure 7.2. The first church on St. Paul was constructed in 1821 of hewn driftwood logs. The polygonal sanctuary is on the left; the belltower rising out of the roof of the narthex on the right was a later addition. (Courtesy Bancroft Library, University of California, Berkeley)

Paul. Although the Russian-American Company's second charter had stipulated that it support the establishment of churches, Cherkashenin and Shayashnikov built this one without aid from the company. Cherkashenin died soon after construction, but Shayashnikov continued as church warden for several decades.[5] The church was tended by the priest assigned to Unalaska, 250 miles to the south, who could make the trip only in alternate years.

Saints Peter and Paul Russian Orthodox Church was built of hewn driftwood logs in a manner typical of Russian house construction (figs. 7.2, 7.3). The square nave, in the center, was similar in form to the Russian *izba,* or cube-shaped peasant cottage. The nave had a large cupola rising from the pyramidal roof. On the east was the polygonal sanctuary, containing the altar, which was separated from the nave by the iconostas, a partition wall covered with icons and penetrated by three doors. On the west an attached belltower was added several decades after the church was constructed.[6] The three elements of the church—sanctuary, nave, and belltower—were topped by small onion domes. In 1833 a similar church was built on St. George, where Russian-built log structures combined with Aleut barabaras to form a small community.

In 1867 the United States acquired Alaska and administered it through the war and navy departments. The Pribilof Islands, however, remained under the control of the Treasury Department—testimony to the incredible income that the islands provided. Between 1870 and 1890 furs from the Pribilofs grossed an average of $2.5 million a year. The profit to the United States over this period was $9.6 million, an ample return, considering that the price for all of Alaska was only $7.2 million.[7]

To harvest the seals, the Treasury Department granted a twenty-year monopoly to the Alaska Commercial Company (ACC), which leased the islands for $55,000 per year and $2.625 per sealskin. The San Francisco–based fur company had pur-

Figure 7.3. *(Opposite)* St. Paul as drawn by I. G. Voznesenskii in 1843 or 1844. On the far right is the church, before the belltower was added; nearby is the home of the Russian-American Company administrator and between them a warehouse. Below, to the left, are the barabaras of the Aleuts, between which seal skins have been stretched to dry. (Courtesy Oregon Historical Society, neg. no. 1142-8).

chased the stores and ships of the Russian-American Company and was poised to replace it as the primary trader in Alaska. On the Pribilofs, the Treasury Department limited the number of seals killed to seventy-five thousand per year on St. Paul and twenty-five thousand per year on St. George, although these numbers were adjusted over the years. The Alaska Commercial Company was required to provide for the Aleuts, giving them schooling and medical care. In addition, the company furnished free fuel, oil, and salmon to supplement the natives' seal-meat diet; other necessities could be purchased at the company store at no more than 25 percent above the cost of wholesale in San Francisco. The natives were paid forty cents per seal skin, and as before, they divided the payment among them "according to their standing as workmen." In one instance where fifty-six men worked, they divided the proceeds into seventy-four shares, the extra shares providing for the church, priest, and widows.[8] The Treasury Department stationed special agents on both St. Paul and St. George islands to oversee the harvest and the company's treatment of the natives. The views of these men—well documented in the official record—provide insights into American attitudes at this pivotal moment of administrative and cultural change.

With the encouragement of the Treasury Department, the Alaska Commercial Company immediately began to build houses for the Aleuts (fig. 7.4). The one-story, wood-framed houses measured 20' x 14' on the ground, and 8' between floor and ceiling. Constructed of imported lumber and furnished with stoves, the houses had two rooms, lean-to extensions to the side, and a variety of outbuildings. ACC agent H. W. McIntyre designed the buildings and arranged the townsite in neat rows, in contrast to the haphazard arrangement of the barabaras. And also unlike the barabaras, which had been set below the hill holding the church, the new houses, particularly on St. Paul, clustered around the church (fig. 7.5). The church was no longer set apart on the landscape. By 1879, the company had built sixty-two houses on St. Paul and twenty-one on St. George.[9]

American motivation for the replacement of the native housing was on the surface noble; officials proclaimed health and sanitation to be their primary concerns. A more selfish reason, however, was the general belief that improved housing made better workers. The Americans, of course, had nothing but contempt for the Russians' tolerance of the Aleut dwellings. Discussing the natives' poor living conditions, assistant special agent Henry W. Elliott noted, "It seemed to be the policy of the short-sighted Russian management to keep them so, and to treat the natives not near so well as they treated the few hogs and dogs which they brought up here for food and for company."[10] The Americans' solution to the housing situation was not altogether altruistic, for their underlying desire to Americanize the natives permeates the written record.

Special agent Charles Bryant initially objected to the company providing houses

Figure 7.4. Three Aleuts in stylish clothes sit in front of their wood-framed house, built by the Alaska Commercial Company in the 1870s. (Courtesy Alaska State Library, PCA 185)

Figure 7.5. The church is the dominant structure in this 1891 view of St. Paul. Wood-framed houses built by the Alaska Commercial Company in the 1870s stand in neat rows. (Courtesy National Archives)

for the natives, fearing that it would only increase their dependence on the company. The company proposed to let the natives live in the houses rent free, but not own them, "being averse to the Natives acquiring any right or title to such property on the island." Bryant thought it was the government's role to build and give them houses, as homeownership would increase their adoption of sanitary ways: "It is doubtful whether, without the right of ownership in their houses, they can be induced to change their confirmed habits so as to secure the necessary conditions of cleanliness and comfort desirable for their better health."[11]

U.S. Treasury agents, men who usually obtained this political appointment without previous experience in Alaska, were generally appalled at the living conditions of the Aleuts, finding the "huts" "damp, dark, and exceedingly filthy." Americans most often cited the lack of ventilation of the barabaras as causing disease, but it was the very lack of ventilation that made these sod-covered dwellings so warm. They also objected to the odor of the blubber that was burned as a fuel: "the use of seal fat for fuel caused the deposit upon everything within doors of a thick coat of greasy, black soot, strongly impregnated with a damp, moldy, and indescribably offensive odor." The wood-framed, above-ground houses that the Americans built had their drawbacks, too. Mostly, they were too drafty, and, as a result, Bryant was soon pleading for additional coal, noting that "having placed [the natives] in houses above ground and rendered this a prime necessity, it belongs to [the company] to furnish this supply, for which they are abundantly able and willing to pay." There was also apparently a problem with the design of the buildings, as the initial buildings "have not proved wholly a success for comfort and convenience." After some experimentation, it was discovered that lining the walls with thick tar paper helped reduce the pervasive dampness.[12]

Two Treasury Department special agents stand out for their conflicting views on how the Aleuts should be treated. As it happened, one worked for the other. Charles Bryant, a retired whaling captain who returned to his home in Fairhaven, Massachusetts, each winter, served as special agent on St. Paul from 1870 to 1877. His assistant was a brash young scientist, Henry Wood Elliott. Elliott, who claimed ties to the Smithsonian Institution, had a long career as an outspoken defender of the fur seals, arguing for their protection at numerous congressional hearings over the years until his death in 1930. In the 1870s, however, he was an advocate of the seal harvest, assuring the Treasury Department that there was an ample quantity of seals, and that the Alaska Commercial Company was executing its task superbly. Despite his marriage to a creole from Sitka, Alexandra Melovidov, Elliott strongly objected to the Aleuts' traditional ways and saw nothing but improvement in the new company houses. Bryant, on the other hand, found fault with the new houses and demanded an increased ration of coal for the natives, while questioning whether the natives should be made so dependent on the company. When Elliott resigned after the 1873 season,

Figure 7.6. Built in 1873–75, the second church on St. Paul is architecturally more sophisticated than its predecessor, but has the same basic form. (Courtesy Alaska State Library, PCA 185)

he accused Bryant of filing inaccurate reports and generally demoralizing the Aleut community. William J. McIntyre, the assistant agent on St. George, supported Elliott's claim, charging Bryant with "rile and infamous conduct," accusing him of "debauch[ing] the minds of the native women and young girls by his beastly sensuality," calling his administration a "farce," and alleging that he was "despised by the natives and detested by every white person upon both islands."[13] Despite his conduct, Bryant seemed to have a keener sensibility of the Aleuts' rights than his critics.

Although the first three native families to obtain new houses were described as "highly elated," the Aleut community "unanimously desired" that a new church be built before any additional houses were constructed.[14] The U.S. government had studiously avoided interfering with the existing church in Alaska; terms of the sale of Alaska had provided that the Russian Orthodox church be permitted to continue to operate, and the government wished to observe the traditional separation of church and state. The Alaska Commercial Company was explicitly instructed not to interfere with the church on the Pribilofs. When the natives requested that a church and priest's house be built, the company obligingly built them, charging the congregation fifteen thousand dollars for its services and materials. Elsewhere in Alaska the Russian church continued to assist the native congregations both in construction of new buildings and in payment of priest's salaries. The worshippers in the Pribilofs, however, had a cash income, and were able to finance construction themselves by setting aside two first-class sealing shares.[15]

Built in 1873–75, the new church, also named Saints Peter and Paul, had the same general form as the previous church, but had more architectural detail (fig. 7.6). The hip-roofed nave was crowned with a windowed cupola and onion dome. The sanctuary on the east and belltower with clock on the west were also topped with onion domes. Pediments over the windows, paired brackets at the cornice, and balustrades at the belltower windows were architectural flourishes imported from San Francisco. Inside, the carved, mahogany iconostas held icons from Russia; interior furnishings such as carpets and curtains cost over one thousand dollars. The colors of the icons, the golden implements sparkling in the candlelight, the richness of the furnishings—all would have been especially striking in contrast to the bleakness of the fog-enshrouded landscape outside. Although the designer of this new church is not known, the company provided two San Francisco carpenters to oversee the building of the church, and the Aleuts performed much of the labor themselves.[16]

The Aleut community on St. George also paid for construction of a new church there, again named after St. George (fig. 7.7). James C. Redpath, a San Francisco carpenter, was described as architect and builder.[17] This church, built in 1875–76, had a gable-roofed nave and sanctuary, and the open belfry was topped by a Roman dome. The paneled doors were set in a pedimented and pilastered surround, and as at St. Paul, the churchyard was encircled by a picket fence.

With the construction of these new churches, the two islands attracted clergy. By assigning them first-class sealing shares, the St. Paul and St. George natives paid the entire salary of their priests. Fr. Paul Shayashnikoff, an Aleut from St. Paul and brother of Innocent Shayashnikoff, archpriest of Unalaska, arrived on St. Paul in 1875. In 1882, Fr. Innokenty Lestenkof was assigned to St. George.

Although the U.S. government professed initially to have no argument with the orthodox church—even welcoming the moral guidance it provided—conflict arose when the priests interfered with the U.S. education system. Long before the resident priests arrived in the Pribilofs, the warden Kassian Shayashnikov had instructed the Aleuts in reading and writing Russian—the language of the church—as well as in Aleut language. By 1838, nearly every male on St. Paul could read. By terms of its contract, the Alaska Commercial Company established English language schools and required children to attend. The Aleuts objected, however, fearing that the chil-

Figure 7.7. St. George church and village, from the water. To the left of the church, built in 1875–76, are the houses built for the natives at the same time. To the right are the company buildings. (Courtesy National Archives)

dren would then not be able to learn Russian and thus would be unable to participate in church services.[18] The priests assigned to the islands, who conducted their own Russian language schools, spoke no English. As education was a vital part of any Americanization program, the Americans continued to require an American education. Resistance to an English language education continued throughout the nineteenth century.

In 1890, the Alaska Commercial Company's lease expired and a new twenty-year lease was granted to the North American Commercial Company. By this time the seal herd had been seriously depleted and the overwhelming riches of the previous twenty years were no longer to be had. The 1890s also saw an increase of pelagic sealing (the taking of seals at sea), which further reduced the population. In 1910, at the end of the North American Commercial Company's lease, the U.S. Department of Commerce assumed direct administration of the islands. With the fur seal population facing extinction in 1911, an international conference resulted in a moratorium on sealing in the Pribilofs until after World War I.

By the 1890s, the housing built by the Alaska Commercial Company was deemed inadequate. Treasury agents now raised some of the same complaints as earlier, pointing to overcrowding and a lack of sanitation. Most houses now had privies (previously, the natives had used a chamberpot-like arrangement), but were spatially inadequate. The agent on St. George cited an example of a seven-member family "of all ages and sexes" sleeping in a 10' x 10' room. Further complicating matters was the fact that in 1892 and 1893 no seals were harvested except those the Aleuts needed for subsistence. The drastic reduction in the natives' income caused the American officials great concern, one noting "now that the seals have disappeared the natives are very much alarmed, and they anxiously inquire what will the Government do for them in their destitution."[19] Unable to earn a living, the Aleuts were at the mercy of the government and its contractor.

Given the severe drop in income, neither the North American Commercial Company nor the government felt obliged to replace the deteriorating dwellings of the Pribilof natives. Twenty years later, the houses were still overcrowded. "Many of [the houses] are far too small," said one observer, "with the result that in some cases mothers, fathers, and children sleep, eat, and live in one ill-ventilated room." The agent on St. George cited an example of a fourteen-member family living in the largest house on the island, which was still inadequate—four rooms ranging in size from 11' x 12' to 7' x 11'.[20]

When sealing began again in the 1920s, the Department of Commerce finally began replacing the nineteenth-century dwellings one by one, while retaining the village plan (fig. 7.8). Three-, four-, and five-room houses, one-and-a-half stories, were built. On St. Paul, the houses were constructed of reinforced concrete. Although practical for construction because gravel from the island could be mixed with cement on site, the concrete proved unsuited to St. Paul's wet and windy climate. Cold and damp were conducted indoors by the concrete walls; as a result, as soon as private owners acquired the houses they sided them with wood. The wood siding had the added effect of individualizing the houses, bringing different colors and textures to the streetscape. On St. George, no satisfactory gravel to use as aggregate could be found and the houses were constructed of imported lumber. None of the houses was built with plumbing, although electricity was provided in the 1930s.[21] On both islands, slightly larger houses were constructed for white government employees (fig. 7.9).

The Aleut houses are functional, if plain. The natives' clearest architectural expression, however, remains in the present churches, both built in the twentieth century. On St. Paul, the 1875 church was replaced in 1905–6 (figs. 7.10, 7.11, and 7.12).

Figure 7.8. The U.S. government built concrete houses, later sided with wood, for the Aleuts on St. Paul in the 1920s. (Photo by Jet Lowe, 1989, Historic American Buildings Survey)

Figure 7.9. The whites on St. Paul received slightly larger concrete houses. On the left is the only house with the concrete exterior still showing; all the others have been sided with wood. In the foreground is the churchyard of the Russian Orthodox church. (Photo by Jet Lowe, 1989, Historic American Buildings Survey)

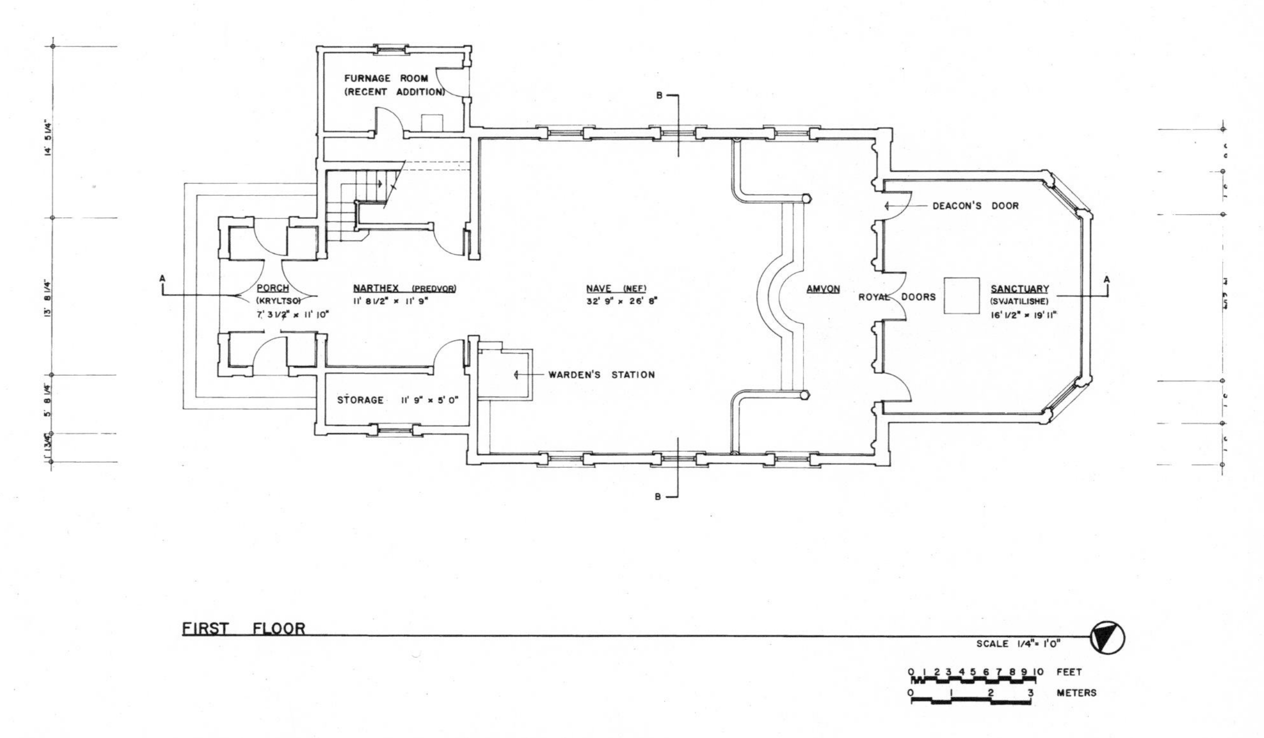

Figure 7.10. The plan of Saints Peter and Paul Russian Orthodox Church, built in 1905–6, shows the traditional progression of spaces, from the outside porch, to the narthex, to the nave where the congregation gathers, to the sanctuary where only the priest and his assistants are allowed. (Delineated by Andrew Feinberg and Lidiya Velichko, 1989, and by Kate Solovjova, 1990, Historic American Buildings Survey)

Designed by Nathaniel Blaisdell, an architect from San Francisco, and built by four San Francisco carpenters aided by the congregation, the new Saints Peter and Paul Church had the same elements as the previous church—a nave, sanctuary, narthex, and belltower, each crowned with gable roofs. Apparently the Pribilofs' strong winds were hard on the onion domes of the previous church, for this church was designed without any. In their place, Blaisdell used an ironwork stylization of an onion dome atop the belltower. Corner pilasters, cornice returns on the gable ends, and entablatures over every opening added to the architectural splendor. Now somewhat altered on the exterior through the application of cement-asbestos shingles and the consequent removal of ornament, the church still has a breathtaking interior. The

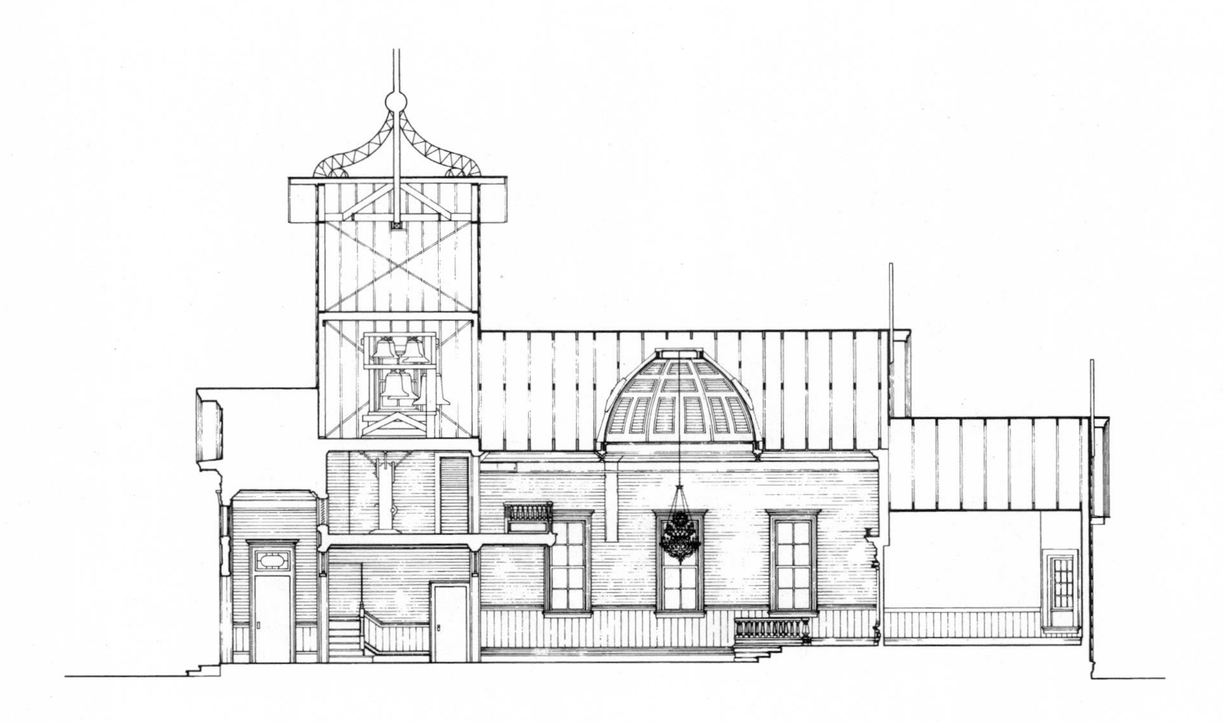

Figure 7.11. Unlike most Russian Orthodox churches in Alaska, Saints Peter and Paul has no onion dome. Instead, an ironwork stylized version of a dome crowns the belltower; above the nave is an interior dome. (Delineated by Raymond Todd and Lidiya Velichko, 1989, and by Kate Solovjova, 1990, Historic American Buildings Survey)

iconostas from the previous church was installed in the new one, as were the bells. A balustraded choir loft and a dome over the nave add to the lofty interior.

In 1935, St. George also received a new church (figs. 7.13, 7.14, 7.15, 7.16). The architect is not known, but the church's elements of nave, sanctuary, narthex, belltower, and porch are all expressed on the exterior in the traditional manner. The church has an unusual ogee-arched doorway and pointed-arched windows uncharacteristic of Russian wooden construction. The nave's ceiling is in the form of a modified triple barrel arch, and a mural of the Madonna above the iconostas adds to the visual impact. Both churches were financed by the congregations themselves, and as in the past, materials and building expertise were brought in from outside.

Figure 7.12. The elaborate iconostas of Saints Peter and Paul. The iconostas was saved from the previous church; the icons were imported from Russia. (Photo by Jet Lowe, 1989, Historic American Buildings Survey)

Although outsiders designed and directed the construction of both churches in the Pribilofs, the churches are nevertheless significant to the Aleuts. Church buildings are the one element in the landscape that they traditionally control (fig. 7.17). They decide when a new church is needed and then pay for it. Because the orthodox church form has a long history, being derived from churches the Russians built throughout Alaska as well as the churches' predecessors in the Pribilofs, there is a consistency in design that is comforting. The bishop in San Francisco might approve the drawings (as he did for the church on St. Paul), but the natives instigated the planning, participated in the construction, and maintained the buildings.

By contrast, the natives had no control over their housing. It had always been imposed on the Aleuts, and the very standardization of the houses illustrates decisions by outside agencies, not individual selection. The immediate individualizing

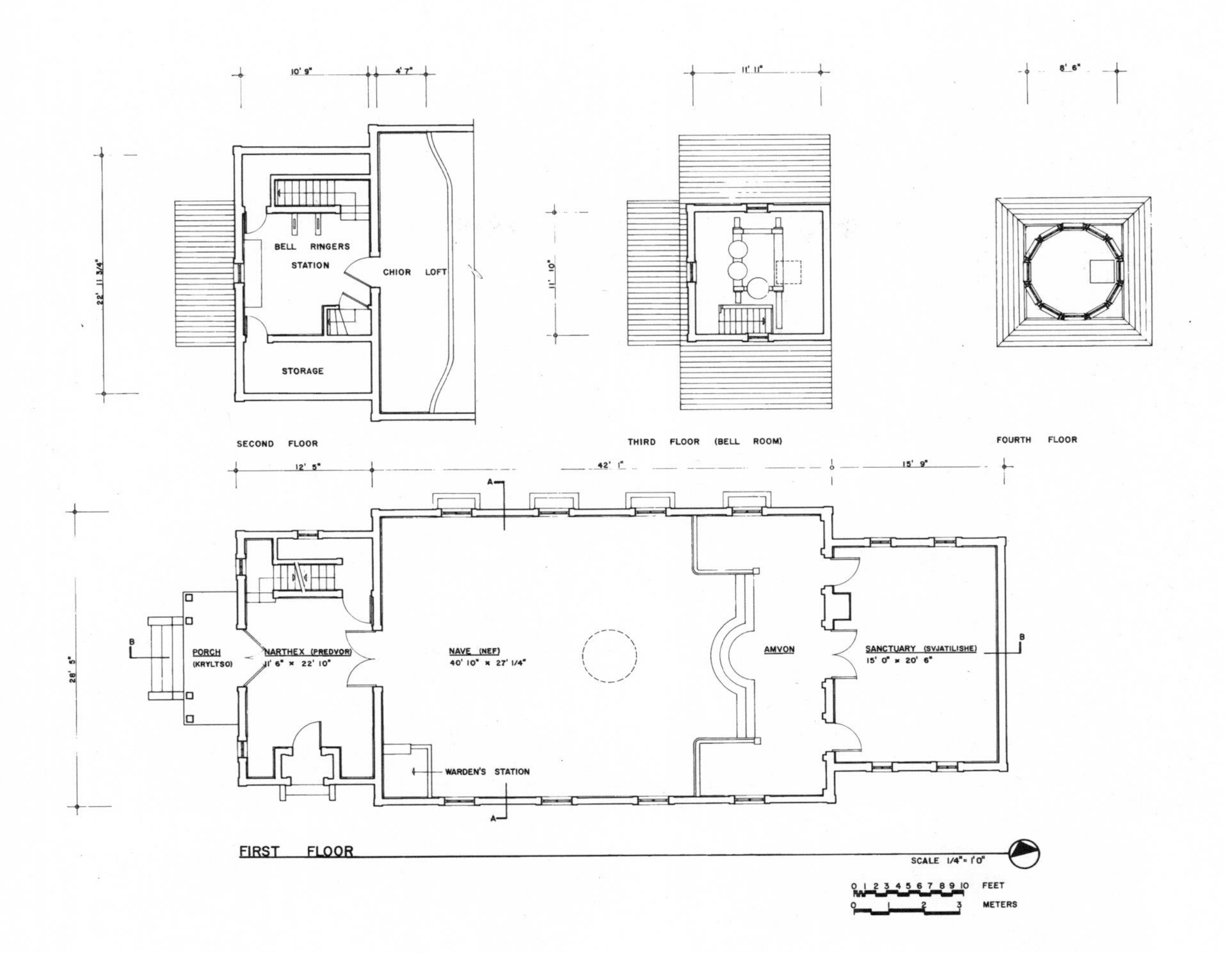

Figure 7.13. Although the Church of St. George the Great Martyr, built in 1935–36, is stylistically very different from Saints Peter and Paul, the plan reveals the same progression of spaces. (Delineated by Alex Lashkevich, 1989, and by Kate Solovjova, 1990, Historic American Buildings Survey)

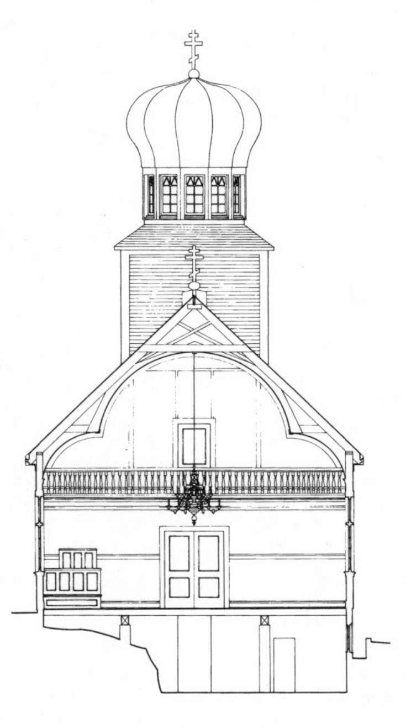

Figure 7.14. The section of the Church of St. George, looking back toward the entrance and choir loft, shows the unusual barrel-arched ceiling. St. George's belltower has a traditional onion dome and three-bar cross. (Delineated by Alex Lashkevich, 1989, and by Kate Solovjova, 1990, Historic American Buildings Survey)

of the houses as soon as they were acquired by private owners was a clear expression of distaste for this imposed uniformity. Before private ownership in the 1980s, the uniform appearance of the village reflected an autocratic administration.

An even stronger governmental presence is visible in the industrial buildings found along the waterfront. Although neither St. Paul nor St. George had a harbor, both had landing sites from which freight was lightered on or off ships. Near the landing sites were located large, gable-roofed buildings that housed the fur processing activities. Here the native workers washed the furs, removed blubber from them, soaked them in brine, salted them down, and loaded them in barrels for shipment.

Under U.S. rule, the Aleuts' behavior was carefully monitored and controlled. Although technically free to leave the islands at any time, the Aleuts were bound to wait for space on ships, and their comings and goings were noted by the resident government agents. With no bank on the island, the agents also held the Aleuts' savings, and oversaw its disbursement. The government, or its contractor, provided food, shelter, education, medical care, and employment. During World War II, the government evacuated both islands, fearing an attack. The natives were interned at canneries in southeast Alaska, then returned to the Pribilofs after the war.

In the last two decades, the situation has changed dramatically for the natives. Pribilof residents have received millions of dollars as part of the settlement of Alaskan land claims, as compensation for ill treatment at the hands of the government, and as reparations for internment during World War II.[22] They now own their land and houses and administer the villages themselves. The paternalistic treatment policies have been abandoned. At the same time, the sealing industry is moribund. Due to an international agreement in 1985, there is no market for seal pelts, worldwide. The village corporations are endeavoring to develop the fishing industry, beginning with construction of harbors on both islands.

(Opposite) Figure 7.15. St. George Russian Orthodox Church has an unusual ogee-shaped entrance and pointed-arch windows, yet the church exhibits the traditional elements of sanctuary, nave, and belltower. (Photo by Jet Lowe, 1989, Historic American Buildings Survey)

(Opposite) Figure 7.16. The iconostas of the St. George church is ornamented with colored light bulbs in porcelain sconces, as well as the traditional icons. The ceiling has a modified triple barrel arch, and the paintings above the iconostas are striking: the Madonna in the center, on a sea of clouds, and Hollywood blond angels in the corners. (Photo by Jet Lowe, 1989, Historic American Buildings Survey)

Figure 7.17. The fog-enshrouded village of St. George. In the center is the Russian Orthodox church and beside it the hotel, or housing for transient company employees. On the left are the buildings of the sealing plant, on the shore of the Bering Sea. On the right are the houses built for whites, and beyond them, the slightly smaller housing for Aleuts. (Photo by Jet Lowe, 1989, Historic American Buildings Survey)

Settlement history on the Pribilofs is in many ways a distillation of Alaskan settlement in general. Attracted to the islands by the incredible riches of the fur seal industry, the Russians brought in Aleuts to perform the harvest, thereby establishing a settlement where none had been before. The U.S. government, while virtually ignoring the Alaskan mainland for the first thirty years after acquisition, kept tight control over the Pribilofs, ceding authority only recently when it was clear the fur seal industry was defunct. Because of the national attention the Pribilofs received, they were also the site of the U.S. government's only nineteenth-century efforts in Alaska to provide housing for natives. Although well intentioned, the housing illustrates the Americans' confidence in their own cultural tradition, as well as the paternalism inherent in the U.S. colonial policies. The Aleuts look to the Russian Orthodox church that, although an adopted religion, has become a part of their culture over the last two centuries. In a curious twist of the usual situation, in the Pribilofs it is the modest housing that represents the imposition of outside values, whereas in the architecturally elaborate church buildings, we find symbols of the native culture. On the Pribilofs, two aspects of culture, Russian churches and American houses, coexist in a landscape of exploitation that is quintessentially western, and American.

Notes

1. Basil Dmytryshyn, E. A. P. Crownhart-Vaughan, and Thomas Vaughan, eds. and trans., *The Russian American Colonies: A Documentary Record, 1798–1867* (Portland: Oregon Historical Society Press, 1989), lvii.

2. P. A. Tikhmenev, *A History of the Russian-American Company* (1861), trans. and ed. Richard A. Pierce and Alton S. Donnelly (Seattle: University of Washington Press, 1978), 88, 409; Main Administration, Russian American Company, to Osip P. Kozodavlev, Minister of Internal Affairs, 30 September 1813, in *The Russian American Colonies,* 210.

3. H. H. McIntyre, Special Agent, Treasury Department, to the Hon. George S. Boutwell, Secretary of the Treasury, 31 May 1869, Alaska File of the Special Agents, Division of the Department of the Treasury, 1867–1903, National Archives, microfilm roll 1; Main Administration, Russian American Company, to Matvei I. Muravev, Chief Administrator, 6 January 1821, in *The Russian American Colonies,* 337.

4. Charles Bryant, Special Agent, Treasury Department, 30 November 1869, Alaska File of the Special Agents, National Archives, microfilm 1; Bryant to Boutwell, 10 November 1871, in *Seal and Salmon Fisheries and General Resources of Alaska* (Washington, D.C.: Government Printing Office, 1898), 1:26.

5. Report of the priest Gregory Golovin to Bishop Innokenty, n.d., response dated 26 September 1844, both in "Documents Relative to the History of Alaska," vol. 1, p. 292, Library of Congress, microfilm.

6. Belltower added after 1843, as it does not appear in the drawing by Voznesenskii made in that year. E. E. Blomskvist, "A Russian Scientific Expedition to California and Alaska, 1839–1849: The Drawings of I. G. Voznesenskii," *Oregon Historical Society* 73 (June 1972): 128.

7. This $9.6 million included custom duty on furs that were shipped to London for processing and then reimported into the United States. Lois D. Kitchener, *Flag over the North: The Story of the Northern Commercial Company* (Seattle: Superior Publishing, 1954), 39.

8. John F. Miller, President, Alaska Commercial Co., "Regulations for Conduct of Affairs on the Seal Islands," January 1872, in *Seal and Salmon Fisheries,* 3:255–56; Henry W. Elliott, "Report on the Seal Islands of Alaska," 31 March 1880, in *Seal and Salmon Fisheries,* 3:38.

9. Wilfred H. Osgood, Edward A. Preble, and George H. Parker, "The Fur Seals and Other Life of the Pribilof Islands, Alaska, in 1914," *Bulletin of the Bureau of Fisheries* (Washington, D.C.: Government Printing Office, 1915), 34 (1914): 142; Elliott, "Report on the Seal Islands," 3:137; Harrison G. Otis, Special Agent, to the Hon. John Sherman, Secretary of the Treasury, 25 August 1879, in *Seal and Salmon Fisheries,* 1:119.

10. Elliott, "Report on the Seal Islands," 3:28, 35.

11. Bryant to Boutwell, 10 November 1871, 1:26-27.

12. Elliott, "Report on the Seal Islands," 3:28, 262; Bryant to Sherman, 1 August 1877, 1:100; Bryant to Boutwell, 5 September 1872, 1:37.

13. William J. McIntyre, Assistant Special Agent, to O. D. Madge, Supervisor of Special Agents, 12 July 1874, Alaska File of the Special

Agents, National Archives, microfilm roll 1. Citing McIntyre's mistreatment of a native, Bryant requested his removal. Bryant to Hon. B. H. Bristow, Secretary of the Treasury, 28 May 1875, in *Seal and Salmon Fisheries,* 1:79-80. McIntyre was dismissed at the end of the 1876 season, and Bryant six months later.

14. Samuel Falconer, Assistant Special Agent, to Bryant, 4 May 1872, Alaska File of the Special Agents, National Archives, microfilm roll 1; Bryant to the Hon. William A. Richardson, Secretary of the Treasury, 30 September 1873, in *Seal and Salmon Fisheries,* 1:45.

15. Miller, "Regulations for Conduct of Affairs," 3:256; Bryant to Richardson, 30 September 1873, 1:44.

16. "Abstract of Statement of Cost of Church," [1881], Alaska Russian Church Archives, Library of Congress; Bryant to Richardson, 30 September 1873, 1:44; Bryant to Richardson, 4 December 1873, 1:50; Bryant to Bristow, 1:73; Log of the Treasury Agents, 1 and 13 September 1874, 26 May 1875, St. Paul Island, Pribilof Islands Collection, University of Alaska Fairbanks, on microfilm.

17. Falconer to Bryant, 17 May 1876, correspondence received by Treasury Agent on St. Paul Island, Pribilof Islands Collection, University of Alaska Fairbanks, microfilm.

18. Bishop Innocent (Veniaminov), *Zapieska ob Ostrova* (St. Petersburg: Russian-American Company, 1840), trans. Elliott, in *Seal and Salmon Fisheries,* 3:240; Elliott, "Report on the Seal Islands," 3:36.

19. Joseph B. Crowley, Special Agent, to the Hon. John G. Carlisle, Secretary of the Treasury, 1 December 1895, in *Seal and Salmon Fisheries,* 1:474; Crowley to Secretary of Treasury, 20 November 1893, ibid., 1:412; Joseph Murray, First Assistant Agent, to the Hon. Charles J. Goff, Special Agent, 31 July 1890, ibid., 1:237–38; Murray to Goff, 31 July 1890, ibid., 1:239.

20. E. Lester Jones, Deputy Commissioner of Fisheries, *Report of Alaska Investigations in 1914* (Washington, D.C.: Government Printing Office, 1915), 126; Osgood, Preble, and Parker, "Fur Seals and Other Life of the Pribilof Islands," 142.

21. Fredericka Martin, "Pribilof Sealers—Serfs of the North," *Newsletter of the Institute of Ethnic Affairs* 3 (May–June 1948): 2.

22. Lael Morgan, "The Promising Pribilofs," *Alaska* 41 (January 1975): 36; Susan Hackley Johnson, "New Choices for the People of the Pribilofs," *Alaska* 45 (May 1979): 6; Anna Pickett, "APIA Seeks Aleuts Relocated During War," *Tundra Times,* 21 May 1990, p. 5.

Cultural Diversity

CHAPTER EIGHT

A Chinatown of Gold Mountain

The Chinese in Locke, California

CHRISTOPHER L. YIP

Locke, California, sits on the Sacramento River in the heart of the rich delta farmland that has produced huge quantities of pears, asparagus, and various other fruits and vegetables. The town itself, hardly more than two blocks of tumbledown buildings with a certain raffish charm, does not appear remarkable at first glance (fig. 8.1). But the busloads of tourists from San Francisco and Sacramento that pour into the tiny Chinese rural community are immediate evidence that this town is different. Perhaps the bus lines that bring in their patrons in ever-increasing numbers sense the end of an era for Locke. The town recently was purchased by a Hong Kong investor, who has disclaimed early reports of plans to build Asian City on the site—a development that would include four hundred houses of Chinese design, pavilions representing Japan, Taiwan, Korea, the Philippines, Hong Kong, and Thailand, as well as a floating restaurant, shopping center, country club, and boat racing facilities. County officials reacted, and subsequent versions of the financier's plans were much toned down. The question of Locke's future is unresolved. This is the most complete surviving rural Chinatown, yet no one yet has come up with an acceptable plan for preserving a landscape that so clearly records an immigrant subculture's struggle for survival (fig. 8.2).

The subcultures of the United States have not selected nor fully created their own environmental settings. The dominant culture largely has determined the location and form of ghettos as much by social and economic constraints as legal restrictions and the threat of physical violence. Chinese settlement in the Sacramento–San Joaquin Delta depended upon the availability of agricultural employment. The laborers found inexpensive dwellings, which often were separate from the European American community. The Chinese viewed the ghettos as temporary residences until the time for "bitter strength" was over and the laborer could return to his native village in China to live out the remainder of his life in comfort. Although the dream

Figure 8.1. Main Street, Locke, California. (Photo by author)

Figure 8.2. Levee Street, Locke, California. (Photo by author)

rarely was realized, as late as 1949 many Chinese Americans still expected to return, and most first-generation immigrants espoused the familiar hope even if they did not hold the conviction.

The social prejudices against the Chinese were based on European American images of the Chinese that were a confused mixture of positive and negative elements formed before the first major wave of immigration had occurred in the early 1850s. These elements had come from eighteenth-century accounts of China, Yankee traders, the writings of Western diplomats, and Protestant missionaries.[1] The eighteenth-century accounts depicted a country of great age and wisdom that had arrived at a cultural plateau, whereas Yankee traders returned with accounts of a peculiar people with a strange and repulsive cuisine who were being degraded by a corrupt, cowardly, venal, and deceitful government. Yankee participation in the opium trade and their dealings at the edge of Chinese society did not give them the best of perspectives. Western diplomatic writers, who were influential among the American intelligentsia, introduced the notion of racial prejudice against the Chinese based upon theories of inherent biological and moral defects. Protestant missionaries added the notion that the Chinese were the poor victims of Satan, and many missionaries became obsessed with Chinese idolatry, gambling, sexual immorality, paganism, and opium use. The result of these influences was a latent hostility and racially based prejudice toward the Chinese before any significant immigration had occurred.

These attitudes were captured in a comment by Ralph Waldo Emerson in 1824: "The closer contemplation we condescend to bestow the more disgustful is that booby nation. The Chinese Empire enjoys precisely a mummy's reputation, that of having preserved for 3 or 4,000 years the ugliest features in the world. . . . They are tools for other nations to use . . . all she [China] can say at the convocation of nations must be—'I made the tea.'"[2]

Defamatory depictions of the Chinese gradually found their way into textbooks on geography and social studies. From 1839 on, reports on events in China were colored by these unsavory images. In 1859 four gunboats in a British fleet attempting to force its way to Tientsin were lost after being caught in a cross fire. S. C. Miller notes, "It was in battle that the American Commodore Tattnall rushed to aid the English with the now famous remark attributed to him, 'blood is thicker than water.'. . . Stephen Decatur's diary records that he heard Tattnall swear that he would 'be damned if he'd stand by and see white men butchered before his eyes.'"[3] By 1859 the negative image of the Chinese was firmly established in the American consciousness, making them an easily exploited scapegoat in times of crisis or economic distress.

Prejudice, discrimination, disenfranchisement, exclusion, and physical violence were the legacies of these attitudes. The discovery of gold in California generated a migration led by New Englanders and southerners and followed by Latin Americans, Europeans, and Chinese. As the good sites filled up, "non-American" groups were driven out by law and force in whatever amount and combination proved necessary. The Chinese became menials in the mining camps, washing clothes and cooking for the white miners. Later, hydraulic mining companies hired them to work the low-yield sites, which led white miners to blame the rise of the mining companies on the Chinese. Since Chinese labor helped to build the empires of railroad barons after the Civil War, the Chinese also were accused of undermining American independence, equality, and democracy. New theories of biological racism and the common characterizations of Chinese as subhuman, docile hard workers, incapable of original thought were used to justify hostility and discrimination. White labor raised a cry against Chinese workers, and in California the labor movement and anticoolie clubs became one and the same. Samuel Gompers, the president of the American Federation of Labor and a major anti-Asian activist, expressed his hostility to Asians and his belief in their racial inferiority in his widely circulated pamphlet *Meat vs. Rice, American Manhood against Asiatic Coolieism. Which Shall Survive?*[4]

The panic of 1873 and the depression of 1877 fired social and economic tensions, which were unleashed on the Chinese. The revised California Constitution of 1878 provided "no native of China, no idiot, no insane person convicted of any crime . . . shall ever exercise the privileges of an elector of this state." Another clause prohibited state-licensed corporations from employing Chinese. In 1882 Congress passed the first Chinese Exclusion Act banning immigration. The act, which had a ten-year limit, was renewed in 1892 for another decade and continued in 1900 with no time limit specified. A 1924 addition to the Exclusion Acts excluded all Chinese females and limited the immigration of males to only 105 per year. With the passage of the Exclusion Acts, hatred of the Chinese faded into the pool of hostile feelings directed at all nonwhite peoples and ethnic groups. Only the Sino-American alliance of World War II altered the image of the Chinese in the media, but the Chinese Communist Revolution and the Korean War reversed the favorable trend. Richard Nixon's rapprochement and the growing interest in Eastern religions and the martial arts have added more layers of confusion.

Discrimination and hostility turned the Chinese American community inward. Unable to procure fair and equal treatment from either the legal system or the majority society, the immigrants from China created their own institutions for protection, as well as social and cultural support. Many institutions and organizations were transported from China to help the oppressed community cope with its problems. Others were hybrid adaptations specifically developed to meet conditions in the United States. Almost all of the first wave of Chinese immigrants came from the Pearl River Delta of Guangdong (Kwangtung) Province. During the nineteenth century, the population of Guangdong grew rapidly, making it one of the most densely populated provinces in China. The Pearl River Delta also had high rates of farm tenancy and shrinking per capita acreage. These problems were compounded by droughts in 1848, 1849, and 1850, which led to a growing disrespect and mistrust for the Ch'ing government, paralleled by a growing fear and hostility toward Westerners and the pressures of imperialism.[5] Many secret societies, such as the Triads who advocated rebellion and the restoration of the fallen Ming Dynasty (1368–1644), were active in Guangdong. Qing Dynasty (1644–1911) efforts to stamp out the secret societies only drove them underground. Many poverty-stricken peasants turned to banditry, and some complete districts joined bandit gangs or secret societies to gain their protection. Conditions worsened with the rise of the Taiping Rebellion of 1850–64, which was led by a disillusioned scholar, a descendant of the Hakkas, an oppressed minority in Guangdong.

Banditry, rebellion, government retaliation, famine, and economic dislocation forced the people of Guangdong to desperate measures. Thousands emigrated to Southeast Asia or to California.[6] The discovery of gold in California (known to the Chinese as Gum Shan or Gold Mountain) drew many males seeking a quick way of saving themselves and their families. By the end of 1852, about twenty-five thousand Chinese, almost all of them males, were in California. They quickly formed a social structure to support their traditional way of life.[7] Since Guangdong was divided into a number of distinct dialect groups, it was natural for the relatively few Chinese in California to establish district associations (huiguan) based on dialect. These associations effectively grouped the largest number of people into the fewest number of organizations capable of maintaining social and cultural bonds. In 1851 the first huiguan, the Kong Chow (literally the Pearl River Delta), was established, which later split into dialect- and district-based associations. One of these was the Yeong Wo, which represented Chinese from Chungshan district, the group that founded Locke.

The huiguan formed the Chinese Consolidated Benevolent Association (later known as the Six Companies), which became the central organization representing the Chinese community to the various levels of government and the white community.[8] As in Guangdong, the Chinese in America had little control over the political institutions to which they were subjected. An 1854 ruling of the California courts removed, for a short time, the right of Chinese to testify in a state court against white people and admirably represented the position in which Chinese Americans found themselves.[9] The federal government prevented Chinese from becoming naturalized citizens, barred Chinese laborers from immigrating, and later banned the immigration of wives of resident Chinese. The ability of the Six Companies to act as a quasi government and buffer was in part due to the way their members had been driven into urban and rural ghettos, which kept them within the sphere of huiguan influence.

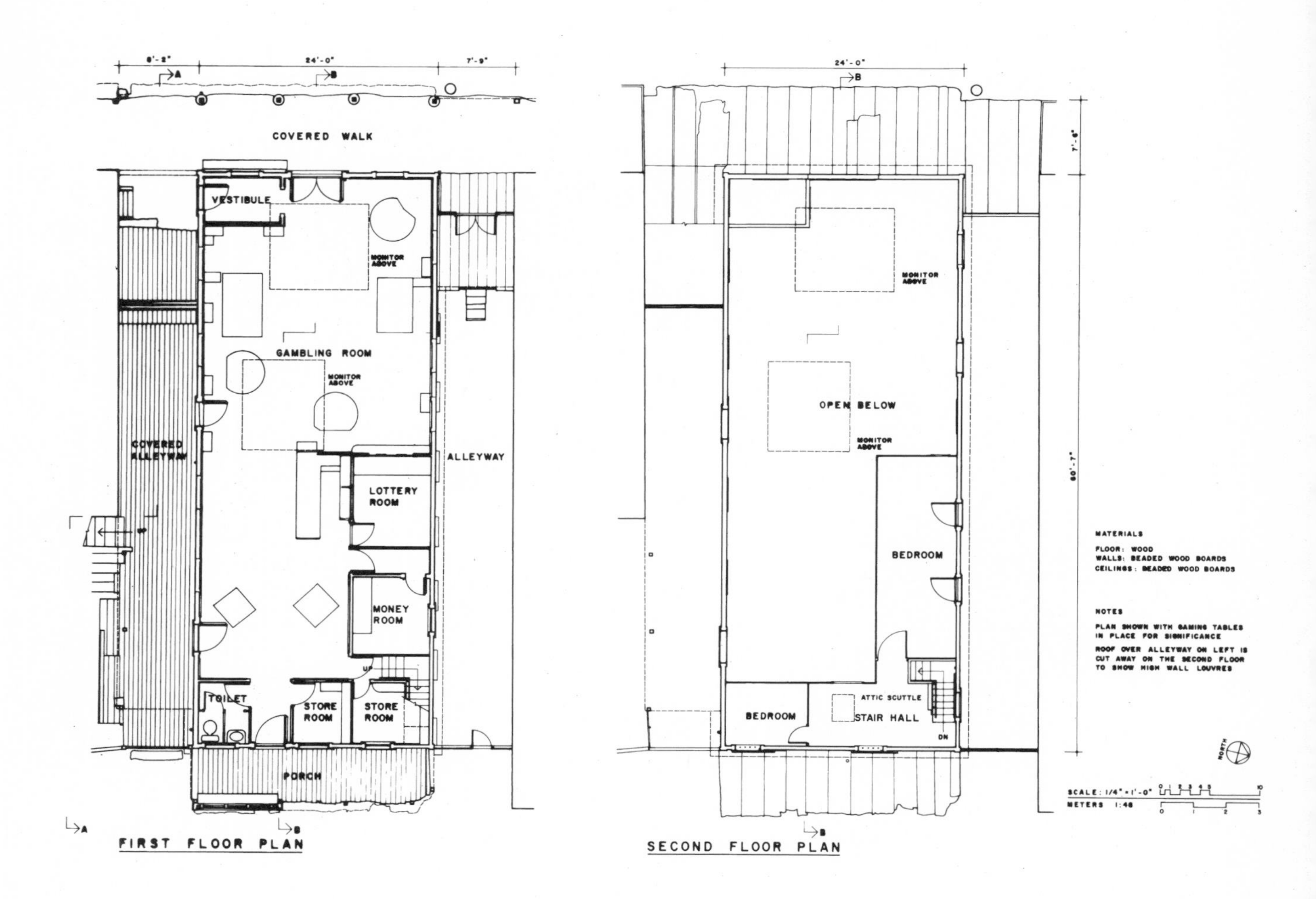

Figure 8.3. HABS Drawing, Dai Loy Gambling Museum, plans.

Overcrowding and tight community organization often were the only insurance against the hostile world beyond. The huiguan also maintained contact with immigrants' native places, which kept communication alive and ensured that individuals could not escape their debts and responsibilities by returning to Guangdong. Discrimination in California fostered an intense dependence on the institutions of the Chinese American community. The pressures that forced the Chinese to seek solace and comfort inside a shrinking circle also intensified the aberrations that lurked within the cultural baggage the Chinese had transported to the new land. Given the conditions, it is not surprising that prostitution, gambling, and opium thrived in this isolated "bachelor" community. Although many men were married, their wives often remained in Guangdong to take care of aging parents, raise children, and guarantee the husband's loyalty to the family. Many women who made the journey to

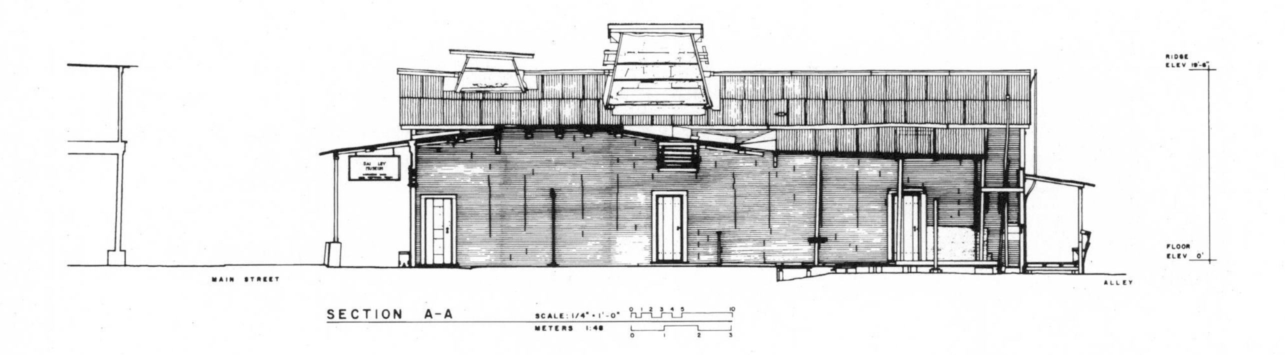

MATERIALS

FOUNDATION: CONCRETE FOOTINGS WOOD PIER AND BEAM
WALLS: NARROW-BOARD WOOD SIDING
ROOF: CORRUGATED SHEET METAL
FASCIA: WOOD

Figure 8.4. HABS Drawing, Dai Loy Gambling Museum, elevations.

Figure 8.5. HABS Drawing, Dai Loy Gambling Museum, section.

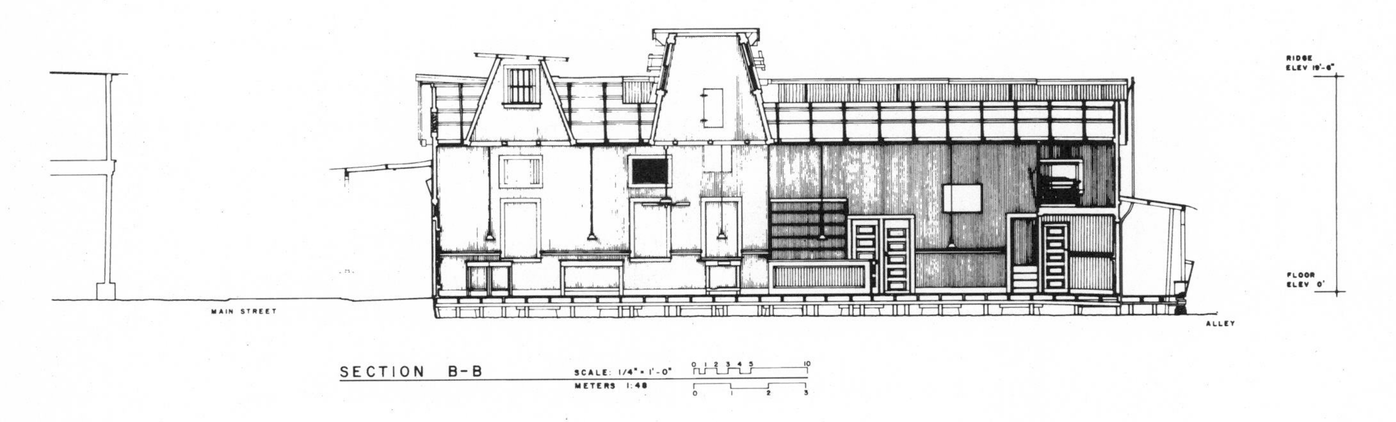

California were semi-enslaved prostitutes. Thirty-nine states passed miscegenation laws, so dependence upon prostitution for female companionship was assured. Gambling and opium traffic also helped to pass the time within the almost totally male ghettos (figs. 8.3, 8.4, 8.5). Quite often, the sons of immigrant males would establish a family in Guangdong and follow their fathers to California in search of work, which continued the pattern of life in California and kept the Chinese in California oriented toward Guangdong. Fifty years after the first influx, the Chinese still had not been allowed to assimilate in their own way.

During the Gold Rush, the Sacramento River served as the major route from San Francisco to the gold fields in the Sierra foothills. Like others, the Chinese followed this passage and the ports of Northern California were known to them as the First (San Francisco), the Second (Sacramento), and the Third (Marysville) ports of Gold Mountain. Traveling the river made the Chinese familiar with the delta long before it became a major agricultural area, but few were interested in performing the arduous labor necessary to reclaim the marshlands for agriculture. The first efforts at farming by Chinese Americans involved the development of market gardens that served the mining camps and major urban centers.[10] However, with the completion of the transcontinental railroad in 1869, many unemployed Chinese migrated to the delta where they were hired by speculators who had acquired huge land holdings.[11] Racial violence and the burning of Chinatowns in western states during the 1870s and 1880s also added to the delta's pool of Chinese laborers. Chinese labor offered the employer a contract labor system in which the laborers were organized under Chinese bosses who kept accounts and hired, directed, and paid the workers. The crews tended to share a common dialect since contractors organized their crews based on village, family, and district loyalties. The crews prepared the land and planted orchards on the large ranches and company-owned lands. Competition between the new railroad lines and the steamboat lines worked to keep freight rates low, and the availability of cheap transportation spurred a rapid development of farming in the delta.

Along the levees of the Sacramento River, small clusters of shanties sprang up to house the farm laborers. Walnut Grove, which may have been settled as early as 1851, contained one of the occasional Chinatowns interspersed along the route. The lands around the town eventually became the world center of Bartlett pear production. Before 1921 the Walnut Grove Chinatown contained two Chinese dialect groups—Sze Yup and Chungshanese. Their joint occupation of one rural ghetto may have been related to crop distribution in that part of the delta. Walnut Grove straddled the orchard lands centered to its north and the field croplands to the south. Since Chungshanese often worked in orchards and the Sze Yup generally worked field crops—particularly potatoes and onions—Walnut Grove's Chinatown might have marked a geographic intersection in the delta's farming pattern.

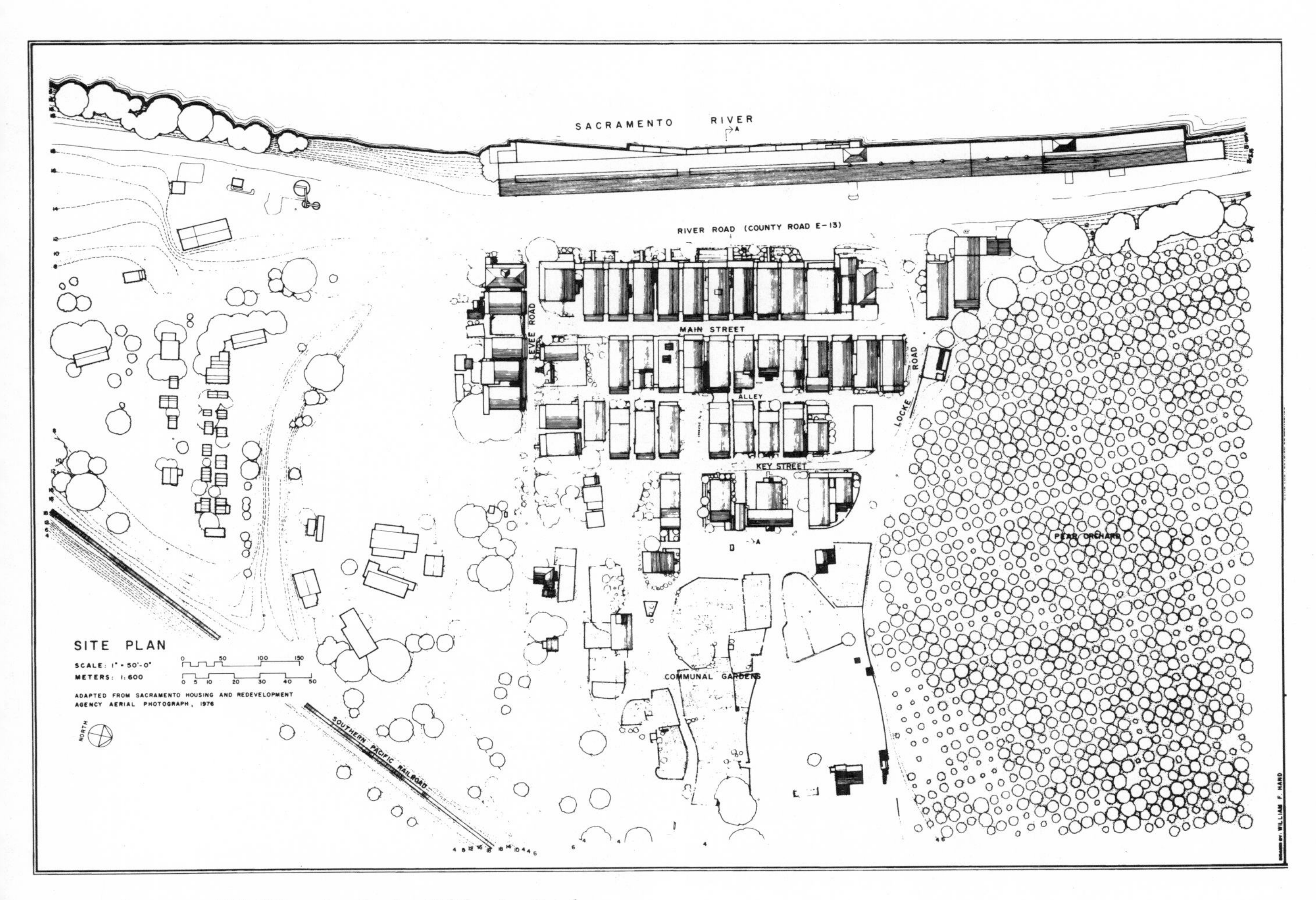

Figure 8.6. HABS Drawing, Locke, California, site plan.

In 1915 a fire destroyed Walnut Grove's Chinatown, and rather than rebuild many Chungshanese decided to found a new community about half a mile north on a site known as Lockeport. The land belonged to a farmer named George Locke who owned orchards on and around the site. Locke made a verbal agreement to lease land to the Chinese, who were prohibited from owning land by the California Alien Land Law of 1913. The fixed rate per lot was based on the size of the building constructed: five dollars per month for a house and ten dollars per month for a commercial building; the tenants would own the buildings they erected on the leased land (fig. 8.6).

For most early settlers, the cost of moving to the new site had to be raised through the use of Hui, a rotating credit system. A Hui was a system by which a number of people got together and pooled an agreed-upon amount of money at regular intervals until each member had received the lump sum once. For instance, a man who needed five hundred dollars to set himself up in Locke would organize ten friends

Figure 8.7. Alley, Locke, California. (Photo by author)

and relatives into a Hui. Members would meet at a prearranged dinner and each would place the agreed-upon amount of fifty dollars into a common pool. The organizer would pay for the first dinner and receive the first lump sum. The group would then meet for nine more dinners at which each member would donate fifty dollars to the evening's pool. This system of rotating credit was very important in the rise of small-scale Chinese businesses in the United States, and it continued to be widely used well into the 1950s.[12]

At its peak in the 1920s, Locke probably never exceeded a population of about six hundred. Besides the merchants, a few families, labor contractors, prostitutes, and workers at the Locke dock, the only inhabitants were farm laborers who worked near the town or were between jobs. The town layout adjusted to several existing conditions. A rail siding looped around the south end of the site to the dock built by Locke in 1907 to facilitate shipping. The short, projecting levee between two existing buildings became a street. The Chinese agreed to construct their town along the Sacramento levee, so they began by laying out lots about thirty-two feet wide and seventy-five feet deep in a row facing the highway that ran along the top of the levee. Just behind this row was Main Street. A farsighted leader suggested that a wide Main Street was needed to accommodate the automobiles that were beginning to appear in the delta and to reduce the chance of another disastrous fire. The eight-foot-wide spaces left between buildings for fire safety eventually became alleys and enclosed yards used for storage, hanging laundry, and later for propane tanks (figs. 8.7, 8.8, 8.9).

Locke was closer to the center of the orchard belt than Walnut Grove, and as the number of Chungshanese declined from emigration and mortality, those remaining gathered at Locke where they had a good chance of finding orchard work. Fires in the Chungshan Chinatowns on the Sacramento River to the north of Locke also helped concentrate the dwindling population at the new site. Locke was more a service center of the farm laborers than a residential community. Laborers could purchase clothes, food, and other necessities that could not be raised or made on the farm. The town had a post office, so many laborers and tenant farmers used Locke as their mailing address. Some came to have letters written for them.

Locke also offered relaxation, entertainment, and diversion for the men on their rare days off or during the rainy season when the fields and orchards were too soggy to work. The benches in front of the buildings along Main Street (which have since been stolen by tourists) provided a place to watch the traffic and greet friends. Gambling houses where tenant farmers and laborers could be parted from their hard-earned money lined the streets, and Main Street had at least one bar. In many stores, friends passed the time playing mah-jongg. The brothels were on the back street.

Chinese farm children went to a public school only if they lived near one. The elementary schools in the area were segregated, with the Oriental school located in Walnut Grove. Children living in or near Locke also attended Chinese school, where they learned to read and write Chinese while becoming acquainted with the Chinese classics and culture.

All the buildings were simple, wood-frame structures placed directly on the ground without foundations. Clapboard or board-and-batten sheathing formed the exterior skin of these gabled structures. Almost all the buildings were roofed with corrugated metal, which was

Figure 8.8. Alley, Locke, California. (Photo by author)

Figure 8.9. Alley, Locke, California. (Photo by author)

Figure 8.10. Levee Street, Locke, California. (Photo by author)

cheap, easily installed, and relatively fire resistant. Two-story buildings provided more interior space per lot and a refuge in case of flood. Most single-story buildings were residences at the back of town on Key Street. The emphasis on utility and economy was largely due to the California law, which barred Chinese from land ownership. Brick or stone would have offered greater fire protection, but such expense and permanence must have seemed unreasonable to people who did not own the land and did not expect to spend the rest of their lives in America.

The local European American carpenters who "designed" and built the buildings probably used standard layouts modified to meet particular requests of the Chinese. The two-story buildings between Main Street and the levee typically have two main entrances, one on the first floor opening onto the levee highway (fig. 8.10). The ground-floor facade facing Main Street was usually the display area of a store. The sidewalk was protected by an overhanging second-floor balcony and offered a haven from the summer sun and winter rain. The ground-floor spaces farthest from the street were used for storage, living quarters, and possibly opium dens (fig. 8.11). The second floor commonly had provisions for another store accessible from the levee highway. Behind this space often were a series of rooms opening onto a double-loaded corridor. These rooms could be rented to farm laborers during off-season or to people employed at the Locke dock and warehouse. As building owners started having families, they often converted part of the upper floor for the family residence. The simple wood construction and the rectangular plan facilitated the continual alteration of the buildings to fit changing conditions (fig. 8.12). One versatile structure was built about 1925 by a carpenter to serve as a small bar next to the brothel he had built earlier. The brothel was a simple rectangular structure with central corridor and five small rooms on either side. In 1937, the brothel and bar were sold as a package for back rent, and the new owner converted the structures to conform to the needs of a modified version of the traditional Chinese extended family.

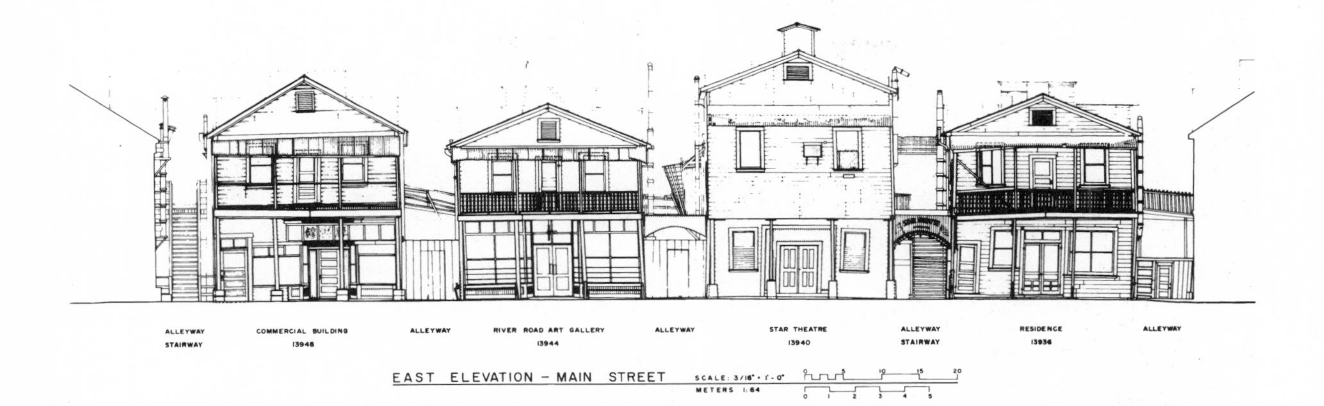

Behind the town stood one of George Locke's barns and an open area developed into small vegetable gardens (fig. 8.13). Produce from these gardens included potatoes, celery, tomatoes, onions, corn, carrots, lettuce, melons, bok choy, and other Chinese vegetables. A few paths continued back to a branch of Snodgrass Slough where people could fish or hunt game birds. The less fortunate Chinese sojourners are buried behind the town in what are now lost, unmarked graves. It was the common practice to disinter them after a number of years, clean their bones and send them back to China for burial at their native place.

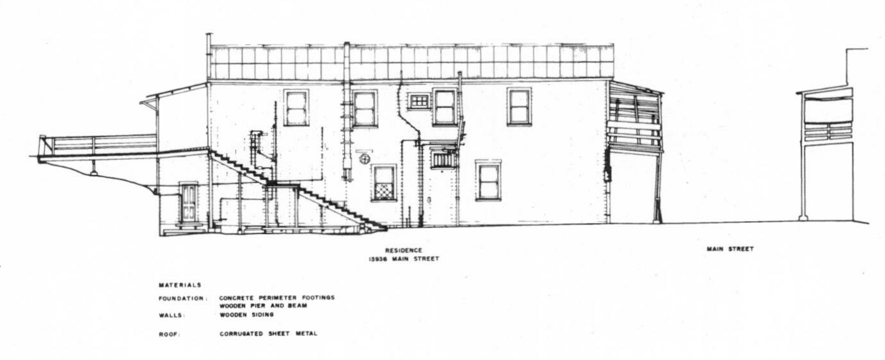

Figure 8.11. HABS drawing, Main Street, east elevation, Locke, California.

Figure 8.12. 13936 Main Street, elevation, Locke, California. (Drawing by author)

Locke had neither the population nor the diversity to support the range of organizations found in the Chinese American social structure of large cities such as San Francisco. Locke's major organization was a branch of the Triad Society known as the Chee Kung Tong. By the nineteenth century the Triads had degenerated into a pseudopolitical, loosely organized underworld organization with a

Figure 8.13. Vegetable gardens, Locke, California. (Photo by author)

large following among the Chungshanese. It was a natural choice for the focal organization in Locke, because the Chungshanese dominated the Chee Kung Tong branches in the Sacramento Delta. The merchants could use the organization to provide protection and to arbitrate disputes over gambling, prostitution, and drug activities. Individuals could use the tong as a social institution and as a vehicle to express their desire for change, social justice, and a strong China of which they could be proud. The presence of the Chee Kung Tong reflected the degree to which the Chinese laborers saw themselves as Chinese first and foremost.[13]

Trapped in low-status jobs, barred from citizenship and landownership, how could they consider themselves Americans? Powerless against the forces that manipulated them in America, they looked back to the land of their birth where many had parents, wives, and children. China's degradation was their degradation; China's salvation would be their salvation. The Chinese in Locke (and in the United States in general) viewed Sun Yat-sen's movement to liberate China as their hope for liberation. Also, the Chungshanese must have liked the idea of one of their own becoming the leader of China. Sun Yat-sen was both Chungshanese and a member of the Triad Society. It required a change in the political and economic climate in the United States fostered by the country's involvement in the Second World War to significantly alter the Chinese American's hopes for the future (fig. 8.14).

The fortunes of delta communities such as Locke waxed and waned according to developments in agriculture. Between 1867 and 1885, wheat was raised on large ranches as cash crops, while smaller farms diversified into a variety of crops for local, national, and international markets. Instability in the wheat market and the growing profitability of the orchards led to a shift in the pattern of delta agriculture. With a smaller initial investment and a steady supply of cheap labor, a landowner could plant about a hundred acres with orchards and make as much or more than he could with ten times as large a wheat farm. The Chinese supplied the cheap labor. As methods for shipping fruit improved, the orchard and field crops drove wheat out of the delta.[14]

The center of the orchard district lay along the banks of the Sacramento River between Hood and Walnut Grove. Pear orchards were the most profitable crop in this productive area, but secondary orchards of apples, peaches, cherries, and plums were also planted. The river was a good source for irrigation water and cheap transportation. Since orchards and field crops required close supervision and a lot of seasonal labor, landowners relied heavily upon tenant farmers, sharecroppers, and farm laborers to do the actual farming. The shift from wheat to orchards and field crops meant an increase in farm laborers rather than an increase in family farms. The average Chinese agricultural worker started off as a farm laborer working under a Chinese tenant farmer and strove to become a tenant farmer himself. Contractors naturally looked to their own clan, village, tong, and district connections to find workers, so laborers of the same dialect generally worked together. Many labor contractors also were town merchants.

Chinese tenant farmers leased or sharecropped the land. For a leasing arrangement, the tenant farmer would check out land that would be available in the next farming year, which usually began in October. Owners specified the crops to be raised, and the leaseholder paid the owner for the use of the land. The first payment commonly was made at the signing of the agreement or just before harvest, the last payment with the sale of the crop. Under this system, the risk lay with the tenant, who had to raise money for the lease and bring in the crop and market it at the best possible price. Contracts usually ran for one year, so the Chinese tenant had to make enough from the crop to pay off the lease and start a new season. Landowners may have used the one-year lease to rotate crops by rotating tenants with different specialties. In lands that had not yet been brought under cultivation, leases could be

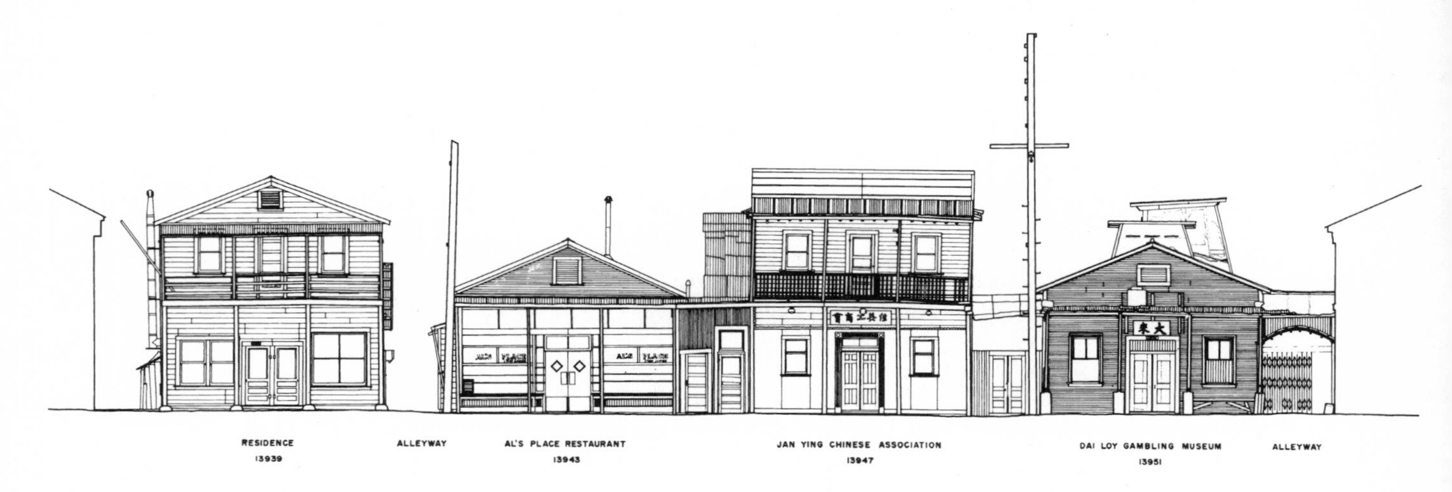

Figure 8.14. HABS Drawing, Main Street, west elevation, Locke, California.

about five years, giving the tenant time to develop the land and bring in one or two crops to cover his efforts.

Sharecropping was the other common form of farm tenancy. The Chinese sharecropper received about half the gross from the sale of the crop. From his share he paid the costs of running the farm and buying seed, chemicals, and labor. The landowner supplied farm equipment, barns, and dwellings. Successful tenant farmers moved carefully on these arrangements, weighing the condition of the land and deciding whether the crop the landowner specified would bring a profit.

The tenant farmer and his family, if he was able to bring them to the United States, lived in a one- or two-room shack next to the fields or orchards. Families often slept on the floor, and cooking was done on makeshift stoves. Outhouses were built downwind from the dwellings. Workers usually lived in a separate shack and stored whatever possessions they had in piles or boxes. The more sophisticated dwellings were equipped with bunk beds.

Pear orchards were the first major source of employment for the Chungshan laborers, but the asparagus boom from about 1900 until World War II kept the demand for farm labor high in the area around Locke. By 1920, almost all the field cropland had been planted in asparagus. At one point, the delta produced 90 percent of the asparagus grown in the United States.[15] Other common field crops were beans, sugar beets, carrots, celery, and tomatoes, which were replacing citrus production. The pear orchards, the asparagus boom, and the increased food demand and higher prices induced by World War I made Locke a lively community in the 1920s, even though the Chinese American population in the United States had dropped from 107,488 in 1890 to 61,639 in 1920 because of the Exclusion Acts.[16]

Local economic conditions were strong enough to make the creation and survival of a new Chinatown possible, although the subculture was facing demographic decline. The Prohibition Act of 30 June 1919, also helped by turning Locke—which had no court and no police force—into a small mecca for drinkers from Sacramento. One local bar became popular with political figures from Sacramento, who found Locke to be a safe distance from the state capital. The bars did not cater to the Chungshanese, who did not view drinking as an important form of social escape.

Technological changes also had a great impact on Locke's fortunes. On the one hand, improved methods of shipping and storage greatly expanded the markets for delta produce, but mechanization cut down the number of farm laborers needed to work a farm. The expansion of the canning industry took up some of the slack. The growth of the asparagus market led to an increase in cannery activity, which in turn led to pressure for crop diversification as asparagus production started moving south into the San Joaquin Delta. Tomatoes were a good canning crop because of their lengthy harvesting season.[17] Increased crop varieties extended the canneries' operating season, which meant more employment for the laborers that supported Locke. Better canning techniques, and the opening of the Panama Canal in 1914 improved the position of canned delta fruits and vegetables in both the Atlantic seaboard and European markets. The ethnic specialization common on the farms soon transferred to the canneries. The Chinese trucked the asparagus to the cannery, washed, sorted, canned, and soldered. Japanese and Caucasians did the warehousing, labeling, storing, and shipping.

Transportation and canning improvements enhanced Locke's position, but the development of farm machinery dealt the town its death blow. World War I generated a bigger market and higher prices for delta produce, which provided farmers with the capital to buy new equipment. With pruning towers, fog-spraying machines, forklifts, and trucks, fewer orchard workers were needed.[18] The increasing use of trucks meant farmers could speed their produce to large, centralized canneries. Locke's cannery was one of the small operations that did not survive.

After World War II, farmers made more widespread use of airplanes for seeding, spraying, fertilizing, and dusting fields. By the 1950s the Sacramento Delta had become one of the world's largest markets for farm machinery. Mechanization, along with the declining Chinese population, doomed Locke and other Chinatowns in the delta.

Yet Locke's decline from the boom days of the 1920s was gradual. Although the adult male Chinese population steadily dropped after 1900, the 1930 census showed the Chinese population in the United States included about 15 percent children under fourteen. At that time, Locke began to take on the character of a family community. The social structure created by the first-generation immigrants had shunned novel ideas, which might threaten the established order, but the children were learning English in the segregated public school. They were more assimilated and did not necessarily share their parents' strong ties to China. They often considered the fraternal solidarity of the immigrant organizations archaic, sentimental, and parochial.

Their career ambitions went beyond field laborer and, with their parents' blessings, they sought education and better jobs. Often by the late 1950s, only elderly Chinese worked in the fields. Many second-generation Chinese Americans pursued technical training that demanded less reliance upon English than other fields and offered the possibility of professional employment. The college experience furthered the growing split between traditionalist parents and the more assimilated children. Going to dances, courtship, romantic love, physical attraction as a basis for marriage, church weddings, embracing in public, divorce, and remarriage were all signs of change. Skills learned in college could not be put to use in small Chinatowns, such as Locke, but discrimination in hiring and the depressed economy of the 1930s ruled out professional employment. Some college graduates worked in their parents' stores; some did farm work. A few returned to China, but the exodus was small since technical work was difficult to find in China, and many second-generation Chinese Americans lacked a sophisticated knowledge of the language. Also, China was a land that the second-generation Chinese American had never known.

World War II opened up the job market to Chinese American college graduates. Through the G.I. Bill, many poor Chinese Americans were able to attend college, so even more of the second generation were destined to leave Locke and the delta region.[19] Second-generation women also began to seek careers beyond the family, further increasing the generational split. A major change in the position of the Chinese American came with the repeal of the Exclusion Acts during World War II. Suddenly China was an ally. Finally, in 1947 California repealed its antimiscegenation law.

Although most of the second generation who found jobs did not return to Locke, the town had its own postwar baby boom. The Chinese language school that had lapsed between 1947 and 1953 was reopened and reached a peak enrollment of about fifty children.

In 1952, the Alien Land Law, which had barred Locke's early residents from owning land, was found unconstitutional, but the Chinese American community had moved away from agriculture. The end of the immigration quota system in 1965 had no impact on Locke either, since the new immigrants from Hong Kong, Taiwan, China, and Southeast Asia sought employment in large American metropolitan areas.

Today the population of Locke is less than one hundred. Many residents are elderly bachelors who had harbored hopes of returning to China in their earlier years. A few have saved a little money, but most receive welfare and other forms of government assistance. Those who remain in Locke enjoy the landscape and a slow pace of life measured by changes of seasons and crops. They sit on the benches that have not been stolen by tourists and walk down to the Chee Kung Tong clubhouse on Main Street to see if there is anything going on.

Figure 8.15. Key Street, Locke, California.
(Photo by author)

The delta has become a major boating and recreation area for Sacramento and San Francisco area residents. There are fishing and boating on the delta waters and vacation houseboats in Snodgrass Slough behind the town. The dock, now named the Boathouse, stores pleasure craft and sells fuel to boaters; in duck season the delta is full of hunters. The town's life has ebbed along with the population it once served (fig. 8.15).

Old Locke and its world are gone forever, but the physical setting remains. Somehow the majority of dry, unfinished wood buildings have survived ever-present threats of fire and flood. Locke is now the largest and most complete surviving rural Chinese American community. Because it was built as a separate entity unattached to a larger town, it is both unique and archetypal. The physical forms of this small rural ghetto are derived from the American experience, but the understanding of these forms lies in the history of the Chinese in America.

Notes

1. This argument is developed in S. C. Miller, *The Unwelcome Immigrant: The American Image of the Chinese, 1785–1882* (Berkeley: University of California Press, 1969). See also Harold Isaacs, *Images of Asia: American Views of China and India* (1958; reprint, New York: Harper and Row, 1972).

2. Miller, *The Unwelcome Immigrant,* 16, quoting from *The Journal and Miscellaneous Notebooks of Ralph Waldo Emerson,* ed. W. H. Gilman et al. (Cambridge: Harvard University Press, 1961), 2:224.

3. Miller, *The Unwelcome Immigrant,* 126.

4. S. Gompers and H. Gutstadt, *Meat vs. Rice, American Manhood against Asiatic Coolieism. Which Shall Survive?* (1902; reprint, San Francisco: Asiatic Exclusion League, 1908).

5. Frederic Wakeman, *Strangers at the Gate* (Berkeley: University of California Press, 1966), 127.

6. See C. P. Fitzgerald, *The Southern Expansion of the Chinese People* (New York: Praeger, 1972); and Lynn Pan, *Sons of the Yellow Emperor* (Boston: Little Brown, 1990).

7. Lawrence Crissman, "The Segmentary Structures of Urban Overseas Chinese Communities," *Man* 2, no. 2 (June 1967): 185–204.

8. Him Mark Lai, "Historical Development of the Chinese Consolidated Benevolent Association/Huiguan System" in *Chinese America: History and Perspectives* (1987), 23–29; see also William Hoy, *The Chinese Six Companies* (San Francisco: Chinese Consolidated Benevolent Association, 1942).

9. See *People* vs. *George W. Hall.*

10. S. Chan, *This Bitter-Sweet Soil: The Chinese in California Agriculture, 1860–1910* (Berkeley: University of California Press, 1986), 106–57.

11. George Chu, "Chinatowns in the Delta: The Chinese in the Sacramento–San Joaquin Delta, 1870–1960," *California Historical Quarterly* 49, no. 1 (March 1970): 21–37.

12. See Ivan H. Light, *Ethnic Enterprise in America* (Berkeley: University of California Press, 1972).

13. For information on secret societies see Jean Chesneaux, *Secret Societies in China in the Nineteenth and Twentieth Centuries* (Ann Arbor: University of Michigan Press, 1971); for an examination of Chinese American political activity and China, see L. E. Armentrout Ma, *Revolutionaries, Monarchists, and Chinatowns: Chinese Politics in the Americas and the 1911 Revolution* (Honolulu: University of Hawaii Press, 1990).

14. J. A. McGowan, *The History of the Sacramento Valley* (New York: Lewis Historical Publishing, 1961), 1:268, 275–77, 385–87, 2:1.

15. George Chu, "Chinatowns in the Delta," 32.

16. U.S. Census, 1890, 1920.

17. J. A. McGowan, *History of the Sacramento Valley,* 2:16.

18. A. Allen, *Stories of the Sacramento Delta* (Rio Vista: Delta Herald, 1952), 34–35.

19. Melford S. Weiss. *Valley City: A Chinese Community in America* (Cambridge, Mass.: Schenkman Publishing, 1974) 95.

CHAPTER NINE

Keeping House

Women, Domesticity, and the Use of Domestic Space in Nineteenth-Century Nevada

MARGARET PURSER

There is an old photograph from Paradise Valley, Nevada, of three women doing laundry in their back yard (fig. 9.1).[1] The blurry snapshot dates to the early 1870s, when the small Great Basin town was less than a decade old. The rough edges of the captured details seem to convey that raw, new sense perfectly.

The outbuilding behind the women, which housed the wellhead, is sod-constructed right up to its roof, which sprouts new grass. The yard beneath the women's feet is bare earth. The bleached light of the Nevada desert has nearly blinded the old camera lens, blurring the margins of the shot and speaking eloquently of chalky alkali, searing heat, and dry winds.

Set in this context, everything about the women, including their task at hand, seems quaintly incongruous: proper Victorian ladies striving to bring a touch of civilization to the "unsettled" wilderness. Their dress is plain but decorous, with its long-sleeved, high-necked modesty. Waists are corseted, legs encased in black stockings, full skirts cover layers of multiple petticoats. The props making up the tableau likewise speak of middle-class prosperity and decorum, from the mail order hand-cranked laundry wringer to the bentwood chair supporting the reader. She is perhaps the most proper of all the figures, sitting straight-backed with her ankles primly crossed, absorbed in her book, while her mother and sister crank out the snowy yards of that week's washing.

This rather simple, stereotypical view of Victorian gender roles and western expansion masks a more complex spatial and social history. The activities depicted in the photograph unquestionably document an effort by these Paradise women to impose an urban, and urbane, pattern of spatial organization and land use on the settlement during its first years. But the curious fact remains that this initial taste for cultivated eastern styles did not persist. Contrary to expectations, the urban aspirations of the pioneering generation were gradually replaced by a more rural, ex-

Figure 9.1. Wash-day in the backyard, ca. 1875. (Courtesy the late Fredrick Charles Buckingham Sr., Paradise Valley, Nevada)

pedient, and opportunistic way of life during the closing years of the nineteenth century and the first decades of the twentieth. In short, Paradise acquired, as it matured, more of the qualities associated with the western "frontier." The change is not outwardly perceptible, at least judging from the normal perspective of architectural history. The material world of the small town appears to have moved along, like other small American towns, quite predictably from nineteenth- to twentieth-century styles. Later photographs (and surviving examples) show larger, more stylish houses, more mass-produced goods, landscaped front yards, wide streets, and well-dressed citizens. Yet, if we look at interior space, at how that space was organized and used, it is possible to see the reversal of this pattern, from urban to rural, that characterizes so much of the later industrial West.

The question addressed in this essay concerns the role that gender played in this masked transition. How can architectural practice, in this case the organization and use of space, tell us more about the gender relations of a small community and the larger social and cultural fabric of which such relations were an integral part? The answers lie not in the stereotyped tableaux of period accessories and demeanor, but are, instead, embedded in the complex and diverse material life created in this small community over the course of sixty or seventy years.

Most current treatments of gender relations in the United States acknowledge variability across racial, ethnic, and class lines. For example, the experiences and expectations of an African American woman working in an eastern, urban factory varied dramatically from the lives of either a wealthy white woman living in the same city, or a Hispanic woman homesteading in the Southwest. An increasing number of studies examine this variability under specific historical conditions.[2] But relatively few describe the relationships between gender and the objects, structures, spaces, and technologies that made up the material culture of a given place and time. It has been particularly difficult to get beyond "sexing" the object: to move from identifying women's (and men's) things, spaces, and activities toward an understanding of gender as a social construct and its influence on the ways that things were made and used.

Changes visible in the domestic architecture of Paradise Valley, Nevada, between 1860 and 1920 offer a chance to see the important role gender played, in conjunction with race, ethnicity, and class, in determining the complex system of local social relations and material life. Townspeople dramatically redesigned their houses and their town over these decades, as they struggled to survive a downward economic cycle that turned many neighboring communities into ghost towns. Individual households and the town as a whole lost their earlier urban pretensions. Houses and lots turned into miniature ranch headquarters; streets lost their shops, saloons, and crowds; urban style alleys became driveways or side yards; barns and sheep pens sprouted on lots once facing thoroughfares optimistically named "University Avenue" and "Second West Street." At the same time, radical changes transformed the spaces in which men and women worked, the tools and equipment they used, the places where they took their leisure, the rooms where they slept, ate, and entertained. These two transformations were not only related, but the transition from urban to rural would not have worked the way it did without the increasingly sharp division of living spaces into women's and men's realms. In particular, there would have been no ambiguity in the process: no way to hide rural functions inside an urban facade; no way to mask the local economic struggle as participation in a national myth of industrial progress and Victorian propriety.

Paradise was (and is) a small community in north central Nevada, forty miles north of Winnemucca in Humboldt County. Initial settlement by Euro-American immigrants began in the early 1860s, as people were drawn by the proximity of the valley's lush agricultural lands and water to the nearby boomtown markets of the

Humboldt Range silver mines. Over the next sixty years, the local economy cycled through a commercial agriculture based on export grain crops, a small but rich local mining strike, and finally a large-scale range livestock industry based on cattle and sheep. Paradise attracted settlers from Germany, Italy, the Basque country, and China, and from the northeastern, midwestern, and southern regions of the United States.

Commercial as well as agricultural profits drew people to the valley, and these residents had begun construction of a small centrally located town called Paradise City by the early 1870s (fig. 9.2). By the time the town plat was filed in 1879, there were blacksmiths, carpenters, wheelwrights, livery stables, hotels, saloons, and a brewery, as well as three competing general stores.

The valley's fortunes declined beginning in the mid-1890s, and Paradise City ultimately lost its struggle to compete with larger county commercial centers. But the valley settlement and its central town survived. For town residents this survival was predicated on adopting increasingly flexible, opportunistic economic strategies for their households. The town gradually lost most of its urban aspirations and functions, and town households increasingly participated in the agricultural production of the broader valley economy.

The private residences built in Paradise during the course of this history are the primary concern of this essay. The term "private residence" in this case marks a selection of a particular structural type, the single-family dwelling. It does not include all the places where Paradise residents lived. It excludes, for example, the temporary willow-frame homes of seasonally migrating Paiutes and the sod-walled dugouts of a group of Chinese laborers who lived at the margins of town. It also excludes all those people who occupied the town's various residential hotels and boarding houses: seasonal laborers, single males from all social levels, and newly arrived immigrant families lacking the capital to buy or possibly even to rent separate houses. Finally, it leaves out the more urban style, dual-purpose buildings that housed both commercial shop and private residence for a number of the town's early tradespeople. These exclusions reduce the sample to thirty houses either currently standing or recorded in documentary records and oral history. Measured plans are available for seventeen of these; physical descriptions for six more. In addition to type of residence, several environmental and economic factors also shaped the domestic architecture of nineteenth-century Paradise. The great majority of the town's houses were small frame structures; most began with four rooms or less. Oddly, in an aspiring boomtown populated by immigrants from several continents, neither the ethnic diversity nor the considerable range of social status, amply documented in newspapers and tax assessments of the time, had much impact on residential architecture. Even when individual families gained in wealth and prestige, their residences remained relatively unassuming, in marked contrast to the houses of their successful

Figure 9.2. Main Street, Paradise Valley, ca. 1890. (Courtesy the late Fredrick Charles Buckingham Sr., Paradise Valley, Nevada)

ranching neighbors and to the commercial stores, shops, and hotels in their own town.

Furthermore, the same three basic house types were built by German, Italian, and Basque immigrants as well as other settlers from the United States over a span of nearly seventy years. The most popular house plan laid out four rooms in a box: two rooms front and rear, with interior partitions that formed either a simple or staggered cross (fig. 9.3a). The front entrance always opened into a larger, more public "front room," with bedrooms to the side and a kitchen in the rear. Another house plan organized three small rooms into a line, with a small (sometimes partitioned) kitchen lean-to running across the rear wall (9.3b). The smallest of these house types sorted front room, bedroom, and kitchen into a T- or L-shaped plan (9.3c). Even with the accumulated diversity of later additions and modifications, the houses retained a sameness evoked in a contemporary description that counted "thirty-five pretty little cottage homes" in town by 1905.[3]

There is also a marked hand-me-down character to Paradise town houses. The town experienced an initial domestic building boom during the 1860s and 1870s, followed by several decades in which new construction focused on commercial rather than residential structures. Because of the high cost of importing lumber to their relatively treeless Great Basin valley, Paradise residents proved reluctant to build entirely new homes. Instead, they would add to, renovate, and rearrange existing structures—even move them from place to place. The surviving built environment records many of the choices and changes three generations of townspeople made in their immediate surroundings.

Several broad trends link the changes wrought in Paradise City's domestic architecture through the early twentieth century. Direct physical changes are the most readily apparent. First, by the 1920s, larger houses sat on much bigger lots. Second, later residences exhibited many more specialized uses of both internal and external space than had their counterparts of the 1870s: more rooms were exclusively designated as bedrooms, closets, cellars, parlors, and so on. Third, although they did so with minimal cost and stylistic elaboration, Paradise houses of the early twentieth century did physically document the new social distinctions that had grown with the maturing frontier community. Using the simplest refinements, like mail order picket fencing and architectural gingerbread, even mundane cottages began to sort wealthier from poorer residents, older from more recent immigrant families, and larger property owners from smaller ones. In addition to these alterations in the appearance of the houses, more subtle changes occurred in the ways people lived in them. A fourth major category of change reflected the increasing demands Paradise residents made on their houses and lots as sites for small-scale economic production. Unlike people living in more urban settings, who found the economic productivity of the private household increasingly supplanted by factories and other corporate enterprises, Paradise family households had actually increased their economic significance over time. To be sure, wage labor outside the home was increasingly important in this cattle ranching valley through the turn of the century. But town families in particular continued and even increased the amount of independent economic activities carried out at the individual household level. Residential structures and lots were further diversified to accommodate livestock-raising, farming, crafts such as smithing or carpentry, and even small commercial enterprises such as freight lines.

Finally, domestic structures changed to reflect changing local definitions for and roles of private versus public spaces and structures. These new spatial and social definitions echoed not only the increasing isolation of individuals and families as a result of local social competition and economic decline, but a more pervasive separation of public and private spheres in American society. Public life shifted from more informally social to more formally commercial. Private life became more isolated from the immediate public sphere of the town and was increasingly graded across lines of ethnicity and social status in the emerging hierarchy of the maturing town. But at the same time, nationwide marketing was making the private lives of all Paradise residents *appear* less isolated and more homogenized by the myriad consumer goods, architectural embellishments, and social behavior that accessorized late Victorian popular culture.

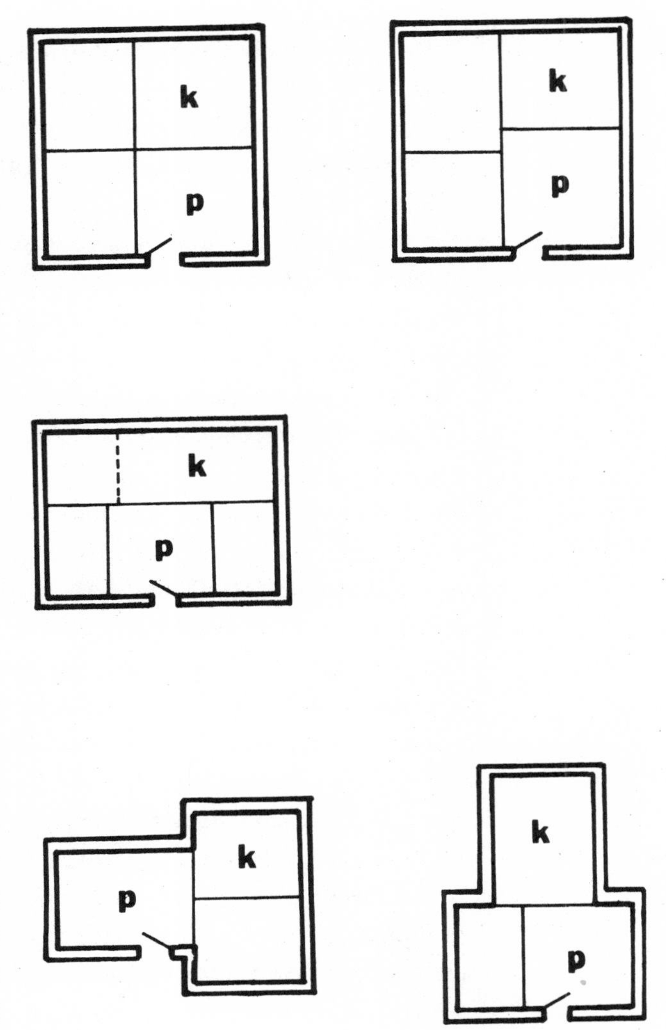

Figure 9.3. Schematic of townhouse floor plan types. Internal piercings too variable to depict. (Drawing by Alan Burnett)

Most of these trends should have a familiar ring to them; in one form or another they have been identified in many nineteenth-century contexts, both early and late, urban and rural, eastern and western. They are also among those features most often described as varying sharply across the cultural and class lines that divided Victorian society in America. Conformity to these behaviors was associated strongly with upward mobility and the (Anglo-European) upper middle class. Members of urban laboring classes could rarely control enough of their domestic environment or afford the new construction of specialized spaces that new codes of "privacy" demanded. Members of other cultural and ethnic groups resisted or rejected the new definitions of appropriate social and spatial organization as uncomfortable, alien, or harmful to their cultural identity.[4]

One configuration of this powerful

social ideology has been called the "cult of domesticity." This was a mid-nineteenth-century phenomenon that linked social reform, postcharismatic Christianity, and emerging transformations of the family, work behavior, and class consciousness brought on by industrialism to produce an idealized version of urban industrial culture centered around the middle-class home.[5] The link between the cult and architectural reform is well documented, particularly for the wealthier classes of eastern, urban centers.[6] Reformers citing the cult's basic tenets advocated the construction of houses that exhibited greater specialization of space, more consumer-oriented furnishings, and new concerns with efficiency, technological innovation, and status display as the means to inculcate a "morality" appropriate to the times.

The connections between domesticity ideologies and concurrent transformations in gender roles likewise have attracted considerable attention.[7] The social and economic transformations of later nineteenth-century industrialism increasingly removed men from active participation in their own domestic lives, and restricted their social and cultural roles to wage labor income producers. These changes simultaneously reduced the recognition of women's productive economic activities both in and outside the household, sharply separated men's and women's spheres of influence, and considerably expanded women's perceived responsibilities as the primary, if not sole, household members in charge of the adequate socialization of children, coordination of household consumption, and maintenance of the outward signs of social status and competition.

Much recent debate has centered on whether the "cult" really merits such a label, and the degree to which its influence penetrated beyond the upper middle class or the dominant Anglicized culture.[8] The changes seen in Paradise Valley houses testify to some level of currency for these ideas within the community. However, the changes in Paradise Valley material life do not merely reflect the more general power of the cult of domesticity as an element of national popular culture. Over the course of half a century, the relative popularity of the movement's ideals rose and fell, both in Paradise and across the country at large.

It is also important to recognize that people in the western United States experienced the latter decades of nineteenth-century industrialism very differently from their eastern, urban cousins. In the West, industrialism brought depopulation rather than population growth, economic reduction rather than expansion, and increasing ruralization rather than urbanization. Struggling against this threat, Paradise houses and households failed in many ways to conform to the principles of the national reform movement.

Instead, the spatial and architectural changes that occurred in Paradise housing indicate the ways that local people manipulated elements of the movement to deal with the economic stresses and social competition surrounding them. And gender roles proved crucial in that manipulation. Specifically, the division of labor along gender lines that had characterized earlier town households regardless of class and ethnic identity was now codified by a greater spatial segregation of gendered places. The cooking, cleaning, food production, and childcare tasks that made up women's work had been understood as separate from men's cash-producing labor since at least the early 1800s in American society. But in the Paradise Valley of the 1860s and 1870s, these different tasks could take place in kitchens, yards, shops, and fields that did not necessarily physically separate the two types of labor.

By 1900 a clear physical segregation of labor along gender lines existed in most of the town houses, regardless of ethnic background or social status. Increasingly, women worked indoors; men worked outside. Women ran kitchens and entertained in parlors; men labored in shops and sheds. New technologies like washing machines, cook stoves, bathroom plumbing, engines, and vehicles further specialized the individual tasks conducted in houses, porches, yards, lots, and streets.

And yet these trends toward spatial segregation and specialization masked an actual increase in the opportunistic diversity of *both* men's and women's activities, and the economic strategies of town households, and a sharp decline in the economic health of the community in general. In effect, Paradise residents participated in the national cult of domesticity in ways that disguised local economic hardship as middle-class prosperity, confounded urban land use patterns with rural ones, and translated ethnic diversity into class difference. The key to all this sleight-of-hand lay in the links that developed between gender and the use of domestic space between the 1860s and the turn of the twentieth century.

The first components of the town's built environment held no such ambiguity or double meaning. Early Paradise developers built their urban aspirations quite explicitly into the town plat they filed in 1879 (fig. 9.4). The town grid followed the standard practice of the day: it occasionally ignored local geography (dumping East Street unceremoniously into Cottonwood Creek), but promised the prosperity of infinite expansion. Small, city-scale lots of 50' x 100' fronted onto wide streets and backed up against narrow alleys, then the hallmark of accepted urban spatial planning. Houses sat near the street front of the lot, leaving a long, narrow back yard for gardens, wells, and domestic outbuildings. Alleys ran along the rear of the lots, and were intended to provide service access, convenient for the delivery of coal and hay, and the removal of rubbish.[9]

The town's first residents apparently seconded these aspirations, even though they began to alter the original grid almost immediately (fig. 9.5). For example, newcomers buying lots along the northern side of West Bridge Street opted to turn their property to face the busier Bridge Street, rather than the quieter stretches of West and 2nd West (fig. 9.4). But they retained the general lot dimensions and intervening alleys nonetheless. Evidence that these alleys did serve their intended purpose still trickles from beneath the sheds that line the alleyway beside the Liotard house

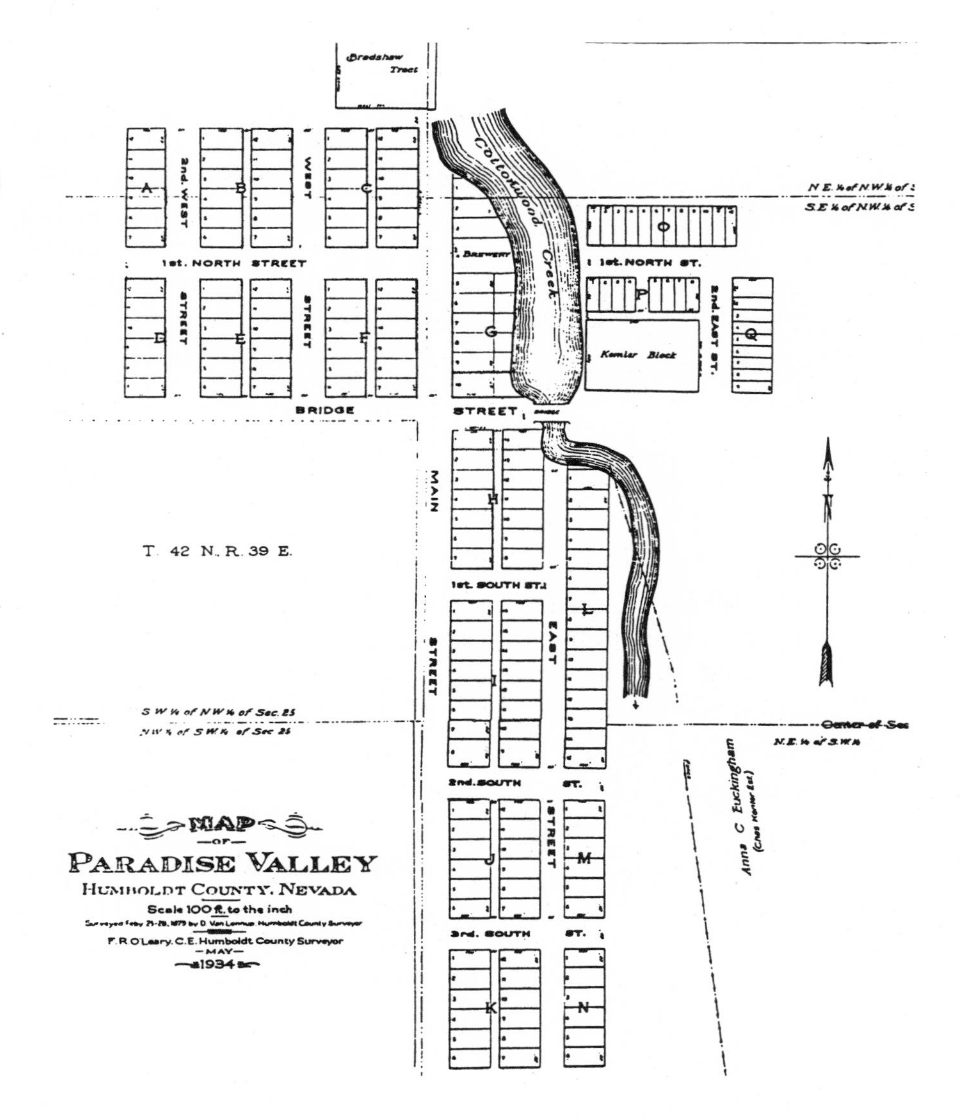

Figure 9.4. Town plat map, filed in 1879. (Humboldt County Recorder's Office, Winnemucca, Nevada)

in block F: coal dust drifts out beneath one alley door, wood scraps from beneath another, testimony to convenient alley deliveries of household necessities.

It was in this earlier context that the wash day tasks of the women in the photograph spoke of a more cosmopolitan frame of reference, however rough their immediate surroundings. Midcentury town backlots were places for the execution of household chores: laundering, some food processing and storage, and the necessary accompaniments of household cleaning, maintenance, and hygiene: wells, woodsheds, coal sheds, and outhouses. Although some early residents originally purchased half of an adjoining lot to expand the overall lot size to 150 feet, most kept the smaller, urban scale dimensions, at least initially. The small three- and four-room frame houses sat close to the street. There was little or no front yard, which conserved all available space at the rear for domestic outbuildings and activities.

By the turn of the century, this pattern was gone. Later owners bought up second

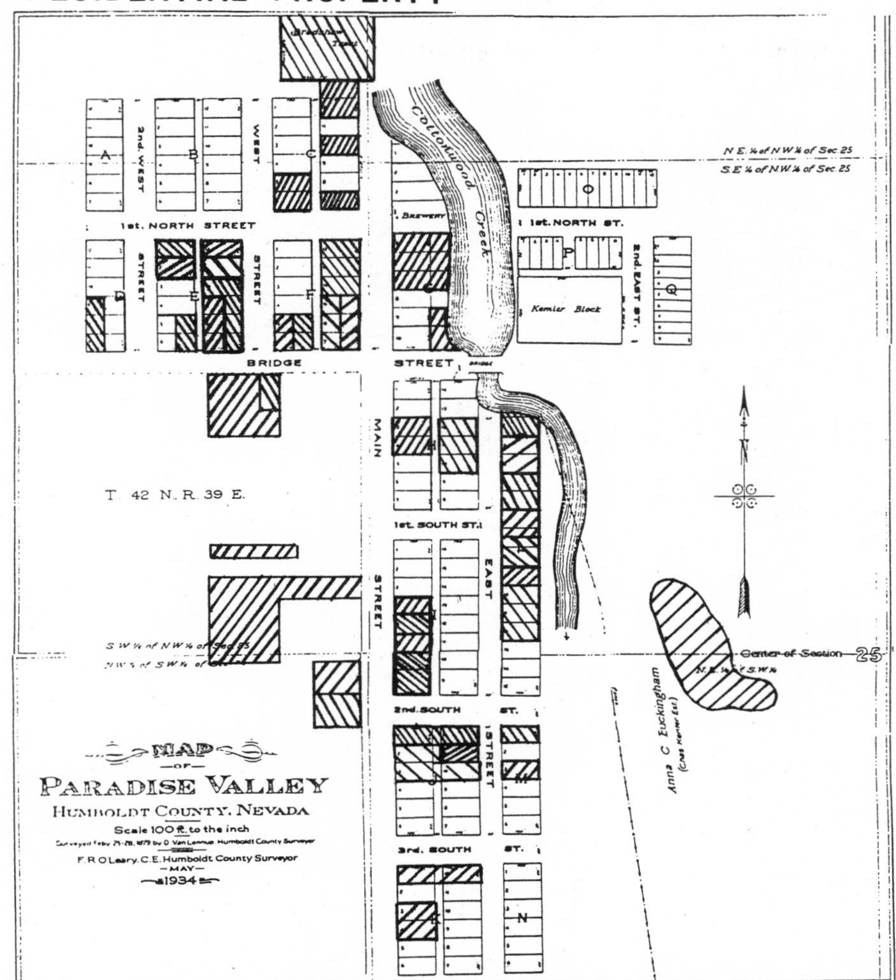

Figure 9.5. Residential property, ca. 1900. Different hatching patterns distinguish individual parcels; irregular circled area to southeast represents location of Chinese laborers' dug-out houses. (Humboldt County Recorder's Office, Winnemucca, Nevada; details added by author)

and third adjacent lots, greatly expanding the available space. New, larger outbuildings sprouted in the larger yards. These new sheds and shops often lay at some distance from the house proper, unlike earlier structures that had clustered near the back kitchen door and the well. Unlike the earlier outbuildings, the new structures had little or nothing to do with domestic chores. Instead, they were barns for livestock, wagon sheds (and later garages) for new vehicles and agricultural equipment, or machine shops that housed the tools and workspaces for smithing or carpentry.

But it is in the houses themselves that the greatest modifications occurred. Here the changes were not just the inevitable additions signaling larger families or greater prosperity. The alterations signaled a new way of living in houses altogether. Between the 1870s and the 1920s, townspeople added just about everything, including bedrooms, bathrooms, kitchens, cellars, parlors, front and back porches, and closets. But fundamental shifts centered around kitchens and parlors, areas at the back and

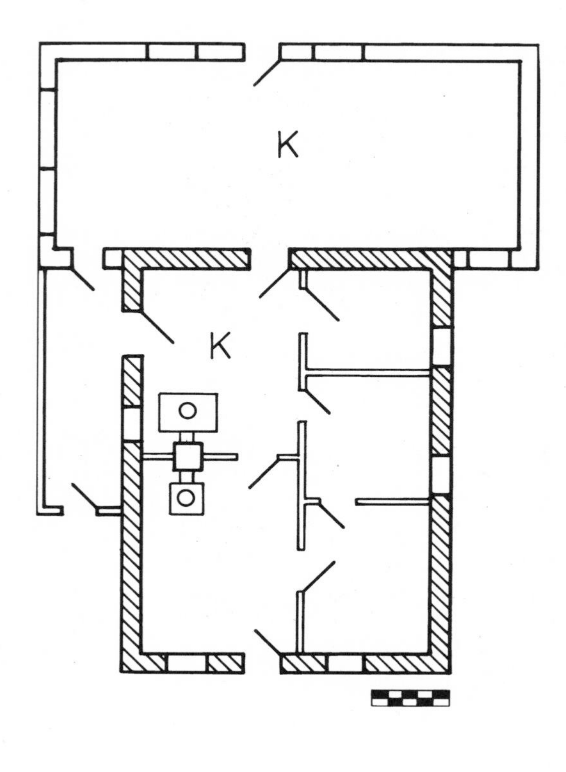

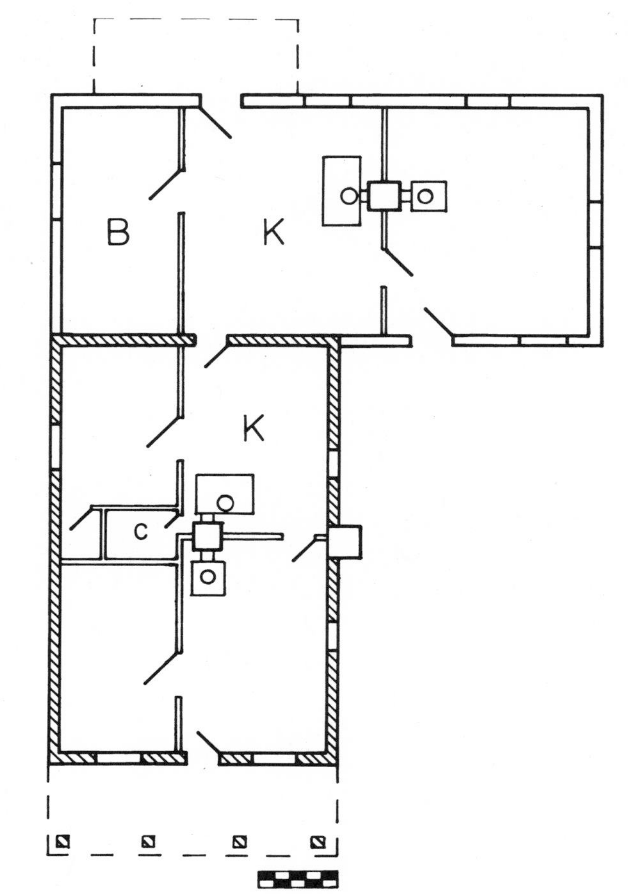

Figure 9.6. Meyer-Echeverria House plan, ca. 1881–1910. (Drawing by Alan Burnett)

Figure 9.7. Freemont-Gastenaga House plan, ca. 1900–1910. (Drawing by Alan Burnett)

front of the house, relating specifically to changes in how the houses were used. In particular, they indicated changes produced by the gender-based definitions of work and activity spheres on the one hand, and the strongly gendered language of the cult of domesticity on the other. But different households chose different additions at different times in their life cycle. The relevance of ethnic and economic difference to the variability of these choices gives some indication of the way that gender interacted with other social factors that made up the small town community.

The greatest number of additions were made to houses between about 1890 and 1910, well beyond the peak years of the cult of domesticity's popularity.[10] In part this lateness may indicate the length of time it took newly immigrated families to develop the capital base needed to build additions and expand their household economies. In part it also indicates a retention of some domesticity ideals locally because of the role they played in competition between households, and in strategies for

Figu-e 9.8. Read-Case House, ca. 1895–1920. (Photo by author)

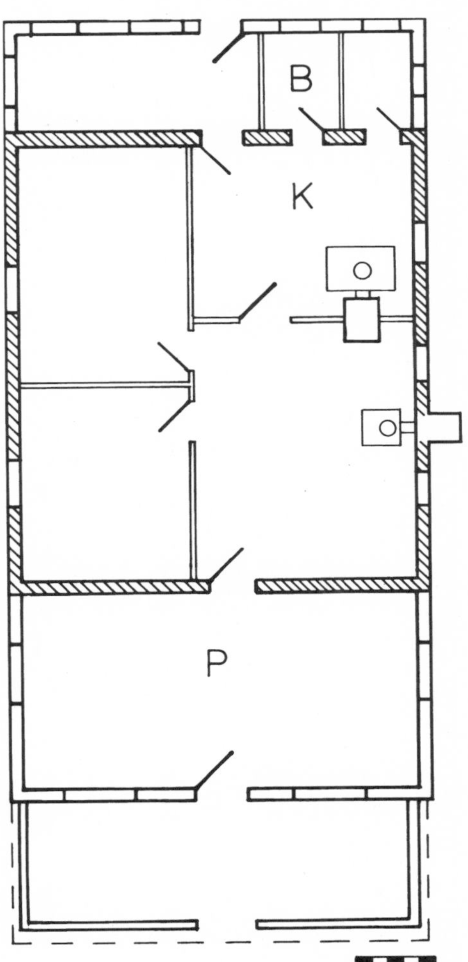

Figure 9.9. Read-Case House plan, ca. 1895–1920. (Drawing by Alan Burnett)

surviving the broader regional and national economic transformations that were stressing town households severely by the early 1900s.

It was the changes made at the rear of houses that document most clearly the kinds of strategies Paradise families employed to weather the economic vicissitudes brought on by the collapse of the local silver boom, a declining water table that removed much of the surrounding valley land from agricultural production, and the general decline of their town as

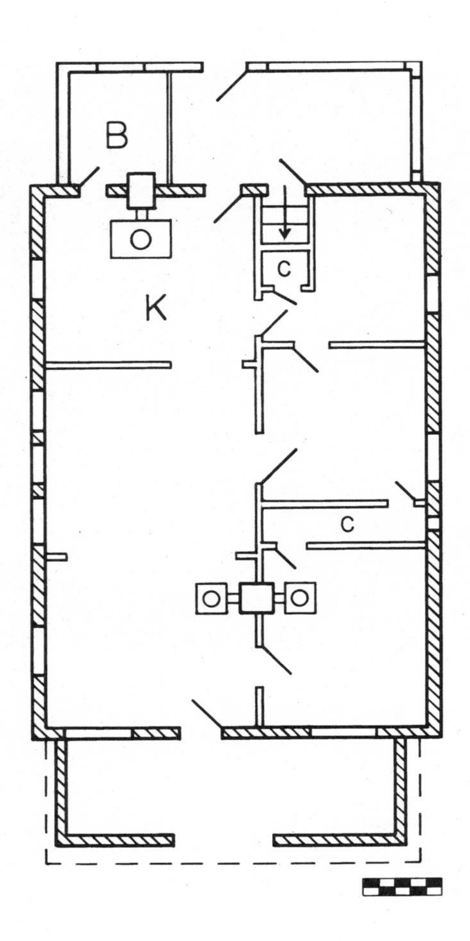

Figure 9.10. Byrnes House plan, ca. 1915–20. (Drawing by Alan Burnett)

a commercial center. At this time, there was a fundamental shift from a more commercial, town-oriented economy to a more agricultural, ranch-oriented one. Townspeople opportunistically combined the partial and often seasonal incomes produced by hauling freight, running small herds of sheep or cattle, or raising hay on outlying valley parcels, as well as working as day laborers on the larger ranches, or practicing crafts such as stonemasonry and carpentry. Many towns and lots became centers of operation for such diverse enterprises by providing storage and maintenance facilities, stabling draft animals and other livestock, or housing production and transportation equipment. This intensified, transitional land use pattern produced the considerably expanded lot sizes and general increases in the number and size of household outbuildings over the earlier, traditionally "urban" land use patterns seen in the more prosperous Paradise of the 1870s and 1880s.

One major impact of larger, more intensively used lots was that activities previously carried on in the back yard moved into the house proper. This shift affected women of the household most, because it was their activities of laundering, food production and processing, and household maintenance, traditionally female occupations, that now moved exclusively indoors to back porches, kitchens, and cellars. In fact, much of the architectural modification to houses took the form of adding new versions of these three rooms, and repeatedly occurred in conjunction with the expanding lot size and increase in outbuilding construction.

The contraction of women's workplaces from the yard into the house took place at least in part through the medium of changing kitchen and household production technologies. By the 1890s the local availability of bigger cookstoves, iceboxes, washing machines, and so on had further specialized the use of kitchen spaces. Period treatises on efficient kitchen organization and the emerging literature on sanitation and germ theory supported the introduction of new appliances, and the reorganization

Figure 9.11. Ugaldea House, ca. 1917–30. (Photo by author)

Figure 9.12. Ugaldea House plan, ca. 1917–30. (Drawing by Alan Burnett)

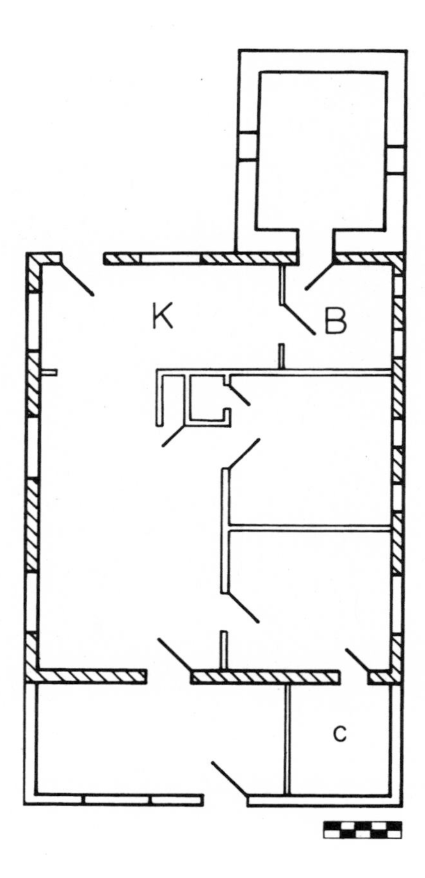

Figure 9.13. Taylor-Riley House plan, ca. 1900–1920. (Drawing by Alan Burnett)

of workspace to accommodate them.[11] Paradise kitchens appear to have followed this national trend to a considerable extent, either by adding entirely new, larger rooms to serve as kitchens, or by adding smaller porches, cellars, or closets to remove other activities from the kitchen proper, and free up more space.

Whole kitchens were generally added to earlier or smaller buildings, such as the Meyer-Echeverria house, ca. 1881–1910 (fig. 9.6) and Freemont-Gastenaga house, ca. 1900–1910 (fig. 9.7). Later or larger houses more often simply got large, enclosed back porches, sometimes accompanied by bathrooms, as in the Read-Case house, ca. 1895–1920 (figs. 9.8, 9.9), Byrnes house, ca. 1915–20 (fig. 9.10), and the very late example of the Ugaldea house, ca. 1917–30 (figs. 9.11, 9.12).

The Ugaldea house also acquired a cellar, a subterranean room used for food storage. Local accounts say the valley's Italian immigrants brought the tradition of building cellars to the area, beginning in the 1860s. Built on ranches as well as in town, a number of examples survive as freestanding structures in back yards, making up part of the domestic outbuildings closest to the house. By the turn of the century, a far more common practice was to attach the cellar to the house proper, with access through the kitchen or (new) back porch. A cellar was even added to an Aladdin prefabricated house, as late as about 1920 (fig. 9.13).

These back-of-the-house additions dramatically altered the patterns of women's daily labor. Some enlarged kitchens seem to have been built to accommodate larger cooking ranges (often with their own chimneys added to exterior rather than interior walls) and new specialized food processing and storage equipment. But even without the new technologies, women's earlier work areas in and around domestic outbuildings were absorbed into the interior of the house and sorted into new, specialized spaces. Perhaps no clearer example exists than the modification to the O'Neal-Harvey house, ca. 1885–90 (figs. 9.14, 9.15), in which a large enclosed back

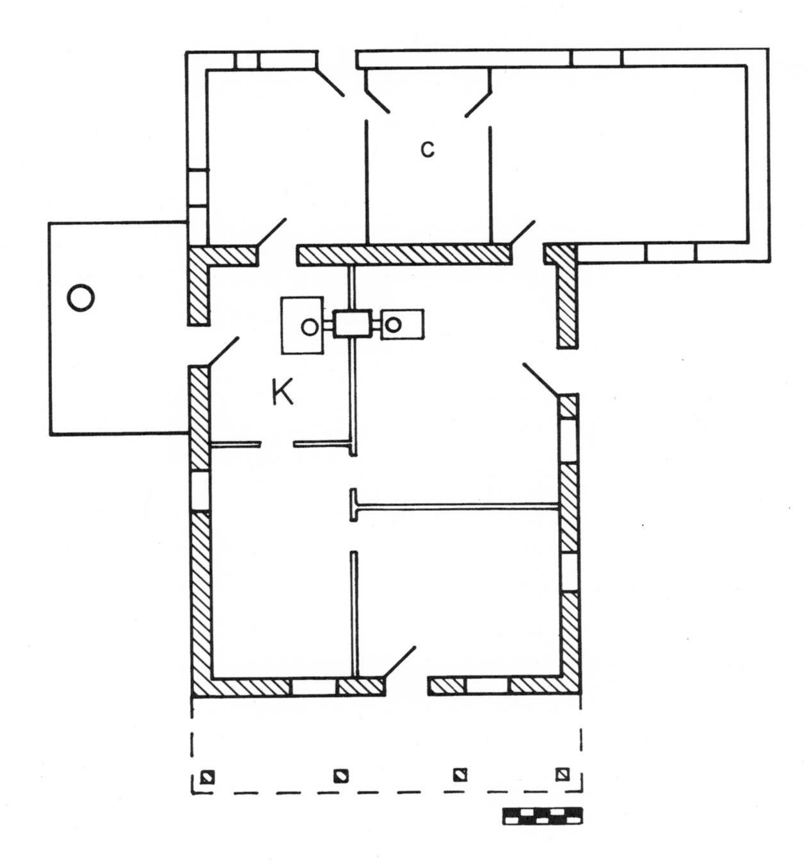

Figure 9.14. O'Neal-Harvey House, ca. 1885–90. (Photo by author)

Figure 9.15. O'Neal-Harvey House plan, ca. 1885–90. (Drawing by Alan Burnett)

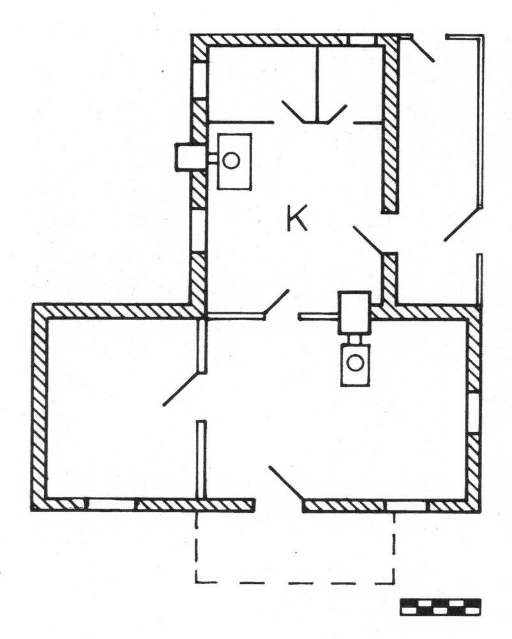

Figure 9.16. Riley House plan, ca. 1910–18. (Drawing by Alan Burnett)

porch was built around the existing outdoor well and pump: not exactly indoor plumbing, but the laundry area was now indoors, not out. Interestingly enough, the O'Neals and the Harveys were ranch families, with large properties in the surrounding valley, so the addition does not indicate a major shift in family occupation. However, at roughly the same time the Harveys enclosed the kitchen pump, they also added a series of large, attached sheds across the back of the property to house equipment used on their ranches and at their newly purchased livery stable next door.

The movement indoors was accompanied by a strong emphasis on more specialized uses of the new rooms, with tasks and equipment sorted between kitchens, cellars, and porches. Similar segregations occurred throughout the house. Many bedrooms were partitioned to create closets at about the same time that other, kitchen-oriented changes were made. The migration of the privy from the back yard into the house (though in most early cases, only as far as the back porch), also brought a new and highly specialized room into play. This perceived need for specialization did not necessarily mean enlargement. At the smallest, poorest house in town that still survives, Lizzie Riley added an enclosed side porch off the kitchen for laundering and two internal pantrylike divisions inside the kitchen that actually decreased the overall size of her room. At the same time, she had a second chimney added to an exterior kitchen wall, possibly to provide more room for a larger stove (fig. 9.16).

To the extent that back porches and cellars, as well as bathrooms and to some extent even kitchens, served to enclose activities that had gone on in the back yard, these additions meant some greater degree of comfort to women's daily labor: outdoor laundering in a Nevada winter could not have been pleasant.[12] The new rooms and their stoves, cabinets, closets, plumbing, or laundry machines also testified to a

Figure 9.17. Ritchie-Harvey House, ca. 1890–1905. (Courtesy Mr. and Mrs. Joseph Boggio, Winnemucca, Nevada)

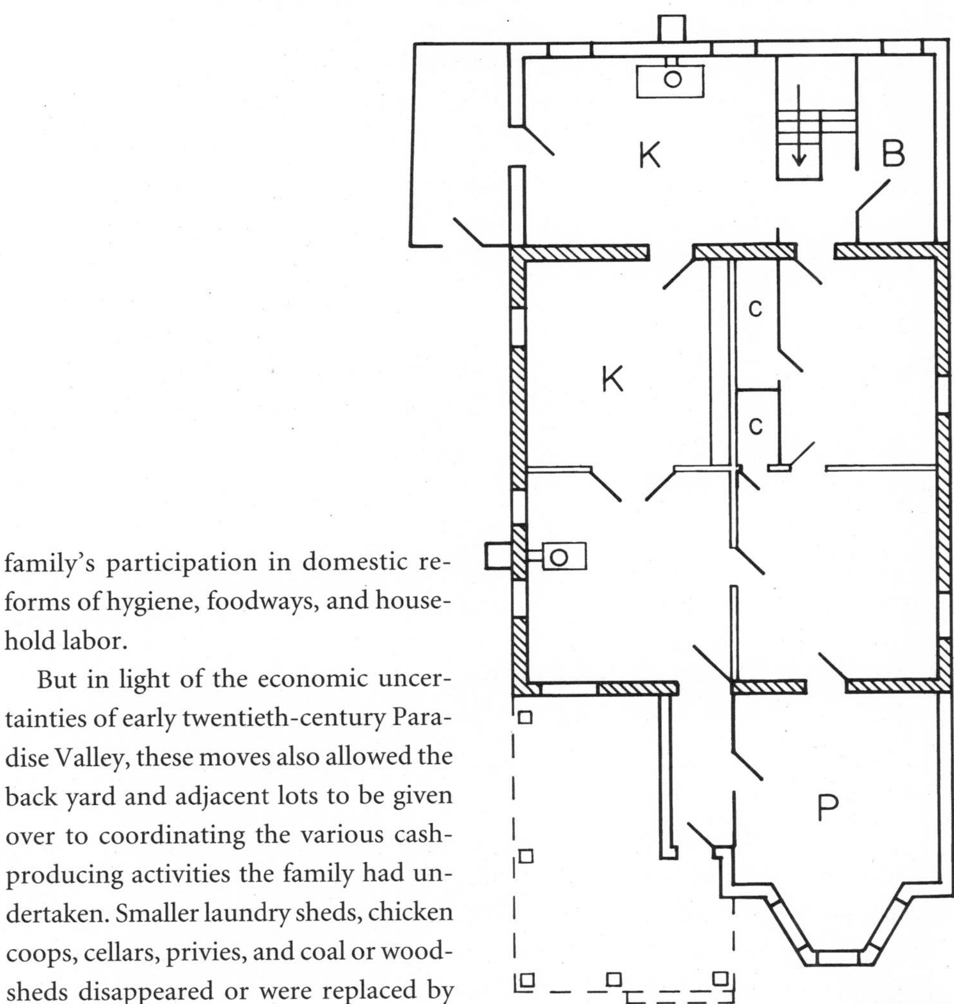

Figure 9.18. Ritchie-Harvey House plan, ca. 1890–1905. (Drawing by Alan Burnett)

family's participation in domestic reforms of hygiene, foodways, and household labor.

But in light of the economic uncertainties of early twentieth-century Paradise Valley, these moves also allowed the back yard and adjacent lots to be given over to coordinating the various cash-producing activities the family had undertaken. Smaller laundry sheds, chicken coops, cellars, privies, and coal or woodsheds disappeared or were replaced by rooms inside the house. Now larger livestock could be stabled; wagons, plows, and reapers sheltered or repaired; carpentry, stoneworking, or smithing workshops operated. This opportunistic strategizing, and the kind of spatial reorganization that accompanied it, shows relatively little social or ethnic variability: to some extent it affected richest and poorest households, newest and oldest immigrant families, Basques, Italians, and Anglo-Americans alike.

Moving from the back to the front of the house, however, the importance of local social distinctions becomes more evident. Paradise residents added parlors and front porches to the fronts of their houses, but far fewer of these additions were made than were kitchen–back porch complexes. Even more important, most Paradise parlors were added at a time when the national popularity of such rooms was declining sharply.[13] These additions were designed explicitly for competitive social display. Exterior ornamentation was important, as was appropriate interior furnishing.

The two most dramatic parlor-porch additions were those made to the Ritchie-Harvey house, ca. 1890–1905 (figs. 9.17, 9.18) and the Read-Case house, ca. 1895–1920 (figs. 9.8, 9.9). Both houses began as relatively large four-room plan structures built by upper-middle and middle-class families, respectively: staunch representatives of the small town's early commercial elite. James Ritchie had been an important town merchant and a justice of the peace. When he died in 1895, his wife, Josephine, listed an estate that indicated the small home contained comfortable, almost luxurious furnishings. These included a cooking stove, two parlor stoves, two beds and bedding, twelve chairs, two tables, five carpets, one sofa parlor set, one lounge, one bureau, one secretary, one clock, lamps, a commode, and a bathtub. These can be compared to the estate left by town blacksmith Capt. James Elliott to his wife, Cassandra, and their four young children in 1882, which consisted of a small house furnished with six chairs, two beds and bedding, one bureau, one wardrobe, a sewing machine, cook stove, and parlor stove.[14]

Rancher and livery stable owner James R. Harvey purchased the Ritchie house in 1905. In spite of the fact that Josephine Ritchie obviously already had a parlor room in the earlier house, the Harveys added a large, new front parlor with bay window, and an L-shaped front porch with turned railings and gingerbread trim. The building's decorative finery matched new imported picket fencing for the front yard. At roughly the same time, a new kitchen, small screened back porch, and bathroom were added to the rear of the house.

The Read-Case house presents a similar story. Irving Case was the son of a prominent local merchant, and by 1919 his father's business partner. In 1920 he and his wife purchased a small four-room house on a back street and moved it to a Main Street lot near the store and other Case family homes. They added a large front parlor and front porch, this time in imitation of the popular bungalow style, more current than the late Victorian finery of their in-laws the Harveys. But the room was still called a parlor, gave pride of place to a grand piano, and was intended to provide family daughters with an appropriate place to court potential spouses.[15]

Oral history accounts of both these cases, as well as two other formal parlors in town houses, similarly associate these rooms, the impetus for their construction, and their intended function with women of the households in their roles as mothers and daughters. Parlors were specifically associated with the family's rising social status, the responsibility of

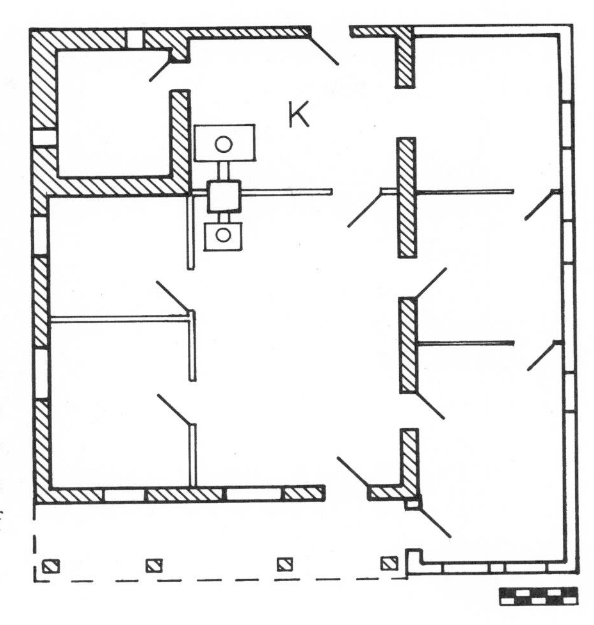

Figure 9.19. Morey-Liotard House plan, ca. 1885. (Drawing by Alan Burnett)

Figure 9.20. The Liotard family in the alley beside their newly clapboarded home, ca. 1910. (Courtesy the late Fredrick Charles Buckingham Sr., Paradise Valley, Nevada)

the women of the household to display that status, and their efforts to maintain and advance it through marriage.

These status-marking functions of women's parlors, as well as the associated front porches and incidental decorative gingerbread, were crucially important in the declining economy of the local town and the increasing competition among local merchants and tradespeople for a shrinking profit base. Although the results of these modifications might not have lifted a house beyond the status of "cottage" to an outsider's eye, in the face-to-face community of the small town, their impact was significant. Everyone would know who had added parlors, and who had not. Parlors and external display also set these houses off sharply from the smaller, less display-oriented town houses being used as bases of operation for widely scattered agricultural and day-labor activities. In those houses, non-kitchen additions were most often bedrooms, which in at least two cases were added deliberately to remove sleeping functions from a central front room, so that guests could be entertained there (fig. 9.19; fig. 9.12).[16] In several such cases, new front porches with decorative trim were added along with the new bedrooms. In the Morey-Liotard example, novelty siding was also added—but only to the front facade and the eastern side most visible from Bridge Street (fig. 9.20). The rest of the house cladding remained board-and-batten.

Ethnicity may also have played a significant role here. The great majority of working-class houses in town were modified by Italian and particularly Basque families like the Liotards, who may have rejected the inclusion of a parlor because of cultural preferences for larger and less formal social gathering places.[17] The differing values that working-class and aspiring upper-class families placed on social display and competition may also have been a factor.

Parlors were added primarily by wealthier German immigrants and by families like the Harveys and Cases who came to Paradise from New York and Ohio. Interestingly, several of the marriage alliances formed by the daughters of these upper-middle-class townspeople in the following generation were not with merchant families, or with other town families at all. Instead, these marriages were between merchants' families and newly successful ranching families. These alliances often crossed ethnic and religious lines, with English-descendant Protestants marrying Italian or Basque Catholics. Ethnicity seems to have been far less a factor than social status, or perhaps economic potential, for the aspiring elite in the declining town.

The increasing importance of parlors and front rooms by the 1910s also paralleled a decline in the more informal public gathering areas that had characterized earlier town life. Open lots near the center of town, which had been used for meeting places and town events through the early 1880s, were sold and fenced off. Free-standing saloon buildings were abandoned or converted to other functions, and the remaining saloon businesses moved inside the larger hotel structures. The hotels themselves were fenced off from the street, excluding their large lots from any informal gathering by a nonpaying public. The size and number of shops and general stores declined sharply, and the earlier encouragement storekeepers had given to multiple uses of their buildings for meeting halls, dances, and informal porch gathering gave way to a more formal restriction to commercial transactions with paying customers.[18]

Oral histories record an increasing emphasis on family gatherings over general public events and a loss of the local community identity as a place that sponsored large public celebrations and gatherings.[19] The shift to family-based gatherings also had the effect of sorting the town population by both class and ethnicity. It was in this context that the rise in popularity of parlors and the less elaborate front rooms took place and, to differing degrees, formalized a place within the home for public gathering.

It is important to reconsider the association of these rooms with women. These accounts come from daughters, grandsons, and nephews living today and may be influenced by romanticized notions of women's roles and activities in the past. Furthermore, these rooms were areas of relative leisure or ceremony, not labor. There are far fewer contemporary accounts explicitly linking parlors and front rooms to town women, or linking women per se to kitchens, back porches, and cellars, for that matter.

Nonetheless, the connection with women in general is a persistent thread through all the descriptions of parlor–front room additions. It may be that the links that parlors and front rooms had with earlier concepts of domesticity (by 1910 somewhat anachronistic) allowed Paradise households from a variety of social and ethnic categories to interpret what was actually an economically negative, socially divisive series of changes as evidence of individual upward mobility and unifying participation in a national popular culture.

In a similarly indirect manner, the removal of women from the back yards of Paradise houses, and the conversion of this space to the workshops and sheds of economic opportunism, apparently did not render the house lot particularly male. People today describe the enterprises run from these lots, the freight lines, sheep herds, and carpentry shops, as family enterprises. Only property is explicitly gendered male: men owned the lots and houses. (At least this exclusively male view of ownership is the case in vernacular parlance; property records regularly indicate otherwise.) But yards did not so much become male territory as they ceased to be female, or at least associated with female labor.

The house proper *did* become an increasingly female place. But the connections remained somewhat abstract, and confounded with the status of the house as display item. It is this double association that lay behind an 1890 newspaper column describing Paradise Valley celebrations of the New Year, which noted that "a number of ladies kept open house and entertained callers."[20] Whether in the case of parlors, kitchens, houses, or yards, gender associations would seem to have been less an explicit statement than the language through which economic decline was translated into prosperity, and social isolation into social aspiration.

Social diversity can be a difficult issue to address in the material culture of the town of Paradise. One can lay aside the homogenizing effect of mass-produced, standardized goods, equipment, and building materials imported great distances in vast quantities to a treeless, nonindustrial desert. But even the objects and material categories that usually provide reliable indices of social or ethnic variety are surprisingly muted.

For example, one of the puzzling things about the domestic architecture in town has always been that it generally fails to reflect, at least externally, the complex ethnic diversity of the nineteenth-century community, or the intense competition that shaped its social categories. Most houses were more or less the same type. This is in sharp contrast to the architectural assemblages of the surrounding ranch lands, which contain a rich array of Italian and Basque structures, and clearly sorted the propertied ranchers from their transient hands and buckaroos.[21]

In like manner, the flexible, opportunistic working world of late nineteenth-century Paradise women and men did not fall neatly into the assumed roles dictated by the cult of domesticity. Women in particular could not be stereotyped in terms of nineteenth-century census phrases like "keeping house." Individual women operated farms, ranches, stage stations, freight lines, general stores, hotels, boarding houses, millinery shops, and telegraph offices, starting as early as the 1860s and continuing through the 1920s and beyond. As family members, women played important roles in the increasingly far-flung economic enterprises of their households.

And yet most of these women's houses would seem to reflect, at least superficially, the basic trends associated with the domesticity movement: the economic restriction of women to the household and their increasingly narrow association with social competition and the enculturation of the young.

In part the reasons for this mutedness may lie in the overall economic trajectory of the town's history. At a general level, the trends in the use of domestic space in Paradise confirm patterns documented for more eastern, urban contexts. But this similarity does not merely mark the upward mobility of individual households or a general increase in the community's participation in a national economy and society. Rather, economic decline forced households of all ethnic groups and social strata into very similar strategies.

Yet this superficial similarity belies a complex set of locally significant differences among individuals, families, households, and occupational groups. Most Paradise residents did not (and could not afford to) move mindlessly into the thrall of a national popular culture, drawn by the ineluctable siren song of Sears Roebuck and

Ladies Home Companion. Instead, they took what was available and made it make sense in a local context of porches and parlors and indoor plumbing. New kitchens and parlors also fit into the expedient innovations of individual household economies and into more subtle, pervasive shifts in where townspeople spent their free time—and with whom. The new rooms marked an ongoing negotiation between local and national culture, public and private spheres of daily life, and male and female spaces and activities. Diversity lay at a much finer and less obvious scale, in the local manipulation of national themes and symbols, and in the material culture that could simultaneously communicate and subtly restate such messages. Over the decades, gender increasingly became the language of both message and material culture, and thus was a vital component of these negotiations. The gendered architecture of local households provided a crucial articulation between these differing scales of nation, region, community, and individuals, and the constant negotiations between social and ethnic groups that made up the social and material life of one small town.

Notes

1. Photograph courtesy of the late F. C. Buckingham Sr. The women are his grandmother Catherine Kemler, his mother, Anna Kemler Buckingham, and his aunt Johanna Kemler, ca. 1875, outside their home in Paradise Valley, Nevada.

2. For some western examples, see Sylvia Van Kirk, "The Role of Native Women in the Creation of Fur Trade Society in Western Canada, 1670–1830," and Susan L. Johnson, "Sharing Bed and Board: Cohabitation and Cultural Difference in Central Arizona Mining Towns, 1863–1873," both in *The Women's West,* ed. Susan Armitage and Elizabeth Jameson (Norman: University of Oklahoma Press, 1987). See also the discussion of ethnic diversity from several perspectives in *Western Women: Their Land, Their Lives,* ed. Lillian Schlissel et al., (Albuquerque: University of New Mexico Press, 1988).

3. Allen Bragg, *Humboldt County 1905* (Winnemucca, Nev.: North Central Historical Society, 1976), 113. For more detailed descriptions of the recorded structures, see Margaret Purser, "Community and Material Culture in Nineteenth-Century Paradise Valley, Nevada" (Ph.D. diss., University of California, Berkeley, 1987), 157–211.

4. Compare Lizabeth A. Cohen, "Embellishing a Life of Labor: An Interpretation of Working-Class Homes, 1885–1915," in *Common Places: Readings in American Vernacular Architecture,* ed. Dell Upton and John M. Vlach (Athens: University of Georgia Press, 1982), 261–73; R. L. Griswold, "Anglo Women and Domestic Ideology in the American West in the Nineteenth and Early Twentieth Centuries," in *Western Women,* 15–34; Roy Rosenzweig, *Eight Hours for What We Will: Workers and Leisure*

in an Industrial City, 1870–1920 (Cambridge: Cambridge University Press, 1983); John M. Vlach, "The Shotgun House: An African-American Legacy," *Pioneer America: Journal of Historic American Material Culture* 8 (1976): 47–70; Gwendolyn Wright, *Building the Dream: A Social History of Housing in America* (New York: Pantheon Books, 1981).

5. For a discussion of the development of domesticity as a historical phenomenon, see Mary Ryan, *Cradle of the Middle Class: The Family in Oneida County, New York, 1790–1865* (New York: Cambridge University Press, 1981); for a related concept, see Barbara Welter, "The Cult of True Womanhood," *American Quarterly* 18, no. 2 (summer 1966): 151–74.

6. For example, Wright, *Building the Dream;* Daniel P. Handlin, *The American Home: Architecture an Society, 1815–1915* (Boston: Little, Brown, 1979); Clifford E. Clark, "Domestic Architecture as an Index to Social History: The Romantic Revival and the Cult of Domesticity in America, 1840–1870," in *Material Life in American, 1600–1860,* ed. Robert Blair St. George (Boston: Northeastern University Press, 1988), 535–49; for rural midwestern material see Sally McMurry, *Families and Farmhouses in Nineteenth-Century America: Vernacular Design and Social Change* (New York: Oxford University Press, 1988).

7. Griswold, "Anglo Women and Domestic Ideology"; Judith A. McGaw, "No Passive Victims, No Separate Spheres: A Feminist Perspective on Technology's History," in *In Context: History and the History of Technology, Essays in Honor of Melvin Krantzberg,* Research in Technology Series, no. 1 (Bethlehem, Penn.: Lehigh University Press, 1989): 172–91; Ryan, *Cradle of the Middle Class;* for contemporary references see Catherine Beecher and Harriet Beecher Stowe, *The American Woman's Home* (New York, 1869).

8. For positions in the debate that discuss western examples, see Elizabeth Jameson, "Women as Workers, Women as Civilizers: True Womanhood in the American West," and Rosalinda Mendez Gonzalez, "Distinctions in Western Women's Experience: Ethnicity, Class, and Social Change" both in *The Women's West.*

9. See James Borchert, "The Alleys of Washington," *Landscape* 23, no. 3 (spring 1979): 3–10; John W. Reps, *The Forgotten Frontier: Urban Planning in the American West before 1890* (Columbia: University of Missouri Press, 1981).

10. Where possible, dates for individual additions will be given. (In the text, the first date is the approximate date of construction, the second the date of additions). The habit of renting or leasing rather than buying houses, which increased following the turn of the century, means that much of this information comes from oral history rather than property records and refers to the period of tenancy by a particular family, rather than a more precise reference to specific years of construction or alteration.

11. Compare McMurry, *Families and Farmhouses,* 103–29.

12. For descriptions of the daily round of chores that made up women's labor on the late nineteenth-century frontier, see *So Much to Be Done: Women Settlers on the Mining and Ranching Frontier,* ed. Ruth B. Moynihan et al., (Lincoln: University of Nebraska Press, 1990), particularly 59–109, 147–66.

13. See McMurry, *Families and Farmhouses,* 135–76.

14. James Ritchie probate document, 1895, Humboldt County Courthouse, Winnemucca, Nevada; James Elliott, probate inventory, 1882, Humboldt County Courthouse, Winnemucca, Nevada.

15. Interview with Geraldine Harvey Boggio, Winnemucca, Nevada, 6 September 1984.

16. Interviews with Gerald Edwards, Paradise Valley, Nevada, 16 June 1984; Virgil Ugaldea, Paradise Valley, Nevada, 16 June 1984.

17. Cohen, "Embellishing a Life of Labor."

18. For further details on this process of change in the commercial architecture of the town, see Purser, "Community and Material Culture."

19. Interviews with Albert Pasquale, Reno, Nevada, 23 August 1983; Ernest Miller, Paradise Valley, Nevada, 28 June 1984; Leslie Stewart, Paradise Valley, Nevada, 1 July 1984.

20. An item in a column authored from Paradise, entitled "A La Mode" in the Winnemucca (Nevada) *Silver State,* 4 January 1898, p. 3.

21. Compare Howard W. Marshall and Richard Ahlborn, *Buckaroos in Paradise: Cowboy Life in Northern Nevada* (Washington, D.C.: Library of Congress, 1980); Marshall, *Paradise Valley, Nevada: Ethnicity and Vernacular Architecture of an American Place* (Tucson: University of Arizona Press, forthcoming).

Urbanization

Figure 10.1. The Real Estate Associates (T.R.E.A.), 2643–2667 Clay Street, San Francisco, 1874–75. (Photo by author)

CHAPTER TEN

The Real Estate Associates

A Land and Housing Developer of the 1870s in San Francisco

ANNE BLOOMFIELD

From the acquisition of California by the United States in 1846 until the great earthquake and fire of 1906, San Francisco grew from a sleepy town of fewer than 500 inhabitants to a proud metropolis of 350,000.[1] This growth created a sixty-year-long housing boom that, as in other cities such as New York and Boston, slowed only during depressions.[2] Almost nothing has been known about the builders. This chapter reviews work and circumstances of the most productive builder from the middle period of these sixty years, the Real Estate Associates (T.R.E.A.) (fig. 10.1).

Before the boom, about 250 houses "of all descriptions" were scattered thinly about the townsite, most of heavy frame construction, some of adobe. Those who stayed in San Francisco during the gold rush instead of going to the diggings were too busy making money from the transients to pay much attention to their own shelter. "Whole streets are built up in a week and whole blocks swept away in an hour . . . a large portion of the fixed inhabitants live in tents and places which cannot be described with any accuracy."[3] Since all were intent on making money quickly, wives and families were left behind, the hotel or boarding house became a way of life, and the market for family housing—such as the rows then going up in New York, Boston, and Philadelphia—was minimal.[4]

Speculation in vacant land flowered in San Francisco, aided by surveying efforts that established rectangular grids. The first survey, made in 1839 during the Mexican possession of California, laid out a few blocks, not quite aligned to north, measured in Spanish varas (1 vara = 2.75 feet). Each block contained six lots of 50 varas, or 137.5 feet to a side, making blocks 275' x 412.5'. In 1847 another survey continued this pattern, locating Market Street at a diagonal to the other streets and on the route to the old Franciscan Mission church. The 1849 survey extended the grid of six 50-vara lots and divided the south of Market area into 100 x 100-vara lots, six to a block. Speculators were soon dividing 50- and 100-vara lots into smaller parcels of various sizes; later builders of mass housing followed their example.[5]

San Francisco's first speculative housing tract was erected early in 1850. The previous November, merchant William Howard had received a consignment of twenty-five prefabricated houses shipped from Boston. They were clapboard with peaked roofs and Gothic trim. Howard set most of them up south of Market Street, a good half a mile away from the main settlement.[6]

Even farther away was the best-known early housing tract, South Park, a speculation of pioneer industrialist and businessman George Gordon. "Tract" is hardly the word for these elegant, two- and three-story houses built of stuccoed brick. Gordon planned his development for the elite, included fire ordinances and zoning restrictions, and carved an oval park out of the center of the 100-vara block. With George H. Goddard as architect, the first seventeen houses went up during the winter of 1854–55, completing one-fourth of the intended London-style crescents. Gordon's plan succeeded, in that South Park did become the city's "center of fashion" in the 1850s and 1860s. But the unimproved lots sold slowly, so that less than half the intended development was built.[7]

Most other early San Francisco developments were like those of the Mount Vernon Proprietors on Beacon Hill in Boston or John Jacob Astor in New York: the speculators acquired land, laid out streets, subdivided and sold lots for houses.[8] The Hayes Tract, for example, was a 160-acre square two miles west of the city hall. Thomas Hayes, county clerk from 1853 to 1856, very likely arranged some deal with mayor T. C. Van Ness. In 1859 Hayes commenced construction of a railway from the main city through the sand hills where Market Street was supposed to be and out beyond his tract. Van Ness accepted a block from Hayes and built his residence facing the wide avenue that bears his name. Hayes himself lived on the next block north. He reserved nearly two blocks in the western part of the tract for the Hayes Park Pavilion, a public pleasure grounds served by a spur of his Market Street Railway. In 1859, the remainder of the land was offered at public auction in 27.5 foot lots, but not many purchasers came forward. Housing was slow to develop so far out from the business district (fig. 10.2).[9]

Hayes may have offered his lots just a bit too soon. The population growth that could support such far-flung speculation was recorded in the censuses: 35,000 in 1852, 57,000 in 1860, 149,000 in 1870, 234,000 in 1880, 299,000 in 1890, and 343,000 in 1900.[10] However pattern-setting the gold rush may have been, the 1860s and 1870s witnessed the greatest increases in San Francisco's population during the nineteenth century, creating the greatest pressure for new housing.

Each *San Francisco Directory* of these two decades boasted about the increases in new buildings erected since the previous *Directory* (fig. 10.3). It can be assumed that almost all the brick buildings listed were for downtown businesses, since wooden

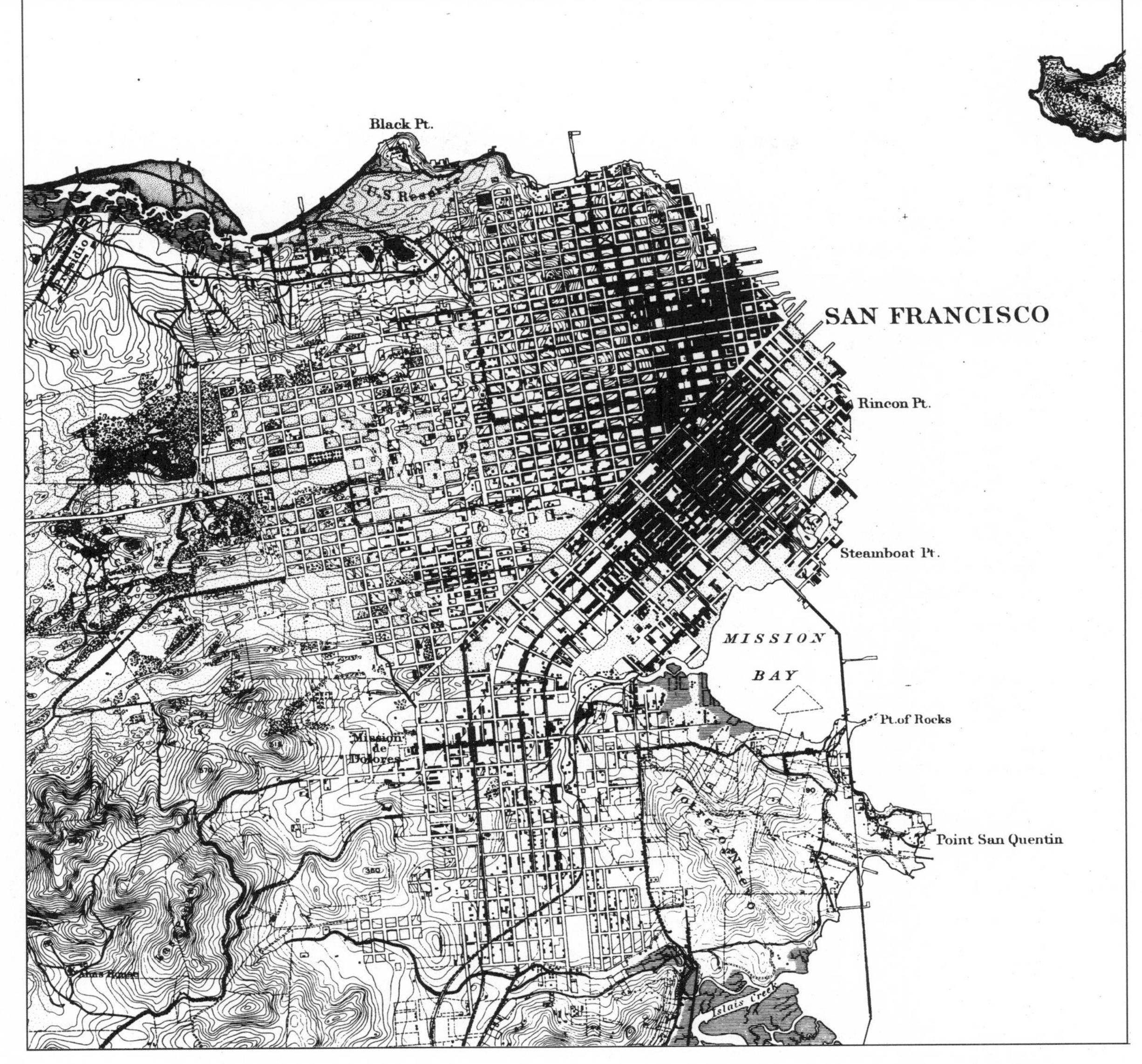

Figure 10.2. San Francisco, northeast portion, showing improvements through 1867–68. (U.S. Coast Survey, 1869; courtesy Bancroft Library, University of California, Berkeley)

buildings were forbidden in a thirty-block area at center city since 1853. But wood was preferred for housing because it had proved safer in the 1868 earthquake and was assumed to promote a healthy living environment. Moreover, it was inexpensive, could be easily ornamented, and assured low insurance rates due to a well-organized fire department. Even discounting for editors' boastfulness and for claim shanties and factory buildings, a considerable number of wooden residences were erected, a reflection of population increase and economic cycles.[11]

The wooden residences of the 1860s were modest affairs, many of them "cottages," or one-story dwellings. In 1861 Judge H. C. Hastings had "a number" of four-room cottages built south of Market, and made a profit renting them at ten dollars a month. Others followed his example. The 1861 *Directory* remarked upon "the celerity with which long rows of houses spring up." Advertisements mention rows of four or five houses. A 1912 observer remembered "nothing statistically star-

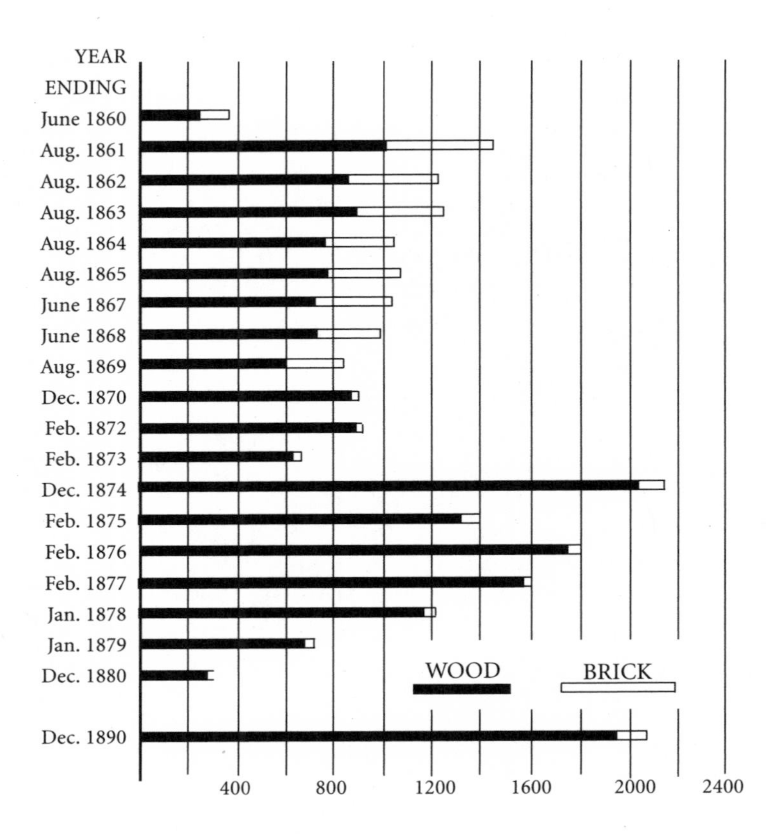

Figure 10.3. Number of buildings erected in San Francisco, 1860–80, 1890. (Graph by author; compiled from data in Langley, *San Francisco Directory;* Bishop, *Directory of San Francisco;* Lewis Publishing, *The Bay of San Francisco*)

tling or architecturally exceptional during the decade."[12] Otherwise little is known about the houses of the 1860s. As the city grew, cottages were replaced by larger structures; moreover, the area where most of them were located was destroyed by the fire of 1906 (fig. 10.2). Those single houses that remain exhibit the lag in house fashion, compared to the East Coast, which Baird and Kirker discuss.[13] Most are in a chaste Italianate style. The flat facade has three window or door openings on each floor; siding is laid horizontally; the roof is expressed in a gable or concealed behind a decorative cornice.

Additional houses were produced by the popular "homestead associations." About 170 of these corporations were formed in the 1860s in order to turn a profit by breaking up large landholdings and encouraging house-lot ownership among workingmen. The "health" and "advantages" of this system were well publicized. The officers would buy a piece of land outside the settled area. Membership was usually bought with an initial fee or deposit of ten to one hundred dollars and monthly payments of ten dollars. When the appropriate sum was collected, the member received title to a lot. Some then built houses.[14]

By 1870 a new type of development, speculative building, had come into its own. The *Directory* of December 1869 reported that architects Johnston and Mooser were putting up a block of eight three-story frame houses (across from today's Hilton Hotel) and that a builder was offering six two-story houses six blocks to the west. The next summer, twenty-four cottages served by horse cars were being sold on a block not far from the old Mission church. The first well-known example of speculative building was put up during the summer and fall of 1870 by David Farquharson (1827–1914), architect of the Bank of California, with the fashionable jeweler J. W. Tucker apparently providing financial backing. Later known as Tuckerville, the development covered one Western Addition block with forty semidetached, bay-windowed cottages, of which only 2209 Jackson remains. Like the homestead association lots, these were sold for a down payment, the remainder to be met in monthly installments with interest. A newly opened extension of a horse car line ran within a block of the property.[15]

Another new extension of the same line ran near the first development of T.R.E.A. Companies such as Rondel's Homesteads and individuals like Henry T. Hinkel were buying 50-vara and larger lots and putting up several houses on each; but the more than one thousand houses erected by T.R.E.A. during the 1870s stood unchallenged for a decade. In 1875 the company claimed to have built more detached houses than any other person or company in the United States in a similar time span.[16] Its work includes familiar rows of detached, nearly identical, Italianate houses such as those on Clay Street facing Alta Plaza Park (fig. 10.1), in the 100 block of Guerrero Street, and on Bush Street between Fillmore and Cottage Row.[17]

The houses were located for the most part on sand west and southwest of the already built up area and well beyond the business district (fig. 10.2), but near street railway lines (fig. 10.4).[18] Such land could be bought cheaply. T.R.E.A. purchased tracts sometimes by the 50-vara lot, sometimes by the whole block, and then subdivided them into appropriately sized lots. It pioneered quality housing in the Mission and Western Addition, two areas immediately west and southwest of the thickly inhabited area. Many T.R.E.A. houses still stand and are still used as residences.[19]

Typically, the company would build a group of virtually identical, detached houses, all with the same setback and equally tall, forming long horizontal lines of cornices and door hoods or marching up a hill in equal steps (figs. 10.1, 10.5, 10.6). The appearance of most of these streetscapes has been changed by alterations, such as stuccoing or raising a house to admit a garage under the bay window. Except for the corner house, each unit along the street had a door on the same side of the facade. A narrow side yard and a bay window or a pair of windows were placed on the other side. The corner house had the bay window toward the side street, but often T.R.E.A. sold the corner as a vacant lot intended for a store. Occasionally it built the store, like Basford's, "one of the most tastily built drugstores in town," which was located at the southeast corner of Bush and Fillmore Streets (demolished).[20] The corner separated streets of more and less expensive houses. Perhaps unconsciously, T.R.E.A. was following principles of Georgian town planning by providing for a whole community: a few larger and several medium-priced houses on the more important streets, slightly less expensive houses on the side streets, inexpensive houses on interior streets that the company cut through the block.[21] Space for markets was also included. The Associates planted evergreens around one block and promised blue gum trees around another, "to add to its attractiveness and health."[22]

T.R.E.A. came near to completing this kind of town planning only once, on the block bounded by Mission, Valencia, Twentieth, and Twenty-first Streets. About

Figure 10.4. San Francisco, northeast portion. Locations of lots with houses built and sold by T.R.E.A. shown by solid areas; street railway routes shown by dotted lines. (Base, R. J. Seib, “Map of the City and County of San Francisco,” Bureau of Engineering, City and County of San Francisco, 1974; street railway routes after *Disturnell's Strangers' Guide to San Francisco and Vicinity,* San Francisco, 1883. Street railway routes and shading for T.R.E.A. areas added by author)

Figure 10.5. T.R.E.A., 929–945 Valencia Street, San Francisco, 1876–77. (Photo by author)

1 June 1875 the company purchased this block for $170,000, less a 40-foot lot on Valencia and subject to a lease on the southern half. The nursery lessee was paid off about six months later for $6,000.[23] Immediately after the original purchase, T.R.E.A. began opening "two narrow streets . . . through the block" and subdividing the whole into about 120 lots (fig. 10.7).[24] House construction must have been begun right away, for the first house, on Twentieth, was sold late in October 1875. By the end of the year six more, on Mission, had found buyers. In 1876 T.R.E.A. sold 8 houses on Mission, 9 on Twentieth, 10 on Twenty-first, 14 on Valencia, 27 on one of the interior streets, and 14 on the other. In 1877 a dozen more houses were put up. After that the company's fortunes produced only resales and a few sales of lots, including three to its plasterer, Henry Helgoth. In sum, T.R.E.A. sold 99 houses on this land for a total of $495,187, or an average of $5,000 apiece.[25]

The most valuable properties of this or any block were the corners, locations

Figure 10.6. T.R.E.A., 330–342 Lexington Street, San Francisco, 1876–77. (Photo by author)

with more light and with commercial possibilities. Here were found the largest lots, 24.5' x 85' to 50' x 90', as well as the highest prices, an average of $9,990. Not a single corner house remains intact, but the prices indicate that they were elaborate, and some were described as "palatial." The original owner-occupants were a real estate office (not T.R.E.A.'s), a couple of grocers, all with residences upstairs, a street contractor, an iron works proprietor, a master mariner, and a salesman.[26]

The price of houses not located on corners was determined by the importance of the street. Mission stood first and foremost. T.R.E.A. subdivided the frontage into lots 25' x 90' and 35' x 90'. On the smaller lots it built its usual houses, but on the larger lots villas, a more expensive and spacious type.[27] The houses cost an average of $7,368 and must have been heavily ornamented. All have been demolished. Owner-residents included an attorney, a photographer, a druggist, and a foundry owner.

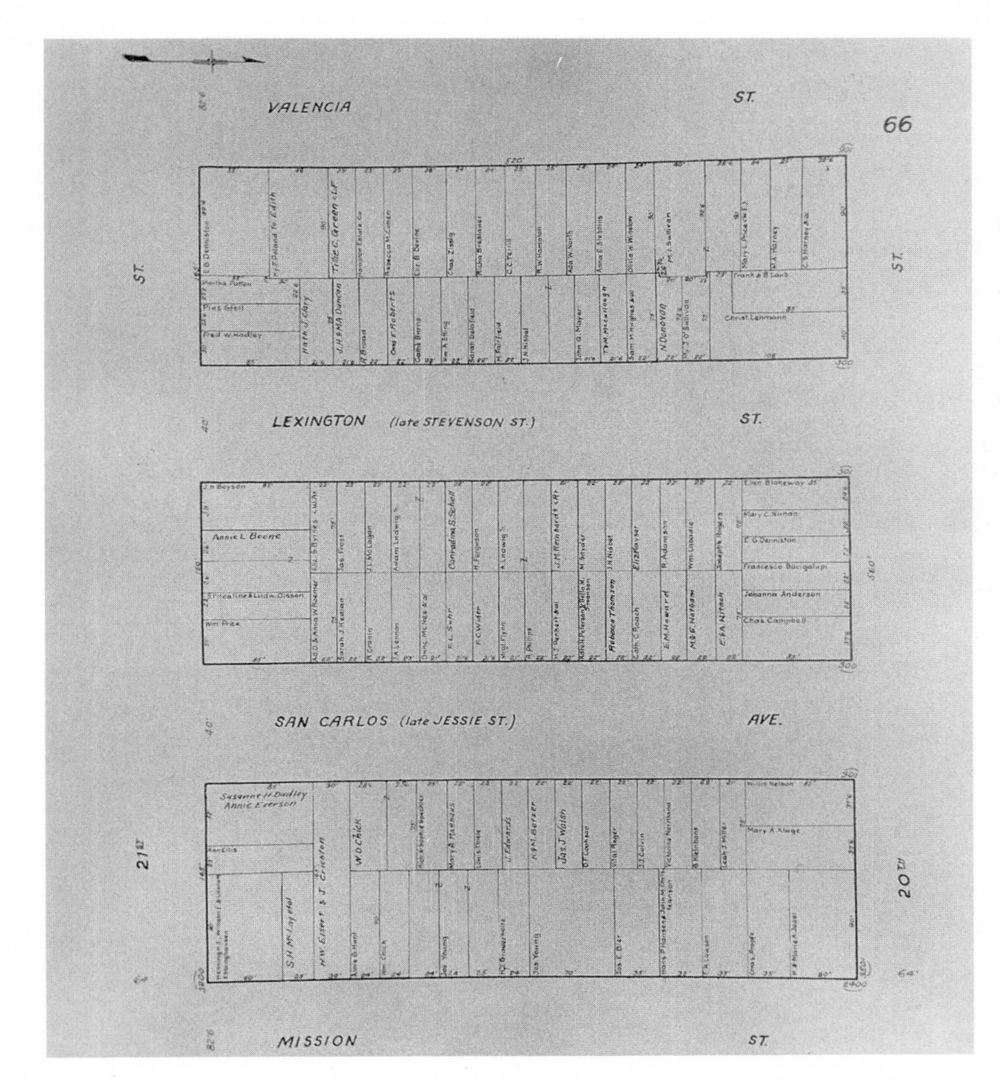

Figure 10.7. San Francisco, block bounded by Mission, Valencia, Twentieth, and Twenty-first Streets, as subdivided by T.R.E.A., 1875–76. (From *Mery's Block Book of San Francisco,* 1909, p. 370) (Courtesy San Francisco Public Library; photo by John Lewis Beckham)

Valencia Street was next in the social and economic hierarchy. Its lots were about 25' x 90'. The houses cost, on the average, $5,841 and had bay windows and conspicuous porticoes (fig. 10.5). The original owner-residents included a lumber dealer, a railway freight agent, a ship joiner, a physician, and several clerks.

Twentieth Street followed in importance, with an average house cost of $5,146; then Twenty-first at $4,576. Lots on both streets had frontages of 22' to 37.5' feet and an 85-foot depth. Probably all the houses had bay windows; some entrances boasted porticoes, others simpler door hoods; some were villas. T.R.E.A.'s customers here included barbers, an attorney, and a teacher.

The Associates cut two narrow streets through the block and named them Jessie, now San Carlos, and Stevenson, now Lexington. It subdivided them into lots about 22' x 75' and charged an average of $3,697 on Jessie, the street nearer Mission, and

Figure 10.8. T.R.E.A., doorway, 1689 Sutter Street, San Francisco, 1875. (Photo by author)

$3,350 on Stevenson. These smaller houses had a reduced version of T.R.E.A.'s typical uniform setback and walkway south of each house (fig. 10.6). Most of these houses remain. All have Italianate details; a few boast arched pediments over the windows. Some on San Carlos have bay windows, all on Lexington have flat facades. The buyer residents were craftsmen, small proprietors, engineers, foremen, and teachers.

Figure 10.9. John Remer for T.R.E.A., 2315–2319 Webster Street, San Francisco, 1878. Original selling prices, *left to right:* $3,800, $4,100, unknown. (William Hollis' residence, 1878–85, mortgage $2,000). (Photo by author)

The company built its houses in the prevailing local fashion so that they are hard to distinguish from their contemporaries. All are made of wood; they have brick foundations, ten- to fifteen-foot ceilings, and are never more than two stories; false fronts mask gable roofs; entrances are up a few steps from the street; detailing is Italianate; and more often than not, a semi-octagonal bay window rises the full height of the house. Invariably the siding was "channell rustic," horizontally laid.[28] Usually an acanthus leaf terminated the door hood bracket (fig. 10.8). The heavy cornices were always the same. One favorite T.R.E.A. device was to alternate details along a particular street, for instance every other house having a bay window (fig. 10.1) or a particular shape of lintel (fig. 10.9).

The house with the bay window would be the more expensive; purchasers could choose variations and pay for extras both inside and out. The expensive houses would have features such as entrance porches, Corinthian columns, dentil moldings, pediments, marble fireplaces (fig. 10.10). When the company was cutting costs for the mass market, it would simplify the ornamentation: moldings around windows instead of colonnettes and cut work, rectangular windows instead of arc-headed, and generally fewer decorative elements (fig. 10.9). All facades were, in Sir John Summerson's term, "collated" from standard offerings of local mills.[29] Some very inexpensive T.R.E.A. houses were described in a local newspaper:

> Each building is two-story, and will have a front stoop, circular arch to the door, double bay windows with corniced segment heads, and a well-finished entablement. The interior will contain a staircase hall and four good rooms on the first floor, while on the second-story there will be three roomy apartments, in addition to a bathroom and closets. Nothing in the shape of ornature will distinguish the interior, all rooms being plainly plastered.[30]

In a very few locations T.R.E.A. built "villas" on lots at least thirty-five feet wide. These house were different in appearance from the usual Italianates. The gable end of their roofs was prominent and the plan L-shaped. Bay and entrance were separate, one-story pieces. The remaining three are textbook examples of the American Italian Villa of the 1850s and 1860s (fig. 10.11).[31] Each is an asymmetrical grouping of rectilinear blocks, which individually are symmetrical. The roof is picturesque, with deeply projecting overhang and eaves supported by brackets. There is a pair of windows and a bay window. However the T.R.E.A. Italian villas lacked tower and veranda. They had eight or nine rooms and cost five thousand to seven thousand dollars. The company built fewer than forty, and later builders did not repeat the type, presumably because its wider lot requirement meant fewer houses could be sold on a given street frontage.

The plan of a typical nineteenth-century San Francisco house contained entrance

Figure 10.10. T.R.E.A., 1712 *(left)* and 1710 Bush Street, San Francisco, 1875. Original selling prices: $10,498 and $9,025, respectively. (Photo by author)

Figure 10.11. T.R.E.A., Villa 2373 California Street, San Francisco, 1876. (Photo by author)

hall and stairs on one side, rooms on the other.[32] Center rooms received light from windows facing a narrow side yard. The house seldom stood more than two stories high, since it could have plenty of well-lighted rooms on each floor. T.R.E.A. used this standard plan and in addition created its own standard relationship to light (fig. 10.12). Bay and side windows admitted maximum light by being placed to the south on north-south streets, or to the east side on east-west streets. Thus the hall was on the north or west side of the house, along the lot line, leaving open yard only to the south or east. Windows facing west were avoided because San Francisco's pronounced westerly winds in the afternoon, combined in that era with great expanses of sand, made them unpleasant and dirty.

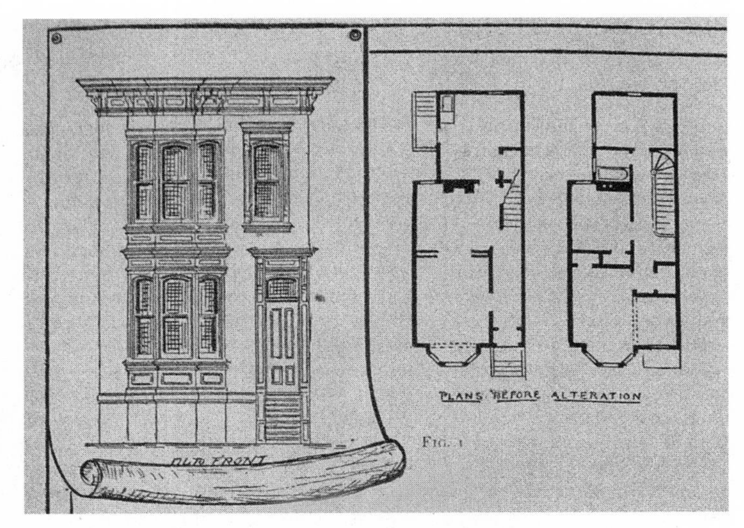

Figure 10.12. T.R.E.A., northeast corner of Twenty-first and Bartlett Streets, San Francisco, 1876; demolished. (From *California Architect and Building News,* plate 6, August 1885, p. 133) (Courtesy Judith Lynch)

The Associates advertised its houses as "of modern style and finish" and having "modern conveniences." Listings for its very first houses, fifteen of them at the northwest corner of Sacramento and Fillmore Streets, invited prospective purchasers to the office "to examine plans."[33] These plans, which did not change during the decade of the Associates' activity, may have come from a pattern book, a company director in the real estate business, or the director who had been a house carpenter in the 1850s.[34] Each house contained six to ten rooms. A T.R.E.A. specialty, even for inexpensive houses, was stairs that curved at the top (figs. 10.12, 10.13). Outside, decorative features did not intrude on the facade's architectural lines. Post and lintel were never broken by lozenge or keystone, and a one-story bay window was seldom built on a two-story house. If bands were indicated for the colonnettes between bay windows, they were placed at the middle sash line. This relative restraint in ornamentation characterizes a T.R.E.A. house.

Although the company publicized its reliance on the architectural profession, the influence is not discernible. The first architectural notice, in 1875, concerned two houses on Sutter built "to order from designs drawn by the architect of the Associates."[35] This was Silas P. Ford, who listed himself as an architect, but only in the 1875 *Directory.* He was really a carpenter-builder-contractor who served from 1874 into 1876 as the superintendent of T.R.E.A.'s Building Department. Probably Ford's designs concerned only ornaments and interior arrangements for customers who were buying unfinished houses.

The first professional architect known to be associated with the company was David Farquharson, who designed not its houses but its office building. His name is

Figure 10.13. T.R.E.A., 1513 Golden Gate Avenue, San Francisco. Stairs seen from entrance hall. (Photo by author)

shown as architect on Eadweard Muybridge's photograph of the T.R.E.A. Building (fig. 10.14). New York theater architect John A. Remer worked on the Associates' later houses. The 1878 *Directory* reported that T.R.E.A.'s "plans, elevations and working drawings are prepared by John A. Remer, the well-known architect of Baldwin's Hotel, who is regularly employed by the company."[36] On 12 January 1880 Remer received fifteen dollars for "Buildings Jackson and Webster," a residual payment as the last of those houses had been sold ten months earlier, and fifty-five dollars for "Buildings Sutter and Buchanan," less than 1 percent of the money T.R.E.A. spent at that location.[37] Remer had his office gratis in the T.R.E.A. Building, bought two T.R.E.A. houses on Buchanan Street, and lived in one of them with his wife and five children from 1878 to 1881.[38] However, the houses Remer worked on (fig. 10.9) are indistinguishable from the company's earlier ones.

The Real Estate Associates was incorporated in September 1866 as a modest enterprise, listed in directories with the homestead associations. The certificate of incorporation declared its business to be the buying, selling, improving, and managing of real estate, and lending money thereon. The stock certificates bore the motto "Land is the basis of all security." In its first year and a half of existence, less than $30,000 was paid in as stock subscriptions; it borrowed an equal amount and spent over $36,000 on real estate. Sales came to only $303. The founding directors were all small fish in the San Francisco pond, four of them bookkeepers, four in insurance, and three in real estate. The president was shortly to open a men's clothing store that still exists, Bullock and Jones. At first the Associates merely bought and sold unimproved land, often breaking tracts into house-sized lots as the homestead associations did. It turned a profit of $116,500 in 1869, the company's only acknowledged net profit on record.[39]

The new decade brought changes. The number of directors decreased, and most of the original ones were replaced by men who could help the company's new venture, house building. B. H. Freeman owned a firm of stair builders, scrollsawyers, and wood turners, and D. A. MacDonald a planing mill. Maurice Dore was a real estate auctioneer, William Sutton bookkeeper of a lumber company. Edward Barry and William Hollis were real estate specialists. C. S. Swenson had money from a waterfront boarding house to invest. None of them appears to have had much, if any, experience in construction. Profit from increasing land values continued to be the company's main interest, and it built houses only on its own land.[40]

These men ventured slowly into house construction. The first dwellings were begun some time in 1870. Their design matched that of T.R.E.A.'s later work (fig. 10.15). In November of that year, the Associates advertised for "subscribers" to houses being built at the northwest corner of Sacramento and Fillmore Streets. In June and July 1871 it sold a complete row of eight detached houses on Sacramento, five on Fillmore, and one each on Clay and Steiner. Of these fifteen buyers, eleven were connected in one way or another with T.R.E.A.'s business. Three owned planing mills, one was a plumber, another a city surveyor, and another the financial editor of the *Daily Evening Bulletin*. The lumber dealer received his house as a "gift." T.R.E.A. directors Hollis, MacDonald, Freeman, and Sutton bought adjacent houses. They were not speculating. Of the fifteen buyers, fourteen moved in immediately, and

Figure 10.14. David Farquharson, T.R.E.A. Building, 230 Montgomery Street, San Francisco, 1876–77; demolished. (Courtesy California Historical Society, San Francisco; photograph by Eadweard Muybridge, FN-16621)

four of them were still there ten years later. Three had moved into other T.R.E.A. houses.[41]

With the start of house construction, the company also began its only structure erected on land other than its own. The lot probably belonged to the New Montgomery Street Real Estate Company, a speculation of William Ralston and Asbury Harpending, which was spending $2,000,000 of the Bank of California's money buying and developing a south-of-Market extension to the main business street. T.R.E.A. president Dore was their auctioneer, and he may have arranged the contract for the Associates on the east side of New Montgomery Street from Minna to Natoma. The two-story brick building was capped by a mansard roof. The second floor contained a hall for the Grand Army of the Republic. This venture presumably generated less profit than the houses, because T.R.E.A. did not construct any more business blocks except, at the height of its activity, its own office building.[42]

Figure 10.15. T.R.E.A., 2564 Sacramento Street, San Francisco, 1871. One of the first group of houses. (Photo by author)

In 1872 the company continued to build and sell houses on its block of land and commenced work near the Hayes Park Pavilion. The next year the Associates purchased its first tract south of Market Street, built and sold 18 houses on it, in addition to houses at other locations. Remarkable increases continued through 1874 and 1875. After that banner year, in which about 350 houses were sold, T.R.E.A.'s activities dwindled until its bankruptcy in 1881.

On the crest of its prosperity in 1875, the company decided to construct its own office building in the heart of the business district. One day late in April, T.R.E.A. bought two parcels from capitalist Daniel Meyer. One was a full Western Addition block where the company immediately erected ten-room houses on 27.5-foot lots. The other was a 44-foot frontage on Montgomery Street across from the Nevada Bank due to open in October, around the corner from the Stock Exchange's building site, and next door to the location where the Mills Building would go up in 1892.

On this $138,000-lot the company decided to erect the Real Estate Associates Building, 230 Montgomery, which would house its own offices as well as a great deal of rental space (fig. 10.14).[43]

Architect David Farquharson designed a flat-fronted, six-story building whose window size and narrow supporting members suggest an iron frame, though contemporary reports speak of a brick building with granite front and slated mansard. Farquharson had already placed bearing columns in the brick walls of the Nevada Bank, which were revealed by the 1906 earthquake. A combination of Greek Revival and Second Empire motifs decorated the building.[44]

Of the $90,000 in construction costs, the facade's incised and carved granite accounted for $25,000. It came from G. Griffith's quarry at Penryn, Placer County, California, which was supplying granite for San Francisco's U.S. Mint (1869–74), its third city hall (1870–94), the stock exchange (1875–77), and portions of the wooden mansions of Stanford, Crocker, and Hopkins. The high-ceilinged interior was served by an elevator and housed numerous offices, all of which were leased for a monthly total of $2,400 during the first year.[45]

All the company's activities must be credited to the initiative of one man, William Hollis (1839–95) (fig. 10.16). T.R.E.A.'s manager throughout its existence, its secretary (1866–73), and president (1874-82), Hollis was "the life and soul of that concern." Born in Iowa en route from Canada, Hollis was the second child in a pioneer family of six. In the year of his birth, his father and uncle settled beside the Mississippi in Elk River Township, Clinton County, Iowa, and helped incorporate it. At the age of thirteen, William come overland to California and searched for gold in Michigan Bluff, Placer County. In 1861 he married Sarah Favor, teacher of German and daughter of an obstetrician there. Probably he spent his entire life west of the Mississippi and never saw the East Coast prototypes of the housing tracts for which he was responsible.[46]

In 1860 Hollis moved to San Francisco and read law. He also served as a clerk, a mining secretary, and a clothing store manager. From 1862 through 1866 he was statewide secretary of the Sons of Temperance, a national, fraternal organization strong enough to have carried the gold country in an 1855 state plebescite for a dry law. Later he joined the Masons. He seems to have drifted into real estate first as a sideline, involving himself with several homestead associations. As president of the Central Park Homestead Association, which had a tract on the north slope of Hunters Point, and secretary-manager of T.R.E.A., he finally moved into real estate full time and stayed there.[47]

Unassuming and "a genial companion," Hollis became "one of the best judges of real estate in this city."[48] He was known for his energy, clear judgment, and ability to buy land cheaply. He was proud to sell houses to "serve the great middle class" and "transform the sandy wastes outside the business part of the city into . . . neighbor-

Figure 10.16. William Hollis, *San Francisco Call,* 30 June 1895, p. 7. (Courtesy Bancroft Library, University of California, Berkeley)

hoods, composed of frugal and industrious people."[49] The 1877 *Directory* presents Hollis as an idealist, who early in 1871 drove the editor out to see three blocks of land the company had acquired. Nothing but sand met the eye. But Hollis "rose up in his buggy" and excitedly proclaimed his vision of creating a community and, given a little more land, of bringing "'the whole of San Francisco out here to reside.'"[50]

This idealism was combined in Hollis with some ruthless and shady business practices. The best demonstration of them appears in the transcript of a land title lawsuit, *Voll vs. Hollis.* Hollis had agreed to purchase land on Buchanan Street if the seller could get clear possession. The process of getting possession came to resemble a grade-B western, with destruction by night, forcible takeover by day in overwhelming numbers, and unceasing armed watch, all punctuated by gunshots that may or may not have been random. Hollis remained in his office downtown and paid his combatants' wages. But when the contesting claimant arrived with police to arrest the participants, who should turn up but William Hollis, with a buggyload of silver, in boxes, for bail. His timely arrival suggests collusion with the police. The rival claimant was told to give up, as "that is the man who runs the Courts," and "here is the money that can take any land, that can buy judges and juries."[51] Hollis won the case.

His knack for getting T.R.E.A. noticed in the press has provided virtually all that is known of the company's finances. A huge publicity article in *Resources of California,* April 1877, timed just before the opening of the T.R.E.A. Building, included extracts from financial statements for the calendar years 1867 through 1876. Thomas Magee, in his *Real Estate Circular,* summarized financial reports for the company's best years, 1869, 1874, 1875, and 1876.[52] It is quite possible that these figures were manipulated to show the company in the most favorable light. For instance, dividends were paid in 1872, 1873, 1875, 1876, and 1877, when the company appears not to have been making a profit. Either the "dividends" were what would now be called interest on deposits, or the company paid them out of capital to bolster the price of its stock by artificially stimulating stockholder confidence. Some additional financial information can be computed from the company's fifteen-page "cash book," covering 19 December 1879 through 24 March 1881, during which time its activities subsided from little to nothing.

From such sources, T.R.E.A.'s financial structure can, in part, be analyzed. It began with capital listed at $120,000, subscribed in monthly payments by stockholders. By 1869 that amount had been doubled twice through new stock issues. The 1875 report claimed a capital stock of $1 million. The company earned income from rents, commissions, interest, profits on land sales, and monthly mortgage payments. In addition, standard bank loans were necessary because Hollis constantly bought land, paying out more than twice the value of his land sales each year through 1872, and well over $1 million in 1875 alone. The company also advertised for funds to be invested in it by prospective customers. It issued special "homestead shares" of stock that were to be paid in monthly installments and exchanged as the down payment on a T.R.E.A. house. Later, customers were invited to deposit funds with the Associates as if it were a bank.[53]

Consideration of the interest paid on these accounts illustrates T.R.E.A.'s fiscal fragility. The company received interest on mortgages and on moneys it deposited with banks. It paid interest to its own depositors and to the banks from which it borrowed money. For interest paid and that received the rates were the same, 8 to 10 percent a year, the local standard.[54] The company made no allowances for its own administrative expenses and usually operated with a fairly heavy debt load. If the San Francisco real estate market had continued rising as it did in the late 1860s and mid-1870s, T.R.E.A. might have been able to pay its real debt costs out of sales at increased land values. Without such rises, the debt load spelled trouble.

The financial reports also show the depth of the company's commitment to land. Estimated value of its real estate never dropped to below 58 percent of assets, and it was 82 percent of assets, or $1,517,450, at the end of 1876, the last year for which information is available. Each year T.R.E.A. bought as much land as possible, $90,000 to $1,090,592 worth, in cash. Most of the purchases were in the Mission or the Western Addition, some in such marginal areas as the vicinity of cemeteries or the lot claimed by the city for a hospital (now Duboce Park). Tracts ranged in size from a 50-foot street frontage to three contiguous 254' x 412.5-foot blocks (fig. 10.4). Often the Associates had to purchase a single parcel from several different claimants, but it sold the product with clear title.

Following purchase, work began on grading, made easier by the sand that covers most of San Francisco. However, in one known case, the block just south of Market Street across from the present U.S. Mint, T.R.E.A.'s laborers removed serpentine

Figure 10.17. T.R.E.A., retaining wall, 1848 *(left)* and 1836 Pine Street, San Francisco, 1875. (Photo by author)

rock thirty feet deep in just one month. In another case, a still-extant retaining wall had to be built on Pine Street, west of Gough (fig. 10.17).[55]

Construction would begin as soon as title was clear. On one tract, house frames were going up within a week of purchase. On another, forty-one houses were completed five months after purchase. Obviously some sort of mass production was taking place, and construction went on at several locations at once.[56]

The Associates constructed its houses by standard methods, with balloon frames. The first known superintendent of the Construction Department was Silas P. Ford (1874–76). After him came John B. Gonyeau (1877–81). Both men had previous experience as carpenters and struck out on their own as master builders after working for T.R.E.A. With foremen, they supervised up to three hundred or four hundred "mechanics" at a time, hired directly by the company in all crafts except plumbing, and collectively paid ten thousand dollars a week. The company boasted that its workmen were all "day labor."[57]

Wages for day labor came to about one-third of construction costs. Another third was spent on lumber—T.R.E.A.'s suppliers had mills in Mendocino, California, where redwoods grow (John Kentfield and Co.), and in Tacoma, Washington (Hanson, Ackerson and Co.). An eighth of construction costs paid for millwork (mills such as D. A. MacDonald's Enterprise, and B. and J. S. Doe). The rest went to suppliers of plumbing, paints and oils, glass, and hardware.[58]

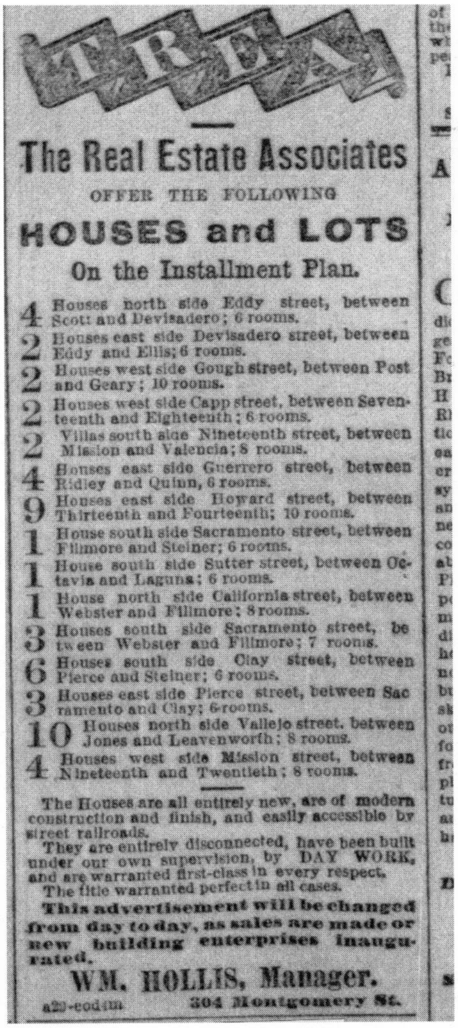

T.R.E.A.

The Real Estate Associates

OFFER THE FOLLOWING

HOUSES and LOTS

On the Installment Plan.

4 Houses north side Eddy street, between Scott and Devisadero; 6 rooms.
2 Houses east side Devisadero street, between Eddy and Ellis; 6 rooms.
2 Houses west side Gough street, between Post and Geary; 10 rooms.
2 Houses west side Capp street, between Seventeenth and Eighteenth; 6 rooms.
2 Villas south side Nineteenth street, between Mission and Valencia; 8 rooms.
4 Houses east side Guerrero street, between Ridley and Quinn, 6 rooms.
9 Houses east side Howard street, between Thirteenth and Fourteenth; 10 rooms.
1 House south side Sacramento street, between Fillmore and Steiner; 6 rooms.
1 House south side Sutter street, between Octavia and Laguna; 6 rooms.
1 House north side California street, between Webster and Fillmore; 8 rooms.
3 Houses south side Sacramento street, between Webster and Fillmore; 7 rooms.
6 Houses south side Clay street, between Pierce and Steiner; 6 rooms.
3 Houses east side Pierce street, between Sacramento and Clay; 6 rooms.
10 Houses north side Vallejo street, between Jones and Leavenworth; 8 rooms.
4 Houses west side Mission street, between Nineteenth and Twentieth; 8 rooms.

The Houses are all entirely new, are of modern construction and finish, and easily accessible by street railroads.

They are entirely disconnected, have been built under our own supervision, by DAY WORK, and are warranted first-class in every respect.

The title warranted perfect in all cases.

This advertisement will be changed from day to day, as sales are made or new building enterprises inaugurated.

WM. HOLLIS, Manager.

a29-eod1m 304 Montgomery St.

Figure 10.18. T.R.E.A., advertisement, *San Francisco Chronicle*, 9 May 1875. (Courtesy San Francisco Public Library; photo by John Lewis Beckham)

To find buyers for all these houses, T.R.E.A. advertised liberally and held auctions almost annually. The monthly *Real Estate Circular* carried adds for the first houses and later a brief announcement. The *Daily Morning Call* published T.R.E.A. ads two or three times a week from October 1871 through December 1878 (fig. 10.18). Headed by the T.R.E.A. logo, these ads emphasized buying on "the installment plan." Their most obvious feature was the lists of locations where houses were being offered for sale. One or two of the five to sixteen locations might feature villas. The fine print mentioned convenience to street railways, title, day labor, the company supervision, and that the houses were all new, detached, and modern. Similar ads were found in the *Examiner,* the *Chronicle,* and the *Bulletin.* The very last T.R.E.A. ad was a three-line mention in the "Improvements in Progress" column of the June 1880 *California Architect and Building Review.* There were also ads for auctions, held in April 1873, November 1875, April 1877, February 1878, and March 1879. Each auction had its own catalogue, detailing payments and showing maps of all the blocks where property was being offered.[59]

Customers usually bought T.R.E.A houses as their own residences. People listed in the *Newsletter* as buyers of the firm's more expensive houses, $6,000 and up, appeared in directories as doctors, lawyers, mining secretaries, "capitalists," publishers, proprietors of stores and factories, and the Spanish consul. The least expensive houses, $2,500 to $4,000, attracted buyers who were craftsmen or in jobs such as were noted on Jessie and Stevenson Streets. Inexpensive houses on Webster were bought by a bartender, a starch factory worker, a plumber, and a porter. One $3,000 house on Pearl Street was bought and lived in by Denis Kearney, drayman, soon to be the famous sandlot orator, a founder of the local Workingmen's Party which elected a San Francisco mayor and passed a new state constitution.[60]

Some consistency existed among buyers on particular streets. People tended to buy near friends and relations, and the limited price range on one street would group buyers of similar means. In addition, certain social restrictions may have been imposed or encouraged by the company in its efforts to boost sales. The 1870 ad promised the first house subscribers a chance to approve all subsequent subscribers. This sentence never appeared again, perhaps because it proved too cumbersome or hindered sales. However, names of a single nationality dominated some T.R.E.A. streets. For instance, Irish names were listed as buyers on the east side of Valencia Street north of Twenty-first, and German names on the same side of the same street in the next block south.

Most of the customers took advantage of T.R.E.A.'s installment plan method of purchase. The company's advertising stressed the ease of payment: only one-fifth to one-half the purchase price down, the rest paid over one to twelve years in monthly installments that included interest of 8 to 10 percent a year. T.R.E.A. claimed that "not over one-third [of its customers] could have ever hoped to have owned a home" were it not for the company's mass construction economies and, especially, financing.[61] The Associates held the mortgages, rather than conveying them to banks, which permitted greater latitude in accepting risks in order to sell more houses, but also proved vulnerable to depression.

Holding mortgages may be considered one of the company's fatal weaknesses, along with borrowing too much at high rates, charging insufficient interest on mortgages, spending more each year for land and construction than sales brought in, and perhaps pricing houses too low in relation to costs. These weaknesses and a four-year-long depression caused the end of the Real Estate Associates.[62]

When mining stocks fell precipitously in January 1877, involving most of the populace, Hollis responded energetically and immediately by selling undeveloped lots in greater numbers than his usual practice. It was not enough. Too many mortgages had to be called in, no one was willing to buy, and construction had already been reduced drastically. T.R.E.A. had to suspend the June 1877 dividend. It hung on, with occasional spurts of activity, but virtually ended all business except sales in November 1878.[63]

Hoping to hang on until the economy would permit him to recover, Hollis took evasive action.[64] After being ousted and reinstated as president, he founded a new company, the Real Estate and Building Associates, incorporated in November 1879 with the same purposes as T.R.E.A. Capital stock worth five hundred thousand dollars was paid in, 99 percent by Hollis. The directors were Hollis's brother, two T.R.E.A. directors, two friendly T.R.E.A. creditors, T.R.E.A.'s long-time secretary Luis Emilio, and John B. Gonyeau, superintendent of the Building Department. All of them, and all the T.R.E.A. directors, owed money to the original company, assets mentioned to the note-holders but never used to pay them. And of course the Building Associates' capital was really the assets of T.R.E.A., as it were, smuggled out to escape creditors. T.R.E.A. stockholders were urged to trade for Building Associates stock. On 1 March 1880 the T.R.E.A. directors resolved to sell a lot of property, including the T.R.E.A. Building, to Hollis for five hundred dollars. He, in turn, sold it to the Building Associates, which proceeded to do what business it could.[65]

On 16 April 1880 the state legislature entered the picture by passing an Insolvent Act. A number of legislators had been elected by the Workingmen's Party, inspired by T.R.E.A.'s former customer Denis Kearney. The Insolvent Act of 1880 was easy on individual debtors (that is, workers) and hard on corporations. If one of the latter went bankrupt, its assets would be sold and distributed to creditors, but it still could not be declared free of debt. Since no corporation would voluntarily go through this process, five or more creditors could petition a court to declare their debtor bankrupt.[66]

And so it happened to T.R.E.A. On 26 February 1881 five creditors petitioned superior court judge Charles Halsey for the bankruptcy of the Associates. He appointed a receiver, attorney William Hale, who had sold the company many land claims, including the disputed land in *Voll* vs. *Hollis.* That very day Hale took possession of the T.R.E.A. Building. Within a week he changed the safe combination, fixed locks, and installed a twenty-four-hour guard with bedding. Hollis made such difficulties about handing over rent and other assets that he was jailed for contempt of court early in May 1881; he got out two months later on habeas corpus petition to the state supreme court. The in-court wrangling and out-of-court evasions continued until the final appeal was turned down. In the squabbling over the remains, some creditors seemed to hope Hollis could recoup the losses, and some simply wanted what money was left.

While this farce was being played out, house construction in San Francisco was recovering from the depression. The *Directory* of April 1880 noticed the first signs: "An almost new town has within a year or so sprang up at the south-western outskirts of the Mission, between Twenty-fifth, Thirtieth, Guerrero and Sanchez streets. The buyers and builders were all people of small means." The 1880s and 1890s became San Francisco's great era for house construction. Over ten thousand of these residences remain, more than three times the number of survivors from the 1860s and 1870s. In the later two decades, six hundred owner-builders have been identified, outstanding among them the Rountree Brothers, who bettered T.R.E.A.'s record, and Fernando Nelson, this city's most prolific nineteenth-century builder, responsible for over four thousand houses.[67]

Amid all this activity the Real Estate Associates were forgotten. But this company had contributed a great deal to the development of San Francisco. It spread more than one thousand houses in the first of "those endless rows . . . which ran in undulant streamers across the empty spaces of the Western Addition."[68] Its impression on the business community earned the flattery of imitation in name as well as in methods, by the Mechanics Real Estate Association, the Installment Homestead Union, and the San Francisco House and Loan Association.[69] It enabled many people of modest means to become homeowners in complete communities. Its model of the setback streetscape near public transportation with houses priced for the mass market was followed by most later builders in San Francisco. To this day, more than two hundred of the Associates' houses provide people with attractive, comfortable, practical living space.

Notes

This article grew out of research I did for the San Francisco Landmarks Preservation Advisory Board under the direction of G. Bland Platt, Albert Shumate, and Edward Michael. For encouragement and suggestions, I thank Richard Longstreth.

1. Gladys Hansen, *San Francisco Almanac: Everything You Want to Know about the City* (San Francisco: Chronicle Books, 1975), 10.

2. Charts of house construction in Charles Lockwood, *Bricks and Brownstone: The New York Row House, 1783–1929* (New York: McGraw Hill, 1972), 77, 254; Bainbridge Bunting, *Houses of Boston's Back Bay: An Architectural History, 1840–1917* (Cambridge, Mass.: Harvard University Press, 1967), 5; Sam B. Warner Jr., *Streetcar Suburbs: The Process of Growth in Boston, 1870–1900* (New York: Athenaeum, 1973), 44.

3. James M. Parker, *San Francisco Directory, 1852–1853* (San Francisco: Monson Haswell, 1852), 6–7; Harold Kirker, *California's Architectural Frontier: Style and Tradition in the Nineteenth Century* (Salt Lake City: Peregrine Smith, 1973), 26–28; Charles P. Kimball, *San Francisco Directory* (San Francisco: Journal of Commerce Press, 1850), 3.

4. Henry G. Langley, *San Francisco Directory*, indicates in 1861, 340 hotels and boarding houses (p. 15), and in 1868, 614 boarding houses (p. 53); B. F. Lloyd, *Lights and Shades in San Francisco* (San Francisco: Bancroft, 1876), 450–51; eastern mass housing seems to have been almost entirely row houses; see Charles Lockwood, *Manhattan Moves Uptown: An Illustrated History* (Boston: Houghton Mifflin, 1976); Lockwood, *Bricks and Brownstone;* Sarah Bradford Landau, "The Row Houses of New York's West Side," *Journal, Society of Architectural Historians* 34 (March 1975): 19–36, hereinafter cited as *JSAH* with vol. and date; Bunting, *Houses of Boston's Back Bay;* Warner, *Streetcar Suburbs;* Warner, *The Private City: Philadelphia in Three Periods of Its Growth* (Philadelphia: University of Pennsylvania Press, 1968); William John Murtagh, "The Philadelphia Row House," *JSAH* 14 (December 1957): 8–13; T. Kaori Kitao, "Philadelphia Row House: Is It Peculiarly American, or Even Uniquely Philadelphian?" *Swarthmore College Bulletin* 74 (April 1977): 6–11; Kenneth Ames, "Robert Mills and the Philadelphia Row House," *JSAH* 27 (May 1968): 140–46. *Avery Index to Architectural Periodicals* (Boston: G. K. Hall, 1973) lists nineteenth-century articles on row houses in Chicago; Omaha, Neb.; Newark, N.J.; Hartford, Conn.; St. Louis, Mo.; St. Paul, Minn.; Yonkers, N.Y.; and Arlington, Brookline, Roxbury, and Somerville, Mass. (12, 531–33).

5. Hansen, *San Francisco Almanac,* 130; Paul W. Gates, "Carpetbaggers Join the Rush for California Land," *California Historical Quarterly* 56 (summer 1977): 98–127.

6. Kirker, *California's Architectural Frontier,* 39–40; Parker, *San Francisco Directory, 1852–1853,* 13.

7. Albert Shumate, *The California of George Gordon* (Glendale, Calif.: Arthur H. Clark, 1976), 119–39; Kirker, *California's Architectural Frontier,* 68–69, plate 21.

8. In the first half of the nineteenth century the Mount Vernon Proprietors syndicate bought land on what is now called Beacon Hill, leveled it, laid out streets, and sold house lots, building a few houses as stimulation for further development. See Bunting, *Houses of Boston's Back Bay,* 27–28; Allen Chamberlain, *Beacon Hill: Its Ancient Pastures and Early Mansions* (Boston: Houghton Mifflin, 1925), 26, 44, 61–62, 92–93, 161–62, 187–89. In the same period, John Jacob Astor frequently bought large tracts on Manhattan, well north of the developed area. He would wait some years, lay out streets, and sell house lots at fantastic profits. See Lockwood, *Manhattan Moves Uptown,* 57–58, 68; Christopher Tunnard and Henry Hope Reed, *American Skyline* (Boston: Houghton Mifflin, 1956), 67–68.

9. Letter by Frank McCoppin of 1894 quoted in Edgar M. Kahn, *Cable Car Days in San Francisco* (1944; reprint, Oakland, Calif.: distributed by Scrimshaw Press for Friends of the San Francisco Public Library, 1976), 10–13; H. A. Cobb, *Great Peremptory Sale of 1000 Homestead Lots in the Hayes Valley Tract . . . on Saturday, June 11, 1859* (San Francisco: B. F. Sterrett, 1859), Collection, California Historical Society, San Francisco; *Map of the Hayes Tract,* ca. 1861, Collection, California Historical Society, San Francisco; Edward A. Morphy, "San Francisco's Thoroughfares," *San Francisco Chronicle,* 30 June 1918, 7 July 1918, 14 July 1918, Scrapbook,

California Historical Society, San Francisco, pp. 4, 12–18; Langley, *San Francisco Directory, 1860,* passim.

10. Figures rounded off from Hansen, *San Francisco Almanac,* 10.

11. Frank Rivers, *San Francisco Directory* (San Francisco: Le Count and Strong, 1854), 214; Langley, *San Francisco Directory, 1860,* 21; *1861,* 19; *1862,* 21; *1863,* 6; *1864,* 10; *1865,* 4; *1867,* 15; *1868,* 3, 19; *1869,* 21; *1871,* 25–26; *1872,* 3, 18; *1875,* 3, 14–15; *1876,* 3, 13; *1877,* 3, 11; *1878,* 3, 11; *1879,* 11; Bishop, *San Francisco Directory, 1875,* 11–12; *The Bay of San Francisco* (Chicago: Lewis Publishing, 1892), 278. In the nineteenth century, economic cycles in California differed from those in the East. The Civil War had very little effect in California, and the panic and depression of 1873 were not felt until the late 1870s. California alone experienced a depression following the completion of the transcontinental railroad in 1869.

12. Langley, *San Francisco Directory, 1861,* 16; *San Francisco Daily Morning Call,* 5 December 1861, 3; 12 September 1868, 2, p. 3; 15 January 1869, p. 4; John P. Young, *San Francisco: A History of the Pacific Coast Metropolis* (San Francisco: Clark Publishing, 1912), 411.

13. Joseph Armstrong Baird Jr., *Time's Wondrous Changes: San Francisco Architecture, 1776–1915* (San Francisco: California Historical Society, 1962), says Italianate was common in the United States from 1850 to 1860, but in San Francisco from 1850 to 1880 (10, 16–20). Kirker's major thesis in *California's Architectural Frontier* is that in typically colonial fashion, California architecture copied that of the immigrants' homes and therefore lagged up to a generation behind East Coast styles (vii–ix, 26–27, 64–66, 91).

14. Langley, *San Francisco Directory, 1861,* 36, 478–80; *1862,* 37, 563–64; *1865,* 616; *1867,* 39; *1868,* 780–81; *San Francisco Newsletter,* 19 June 1869, 19; maps of various homestead associations, California Historical Society, San Francisco.

15. Langley, *San Francisco Directory, 1869,* 21; *1871,* 21, 23; *Call,* 26 July 1870, 4; 27 July 1870, 2; *Newsletter,* 20 August 1870, 7; 19 November 1870, 13; 3 December 1870, 11; 10 December 1870, 11; 17 December 1870, 14; 14 January 1871, 14; 28 January 1871, 14; 4 February 1871, 14; 18 February 1871, 15; 25 February 1871, 15; 4 March 1871, 15; 11 March 1871, 15; 29 April 1871, postscript, 3; 15 July 1871, 12; Thomas Magee, *Real Estate Circular,* November 1870, 2; December 1870, 1; January 1871, 2; February 1871, 2; March 1871, 2; April 1871, 2, hereinafter cited as *Real Estate Circular* with date and page number.

16. An accurate count of the houses T.R.E.A. built is not known to exist. The three main sources disagree. "Real Estate Associates' New Building," in *The Resources of California* (San Francisco: J. P. H. Wentworth, April 1877), 1, which is obviously a publicity article but contains accurate financial data, gives the largest numbers for the four years it cites, 1873–76, a total of 1,057 houses. Next most expansive and also intended as publicity is material in "The Progress of the City" sections of Langley, *San Francisco Directory, 1871,* 23; *1873,* 25–26; *1875,* 15; *1876,* 13; Bishop, *San Francisco Directory, 1877,* 40; *1878,* 41–42. These give a total of 1,133 houses for the six years. Last is a compilation from the daily sales listed in "Real Estate Transactions," *Newsletter,* 1866–81, passim. This total of 938 houses cannot be accurate: it involves interpretation as to how many new houses, if any, were on each lot sold (construction of a house might cost as little as one thousand dollars); the total dollars of these sales differ from those listed in annual reports; and the discrepancies with other sources lead to the conclusion that other sales existed. These are the numbers of houses according to the different sources.

Table 10.1

	Resources	*Directories*	Compilation
1870–71	N/A	13	15
1872	N/A	51	17
1873	117	120	35
1874	320	316	144
1875	385	355 *	320
1876	235	209	201
1877	N/A	69	103
1878	N/A	N/A	86
1879	N/A	N/A	11
1880	N/A	N/A	6
	1,057	1,133	938

* Source: *Real Estate Circular,* January 1876, 2.

17. *Resources,* February 1875, 3; Roger Olmstead and T. H. Watkins, *Here Today: San Francisco's Architectural Heritage* (San Francisco: Chronicle Books, 1968), 32–33, 104–5, 113–18.

18. Young, *San Francisco,* 755.

19. For a list of the surviving houses, see appendix of article in *JSAH* 37 (1978): 31–33.

20. Quotation from *Resources,* February 1875, 3; *Newsletter,* 20 February 1875, postscript, 3; Langley, *San Francisco Directory, 1882,* 187, 1,088.

21. John Summerson, *Georgian London* (London: Pleiades Books, 1945), 90.

22. *Resources,* February 1875, 3; *San Francisco Evening Bulletin,* 4 March 1876, 1.

23. *Newsletter,* 26 June 1875, postscript, 8; 29 January 1876, postscript, 8; William Appleby European Nursery, *Descriptive Catalogue of Plants* (San Francisco: Bruce's Printing House, 1875), cover, Collection California Historical Society, San Francisco.

24. *Circular,* May 1875, 4.

25. Sales listed in *Newsletter,* 6 November 1875 through 29 November 1879, passim.

26. Ibid.; Langley, *San Francisco Directory, 1882,* passim; U.S. Archives and Record Service, *Population Schedules, Tenth Census, 1880,* California, San Francisco County, 11th ward, roll no. 77, leaves 354–59; *Bulletin,* 15 April 1876, 1.

27. T.R.E.A. ad, *Call,* 29 August 1875, 6.

28. *California Architect and Building News* 6 (May 1885): 76.

29. *Resources,* February 1875, 3; Archives of the California Supreme Court (hereinafter cited as Archives), "Copy: Cash Book of The Real Estate and Building Associates" (manuscript), exhibit A, case no. 77866, "In the Matter of The Real Estate Associates, a Corporation, in Insolvency," passim; Summerson, *Georgian London,* 149.

30. *Alta California,* 30 September 1872, 1.

31. Marcus Whiffen, *American Architecture since 1780* (Cambridge, Mass.: MIT Press, 1969), 69; Talbot Hamlin, *Architecture through the Ages* (New York: Putnam, 1940), 594.

32. Lockwood, *Bricks and Brownstone,* shows similar plans in the usual New York row house (14, 70, 164–67, 228).

33. *Call,* 13 October 1871, 1.

34. T.R.E.A. ad *Circular,* January 1870, shows Edward Barry as president, William Hollis as manager, secretary, and a director (4). The *Directory* lists both in real estate. Another director was D. A. MacDonald; see Oscar Shuck, *Sketches of Leading and Representative Men of San Francisco* (New York: News Companies, 1875), 781; *Newsletter,* 30 October 1875, postscript, 3.

35. *Resources,* February 1875, 3.

36. Farquharson was born in Scotland 1827, received British architectural training, came to California in 1850, and died in San Francisco 1914. He built the ten-columned Greek Revival Sacramento Courthouse (1854), the Sansovino-inspired Bank of California (1867), and South Hall, the first and only remaining early building on the Berkeley campus of the University of California. See Anne Bloomfield, "David Farquharson, Pioneer California Architect," *California History* 59 (spring 1980): 16–33.

Remer had come to San Francisco from his native New York in 1875 to design Baldwin's Hotel and Theater, a luxury hotel competing with John P. Gaynor's contemporary Palace. Theater expert Remer had probably been recommended to "Lucky" Baldwin by his theater manager, Thomas Maguire, who was associated with Richard M. Hooley for whom Remer had designed the post–Chicago fire Hooley's Opera House (1872). Remer was also credited with New York's Lyceum Theater (first of that name) and Union Square Theater (1871), and with Wade's Opera House in San Francisco (1876). The last had been commenced in 1873 with S. C. Bugbee and son as architects. Financial reverses caused suspension for a year, and Remer's name may have become associated with the building because he took over the completion. After working for T.R.E.A., Remer executed various works in and near San Francisco. He altered San Jose's Brohaska Opera House (1879). He constructed a brick building to house a gasometer for the Palace and Grand Hotels (1880). He won a competition and designed Bacon Hall (1880) for the University of California at Berkeley. For Reinhardt Daemon, Remer built the Casino restaurant west of the conservatory in Golden Gate Park. Late in 1881 Remer sold his T.R.E.A.-built houses and moved back to New York. See Lloyd, *Lights and Shades,* 155–57, 370–76; Langley, *San Francisco Directory, 1874,* 29–30; *1875,* 31–32; *1876,* 12, 27; Lois Foster Redcape, "Tom Maguire, Napoleon of the Stage," *California Historical Quarterly* 21 (1942): 153–76, 241; John William Snyder, "A Partial Index to the *California Architect and Building News,* 1 April 1879 to 20 June 1900," master's thesis, University of California, Davis, n.d. [ca. 1976], 411, appendix 1, 207, appendix 2, 8, 41; Remer's listings, *Trow's New York City Directory,* 1871–72, 1875, 1877, 1887, 1888, 1893, 1896, 1900–1901 (Remer was not listed in *Trow's* 1862, 1883, 1902, 1910); Langley, *San Francisco Directory, 1878,* 12.

37. Archives, "Cash Book," 3, passim.

38. *California Architect and Building News* 1 (June 1880): viii; 11 (June 1881): viii; *Newsletter* 21 January 1877, postscript, 4; 22 December 1877, 11. Archives, "Cash Book," does not list Remer among those paying rent for offices in the T.R.E.A. Building (6, 12); *Census 1880,* San Francisco, part of 13th ward, roll no. 77, leaf 145.

39. The Real Estate Associates, "Constitution and By-Laws," 1868; *Resources,* April 1877, 1; Langley, *San Francisco Directory,* late 1860s, passim. The company's finances are discussed in more detail later in the text.

40. *Circular,* January 1870, 2; January 1871, 4; September 1873, 4; October 1876, 3; Langley, *San Francisco Directory, 1876,* 13; *1878,* 12; *1870s,* passim.

41. *Circular,* November 1870, 4; *Newsletter,* 3 June 1871, postscript, 2; 10 June 1871, 13; 24 June 1871, 13; 1 July 1871, 13; 8 July 1871, 13; Langley, *San Francisco Directory, 1872, 1873, 1882,* passim.

42. Langley, *San Francisco Directory, 1871,* 25; *1871–93,* passim, for names on photograph; photographs of New Montgomery Street (1885) and the Grand Hotel (ca. 1872), San Francisco Public Library; Asbury Harpending, *The Great Diamond Hoax* (San Francisco: James H. Barry, 1913), 115, 141–42; George D. Lyman, *Ralston's Ring* (New York: Scribner's, 1937), 82, 120–21, 228–29; David Lavender, *Nothing Seemed Impossible: William C. Ralston and Early San Francisco* (Palo Alto: American West Publishing, 1975), 248; "Map of Property of New Montgomery Street between Market and Howard Streets to be sold at AUCTION Thursday May 6th, 1869, by Maurice Dore," San Francisco, 1869.

43. *Newsletter,* 1 May 1875, postscript, 3; *Circular,* March 1875, 1.

44. *Resources,* April 1877, 1; *Circular,* July 1876, 1; John Cotter Pelton, "San Francisco, Its Position in Architectural and Constructive Development," in *Modern San Francisco 1907–1908* (San Francisco: Western Press Association, n.d.)

45. *Newsletter,* 20 December 1879, 28; Archives, "Cash Book," account no. 64, 6, 12; *Circular,* November 1877, 4; sole evidence for existence of the elevator is in a three-page manuscript, Archives, "William Hale, Receiver, The Real Estate Associates, costs of running building," case no. 8160, "In the Matter of The Real Estate Associates, a Corporation, in Insolvency." Submitted to the Court on 11 November 1881, these costs include five small items for "repairs to elevator," total $33.85. Regular monthly costs of running the building included $50 for janitor, $20 for engineer, and $100 for steam.

Opening of the building had been delayed by a plasterers' strike, Early in April 1877 the men went out over the company's refusal to fire two nonunion plasterers and pay four dollars for an eight-hour day. In about a week a placard went up on the uncompleted T.R.E.A. building: "Wanted, 100 plasterers to work ten hours a day, wages four dollars." That no plasters turned up shows the union's remarkable solidarity, especially in the face of the immense and increasing unemployment in the third month after a mining stock panic had burst over California. The ensuing depression lingered into the 1880s and contributed to the failure of T.R.E.A. The brave plasterers' strike was also a casualty, for the union settled on 1 May for the terms on the placard. Fate of the union shop is unknown. See *Newsletter,* 14 April 1877, 16; *San Francisco Examiner,* 7 April 1877, 3; *Bulletin,* 1 May 1877, 2.

46. Quotation from *Circular,* March 1877, 4; *Sixth Census 1840,* Iowa, Clinton County, leaf 13; *Seventh Census 1850,* Iowa, Clinton County, Elk River Township, leaf 292; *Eighth Census 1860,* California, Placer County, Michigan Bluff, 809, dwl. no. 933; *Tenth Census 1880,* California, San Francisco County, part of 12th ward, roll no. 78, leaf 45; Lucius P. Allen, *History of Clinton County, Iowa* (Chicago: Western Historical, 1879), 618; "Death of W. Hollis," *Call,* 30 June 1895, 7.

47. Hollis's listings in San Francisco directories, 1861–95; *Great Register of San Francisco,* 1867; William Hanchett, "The Question of Religion and the Taming of California, 1849–1854," *California Historical Quarterly* 32 (June 1953): 131–32; Langley, *San Francisco Directory, 1867,* 687; Brooks and Rouleau, *Abstract of Title of Lands of the Central Park Homestead Association* (San Francisco: Joseph Winterburn, 1866), map, Collection Bancroft Library.

48. "A Contractor's Death," *Bulletin,* 26 June 1895; *Circular,* March 1877, 4.

49. Langley, *San Francisco Directory, 1877,* 12; *1876,* 13.

50. Langley, *San Francisco Directory, 1877,* 11. Perhaps this writer was the *Bulletin* editor who bought one of the first fifteen houses, which were built on the middle of the three blocks.

51. Archives, *No. 6868, In the Supreme Court of the State of California, F. W. Voll et al., Plaintiffs and Appellants* vs. *William Hollis et. al., Defendants and Respondents, Transcript on Appeal . . .,* San Francisco, 1879, 7, passim.

52. *Circular,* January 1870, 2; January 1875, 4; January 1876, 2, 4; January 1877, 1, 4.

53. *Call,* 5 January 1874, 1; January 1875, 3; The Real Estate Associates, Certificate of Incorporation, San Francisco, 1868.

54. Langley, *San Francisco Directory, 1871,* 23; *Circular,* March 1873, 3; October 1876, 3; January 1878, 3; *Call,* 5 January 1874, 1; 1 January 1875, 1; The Real Estate Associates, *Catalogue of Property for Sale by The Real Estate Associates* (San Francisco: T.R.E.A., 1877), inside front cover and inside back cover; "Mortgages" and "Real Estate Transactions," *Examiner,* 1878, passim; Ira Cross, *Financing an Empire* (Chicago: S. J. Clarke, 1927), 2:797.

55. *Circular,* August 1876, 1; September 1876, 1; *Resources,* February 1875, 3.

56. *Resources,* February 1875, 3.

57. Langley, *San Francisco Directory, 1876,* 13; *Bulletin,* 22 January 1876, 1. Lockwood, *Manhattan Moves Uptown,* explains that in New York men on "day's work . . . were paid by the day [instead of by contract] and expected to do the highest quality work" (68). In San Francisco "day work" may have had the New York connotations. Alternately or in addition it may have carried political overtones in relation to the large numbers of immigrants, the strong union situation, or the factors that made a success of the Workingmen's Party.

58. In building its last three houses, the Associates contracted out the stair building (G. K. Lawson), plastering (Helgoth, Ferguson), dryage (Lane and Pullen), and house painting (Lang and Griffith), as well as the plumbing (Sweeny and Vance). It also made payments to suppliers of embossed and cut glass (John Mallon), marble (J. and F. Kesseler), paints (J. R. Kelly and Company), plaster decorations (Samuel Kellet), stoves and tinware (Schuster Brothers), patent brick (Patent Brick Company), sewerpipe (J. B. Owens), hardware (Huntington and Hopkins), fancy goods (Davis Brothers), and lime and cement (Davis and Cowell). See Langley, *San Francisco Directory, 1876,* 13; Archives, "Cash Book," passim.

59. *Call,* 21 June 1875, 1; *Examiner,* 1 May 1877, 2; *Chronicle,* 2 May 1877, 2; *Bulletin* 11 July 1878, 1; *Circular,* March 1873, 3; November 1875, 3; March 1877, 4; January 1878, 1; February 1878, 1; February 1879, 2; *Resources,* April 1877, 1; Real Estate Associates, *Catalogue,* 1877.

60. *Newsletter,* 6 September 1873, 4; Langley, *San Francisco Directory, 1874,* 365.

61. Langley, *San Francisco Directory, 1876,* 13.

62. *Newsletter,* 5 March 1881, 18; *Resources,* April 1877, 1. Extracts from annual reports show sales in 1874 of $1,479,719 against land purchase and construction costs of $862,509. In 1875 the figures were $1,938,844 against $2,133,437, and in 1876, $1,099,481 against $1,144,471.

63. Compilation of sales from the *Newsletter* shows vacant lots produced 3 percent of sales revenue in 1873, 5.6 percent in 1874, 5.3 percent in 1876, 18.4 percent in 1877, and more thereafter. *Circular,* May 1877, 2; Archives, "Transcript on Appeal," case no. 7866, 22–23.

64. On 14 November 1879, T.R.E.A. and Hollis jointly executed with the German Savings and Loan a $150,000 mortgage of sixty-one land parcels each of which had already been mortgaged separately. Hollis next "prevailed on the unsecured creditors to forbear immediate action" and to accept notes that the company could pay from rents and assets. These eighteen creditors included the National Gold Bank, real estate agent and *Circular* publisher Thomas Magee, B. Doe and J. S. Doe of the sash and door mill, lumber dealer Hansen and Ackerson, and plasterer Henry Helgoth. The notes amounted to some $38,000. Another creditor, J. S. Polack, a realtor whom T.R.E.A. had never paid for a claim to the city's hospital lot in 1872, filed suit and attached property in May 1879. Archives, "Mortgage": exhibit D, case no. 7866; "Affidavit of William Hale," filed 12 November 1881, case no. 7866, 3; "Transcript," case no. 7866, 51–52; Real Estate Associates, *A Complete Transcript of . . . the Meetings of Creditors . . .* (San Francisco: B. F. Sterrett, 1882), passim, Collection Bancroft Library; *Examiner,* 12 May 1879, 3; *Newsletter,* 11 January 1873, postscript, 23.

65. Archives, "Affidavit of William Hall," case no. 7866, 3; Archives, "Articles of Incorporation, Real Estate and Building Associates," exhibit B, case no. 7866; Archives, "Minutes of

Board of Directors, Real Estate and Building Associates," exhibit C, case no. 7866; George H. Smith, reporter, "Ex Parte William Hollis," *Reports of Cases Determined in the Supreme Court of the State of California,* (San Francisco: Bancroft Whitney, 1906), 410 (59 Cal 410).

66. *Statutes of California, 1880,* 1, 82–94.

67. Quotation from Langley, *San Francisco Directory, 1880,* 13; Judith Lynch Waldhorn, "San Francisco's Victorian Heritage: The Carpenter-Builder Revealed," paper presented at the Northern California session, thirtieth annual meeting of the Society of Architectural Historians, Los Angeles, February 1977; Carol Orwell and J. L. Waldhorn, *A Gift to the Street* (San Francisco: Antelope Island Press, 1976), 157–59; Kirker, *California's Architectural Frontier,* 103–10.

68. Baird, *Time's Wondrous Changes,* 23–24.

69. *Chronicle,* 2 May 1877, 2; *Examiner,* 10 April 1877, 3; Langley, *San Francisco Directory, 1877,* 12.

CHAPTER ELEVEN

Innovation without Paradigm

The Many Creators of the Drive-in Market

RICHARD LONGSTRETH

Significant changes in architecture designed for retail purposes as well as for many other functions tend to be associated with individual businesses and often with the individuals who lead them. Among the best-known examples is A. T. Stewart, who conceived the dry goods store as a grand emporium purveying a wide range of wares at reasonable prices in an elegant setting. A radical departure from what was then the norm, Stewart's "marble palace" in New York (1846–50) and second, larger building (1859–62) became springboards for the enormous department stores erected in major cities during the Gilded Age. Similarly, Marshall Field and John Wanamaker were leaders in recasting the department store along even more sumptuous lines at the turn of the twentieth century, setting a new standard in the process. Robert E. Wood guided Sears, Roebuck into the retail field after World War I, creating stores that defied conventional wisdom by locating them on sites that were easily reached by car but were well removed from established business districts of any size—a pattern that would become widespread for major department store branches some twenty years later. Concurrent with the first Sears outlets, Kansas City real estate developer J. C. Nichols was emerging as the nation's foremost exponent of the shopping center as a fully planned, integrated business enterprise that was also oriented to the motorist. Nichols's Country Club Plaza, conceived in 1922 to contain over two hundred stores, afforded a prototype for the regional shopping center that continued to be studied by colleagues well into the 1950s.[1]

Distinguished architectural firms often have contributed significantly to creating paradigms in the commercial sphere. D. H. Burnham and Company designed buildings for Field and Wanamaker in a majestic mode that offered a dramatic contrast to their predecessors at home and abroad—one that aptly symbolized the department store as a nexus of consumerism as well as the shift in hegemony from wholesale to retail operations. George Nimmons gave singular form to the Sears outlets as beacons for the motorist, creating a vocabulary inspired as much from industrial buildings as from those that distinguished the retail core. Victor Gruen and Morris Ketchum were key agents in redefining the nature of small specialty shops just prior to World War II, applying avant-garde design precepts as if they had been conceived to foster merchandising. A decade later, both men became leaders in advocating the efficacy of the pedestrian mall as the organizational spine of the regional shopping center and the redeveloped core shopping district alike.[2]

While the extent to which singular contributions have shaped retail architecture is impressive, they by no means afford a complete picture. As in so many other historiographic realms, focusing on the great figures often occurs first because the documentary material needed is among the easiest to retrieve and analyze. Even when primary sources no longer exist, a substantial amount of evidence can be gleaned from published accounts of the period. The process of investigation can be self-reinforcing since contemporary writings often reflect biases that range from the overt—flattering the most powerful figures in the field—to the wholly unintentional—it is easier for authors and the people they interview to pinpoint a few things that have influenced their work than to sort out the myriad ones that may actually have had an impact.

Probing beyond the titans can be a difficult task. Even if adequate source material exists, the evidence is likely to be so diffuse that reconstructing the historical record entails discovering, then piecing together, small, scattered fragments of information. Yet this kind of inquiry is needed, not only to depict major works in their appropriate context, not only to understand typical patterns as well as extraordinary ones, but also to identify innovations of consequence that have escaped collective memory. Things that fall into this latter group may be hard to recognize because they are neither connected to a well-known person or company nor present a clear paradigmatic example. Their historical import derives from a cumulative rather than a singular occurrence. No clearer illustration of this pattern can be found in commercial architecture than the drive-in market.

At first the subject might seem hardly worth detailed study, for the drive-in market was a very brief phenomenon. The earliest known example was erected in 1924, the last in 1932, and the great majority between 1928 and 1930. The drive-in market was also a localized phenomenon. Most examples were constructed within a twenty-five-mile radius of downtown Los Angeles. Some could be found as far south as San Diego, as far east as Tucson, and as far north as Sacramento, but except in a few isolated cases, these places represent the extremities of the type's geographic dispersal. Finally, the drive-in market has been a long-forgotten phenomenon. Many examples remain extant, but few give clear indication of their original use. These buildings are part of a vast arterial panorama that is presumed yet seldom really seen. Few people are even familiar with the term. Historical accounts of the region's

Figure 11.1. Wilshire at Fourteenth Drive-In Market, Wilshire Boulevard, Santa Monica, California; Fred Nowell Jones, designer-builder, 1927; no longer standing. (Photo by "Dick" Whittington, 1929; courtesy Whittington Collection, Department of Special Collections, University of Southern California)

architecture and urban development as well as of the automobile's impact on commercial work in the United States all but ignore this legacy.[3]

Despite its elusive past, the drive-in market serves as a benchmark in the development of retail outlets beyond the city center, one that in time would have a profound effect on the urban landscape nationwide. The transformation entailed three interrelated aspects: the drive-in concept, one-stop shopping, and business integration. The drive-in concept—arranging a facility so that off-street parking for customers is a major determinant of the entire layout—was a new idea in the 1920s. Among traditional building types, the food store was the first to experience substantial modifications along these lines. The resulting drive-in market offered consumers a new degree of convenience by having the sales area a linear space open to the forecourt, a parking lot situated at the front of the property where patrons could pull off the street and leave their cars while shopping (fig. 11.1). This configuration,

Figure 11.2. Wilshire and Harvard Market, Wilshire Boulevard, Los Angeles; Gable and Wyant, architects, 1929; no longer standing. (From *Chain Store Review*, October 1930, p. 12)

now so ubiquitous as to be taken for granted, seemed revolutionary at that time and was heralded as a dramatic change in the design of retail facilities.[4] The location of these markets away from business nodes was no less a departure, demonstrating that orientation to the motorist demanded different citing criteria than those normally employed to attract streetcar passengers or pedestrians. The drive-in could prosper on a site free from congestion by attracting motorists in transit and even functioning as a destination point in itself.

The drive-in market exerted considerable influence on merchandising techniques, for it helped extend the selling of many related items under one roof beyond the realm of the department and variety stores. The drive-in was a pioneer in the practice of combining retail services for the distribution of everyday goods in outlying parts of a metropolitan area.[5] Concessions existed for all basic types of food products in a single space where purchases could be made quickly and easily (figs. 11.2, 11.3). In many cases, a few other household needs could be satisfied in one or two separate units of the building. These complexes were seldom fully integrated businesses; more often, each food concession was separately owned and the ensemble lacked a central management structure. Yet the coordination of activities between merchants was common, owing to the need for the market proper to function as a more or less unified entity and the support stores to operate in concert. Prior to the depression, the drive-in revealed the economic value of such linkage to as great a degree as any form of business outlet beyond the city center.

The drive-in market became a standard fixture at an early date. No type tailored to the needs of a mobile consumer society was as prevalent in an urban setting during the 1920s save those devoted to the car itself.[6] About 300 drive-in markets were designed in California, out of which at least 250 were realized. Because the drive-in market was at once ubiquitous as a food emporium and anomalous among other

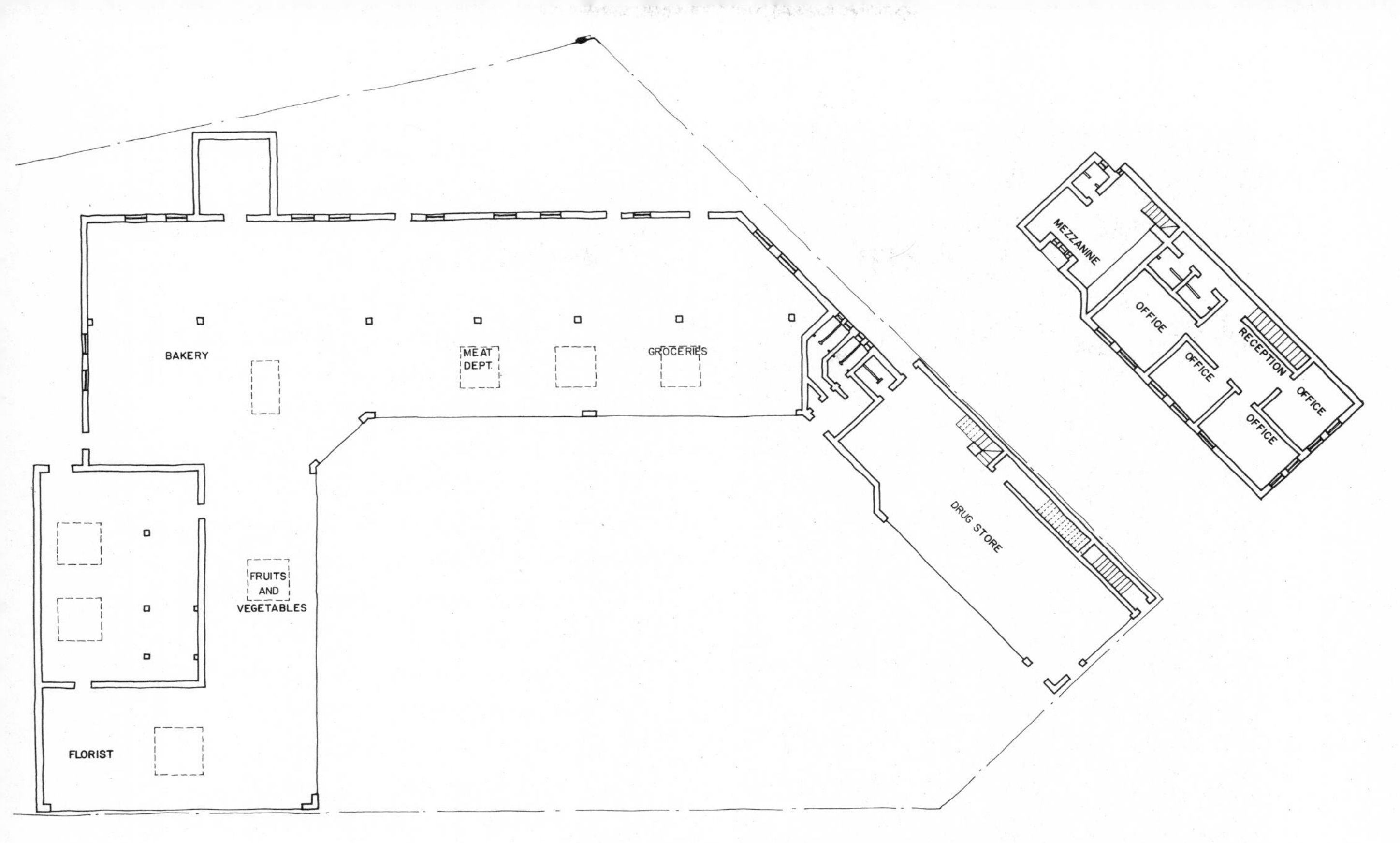

Figure 11.3. Mesa-Vernon Market, Crenshaw Boulevard, Los Angeles; George J. Adams, architect, 1928; burned 1992. (Floor plan drawn by Julie Osborne)

retail types, it was instrumental in acclimating motorists to changes in their routine patterns of movement—changes that affected where, when, and most importantly how they purchased things. While the car greatly facilitated movement from home to shopping place, automobile congestion at the latter imposed a new set of problems. The drive-in underscored how much frustration could be alleviated by a site removed from concentrated business areas where one could park on the premises. The type served as a catalyst to new patterns of consumer conduct in which the automobile played a determining rather than a supportive role.

Despite its innovative attributes, the drive-in market would have remained a peripheral phenomenon in the history of retail architecture were it not for the decisive impact it had on two other building types during the late 1920s and 1930s. These latter facilities—the supermarket and the shopping center—became key agents in reordering the structure of retail development nationwide during the mid-twentieth century. The drive-in laid much of the groundwork for the supermarket by demonstrating the merits of coordinating the sale of all basic food items in a sizable emporium located somewhat apart from business nodes—a place to which more customers would drive than walk and where off-street space existed for their cars. That the supermarket to a large degree also was a child of Southern California was probably no coincidence given the extent to which the two types corresponded.[7]

The drive-in's relation to the shopping center design was equally strong. The small, or "neighborhood," shopping center, containing fewer than twenty store units from which a balanced spectrum of basic goods and services was purveyed under single management, predated the drive-in market by more than a decade. By the mid-1920s examples of the neighborhood center could be found coast-to-coast, albeit in very limited numbers as part of planned residential enclaves. The drive-in subsequently provided a direct model for how the shopping center could be modified to provide generous amounts of off-street parking and also how it could be built independent of a single residential community. Both were important to the shopping center's rise as a significant force in retailing by the eve of World War II. That tendency, in turn, fostered the ascent a decade later of considerably larger shopping centers as the preeminent form of retail development—a form in which the drive-in concept, one-stop shopping, and business integration attained maturity as interrelated facets of a single plan.

The creation of the supermarket, possessing all the attributes that would make it the foremost type of store selling food products coast-to-coast by the 1940s, was primarily the work of the Los Angeles–based Ralphs Grocery Company. Ralphs's first full-fledged supermarket was erected on Wilshire Boulevard in 1928. For well over a decade thereafter, the company continued to bring innovations to the design and operation of its buildings that set a standard for the industry nationwide. On the other hand, adapting lessons learned from the drive-in market to the neighborhood shopping center first occurred in Washington, D.C., through the work of a locally prominent real estate firm, Shannon and Luchs. The company's first project of this genre opened in 1930 on Connecticut Avenue. Although Shannon and Luchs never attained a national stature comparable to Ralphs, it remained a leading local force in shopping center development and its work appears to have been quite influential in other parts of the country. One searches in vain for equivalence with the drive-in market. By 1928 the size, configuration, and tenant mix of these buildings adhered to a relatively consistent norm; however, no one preceding example stands out as the paradigm for these conventions. Likewise, no one party or small group of parties emerges as the central protagonist for advancing the type. There was, in effect, no clear leadership. Profiles of the clients and architects involved resist such neat categorization.[8]

Figure 11.4. Taxpayer block, South Vermont Avenue, Los Angeles, ca. 1925. (Photo by "Dick" Whittington, 1931; courtesy Whittington Collection, Department of Special Collections, University of Southern California)

During the 1920s, few buildings that housed food stores in outlying areas of any city were designed for that specific purpose. Typically such an emporium was quartered in a speculative commercial facility, which seldom contained more than a dozen, and often no more than four or five, store units (fig. 11.4). Known as taxpayer blocks—ostensibly because they could generate sufficient revenue to cover building costs and property taxes until such time as demand warranted more intense development—these buildings were so generalized in plan that a property owner could have one designed by an architect or builder without much thought as to what tenants would occupy the space.[9] Variation in store size was not great, and if a prospective lessee required more space than the norm, two or three contiguous units could be leased. Once a real estate broker began to secure leases, either in the course of construction or after the building was completed, preparation of each

Figure 11.5. Commercial buildings, including Mac Marr food store, South Vermont Avenue, Los Angeles, 1925–26; no longer standing. (Photo by "Dick" Whittington, 1931; courtesy Whittington Collection, Department of Special Collections, University of Southern California)

unit for occupancy was minimal. Most of the work entailed installing fixtures and signs. Groceries as well as fruit and vegetable stores in Southern California were distinguished by open fronts, with folding doors or gates to secure the premises after hours, but even this modification could be made quickly and at low cost. Flexibility was considered an attribute of the taxpayer block since it was difficult for the owner or his agent to anticipate the precise tenant composition at the start and that composition was expected to change over time.

Chain companies in the food business assumed a more aggressive role than independent merchants in order to secure prime locations for their outlets. If a chain did not find space to its liking in a taxpayer block it could work through a real estate broker to purchase or lease a site and erect a facility. However, the product seldom differed to any substantial degree from its generic counterparts and, like them, could be easily adapted to other functions if the venture proved unsatisfactory (fig. 11.5).[10]

The process of developing a drive-in market was more complex. The configuration of both interior and exterior space was function-specific and ill-suited to most other uses. Planning the facility necessitated careful site selection and no less care in choosing at least three or four, and more commonly six or seven, merchants who were adept in their respective trades and could operate in concert. Property management entailed not only the building but its paved forecourt. The retailers who participated in such enterprises generally had small businesses; few possessed either the ability or the inclination to undertake a project of this scope. A grocer such as the locally well-known I. M. Hattem, who built and operated two drive-in markets, was an exception. Either the owner or someone acting on his behalf had to devote a considerable amount of expertise as well as time and money if the undertaking was to be a success.[11]

The principal forces behind both the emergence and subsequent proliferation of the drive-in market were the real estate developer and broker. Working together, these parties, who were sometimes one and the same, picked the site (or how best to utilize a site already in hand), determined the building's basic characteristics, chose someone to design the facility, secured the tenants, and oversaw the completed project. The real estate industry was in effect an instigator and guide, the catalyst of the phenomenon itself. The success of that phenomenon came from a series of clever, intuitive responses to the desire among many small-scale businessmen to bolster their trade in an increasingly competitive field, to the mounting anxiety among shoppers over traffic congestion in outlying areas, and to the insatiable appetite among Southern Californians for real estate as a means of increasing their assets.

An indication of the real estate field's pivotal role in the development of drive-in markets is given by the fact that many persons so engaged also were the owners. In Los Angeles proper, approximately half of those drive-in market owners whose occupations have been documented were in some aspect of the real estate business, including a major share of those who undertook such building projects in the formative period between 1924 and 1928. Sometimes individuals entered the field to develop land holdings as rapid growth occurred nearby. Frank Dishbrow had purchased his nine-acre tract shortly after moving to Pasadena in 1902 and used the land as a citrus nursery until pursuing his plans for the Mother Goose Market and a group of adjacent houses in 1926. E. F. Bagardus, owner of the Sunset-Western Market in Hollywood (1928), had acquired the land in 1900 as a site for his country house. The accelerated pace of urbanization that took place in the vicinity following World War I induced him to develop the land in increments, first with a small office building, then a block of shops, and finally the market complex. In other instances, the land was purchased with the intent of concentrated development. Louis McCray, president of a local oil company, entered into partnership with two other businessmen to undertake the large Toluca Lake Park subdivision in the San Fernando Valley, for which the Toluca Market (1929) was a service center. Charles Chapman was a rancher, but also president of the company that bore his name and controlled numerous real estate holdings in Southern California. Chapman's portfolio included an office building in downtown Los Angeles, mines, and oil fields as well as the eighty-five-acre tract in the mid-Wilshire district where he erected the enormous Chapman Park Market in 1928–29.[12]

A number of owners were in the real estate business full-time and built a drive-in market to supplement their regular income. Often, too, a real estate firm initiated a project. Some of these companies appear to have been modest in scope, run by a few shareholders and concentrating on parcels within a limited precinct. On the other hand, the Taft organization, which included companies specializing in real estate sales, land development, construction, and mining, was headquartered in Hollywood and involved in projects throughout much of the metropolitan area as well as further afield. Burton and Company was a smaller operation, dealing in commercial property scattered from the mid-Wilshire district to Inglewood. The Walter H. Leimert Company had yet another focus—developing sizable tracts principally with moderate-priced single-family houses—and was unusual in the attention it gave to long-term planning. Some companies were organized as real estate syndicates, pooling the resources of a limited number of rich investors, or as real estate investment trusts, tapping the huge market for participation in speculative development among people of lesser means.[13]

The importance of the real estate field to the development of the drive-in market is further indicated by the fact that most owners who were not in that business had little or no experience in work that would prepare them for undertaking such a project on their own. These people were a diverse lot in terms of background, occupation, and resources at their disposal. Collectively, they represent a cross-section of both the elite and the huge middle class that so characterized the Los Angeles metropolitan area's populace. Some owners were rich and had numerous business interests. Many others had limited funds; for them, constructing a drive-in market may have represented the largest single investment they made. A few people were engaged in vaguely related work such as building construction, paving, or house moving. Some businesses were related to the automobile. The Muller Brothers of Hollywood had built one of the region's largest service stations. Karl Woestman made a rare attempt to combine an auto service facility, which he ran, with the drive-in market he built in Pasadena. Elmer Johnson operated a garage in Santa Barbara. Herman Shapiro was president of an automobile loan corporation. Louis Smith sold used cars. Other merchants were involved as well. Samuel Leess was a florist. W. R. Bryant of San Fernando and Cary Johnson of Santa Ana operated drug stores.[14]

Just as many owners were employed in entirely different fields as salesmen, clerks, photographers, or civil servants. C. L. Peckham, who was responsible for the first known drive-in market, was a partner in an insurance adjustment firm. Some were professionals: physicians, dentists, attorneys, and engineers. J. M. Curtis of San Bernardino sat on the California Supreme Court. James McKinley was a state senator. Raymond Griffith and Conrad Nagel were actors. So, of course, was Mary Pickford under whom a company was established to invest the large sums she netted from United Artists.[15] Other owners do not appear to have been employed at all, living on incomes acquired through inheritance, investment, or a career from which they had retired. In several cases, drive-in markets were constructed by executors of estates. Some owners were wives of businessmen; others were widows. In at least one case, the chance to participate in such a venture stemmed from having a house on a site that became opportune for commercial use. Rosa McKenzie moved her dwelling to the rear of the property, facing the side street, so that she could have a drive-in market erected along the Western Avenue frontage, which was rapidly escalating in value.

Among owners, sizable real estate companies and rich investors tended to become involved later; few began to build drive-in markets prior to the closing months of 1928. Many of the latter group owned or were senior officers of businesses and may have taken a conservative approach toward involvement with a type of enterprise still considered new. Max Arnold was sales manager for Miller and Lux, which controlled a large share of the San Joaquin Valley's agricultural production. Edward Murphy headed a wholesaling firm and was vice-president of the Los Angeles Brick Company. Samuel Curson was president of the Security Building and Loan Association; Ellis Bishop, president of the Investment Securities Company in Pasadena. Individuals and organizations with considerable means at their disposal contributed significantly to refinements of the type by commissioning some of the largest, most striking, or the most polished examples, as is evident in Bagardus's Sunset-Western Market (fig. 11.6). For them the market appears to have served as a personal monument much as could an elaborate office building, store block, or apartment house of the period. Yet wealth was by no means the sole, or even the determining, force behind the quality of the product. A number of distinguished drive-in market designs emanated from less affluent parties. Moreover, access to large amounts of capital did not necessarily mean a substantial sum would be lavished on the project. The lackluster appearance of the facility commissioned by the Mary Pickford Company (1930), for example, suggests a minimal investment.[16]

The pioneering drive-in market projects were undertaken, instead, by parties, including real estate operations, with some, but not vast amounts of, capital at their disposal. Before 1928 only two more affluent developers, the Leimert Company and Edward Murphy, became involved. Whether rich or not, none of these early participants nor any among the multitudes who followed emerged as an acknowledged

Figure 11.6. Sunset-Western Market, Sunset Boulevard, Los Angeles; Carl Jules Weyl, architect, 1928; no longer standing. (From *Los Angeles Realtor,* November 1928, p. 42)

leader in the field.[17] Moreover, the overwhelming majority of parties involved erected only one such establishment, and very few are known to have owned or operated more than two. Hattem's markets on Western and Vermont avenues (1927, 1930) and the large establishments of Louis McCray—the Toluca Market and the Palm in Beverly Hills (1928–29)—represent the most ambitious programs realized by a single party. If plans were conceived to develop a network of drive-in markets, they never got beyond the preliminary stage.[18] Since the impetus to build these complexes came primarily from outside the food business, little inducement existed for such specialized development. From the investor's perspective, handsome returns could be made on constructing a number of other types as well. Most retail food chains were still wedded to small outlets, and most independent competitors either lacked the desire or the resources to develop more than one or two facilities. Even if someone had wanted to break away from the standard pattern, there was little time to devise an effective strategy for erecting numerous drive-in markets. By 1928 so many individuals had entered the field that examples more or less saturated the metropolitan region in less than three years.

Ample temptation existed for active and passive parties alike to join the entrepreneurial fray. In the myriad accounts of the profits to be made in Los Angeles real estate, the soaring land values in outlying areas were the most impressive. Property at the intersection of Western Avenue and Santa Monica Boulevard increased over 2,200 percent between 1918 and 1928; at Western and 54th Street, the increase was over 2,100 percent; at Western and Slauson, over 3,600 percent; at Western and 6th, over 800 percent; Vermont and 7th, over 1,200 percent; Crenshaw and Washington, 860 percent.[19] Most of these places were developed with one- or two-story buildings; however, in a few cases the growth was much more intense. The skyscrapers that rose along Wilshire Boulevard near where it crossed Western Avenue, occupying property that for the most part had lain vacant through the mid-1920s, fuelled the hopes of many speculators that their land might eventually undergo a comparable transformation (fig. 11.7). Often the persons involved were savvy in the mercurial realm of real estate development. At the same time, the dream of making a fast fortune also attracted an array of novices.[20] Chronicles of the real estate bonanza often focused on the latter group. One observer depicted what had become a stereotype: the family that had spent most of its life in a small town or rural district of the Midwest, had recently moved to the region, and was enticed into spending its hard-earned reserves: "Ma experiments with clothes and beauty, while Pa may be drawn into building. This is the buildingest town! . . . After fifty years in a corn belt farmhouse, Pa goes Spanish. Or he experiments with business, develops a super-service station, a drive-in market—something just as new as the way of serving customers."[21] As often as not, these accounts emphasized the financial loss, even the financial ruin, experienced by naive investors. A 1927 article written for the *Saturday Evening Post* and given the sardonic title of "Let's Play Store," quoted one local business counselor:

> "People come to California expecting to make millions; they've always thought of it as a wonderland where anything is possible. They bring with them more money than they have ever possessed in their lives. . . . They get all hopped up dreaming about a business of which they know nothing, and it's as much as your life is worth to tell them the truth. . . . Rash epidemics of drug stores or furniture shops break out in certain neighborhoods, for no reason explainable by the rules of business, and run their courses, like an epidemic, and die out with the failure of the stores."
>
> Does [the newcomer] want to play grocery store? [The implication

> was that many of them did.] There are numerous obliging gentlemen who will start the game for as little as $500 and let him play until [his] money is gone, but it will never be anything more than make-believe. With a few thousands of dollars, however, and some good business counsel and some experience in the grocery business, he could have a successful store.[22]

One especially scathing depiction of the scene by an anonymous veteran of the local real estate business detailed the plight of individuals who assumed high mortgages and planned to live off the income generated by the property, only to find the operation marginal and of scant leverage for a sale or exchange. Frequently, too, the author asserted, methods used to entice investors were shady: "Planted tenants and also leases, often of little or no value, figure largely in effecting the sale of various classes of property in Los Angeles. Stores, drive-in markets, rented bungalows, are palmed off on the newcomer in the same way. Buyers are attracted by the classified advertisements in the local papers and are invariably influenced by the high net returns of property is said to earn; these figures are usually from fifteen to forty percent."[23]

Because it was easy to find purchasers who knew little about store location or running a business but harbored dreams of having their acquisition increase exponentially in value, and because land zoned for commercial development commanded higher prices than that designated for residential purposes, speculators pressed for a continuation of strip zoning practices along arteries in new areas of the metropolis. Their efforts almost always met with success, creating a huge oversupply of commercially zoned lots (fig. 11.8). The process fueled itself, as one of the most authoritative contemporary analyses of the situation emphasized: "The purchaser of . . . such lots soon finds that his promising investment is a burden, and he becomes desperate and risks additional funds and credit to erect store buildings. These vacant store buildings [in turn become] . . . an urgent invitation to every individual to open a retail outlet . . . especially a grocery store."[24] As a result, there was a relatively high rate of small business failures as well as store vacancies prior to the depression.

Despite the fact that drive-in markets were among the enterprises singled out as object lessons in poor investment, the degree to which they contributed to this phenomenon is highly problematic. Some owners were no doubt ill-equipped to engage in real estate development; some were probably naive; and some stores were poorly planned, poorly located, poorly run, or all three. The depression, which began to have a major impact on local businesses by 1931, also took its toll, reducing returns from even some of the best operations.

Yet there is no evidence that drive-in markets as a whole constituted a poor investment. To the contrary, the type demonstrated how the spread of poorly conceived businesses in outlying areas could be countered through planning. Developers had ample inducement to take care in selecting tenants, as one poor choice could undermine the entire operation. Furthermore, they could afford to be choosy since many food retailers were anxious to participate in such ventures. The abundant supply existed because many independent merchants saw the drive-in as a means to remain competitive with the chain food stores, which were aggressively expanding into outlying areas by the mid-1920s. Merchants at a drive-in could not match the chains' low prices, but the facility possessed attributes the chains lacked: a wider range of products, the convenience afforded by off-street parking, and a site away from congested commercial nodes. These factors made a critical difference. One study conducted at the height of the drive-in's popularity found that the income they generated ran about four times that of a standard food store in the same approximate location. With most drive-in leases structured on a percentage basis, greater profit for the retailer also meant a greater

Figure 11.7. Wilshire Boulevard, Los Angeles, looking west from Oxford Avenue toward Western Avenue intersection; Pellissier Building, 1930–31 *(left)* and Wilshire Professional Building, 1929–30 *(right)* in midground. (Photo by "Dick" Whittington, ca. 1932; courtesy Whittington Collection, Department of Special Collections, University of Southern California)

Figure 11.8. Beverly Boulevard at La Cienega, Los Angeles. (Photo by "Dick" Whittington, 1932; courtesy Huntington Library)

return for the owner. By 1930 an account written in a trade journal for chain store executives indicated that the drive-in was giving stiff competition to nearby chain outlets and an increasing number of chains were taking leases in new drive-in facilities.[25] Sometimes the company would join independent food merchants as another tenant, a course taken by Von's Grocery at the Palm Market (fig. 11.9). In several cases, however, a chain would operate the entire facility. Billie Bird Markets had four drive-ins in Los Angeles and Alhambra, at least two of which appear to have been commissioned by the firm. Similarly, the then nascent Alpha Beta chain procured the initial lease for all food departments in a complex developed by a Whittier realtor, and the company's first vice-president, J. A. Gerrard, maintained his office on the premises (fig. 11.10).[26]

The capital required to develop a drive-in was also a key factor in the type's success. The buildings themselves generally cost between $5000 and $15,000. A few were less; many others ran between $16,000 and $25,000. Some of the largest complexes entailed considerably greater amounts: $40,000 for the Palm Market, $50,000 for the Sunset-Western, and $115,000 for the Chapman Park. Fixtures and the purchase of the land could make the total investment much more. Base construction cost of the Toluca Market was $25,000, while the total expenditure came to $75,000; Hattem's second outlet cost $50,000, the total, $200,000. The average overall investment was probably about $30,000 to $50,000.[27] Most of the people who were willing and able to commit such resources were capable of securing sound business advice, or at least were far less prone to become the victim of unscrupulous agents.

The amount of funds required to construct a drive-in market was sufficiently great to appeal to sensible investors and helps to explain why so many of them became involved. In 1928 the base construction cost of other types of markets averaged much less than the drive-in; few were more than six thousand dollars. Much the same held true for store blocks generally, although the occasional large retail building, erected to house stylish specialty shops or one of the major variety chains such as F. W. Woolworth or S. H. Kress, could cost many times that amount. Gasoline stations averaged under four thousand dollars except when they included large service facilities.[28]

The other principal realm of speculative building investment to occur in outlying areas of the region was in multi-unit housing, for which there was mounting demand.[29] Within this sphere, by far the most prolific development in 1928 was of small complexes containing ten units or less—edifices classified as "apartments" (two to three stories in height with four to ten units) and as "flats" (generally two stories with four units)—with a base construction cost averaging between $8,000 and $15,000. Duplexes, averaging between $7,000 and $13,000, and apartment buildings, with from ten to twenty units and averaging $15,000 to $30,000, also were popular. The overall cost of such projects may have been somewhat lower than a

Figure 11.9. Von's Grocery unit of Palm Market, Wilshire Boulevard, Beverly Hills; J. Bryon Severence, designer, 1928–29; no longer standing. (Photo by "Dick" Whittington, 1929; courtesy Whittington Collection, Department of Special Collections, University of Southern California)

Figure 11.10. Alpha Beta Market No. 28, Philadelphia Street, Whittier, California; David S. Bushnell, architect, 1930; burned 1970. (Photo ca. 1930; courtesy Edward Schmidt)

drive-in market owing to the smaller parcel of land needed and the fact that, since many of these lots did not front major arteries, they tended to command smaller square-foot prices. Yet in general terms, both the moderate-size, multi-unit dwelling and the drive-in market fell within the middle range of real estate investment—attractive to people who did not have, or want to commit, the substantially greater sums necessary for a large office building, hotel, apartment house, or theater, but who did seek to encumber more than was needed to construct a taxpayer block, which was itself proving to be a risky venture due to poor location and oversupply. The drive-in market probably had further appeal because the base construction cost was low relative to the amount of land occupied, allowing investors to get a handsome return without huge expenditure on a lot that might eventually hold a much larger building if the pressures for urban development continued.

The drive-in market proliferated because of a confluence of favorable circumstances that did not require strong leadership to guide the course. The type was relatively simple in its building and operational programs as well as sufficiently reasonable in its overall cost for participation in the development process to be widespread. Just as a number of parties had independently undertaken the initial work, so a far greater array of individual interests could draw from that aggregate, utilizing what proved to be the most effective practices, to continue the process of diffusion.

When Alexander Haddad erected one of the first drive-in markets in 1925, the idea of securing professional design services probably never occurred to him any more than it would have to a roadside entrepreneur wishing to construct a shelter from which to sell fruits and vegetables (fig. 11.11). The cost would have been too great, the skills involved unnecessary. Some three years later, Richard Neutra, who would soon attain an international reputation as one of the foremost avant-garde architects in the U.S., created several schemes for drive-in markets, in part as a means of illustrating the new, abstract modernism he championed (fig. 11.12). Few subsequent drive-in markets were as unassuming as Haddad's and fewer still fully embodied avant-garde ideals, yet these polarities underscore the remarkable speed with which the drive-in market emerged from a home-grown experiment to a building type that attracted widespread professional interest. The spectrum of people involved in this process encompassed a complete cross-section of building design practice in one of the country's largest metropolises.[30] Yet, much as with the owners, no single practitioner or small group of practitioners assumed the dominant role at any stage of the type's development.

Three of the most prominent firms to design drive-in markets—Walker and Eisen; John and Donald B. Parkinson; and Morgan, Walls, and Clements—ranked among the oldest and largest in Southern California and were the acknowledged local leaders in the commercial sphere. Theodore Eisen had opened his office in the mid-

Figure 11.11. Beverl'y Open Air Market, Beverly Boulevard, Los Angeles, 1925; no longer standing. (From *Chain Store Review,* July 1929, p. 45)

1880s, Octavius Morgan in 1888, and John Parkinson in 1894. Each firm had a much younger partner in charge of design who was a major regenerating force: Albert Walker (partner in 1919), Donald Parkinson (1920), and Stiles Clements (1922). Thus the three offices benefited from long-standing ties to business leaders while keeping abreast of current tendencies in the commercial field. Collectively their work formed a large component of the office blocks, banks, hotels, theaters, and other buildings situated downtown as well as in more recent outlying centers such as Hollywood and the mid-Wilshire district.[31] These firms also produced dozens, indeed probably hundreds, of more modest commercial buildings—from elaborate branch banks to unassuming taxpayer blocks—along the miles of boulevard frontage throughout the greater metropolitan area. This triad exerted a decisive impact in setting the standard and introducing new tendencies in the design for virtually the entire range of commercial architecture in the region. Morgan, Walls, and Clements's contribution beyond the city center was of particular importance, for under the direction of

Figure 11.12. Unidentified design for a drive-in market; Richard Neutra, architect, ca. 1929. (Courtesy Thomas Hines)

its junior partner, the firm made a specialty of small-scale work, giving distinction to buildings that many comparable offices considered worth a minimal allocation of time, albeit an important a source of income. Clements was a pioneer in this respect, marshaling the talent of a large office to leave a strong imprint on the new, decentralized landscape.[32]

Several other architects who designed drive-in markets were known and gained prominence for the caliber of their work generally. Marston, Van Pelt, and Mayberry, considered the leading firm in Pasadena, also had a national reputation. Locally it secured many of the choicest commissions for projects ranging from office blocks to service garages, retail stores to clubs, houses for the rich to apartment buildings for persons of moderate income. The work of Ralph Flewelling was concentrated in Beverly Hills and, while less extensive, was frequently recognized for its high standard of design. Gilbert Stanley Underwood, on the other hand, had projects in many parts of the West, which were as varied as rustic resort hotels at Yosemite and Sun Valley, classicizing federal buildings in San Francisco and Seattle, and Art Deco skyscrapers in Los Angeles. Far better known today, of course, were Southern California modernists Richard Neutra and Lloyd Wright. Each pursued a manifestly different approach to design, the former seeking a cool, yet dramatic, play of form and space embodying a machine aesthetic; the latter, a more naturalistic, expressionist vein. At the same time, both Neutra and Wright were fascinated by the possibilities of a commercial architecture whose character embraced the automobile no less than new, mass-manufactured building products and techniques of illumination. Both men also yearned for the chance to undertake large-scale projects—to have a major impact on the character of their adopted city—even though most of their commissions prior to World War II were limited to the residential sphere.[33]

While this array of the region's leading architects was involved with the drive-in market, none of them, individually or as a group, became a shaping force in the type's development. Their work generally adhered to patterns of size and configuration already established by others. Neutra's and Wright's schemes were prophetic of expressive tendencies in commercial architecture a decade or two later, but had no impact on the drive-in market itself. Morgan, Walls, and Clements's Plaza Market (1928) stood among the most polished examples, and their Chapman Park Market among the most unusual and ambitious (figs. 11.13, 11.14).[34] Nevertheless, their work did not generate the salient expressive qualities for the type in the way that their earlier store blocks did for more conventional forms of retail development. In a few cases, as with the Parkinsons' Leess Drive-In Market (1927), the results were utterly unexceptional (fig. 11.15). Moreover, the contribution of these offices amounted to a small percentage of the total in quantitative terms. Morgan, Walls, and Clements was the most prolific of any firm, with six drive-ins, four of which were realized, to their credit. Neutra's proposals probably were unsolicited and never advanced beyond the schematic stage. One of Wright's two plans saw execution. Flewelling, Underwood, and Marston, Van Pelt, and Mayberry did one each; that designed by Walker and Eisen was not built.

A somewhat larger portion of drive-in markets came from architects who achieved a degree of prominence in their time, but who are virtually forgotten today. Men such as Arthur Kelly, Theodore Pletsch, Allen Ruoff, and Kemper Nomland practiced primarily in the residential field. The Austin Company of California specialized in commercial and industrial buildings. Others, including Gable and Wyant, H. L. Gogerty, Alfred Priest, Carl Jules Weyl, Henry Withey, and A. C. Zimmerman had general practices. A few, such as George Adams and L. G. Scherer, had begun to experiment in a modernist vein; however, most remained tied to the academic tradition, at least until the general thrust of architecture locally began to change dur-

Figure 11.13. Plaza Market, Pico Boulevard, Los Angeles; Morgan, Walls, and Clements, architects, 1928; no longer standing. (From *Architectural Forum*, June 1929, p. 901)

ing the 1930s. More often than not, their offices were modest in size, their buildings modest in scale. None created designs that achieved recognition as major works, then or now. At the same time, these architects represented a high level of competence, which collectively did much to enhance the metropolitan environment.[35]

The largest contingent of architects who designed drive-in markets had bread-and-butter practices, producing plans mostly for small, inexpensive residences, apartments, commercial blocks, and institutional buildings. Their work was almost never covered by the region's professional or trade presses and very little is known about it today. Such architects, however, were among the first to experiment with the drive-in. The designers of the 1926–27 Mission Motor-In Market, one of the initial half dozen examples to be realized, were Cramer and Wise, a small-scale architectural and engineering firm (fig. 11.16). Walter Folland, who was responsible for the slightly earlier plans of the Mother Goose Market had just recently arrived in Pasadena, and much of his practice there focused on designing modest houses and residential hotels. Walter Hegedohm, architect for both of Hattem's markets, trained as a draftsman for the Southern Pacific and Los Angeles electric railroads before he established his own practice in 1927. Many other such architects contributed subsequently, including H. C. Deckbar, Frank Harrington, J. Robert Harris, J. Byron Severence, Frank Stiff, McNeal Swasey, and George M. Thomas. Among them, only Norstrom and Anderson might be considered specialists, preparing plans for numerous taxpayer blocks and similarly small-scale commercial buildings in the region.[36]

Some designers had yet to gain professional status as architects. Men such as Kenneth Albright, Milton Sutton, and Eugene Voght were employed as draftsmen and probably worked on plans such as those they did for drive-in markets as a source of additional experience and income. Others were not pursuing an architectural career. At least three people—C. Waldo Powers, Frank Webster, and H. Sage

Figure 11.14. Chapman Park Market, West Sixth Street, Los Angeles; Morgan, Walls, and Clements, architects, 1928–29. (Courtesy *Progressive Grocer*)

Figure 11.15. Leess Drive-In Market, North Vine Street, Los Angeles; John and Donald B. Parkinson, architects, 1927; altered. (Photo by "Dick" Whittington, 1933; courtesy Whittington Collection, Department of Special Collections, University of Southern California)

Figure 11.16. Mission Motor-In Market, Sunset Boulevard, Los Angeles; Cramer and Wise, architects, 1926–27. (Photo by author)

Webster—practiced as engineers. Some were established contractors. Firms such as the Ted R. Cooper Company, Schumacher Home Builders, and C. W. Wilson and Sons appear to have had sizable construction businesses and were well equipped to draw plans as part of services offered. The Los Angeles Investment Company was a pioneer locally in large-scale residential development. Engaged in land sales and building thousands of houses since the 1890s, the organization provided a host of related services, among them mortgages and loans on property sold; savings accounts for prospective home buyers; and architectural, insurance, and rental departments. Business extended well beyond the company's tracts. Many clients had their own projects, including four who contracted for the design and erection of drive-in markets. Several drive-ins were designed by plan companies such as Bungalowcraft, and at least one was by a manufacturer of prefabricated building components, Safety Steel Products. More frequently, drive-in markets were designed by contractors who seem to have had small, localized practices, including Malcolm Smith (who drew the plans for the first known drive-in) Harry Beall, Charles Buschlen, Robert Eckert, Clyde Jones, L. D. Machado, Harly Martin, and Frank Rasche.[37]

No single firm can readily be given credit for playing the key role in either the early development of the drive-in market or in setting the standard among later examples. It is doubtful whether those involved at the formative stage were interested in conceptualizing some bold departure from basic patterns or retail design. The products suggest instead that these men concentrated on addressing the practical requirements of their clients to develop efficient, economical solutions, with the attributes that became characteristic evolving in modest increments and through repeated use. The "model" was formed by collective experience rather than by singular example. Because that model represented a rather elementary, straightforward solution, it was easy to emulate. As a result, scores of designers who worked for a large building firm or in architectural practices of no great distinction created work on much the same level as that by more prominent colleagues, and did so without the latter group leading the way (fig. 11.17). Little-known designers could be just as inventive as well-recognized architects and were responsible for numerous refinements to the type after its general characteristics were established. Two of the most widely published examples were Adams's Mesa-Vernon Market (1928) and Severence's Palm Market (1928–29), both of which were praised for their strikingly simple exteriors calculated to attract the attention of the passing motorist (fig. 11.18).[38] Yet however practical in nature, few such variations had an impact on the general thrust of subsequent work. In its mature as in its nascent phase, the drive-in market resisted paradigms.

The diffuse nature of the emulation process was at least in part shaped by the involvement of so many independent parties. Like the architectural elite, few designers of less prominence prepared plans for more than one, or at the most two, drive-in markets. The construction firm of Cartwright and Huffman was the exception in designing five. Thus no one office could gain the recognition and with it the potential for influence, by having secured a large share of the business. Architectural specialization in food store design did not coalesce until the next decade when Stiles Clements became the leading figure locally and a well-known one nationally. After creating the prototypical Ralphs supermarket in 1928, he continued to develop new features that set the standard for the type well into the post–World War II era.[39]

In design as in ownership, the drive-in market's development lay in the hands of many people. Lesser-known architects and builders, many of whom had small practices, were the dominant group involved, paralleling the contribution made by the

Figure 11.17. Clock Market, Wilshire Boulevard, Beverly Hills; C. W. Wilson and Sons, designer-builder, 1929. (Photo by "Dick" Whittington, 1930; courtesy Whittington Collection, Department of Special Collections, University of Southern California)

Figure 11.18. Mesa-Vernon Market. (Photo by "Dick" Whittington, 1929; courtesy Whittington Collection, Department of Special Collections, University of Southern California)

numerous small-scale real estate concerns and individual investors. The type remained essentially a vernacular phenomenon to which myriad discrete parties contributed at a grassroots level. Prominent architects and businessmen participated, but introduced no significant modifications that were sustained at the popular level. And while a majority of drive-in markets shared characteristics in their size, configuration, siting, tenancy, and cost that made it easy to delineate what constituted typicality, no one scheme can be identified as the definitive model. Invention occurred in a modest way, with incremental steps taken by people of modest stature, driven by practical objectives and using empirical methods. A paradigm was not needed.

Notes

This essay draws from material gathered in the course of research for a forthcoming book on the drive-in and the supermarket in Southern California. Support for that project included several grants from the University Facilitating Fund and Center for Washington Area Studies at George Washington University as well as from the National Main Street Center at the National Trust for Historic Preservation. Many people have contributed ideas and information during the course of my research. I am especially indebted to Robert Bruegmann, David Gebhard, Thomas Hines, Tom Owen, Ed Whittington, and Robert Winter. I am also very grateful to Randall Mackinson for allowing me to stay on several occasions at the Gamble House in Pasadena, which afforded both sanctuary and inspiration.

1. For general background, see Susan Porter Benson, *Counter Cultures: Saleswomen, Managers, and Customers in American Department Stores, 1890–1940* (Urbana: University of Illinois Press, 1986), chaps. 1–2. Much has been written on Stewart in this regard, including Harry E. Resseguie, "A. T. Stewart's Marble Palace—The Cradle of the Department Store," *New-York Historical Society Quarterly* 48 (April 1964): 130–62; Harry E. Resseguie, "Alexander Turney Stewart and the Development of the Department Store, 1823–1876," *Business History Review* 39 (autumn 1965): 301–22; and Deborah S. Gardner, "A Paradise of Fashion: A. T. Stewart's Department Store, 1862–1875," in *A Needle, a Bobbin, a Strike: Women Needleworkers in America*, ed. Joan M. Jensen and Sue Davidson (Philadelphia: Temple University Press, 1985), 60–80.

For background on Wood's contribution to the company, see Boris Emmet and John E. Jeuck, *Catalogues and Counters: A History of Sears, Roebuck and Company* (Chicago: University of Chicago Press, 1950), chaps. 20–21; and James C. Worthy, *Shaping an American Institution: Robert E. Wood and Sears, Roebuck* (Urbana: University of Illinois Press, 1984).

Concerning the Country Club Plaza, see Richard Longstreth, "J. C. Nichols, the Country Club Plaza, and Notions of Modernity," *Harvard Architecture Review* 5 (1986): 120–35; William S. Worley, *J. C. Nichols and the Shaping of Kansas City* (Columbia: University of Missouri Press, 1990), chap. 8.

2. Concerning Burnham's work, see Thomas S. Hines, *Burnham of Chicago, Architect and Planner* (New York: Oxford University Press, 1974), 303–7; Ann Lorenz Van Zanten, "The Marshall Field Annex and the New Urban Order of Daniel Burnham's Chicago," *Chicago History* 11 (fall–winter 1982): 130-41; and Neil Harris "Shopping—Chicago Style," in *Chicago Architecture 1872–1922, Birth of Metropolis*, ed. John Zukowsky (Munich: Prestel-Verlag, 1987), 142–47.

Many commercial architects have generally been neglected by scholars. For a sampling of period sources on the work Nimmons's firm did for Sears, see George C. Nimmons, "The New Renaissance in Architecture as Seen in the Design of Buildings for Mail Order Houses," *American Architect* 134 (5 August 1928): 142–48; "A Mail Order Store Building in Los Angeles, California," *Architectural Record* 64 (July 1928): 65–69; "No Windows," *Architect and Engineer* 120 (February 1935): 35–38; Leonard E. Dunlap, "Concrete for Sears in Every Climate," *Architectural Concrete* 6, no. 2 (1940): 2–6; and "5 Retail Stores Planned for the Motor Age," *Architectural Record* 88 (September 1940): 32–42.

A good record of Gruen's and Ketchum's early retail work is contained in Emrich Nicholson, *Contemporary Shops in the United States* (New York: Architectural Book Publishing, 1945). For an account of Ketchum's ideas on retail design, see Morris Ketchum Jr., *Shops and Stores* (New York: Reinhold, 1948). Gruen's writing on the subject is voluminous. See, for example, Victor Gruen and Larry Smith, *Shopping Towns USA: The Planning of Shopping Centers* (New York: Reinhold, 1960). Gruen is also the focus of a recent study, Howard Gillette Jr., "The Evolution of the Planned Shopping Center in Suburb and City," *Journal of the American Planning Association* 51 (autumn 1985): 449–60.

3. The drive-in market can be defined as a facility designed for the sale of all basic types of food product (meat, groceries, baked goods, fruit, vegetables, etc.) and open to at least one side of an off-street parking area that is an integral part of the site plan. The selling area was almost always a long, shallow space. Generally each type of food product was sold by a separate concessioner, but never by multiple ones as was standard in municipal and other so-called public markets. The form of the drive-in was generally a rectangle or some variant of an L or U. Size averaged between four thousand and seven thousand square feet of ground floor area, though examples could be found with less than three thousand and more than sixteen thousand square feet. Typically the parking area occupied more than one-half and sometimes as much as two-thirds of the entire lot.

Basic data on the drive-in market noted here and elsewhere in the text were compiled from contract and other notices in the daily *Southwest Builder and Contractor,* period telephone directories and Sanborn fire insurance maps for California and neighboring states, field work, and coverage in Los Angeles area newspapers, including *Alhambra Post Advocate, Beverly Hills Citizen, Glendale News-Press, Hollywood Daily Citizen, Huntington Park Signal, Inglewood Daily News, Los Angeles Times, Long Beach Press-Telegraph, Pasadena Star-News, Santa Ana Daily Register, Santa Monica Evening Outlook, South Gate Tribune, Southwest Wave, Van Nuys News, and Venice Evening Vanguard.*

Work that appears to have been directly inspired by California examples can be found in such distant places as Norfolk, Virginia, New Orleans, and Battle Creek, Michigan; see Louis Fisher Jr., "Putting the New Store Over," *Chain Store Age, Administrative Edition* 9 (February 1933): 14–15; "'10 Stores in One' to Open for Community Shopping," *New Orleans Times-Picayune,* 4 May 1933, 7; W. E. Penick, "Hold that Opening Crowd," *Chain Store Age, Grocery Edition* 9 (June 1933): 16–17, 38, 40; Robert Latimer, "T-Shaped Building Makes Effective Super," *Super Market Merchandising* 6 (February 1941): 46–48; and "Michigan: Short-Lived Shopping Center for Unstable Land," *Architectural Record* 84 (July 1938): 44–45. Nevertheless, these examples entailed modifications in both form and operational structure that differentiated them from their West Coast models. More importantly, such work remained anomalous in other regions.

In some instances, the name "drive-in market" was appropriated and off-street parking was part of the plan; however, no significant correspondence existed between the parking area and the selling space inside. See, for example, "New Food Market Open," *Portland Oregonian,* 20 April 1930, sec. 2, p. 2; "Mac Marr Develops the 'Drive-In' Store," *Chain Store Age, General Merchandise Edition* 6 (October 1930): 59–62, 72; "'Lighthouse Advertises Oregon Drive-In Market," *Chain Store Review* 5 (February 1932): 51; *Indianapolis News,* 3 November 1932, Kroger Section; James R. Branson, "New Drive-In Unit Opened by Kroger In Indianapolis," *Progressive Grocer* 12 (February 1933): 30–31, 80; *Indianapolis News,* 2 November 1933, Kroger Section; "Standard Opens Big Drive-In Market," *Chain Store Age, Grocery Edition* 10 (May 1934): 19; and "Kroger Opens Big Drive-In Market, *Chain Store Age, Grocery Edition* 10 (October 1934): 42, 74.

4. Recently, the drive-in market has been the subject of a brief essay: Richard Longstreth,

"The Perils of a Parkless Town," in *The Car and the City: The Automobile, the Built Environment, and Daily Urban Life,* ed. Martin Wachs and Margaret Crawford (Ann Arbor: University of Michigan Press, 1992), 141–53, 310–13. The best period accounts include a series of articles by Willard D. Morgan, an architectural photographer then living in Los Angeles: "California Drive-In Markets Serve Motorists on the Go," *Chain Store Review* 1 (September 1928): 29–31; "'Drive-Ins' Drive On While Stores Sleep," *Chain Store Review* 2 (May 1929): 15–16, 30–32; "At Last—A Place to Park!" *American Builder* 47 (July 1929): 58–61; "Stores the Road Passes Through," *Nation's Business* 17 (July 1929): 45–46; and "The Super Drive-In Emerges from Competitive Whirl," *Chain Store Review* 3 (October 1930): 10–12, 40. See also "Drive-In Markets Popular in West," *Progressive Grocer* 7 (June 1928): 22–23; Walter Van de Kamp, "An Innovation in Retail Selling," *Magazine of Business* 56 (July 1929): 42–43; Arthur E. Goodwin, *Markets: Public and Private* (Seattle: Montgomery Publishing, 1929), 70–74; Marc N. Goodnow, "Drive In and Shop," *Forbes,* 1 February 1930, 15–17; S. Lewis Brevit, "Drive-in 'Department Stores' Gaining Popularity in West," *Sales Management* 17 January 1931, 118; Crag Dale, "Is Main Street Doomed?" *Popular Mechanics,* May 1931, 765-68; Albert Frey, "Amerikanische Notizen," *Werk* 20 (October 1933): 314; and Clarence S. Stein and Catherine Bauer, "Store Buildings and Neighborhood Shopping Centers," *Architectural Record* 75 (February 1934): 185–86.

5. Several other types also contributed to this process during the 1920s, the most commonplace of which were the chain variety store and the chain drug store. In many sizable outlying business districts of major cities, "neighborhood" department stores, which were generally modest in size, limited in selection, and emphasized practicality over fashion, were constructed at this same time. Finally, Sears Roebuck and Montgomery Ward entered the retail field in the mid-1920s. Among all these developments, Sears had the only retail-specific buildings that were located away from concentrated commercial areas and incorporated off-street parking for customers. These two attributes were an integral part of the company's program beginning with its first two large, purpose-built retail stores, which opened in Chicago on 2 November 1925. See "Sears-Roebuck's 2 Chicago Retail Units Open Today," *Women's Wear Daily,* 2 November 1925, 2, 55.

6. Probings in a number of other metropolitan areas have failed to yield any other building type, aside from automobile service facilities, specifically configured for a motorist clientele that approached anything like the ubiquitousness of the drive-in market. On the other hand, roadside stands and other buildings designed in response to motor travel had become quite numerous in some rural areas by 1930.

7. Fundamental differences between the drive-in market and the supermarket entailed configuration and size. While the drive-in's form was essentially linear, comprised of a shallow selling space oriented to a forecourt, the supermarket of the 1930s tended to be a chunky rectangle—the depth of its selling area generally about twice the width—oriented to the street. If an off-street parking area existed, it lay to one side of the building. Save for Ralphs's stores, scant visual relationship was created between the two components of the site. The drive-in's size was predicated on customers making daily or at least frequent trips to purchase relatively small quantities of goods at a time. The supermarket, on the other hand, depended on a large volume of purchases. Furthermore, pioneering supermarket operations of the 1920s, most notably those of Ralphs in Los Angeles, and Heinke and Pillot in Houston, owned all or nearly all the departments on the premises, a business structure that became widespread in the industry by the end of the next decade.

Good overviews of the development of the supermarket are Chester H. Liebs, *Main Street to Miracle Mile: American Roadside Architecture* (Boston: New York Graphic Society, 1985), 117–35; and James M. Mayo, *The American Grocery Store: The Business Evolution of an Architectural Space* (Westport, Conn.: Greenwood Press, 1993), chaps. 4–5. Whereas two New York–area companies, King Kullen and Big Bear, are generally thought to have been the principal catalysts in the supermarket's emergence as a national phenomenon, Southern California–based firms and, to a somewhat lesser degree, others based in Houston, established all the key attributes of supermarket operation during the 1920s. Furthermore, a close reading of trade literature of the period reveals that the contribution of Southern California, especially, was well recognized by the mid-1930s. See, for example, A. E. Holden, "Is Price-Wrecking Wrecking the Super-Markets?" *Chain Store Age, General Merchandise Edition* 9 (June 1936): 82; Donna Collister, "Inside Story of a Supermarket," *Progressive Grocer* 13 (August 1934): 40; M. M. Zimmerman, "Super-Market!" *Nation's Business* 25 (March 1937): 90–98: M. J. Rowoldt, "How Supers Operate in California," *Progressive Grocer* 16 (October 1937): 30; Emanuel Rapaport, "The Economic Significance of the Super Market," *Super Market Merchandising* 3 (February 1938): 84–85; "Today's Super-Markets," *Progressive Grocer* 17 (July 1938): 23–25; and M. M. Zimmerman, "A Cross Country Impression," *Super Market Merchandising* 5 (April 1940): 37, 40.

8. Concerning the Wilshire Boulevard store, see *Los Angeles Times,* 29 April 1928, sect. 5, p. 1; and Harriet Burdsall, "Thousands Enjoy Opening of Ralphs Market on Wilshire," *Hollywood Daily Citizen,* 21 September 1928, p. 9. Seven additional large stores were opened in the metropolitan area between that year and 1931. Useful accounts include "Ralphs Invite[s] Everyone to Three-Day Opening of New Store," *Hollywood Daily Citizen,* 5 June 1929, Ralphs Section; "Ralphs Alhambra Store Opens Tomorrow," *Alhambra Post-Advocate,* 11 September 1929, Ralphs Section; *Pasadena Star News,* 2 October 1929, Ralphs Section; "Ralphs Opening Sixteenth Store," *Santa Monica Evening Outlook,* 20 November 1929, 14–18; Harriet Burdsall, "Ralphs Adjust[s] Marketing System to Modern Requirements," *Hollywood Daily Citizen,* 2 January 1930, 9–10; "Beautiful New Ralphs Store Ready for Gala Opening," *Southwest Wave,* 13 April 1932, 1–6. For a sampling of material on the company's equally important building campaign of 1937–41, see "New Ralphs Grocery Opens Saturday," *Beverly Hills Citizen,* 11 June 1937, Ralphs Section; J. Gordon Wright, "Sharing Economies with Public, Ralphs' Policy," *Super Market Merchandising* 2 (September 1937): 6, 8, 10; *Los Angeles Times,* 28 April 1929, Ralphs Section; J. Gordon Wright, "Ralphs Twenty-Seventh Unit Makes Debut," *Super Market Merchandising* 4 (June 1939): 10, 19; and "Ralphs Opens 28th Super Unit," *Super Market Merchandising* 5 (March 1940): 14–15, 19.

For background on shopping centers, see Richard Longstreth, "The Neighborhood Shopping Center in Washington, D.C., 1930–1941," *Journal of the Society of Architectural Historians* 51 (March 1992): 5–34.

9. Early accounts of taxpayers in Washington, D.C., indicate that covering expenses on land that might later soar in value may have been the underlying motivation, at least in many instances, but also reveal these buildings were often quite profitable in their own right. See "One-Story Stores Figure in Development of Realty," *Washington Evening Star,* 14 January 1911, sect. 2, p. 2; "Row of One-Story Stores Brings Good Price in Sale," *Washington Evening Star,* 22 July 1911, sect. 2, p. 2; and "Interesting Development along Eighteenth Street," *Washington Evening Star,* 9 November 1912, sect. 2, p. 3. For a historical overview of the type, see Liebs, *Main Street,* 10–15.

10. For a contemporary account describing the practices of Safeway Stores, see H. S. Wright, "Locating Grocery Stores," *Chain Store Age* 1 (August 1925): 10–11, 54–55.

11. For a recent account of Hattem, see Maurice I. Hattem, "I. M. Hattem and His Los Angeles Supermarket," *Western States Jewish Historical Quarterly* 11 (April 1979): 243–51. Documentation has been found on only nine other food retailers who were the initial owners/operators of drive-in markets. Among them, Billie Bird Markets owned at least two and operated two more; Alexander Haddad appears to have operated at least two concurrently; Leonard Redman owned two. The rest owned one each; however, three of them operated a conventional outlet as well.

12. Most of the information concerning owners noted here and in the paragraphs below has been gleaned from notices in the *Southwest Builder and Contractor* and the *Los Angeles Times,* as well as listings in local directories. In only a few instances have biographical accounts been found. Collectively, these sources yield at least the name and occupation of more than one-half of the drive-in market owners in Los Angeles itself and about one-third of those elsewhere in the state.

Concerning Dishbrow, see "Mother Goose Pantry Is to Open," *Pasadena Star-News,* 31 August 1927, pp. 22–23.

On Bogardus, see "E. F. Bogardus Opens Sunset-Western Market Tomorrow," *Hollywood Daily Citizen,* 28 September 1928, p. 17; *Los Angeles Realtor* 9 (November 1928): 42; and Edward Palmer, *History of Hollywood,* vol. 2 (Los Angeles: Arthur H. Cawston, 1937) 237–39.

On Chapman, see William A. Spalding, *History of Los Angeles City and County*, vol. 3 (Los Angeles: J. R. Finnell and Sons, 1931), 587–91; Palmer, *Hollywood*, vol. 2, 49–52; and Ralph Hancock, *Fabulous Boulevard* (New York: Funk and Wagnalls, 1949), 292–93.

13. Concerning the Taft Companies, see *Men of California . . .* , (San Francisco and Los Angeles: Western Press Register, 1925), 38; and *Who's Who in Los Angeles County 1932–1933*, (Los Angeles: Charles J. Lang, 1933), 62. Real estate advertisements provide the best readily available documentation for many of these ventures. Concerning Burton and Company, see, for example, *Los Angeles Times*, 26 February 1922, sect. 5, p. 5. The Leimert Company's first tract was Bellehurst Park in Glendale (*Los Angeles Times*, 16 March 1923, sect. 2, p. 9, 18 March 1923, sect. 5, p. 20). Leimert Park was much more ambitious in both its size and planning; see V. Cahalin, "Spanish Type Houses Pay," *Building Age* 51 (May 1929): 37–40; and "Residence Area Growth Shown," *Los Angeles Times*, 16 August, 1931, sect. 5, p. 2.

14. Concerning the Muller Brothers, see James V. Murray, "Super-Service Station Caters to Stars in Hollywood," *Filling Station and Petroleum Marketer*, 10 January 1927, 24–25; "Everything for the Car on One Lot," *National Petroleum News*, 25 July 1928, 83, 86; Brad Mills, "Mullers' Complete Service," *Petroleum Marketer*, June 1929, 22–23; and *Hollywood Daily Citizen*, 4 October 1929, 13–19. On Woestman, see "Woestman's Drive-In Group of Buildings Opens Tomorrow . . ." *Pasadena Star-News*, 11 July 1930, 25–26; and *Who's Who in Los Angeles County, 1930–1931*, 168.

15. On McKinley, Griffith, and Nagel, see *Who's Who in California . . . 1928–1929* (San Francisco: Who's Who Publishing, 1929), 94, 430, 366–67, respectively. On Pickford, see Robert Windeler, *Sweetheart: The Story of Mary Pickford* (London: W. H. Allen, 1973), 189.

16. The facility still stands, somewhat altered, at 1040–1060 South La Brea Avenue. Base construction cost was only six thousand dollars.

17. Willard Morgan incorrectly credited Alexander Haddad with conceiving the first drive-in market and suggested he was a key figure in establishing practices widely followed by others who entered the field (see especially "California Drive-In," 30–31). Yet Haddad's first building (fig. 11.11) was unusually modest in both physical and operational terms. Haddad appears to have built one other drive-in, slightly more ambitious in nature, and later to have leased space in a third. The evidence found to date shows Haddad to have made a modest contribution as an early figure to experiment with the concept of the food store as a drive-in facility, but gives no support to his role as a seminal innovator.

I. M. Hattem was among the most publicity conscious of drive-in market owners and secured considerable name recognition in the Los Angeles metropolitan area during the late 1920s and early 1930s. Hattem's showmanship no doubt fostered the drive-in's popularity, but his business practices did not provide a direct model. In contrast to the norm, Hattem owned and operated almost all the departments in his two stores, just as would later become commonplace with the supermarket.

18. One account, in noting that "several companies have been formed to establish these markets, build the stalls and lease them," was probably referring to real estate agents rather than owners. See Brevit, "Drive-In 'Department Stores,'" 118. No evidence has been found to suggest that large businesses engaged in the sale of food were behind the drive-in market as would occur later with the supermarket.

19. See, for example, James W. Elliott, "Los Angeles Leads Nation as Realty Hot Spot," *Los Angeles Times*, 17 June 1928, sect. 5, pp. 1, 5; Stuart O'Melveny, "How Is Los Angeles Real Estate?" *Los Angeles Realtor*, 9 (December 1928): 12–13; and Otto G. Wildey, *An Approach to Business Real Estate*, (Los Angeles: Otto G. Wildey, 1930), 6, 8.

20. For contemporary accounts of experienced businessmen who were influential in guiding the growth of modest-size outlying commercial precincts, see "Lilly-Fletcher Company," *Los Angeles Times*, Midwinter Number, 1 January 1921, sect. 3, p. 24; and, "J. D. Farquhar Has Part in Making Western Avenue Section Grow to Present Thriving Proportions," *Hollywood Citizen*, 8 April 1921, sect. 1, p. 2.

21. James Collins, "Los Angeles: Ex-Crossroads Town," *World's Work* 59 (August 1930): 54.

22. James Collins, "Let's Play Store," *Saturday Evening Post*, 19 November 1927, 54.

23. *Sunshine and Grief in Southern California*, (Detroit: St. Claire Publishing, 1931), 47–48.

24. "Retail Store Location: Some Aspects of the Problem," *Eberle Economic Service*, 10 September 1928, 222. See also Carl Bush, "What

About Zoning?" *Los Angeles Realtor* 5 (October 1925): 17, 36; and "Proportion of Neighborhood Stores Vacant in Los Angeles," which appeared biannually in *Eberle Economic Service,* during the 1920s and early 1930s.

25. Morgan, "Super Drive-In," 10, 12; and Van de Kamp, "Innovation in Retail Selling," 42, among other accounts, indicate a high success rate. A later study, commissioned by *Progressive Grocer,* documents the soundness of a well-run operation; see M. J. Rowoldt, "We Study a California Market for You," *Progressive Grocer* 15 (October 1926): 34–35, 99. Concerning chain store involvement, see Morgan, "Super Drive-In," 40.

26. "This Market Largest of Kind in World, Is Claim," *Beverly Hills Citizen,* 18 April 1929; *Alhambra Post-Advocate,* 24 July 1929, Billie Bird Section; "New Store Shows Confidence Placed in City," *Alhambra Post-Advocate,* 14 January 1931, p. 3; *Alhambra Post-Advocate,* 27 July 1931, Billie Bird Section; *Whittier News,* 25 May 1933, Alpha Beta Section; interview with Edward Schmidt, Whittier, California, 9 July 1987.

27. Base construction costs were mostly gleaned from notices in the *Southwest Builder and Contractor.* Less information is available on total expenditures per project; the most reliable information comes from contemporary newspaper accounts. Irrespective of size, cost per square foot was generally between $1.50 and $2.30.

28. Most conventional food markets constructed in 1928 cost between five hundred and four thousand dollars. Figures were obtained for the great majority of markets for which notices appeared in the *Southwest Builder and Contractor.* For stores and other building types cited below, averages are based on a random sampling taken from the *Southwest Builder and Contractor* between January and December 1928, using a total of 225 projects as a data base.

29. Robert M. Fogelson, *The Fragmented Metropolis: Los Angeles 1850–1930* (Cambridge: Harvard University Press, 1967), 146; Scott L. Bottles, *Los Angeles and the Automobile: The Making of the Modern City* (Berkeley: University of California Press, 1987), 187, 189; "Building in Los Angeles and the National Tendency Toward Multi-Family Structures," *Eberle Economic Service,* 5 July 1928, 167–70; "Economic and Sociological Aspects of the Increase in Multifamily Dwelling Construction in Large Cities," *Eberle Economic Service,* 18 July 1928, 173–75; " The Housing Situation," Security–First National Bank of Los Angeles, *Monthly Summary of Business Conditions in the Pacific Southwest,* 2 January 1934, n.p.

30. Little information exists on most of the architects and others involved with the design of drive-in markets. My search for material in conjunction with this study was necessarily limited, focusing on that which could be gleaned from architectural periodicals, biographical compendia, and directories of the period. The most valuable document reconstructing the nature of these individual's practices are the contract and other notices published in the *Southwest Builders and Contractor;* however, time permitted only a cursory sampling. Further information was taken from more recent sources such as Henry F. Withey and Elsie R. Withey, *Biographical Dictionary of American Architects, Deceased* (1956; reprint, Los Angeles: Hennessey and Ingalls, 1970), a few recent scholarly accounts, and the membership files in the Archives of the American Institute of Architects in Washington (hereinafter cited as AIA). David Cameron, Robert Judson Clark, David Gebhard, Tom Owen, Robert Winter, and the staff of the Pasadena Urban Conservation Office generously supplied additional material. The citations in the notes below are not comprehensive, but are intended to give a sense of work done during the period in question.

31. Concerning Walker and Eisen, see Donald Schippers, "Walker and Eisen: Twenty Years of Los Angeles Architecture, 1920–1940," *Southern California Quarterly* 46 (December 1964): 371–94; Harris Allen, "Southern California Architects . . . ," *Building Review* 22 (October 1922): 43–45, plates 48, 51; and F. A. Evans, "Recent Work of Messrs. Walker and Eisen," *Architect and Engineer* 82 (August 1925): 50–89.

Concerning the Parkinsons, see Robert Tracey, "John Parkinson and the Beaux-Arts City Beautiful Movement in Downtown Los Angeles" (Ph.D. diss., University of California, Los Angeles, 1982); *Who's Who in the Pacific Southwest* (Los Angeles: Times Mirror Printing and Binding House, 1913), 285; *Men of California,* 47; *Architect and Engineer* 124 (January 1936): 57; and Withey and Withey, *Biographical Dictionary,* 455–56.

Concerning Morgan, Walls, and Clements, see "Personal Glimpses," *Pacific Coast Architect* 27 (February 1925): 22, 27; *Architect and Engi-*

neer 101 (May 1930): 27; *Who's Who in Los Angeles County, 1930–1931,* 133; and David Gebhard, *The Richfield Building, 1928–1968* ([Los Angeles]: Atlantic Richfield, [1970]), 6, 8.

32. See, for example, Harwood Hewitt, "Is Good Architectural Design a Paying Investment and How Much Does It Cost?" *Pacific Coast Architect* 25 (March 1924): 5–17; "Shops in Los Angeles," *Pacific Coast Architect* 25 (April 1924): 11–24; Arthur Duncombe, "Beautiful Architecture a Magnet of Trade," *California Southland* 6 (September 1924): 7–8; Donald E. Marquis, "The Spanish Stores of Morgan, Walls and Clements," *Architectural Forum* 50 (June 1929): 901–16; and Stiles O. Clements, "Some Considerations in the Design of Small Banks," *Pacific Coast Architect* 33 (December 1928): 11–26.

33. For background on Marston, Van Pelt, and Mayberry, see "Spanish and English Colonial Homes in California," *California Southland* 4 (January 1922): 10–11, 25; Prentice Duell "Some Recent Works of Marston and Van Pelt," *Architectural Record* 52 (July 1922): 16–38; R. W. Sexton, *American Commercial Building of Today* (New York: Architectural Book Publishing Co., 1928), 133–37, 149, 152, 186, 199, 202, 260–61, 274–75; and Withey and Withey, *Biographical Dictionary,* 303–4.

For biographical information on Flewelling, see *Who's Who in California,* 130; and *Architect and Engineer* 155 (April 1941): 44. For illustrations of work, see *Architectural Record* 70 (November 1931): 332–33; 71 (January 1932, 19; 73 (March 1933, 204–7; *Architect and Engineer* 93 (April 1928): 40; 93 (May 1928): 46; 96 (January 1929): 44; 101 (June 1930): 67–81; 108 (January 1932): 62; 113 (April 1933): 14–17; *Pacific Coast Architect* 33 (December 1928): 42–44; 36 (October 1929): 50–55; 37 (May 1930): 24–29; 38 (August 1930): 36–39; *Architectural Digest* 6, no. 3 (1927): 33–35; 8, no. 2 (1931): 18–22; 8, no. 3 (1931): 45–47, 52–55.

For background on Underwood, see Joyce Zaitlin, *Gilbert Stanley Underwood* (Malibu, Calif.: Pangloss Press, 1989).

Concerning Neutra, see Thomas S. Hines, *Richard Neutra and the Search for Modern Architecture* (New York: Oxford University Press, 1982); and Thomas S. Hines, "Designing for the Motor Age: Richard Neutra and the Automobile," *Oppositions* 21 (summer 1980): 34–51. Neutra's drive-in market schemes are discussed at some length in Morgan's accounts, see "California Drive-In," 31; "At Last," 59–61; and "Super Drive-In," 11–12.

Concerning Wright, see David Gebhard and Harriette Von Breton, *Lloyd Wright, Architect* (Santa Barbara: Art Galleries, University of California, Santa Barbara, 1971); "Modern Marketplace Celebrates Opening with Gala Day, Tomorrow," *Hollywood Daily Citizen,* 19 December 1930, 8; and "Corrugated Galvanized Iron, Yucca-Vine Market, Hollywood, California," *American Architect,* 90 ((March 1932): 22–23.

34. The Chapman Market departed from the norm not only in its size but also configuration and tenancy. Here, the parking court was surrounded by the complex, which contained three markets, each oriented toward somewhat different shopping needs. For descriptions, see "Largest Drive-In Market Rising," *Los Angeles Times,* 21 October 1928, sect. 5, p. 6; Olive Gray, "New Market Unusual One," *Los Angeles Times,* 20 June 1929, sect. 2, p. 2; and Frank. H. Williams, "495 Cars Can Park in this New Drive-In Market," *Progressive Grocer* 8 (October 1929): 30–31, 130.

35. On Kelly, see Los Angeles Architectural Club, *Yearbook,* (hereinafter cited as *Yearbook*), 1910, 1911, 1916, 1919; Ellen Leech, *California Homes by California Architects* (Los Angeles: California Southland Magazine, 1922), 32–34; *Architectural Record* 34 (December 1913): 563-65; *Pacific Coast Architect* 27 (March 1928): 41–42; *Architectural Digest* 5 (1925): 66–67; 7, no. 1 (1929): 16–17, 85–93; 7, no. 2, (1929): 102–3, 124–25, 128–29; 8, no. 1 (1930): 33–37; 9, no. 3 (1933): 28–29; 9, no. 4 (1933): 120–21.

On Pletsch see *American Architects Directory,* ed. George S. Koyl (New York: R. R. Bowker, 1955), 437; *Architectural Digest* 10, no. 4 (1934): 109. I am grateful to Mr. Pletsch for providing me with additional information about his work.

On Ruoff see *Pacific Coast Architect* 31 (April 1927): 15; *Architectural Digest* 5 (1922): 58–59, 70–71; 9, no. 4 (1933): 122.

On Nomland see Koyl, *Architects Directory,* 407; AIA; *Architectural Digest* 9, no. 4 (1933): 70–73.

On Gable and Wyant, See *Architectural Forum* 53 (December 1930): 721; *Pacific Coast Architect* 30 (November 1926): 19–25; 32 (December 1927): 28–35; 35 (January 1929): 36–39; *Architectural Digest* 8, no. 1 (1930): 74–77, 82–85; *Shapes of Clay* 3 (September 1927): 7; 6 (March 1930): 14; *California Southland* 9 (December 1927): 14.

On Gogerty, see Koyl, *Architects Directory,* 200; AIA; *Architectural Forum* 53 (December 1930): 713–16.

On Priest, see *Architects and Engineers* 97 (May 1929): 83–90; 105 (June 1931): 84; *Shapes of Clay* 2 (January 1926): 8; 3 (September 1927): 10.

On Weyl, see *Architectural Record* 64 (December 1928): 466–68; *American Architecture* 134 (20 December 1928): 84–86; *Architect and Engineer* 99 (December 1929): 90–97; *Architectural Digest* 7, no. 3 (1929): 153.

On Withey, see Koyl, *Architects Directory,* 614; AIA; *Yearbook,* 1911, 1916, 1919; *Yearbook,* 1922, 24; Leech, *California Homes,* 45, 56; *Architect and Engineer* 94 (August 1928): 81–89; 96 (January 1929): 46.

On Zimmerman, see *Yearbook,* 1922, 62; *Pacific Coast Architect* 28 (August 1925): 37–41; 29 (January 1926): 13–17; *Architect and Engineer* 85 (May 1926): 36; *Architectural Record* 59 (May 1926): 410–11.

On Adams, see AIA; *Architect and Engineer* 96 (March 1929): 14; *Architectural Record* 76 (November 1934): 346–47.

On Scherer, see *Who's Who in Los Angeles County, 1930–1931,* 67, 248; L. G. Scherer, "The Architect Comes to Himself," *Architect and Engineer* 102 (July 1930): 111–12; *Architect and Engineer* 101 (June 1930): 62; 105 (April 1931): 54; 107 (February 1932): 25.

36. On Cramer and Wise, see *Architect and Engineer* 100 (February 1930): 2.

On Folland, see *Pasadena Star-News,* 17 April 1951, and architects' files, Pasadena Urban Conservation Office, Pasadena.

On Hagedohm, see Koyl, *Architects Directory,* 218; and AIA.

On Harrington and Harris, see AIA.

On Norstrom, see Withey, *Biographical Dictionary,* 444; *Los Angeles Times,* 20 May 1928; 14 December 1930, sect. 5, p. 2.

37. For background on the Los Angeles Investment Company see J. M. Guinn, *A History of California . . . ,* vol. 1 (Los Angeles: Historic Record, 1915), 371; *Los Angeles, the Old and the New* (Los Angeles: J. E. Scott, 1911), 55; and the numerous house plan books the company published, such as *Practical Bungalows* (1911), *Inexpensive Bungalows* (1912), and *Modern Homes of California* (1913). Activities during the 1920s are chronicled by numerous real estate advertisements. See, for example, *Los Angeles Times,* 24 September 1922, sect. 5, p. 8; *Los Angeles Evening Herald,* 7 May 1927, B-2, B-3; 6 June 1928, B-3. Concerning the other drive-in market projects, see *Los Angeles Times,* 20 October, 5 November 1929, sect. 5, p. 3. The scale and scope of this company's operations set it quite apart from the stereotypical picture of residential development patterns in the United States during the early twentieth century and deserve further investigation.

The Bungalowcraft Company published a number of plan books for houses and multi-unit dwellings, including *Bungalowcraft* (9th ed., 1921), *New Spanish Bungalows* (1926), and *Homes of the Moment* (1929). Rex Weston, who headed the organization, advertised in these volumes that the company did "all kinds of drafting," listing stores and apartment buildings among the types.

38. Morgan, "'Drive-Ins' Drive On," 15–16, 30–31; Morgan, "At Last," 59–61; Morgan, "Super Drive-In," 11; "Palm Market Is Largest of Type," *Beverly Hills Citizen,* 18 April 1929, 20-A; Cahalin, "Spanish Type Houses," 37; "Store Buildings," *Architectural Record* 65 (June 1929): 603; Frey, "Amerikanische Notizen," 314; Stein and Bauer, "Store Buildings," 185–86.

39. A few of the articles on Ralphs stores designed by Clements are cited in n. 8 above. See also J. Gordon Wright, "Food and Functionalism," *California Arts and Architecture* 54 (October 1938): 28, 36; Ben H. O'Connor, "Planning the Super-Market," *Architect and Engineer* 146 (September 1941): 14–19; and "Super Markets: The Office of Stiles Clements, Architect," *Architectural Record* 86 (October 1941): 72–73.

Exploiting Resources

CHAPTER TWELVE

The Historic Industrial Landscape of Butte and Anaconda, Montana

FREDRIC L. QUIVIK

The human landscape of the American West is certainly the subject of myth but more importantly the product of technology. Historian Thomas Hughes argues effectively in his book *American Genesis* that the large-scale technological systems developed by U.S. corporations during the late nineteenth and early twentieth centuries played a central role in shaping the character of American industrial society.[1] As an integral part of the United States, the West was never insulated from the spread of those technological systems. While it has been customary to view the architectural landscape of the American West as if it were created by many individuals acting alone, the impact of organized capital on the built environment can no longer be ignored. Industrialization as a factor in the history of the American West becomes especially obvious when examining the mining landscape, which resulted not so much from the daring of a few prospectors as it did from the large-scale activities of a few corporate developers. Extraction of mineral values depended on the successful implementation of systems employing complex mining and smelting technologies as well as effective transportation networks and sources of energy.

The pattern developed early. In writing the history of the copper mines on Michigan's Upper Peninsula, Larry Lankton found that the recovery of wealth depended largely on the ability of investors to assemble the great sums of capital needed to wrest pure metal from complex underground ores.[2] Further west, Montana's copper industry—which began to boom in the last quarter of the nineteenth century, a full quarter-century after the beginning of the Michigan boom—produced more copper and consumed more capital than did Michigan's and, not surprisingly, soon took on the physical character of a highly integrated technological system. Developed during the nation's first great period of corporate growth and concentration and founded on the fabulous mineral deposits in the Butte Hill, Montana's copper industry transformed once-remote areas of Montana into an industrial landscape

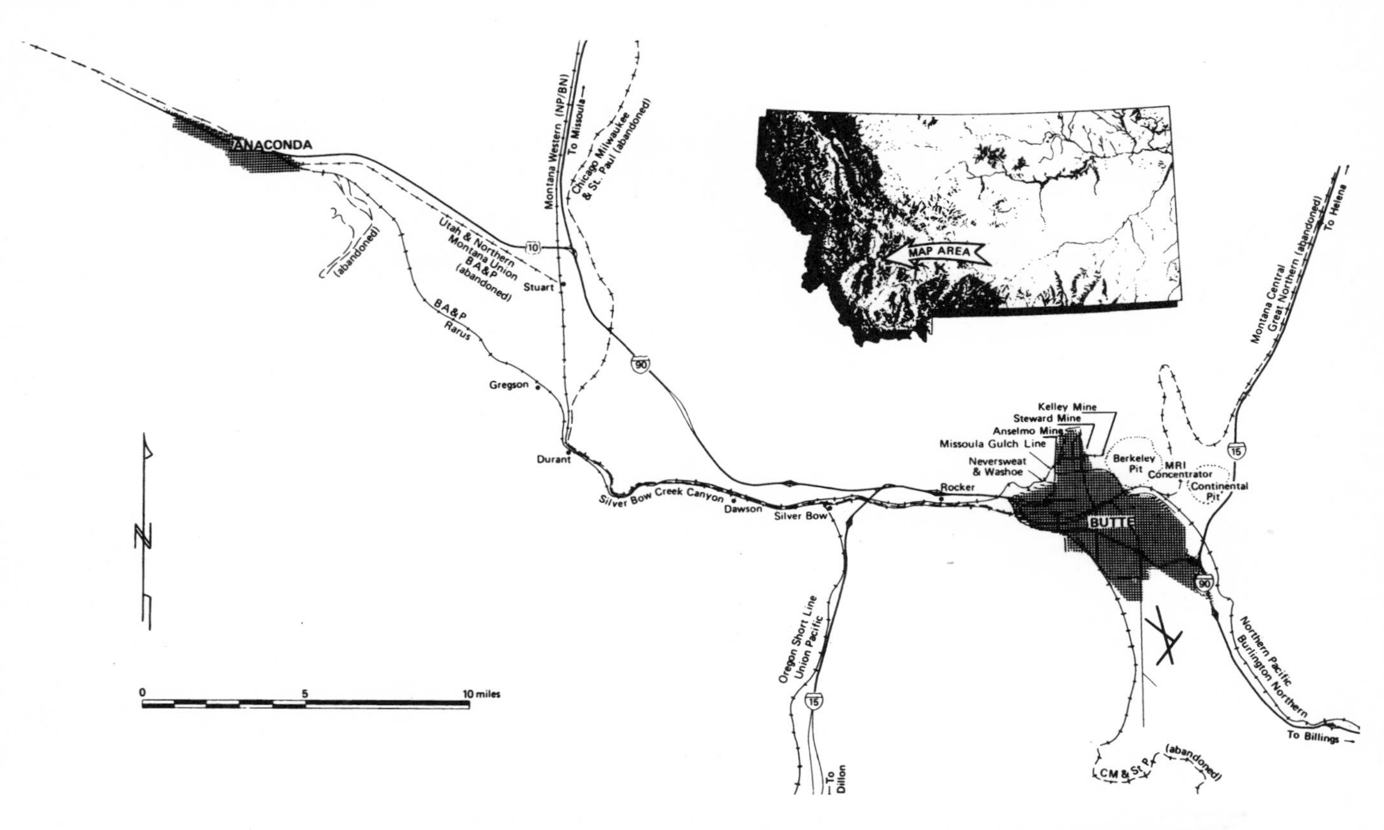

Figure 12.1. Location map of Butte and Anaconda, showing current highways and rail links between the two cities and historic rights-of-way of abandoned rail lines. (Courtesy Montana Bureau of Mines and Geology)

rivaling any in America, east or west. The cities of Butte and Anaconda, located in southwestern Montana, form the heart of this technological system (fig. 12.1). Dominated to this day by structures and landforms associated with the copper industry, these two cities provide an opportunity for us not only to examine the industrial processes that shaped their development but also to interpret the meanings of the surviving landscape as the physical embodiment of larger nationwide technological systems.

In 1864, when prospectors discovered gold in Silver Bow Creek just west of present-day Butte, they unwittingly initiated a series of events that in twenty years transformed a marginal placer camp, inhabited by several hundred transient gold seekers, into a true industrial metropolis and one of the world's greatest mining centers.[3] The infant Silver Bow camp faltered early, lacking enough gold to continue, but the existence of silver in the quartz rock of the area kept the newly established city of Butte from becoming a ghost town. At first, the difficulty of extracting and refining silver discouraged miners from fully exploiting its potential. They had access to neither the technology, capital, nor transportation systems needed to make the profitable recovery of silver from complex ores possible. By 1870 only a few hundred people remained in the area.

During the next decade, however, Butte's miners began to industrialize their operations with the assistance of local banks. Local entrepreneurs financed the construction of stamp mills needed to process the relatively crude ore, and Butte soon had a thriving economy based on silver. In 1876 Irish immigrant Marcus Daly arrived in Butte to assess the possibilities of purchasing a mine for the Utah-based Walker Brothers silver-mining partnership. On Daly's advice, the Walkers bought the claims to the Alice lode, which eventually became one of Butte's more lucrative silver mines. Turning to his own interests, Daly himself purchased the now legendary Anaconda mine and went on to become Butte's most famous mining magnate.

By 1887 several mills, with a total of 290 stamps, were processing silver ore in Butte.[4] Ironically, the hard work and perseverance of many nascent industrialists brought them little wealth compared to the fortunes amassed by subsequent owners who had access to the greater capital needed to develop more complex processes for extracting metals from the hill. The Panic of 1893 eventually led to the demise of Butte's silver economy. The silver boom, however, had allowed some Butte miners to acquire the capital and technology necessary to take advantage of other mineral deposits in the Butte Hill, especially copper. Extracting copper from complex ores required extensive industrial facilities. The shift from silver to copper extraction necessitated the replacement of Butte's early industrial plant. Consequently, the visual record of Butte's first industrial period, a period when the city was in transition from miner's camp to full-blown industrial metropolis, is nearly invisible. The arid, open hills west of the city, however, bear the scars of silver-mining activity, and small waste dumps of yellow, light-brown, and gray rock lie near small discovery pits dug by prospectors hoping to strike it rich. Occasional rock foundations suggest that some diggings attracted enough investment to erect mills (fig. 12.2). The historical record tells of the town of Burlington about four miles west of Butte.[5] Other than the diggings, however, virtually no trace of Burlington survives, underscoring the fact that, were it not for copper and the industrial development it generated, Butte, too, would have gone the way of many of the West's vanished mining camps.

In 1879 the Colorado Smelting Company built the first smelter in Butte to produce a higher grade copper product. Previously, ore had been freighted by wagon to the railroad at Corrine, Utah, some four hundred miles away. From Corrine it was shipped by rail to the East Coast and sometimes from there as far away as Swansea, Wales, for smelting. When the first railroad, the Utah and Northern, arrived in Butte

Figure 12.2. Foundation ruins and waste dumps from silver-mining activity west of Butte. These scars on the landscape are all the physical evidence that remains of the silver-mining activity during Butte's early period of settlement. (Photo by author)

in 1881, the camp had several new mills and smelters that were shipping high-grade copper-silver matte (a semifinished material containing approximately 64 percent copper) to eastern refineries. Eventually, the construction of several other smelters eliminated the need to ship Butte ores elsewhere for processing.

The arrival of railroads spurred growth in the copper-mining industry. In turn, continued expansion of milling and smelting facilities in Butte, coupled with the city's mineral wealth, made Butte a destination point for the railroads' western expansion. Soon after the Utah and Northern Railroad connected Butte with the Union Pacific rail system and thus the rest of the United States, other railroads, such as the Northern Pacific, the Great Northern, and the Milwaukee Road arrived. That Butte became a crossroads of the railroad industry is observable in the several rail lines intersecting at the city: tracks of the Northern Pacific cross the Continental Divide from the east, pass through town, and continue westward; tracks of the Union Pacific still serve the city from the south; and those of the Butte, Anaconda and Pacific link Butte with Anaconda to the west. The rights-of-way of the Milwaukee Road and the Great Northern are still visible although the tracks and ties have been removed. The former passes through Butte from east to west, while the latter approaches Butte from the north. Further evidence of the historical prominence of the railroads in Butte is found in the four surviving passenger depots. This represents a goodly number of a prominent and specialized building type for a city of Butte's size.

The meteoric success of Butte was directly linked to the emergence of the electric industry in the 1880s and the burgeoning need for copper wire. The leading copper-producing area in the United States at the time was Michigan's Upper Peninsula. Mining engineers and investors in Michigan and throughout the industrial world for that matter watched in amazement as Montana copper production increased year after year. Unlike Michigan, where copper was extracted from a geographical area about one hundred miles long, virtually all the copper in Montana came only from Butte. Some contemporary observers were convinced that Butte could not maintain such phenomenal growth in production and that soon the ore would play out. But in 1887 Butte surpassed Michigan in copper mined and remained the world's largest copper producer until 1920.[6]

Miners in Butte encountered some of the richest copper ore the world had ever seen, attracting the attention of capitalists outside the region. Needing money to develop his new Anaconda mine, Daly contacted the successful San Francisco–based mining entrepreneurs, George Hearst, James Ben Ali Haggin, and Lloyd Tevis. The trio responded to Daly's overtures by investing in a mine that soon proved to be a rich silver producer. When Daly's miners encountered copper ore at a depth of three hundred feet, he asked his partners for an even greater stake to construct the mills, smelters, and refineries needed to treat the new ore.

Seeing that the world market for copper was expanding, Hearst, Haggin, and Tevis agreed to commit themselves ever more deeply in Daly's Butte properties. Daly meanwhile continued to buy other Butte mines. He shipped his high-grade ore east to smelters at Swansea and Baltimore and stockpiled the lower-grade ore near his mines while all the time looking for a location with sufficient water for a new smelter of his own.

Butte lies in a semiarid region where the rapid expansion of mining had caused water shortages. Daly chose a site about twenty-five miles west of Butte beside Warm Springs Creek, which forms a narrow valley as it flows out of the mountains from the west. Several miles to the east, the creek joins Silver Bow Creek, forming the Clark Fork River at the head of the much broader Deer Lodge Valley. The site offered Daly ample water and timber for his new smelter.[7] Construction of the concentrator and smelter began along the north side of the Warm Springs Valley during the summer of 1883. At the same time, Daly planned and began construction of a new town to house smelter workers near his new works. He named the town Anaconda for his mine. The Montana Union, a short-line railroad jointly owned by the Utah and Northern and the Northern Pacific, laid tracks between the Anaconda mine in Butte and the smelter in Anaconda, and in September 1884 Daly's crews began firing the smelter furnaces.[8]

The city of Anaconda grew quickly as smelting and related operations expanded (fig. 12.3). Within a year, Daly employed over twelve hundred men there. Although Daly owned the townsite and personally guided the planning of the city, Anaconda did not evolve as a typical "company town." Daly attracted independent merchants rather than establishing a company store system, and instead of requiring smeltermen and their families to live in company housing, he sold lots to real estate developers who speculated on the growth of the city. Although Daly's dream that his smelter city would one day become the capital of Montana went unrealized, Anaconda remains significant today for the role it played in the large-scale industrial system Daly spawned to mine, mill, and smelt copper ore.[9]

As originally built, Daly's Anaconda works had the capacity to treat five hundred tons of ore daily. But because the smelter was only equipped to produce copper matte, Daly still had to ship material east for additional refining. Furthermore, production from the Butte mines continued to increase. In response, Daly immediately began expanding the processing capabilities of his Anaconda works, both in terms of the quantity of ore processed and the quality of the copper produced. Following the example of the Michigan concentrators, he replaced the original crushers with steam-powered stamps, thereby making the first step in the processing of ore more economical. The second step involves the roasting of the finely crushed concentrates to drive off sulphur impurities, yielding a product called calcine. Daly upgraded this step by removing the hand roasters and installing new Bruckner roasting furnaces. Thus began a chain of improvements in metallurgical practice that continued at Anaconda well into the twentieth century.[10]

Daly soon found that although he could improve the technologies employed at his Anaconda smelter, the site itself, located against the base of a steep hill, restricted expansion of the works. A solution was the 1887 construction of another smelter about a mile downstream from the first. Placed along the same side of the valley, the new smelter became known as the Lower Works, while Daly's original smelter became the Upper Works. Wishing to send a purer copper product to market, Daly also built an experimental electrolytic copper refinery in 1888 and his first Bessemer converters at the Upper Works in 1889. (The first successful use of the Bessemer process for treating copper in the United States had taken place at the Parrot smelter at Butte in 1884.) The Lower Works went into operation on 1 October 1889, with a capacity of three thousand tons of ore daily. The combined daily

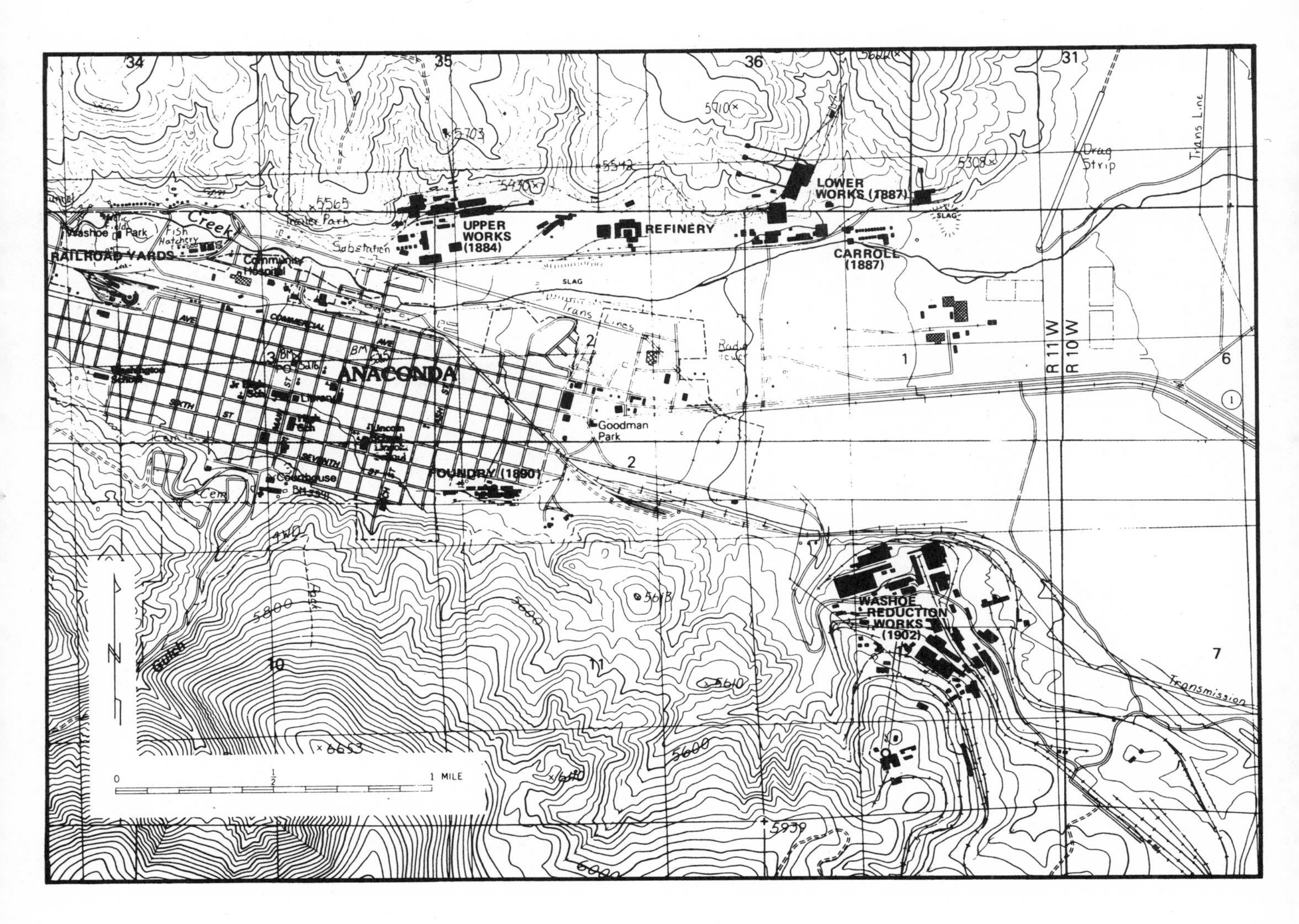

Figure 12.3. Map of Anaconda showing locations of major industrial facilities. The upper and lower works are along the north side of the map; the BA&P yards, roundhouse, and shops are at the west end of the street grid; the foundry complex is at the southeast corner of the street grid; and the Washoe smelter is in the southeast corner of the map. (Courtesy Montana Bureau of Mines and Geology)

capacity of both works was four thousand tons.[11]

The Anaconda works continued to grow during the 1890s. In 1892 a new converter was added at the Lower Works, and the experimental electrolytic refinery was enlarged and went into regular production. Electricity for the plant came from coal-fired steam generators. At the time, the only other electrolytic refinery in the United States was at Baltimore, built in 1887. In 1895, the Anaconda refinery was enlarged and a new silver mill added on

Figure 12.4. Roundhouse *(left)* and shops *(right)* at the BA&P's West Anaconda Yards. These late nineteenth- and early twentieth-century shops are still being used by the Rarus Railway. (Photo by author)

the floodplain between the Upper and Lower Works. The new refinery could produce 120 tons of electrolytic copper per day, the largest electrolytic copper refinery of its time.[12]

In 1894 Daly again closed the Upper Works for repairs and improvements, including the enlargement of the reverberatory furnaces used for melting the calcine to produce slag and copper matte. Early reverberatories at Butte had been only about 20 feet long. By experimenting in lengthening the reverberatories to both increase production capacity and improve efficiency, company engineers at Anaconda contributed greatly to advances in copper metallurgical practice industrywide. The Anaconda experiments showed that the longer reverberatories improved the separation of slag and copper matte. This trend continued well into the twentieth century at Anaconda smelters, where reverberatories eventually reached a length of over 140 feet.[13] The improvement of the reverberatories is representative of a growing awareness among turn-of-the-century company metallurgists and engineers that "today, all the professions engaged in the reduction of ore are parts of a system, and its successful operation is due to the perfection of its component parts."[14]

The railroad linking Butte to the Anaconda works was an important part of the industrial system, but being owned by the Montana Union it was a component Marcus Daly did not control. Beginning about 1889 a dispute arose between Daly and the Montana Union over the freight rate the railroad was charging to haul ore from Butte to Anaconda. The confrontation continued for several years, culminating in a seven-month suspension of the smelter operations in 1891 when the railroad refused to haul ore pending resolution of the conflict. With the promise of help from his friend James J. Hill of the Great Northern Railway, Daly decided to form his own railroad in 1892. The Butte, Anaconda and Pacific Railway (BA&P) was incorporated in September 1892 and began service in December 1893 (fig. 12.4). The company hauled passengers and freight between Butte and Anaconda, but most important was its ore-carrying function. Cognizant of the fact that he was building a technological system, Daly considered the BA&P an integral part of his copper mining and smelting operation. "The road from the Butte Mines to the smelter," he said, "is as much a part and parcel of the works as the Bruckner furnaces or the jigs in the Concentrator."[15]

Figure 12.5. Tuttle Manufacturing and Supply Company. Also known as the Foundry Department of the Anaconda Copper Mining Company, the late nineteenth- and early twentieth-century foundry, machine shop, blacksmith shop, pattern shop, and other historic structures used by the ACM to fabricate mining, milling, and smelting equipment, ornamental iron work, and other metal objects are still being used by AFFCO. (Photo by author)

Before 1891 all of Daly's operations took place within a simple partnership that included himself, George Hearst, James Ben Ali Haggin, and Lloyd Tevis. The company was known variously and unofficially as the Anaconda Mining Company and the Anaconda Gold and Silver Mining Company until 1891 when Daly and his partners incorporated the business under the name Anaconda Mining Company, with headquarters in New York City and principal place of business at Butte. In an 1895 reorganization, the owners incorporated as the Anaconda Copper Mining Company (known for decades in Butte as the ACM). The new entity absorbed many of the ancillary corporations based in Anaconda, which Daly had established to support his operations: the Tuttle Manufacturing and Supply Company, a foundry and fabricating facility that manufactured mining, milling, and smelting equipment (fig. 12.5); the Standard Fire Brick Company, which produced brick for Daly's buildings and furnaces; the Anaconda Water Company, which supplied water to both the smelters and the town; and the Anaconda Townsite Company, which sold lots to businesses, homeowners, and real estate developers.[16]

This corporate consolidation was typical of trends found throughout the U.S. economy during this period. Several giant trusts had been or would soon be created in other segments of American industry, including steel and petroleum, for the purpose of controlling markets and production in the particular commodity. In this climate, Henry H. Rogers and William Rockefeller, both associated with the Standard Oil Trust and intent on forming a copper trust, formed the Amalgamated Copper Company in 1899. Hearst and Tevis had died, and the two surviving partners in

Figure 12.6. Ruins of the Upper Works. Foundation remains of the furnaces *(foreground)* and flues *(right background)* survive on the north side of the Warm Springs Valley adjacent to Anaconda. (Photo by author)

the ACM, Daly and Haggin, sold to the new trust. Haggin received $15 million for his ACM shares, while Daly traded his ACM shares for shares in Amalgamated. Daly became president of the new trust, but died in 1900. Amalgamated continued to acquire Butte properties, including most of the other large mining companies.[17]

The reorganization of Butte's industrial corporate structure paralleled the functional integration and rationalization of activities at the ACM's metallurgical facilities. By the late 1890s Daly's ore production had again outgrown the smelter capacity. But now, instead of enlarging the smelters and forcing his operations into ever more confined quarters, he decided to build yet another facility, this time on the south side of the valley. To plan and supervise construction of the new Anaconda works, Daly hired Frank Klepetko, who earlier had completed a large milling, smelting, and refining complex for the Boston and Montana Consolidated Copper and Silver Mining Company (second only to the Anaconda in Butte copper production) at Great Falls, Montana. In keeping with the rationalized, progressive ideas of plant layout sweeping the nation at the time, Klepetko designed the new works so that each department could be expanded as needed in an orderly fashion without impinging on the other departments or lessening the overall efficiency of the facility. The new plant would make the old Upper and Lower Works obsolete.[18]

Construction of the new works, called the Washoe smelter, began in 1900. By 1902 it operated with a capacity of forty-eight hundred tons of ore daily. Amalgamated expanded the new works to a capacity of twelve thousand tons by 1908 and to even greater levels just before World War I. Meanwhile, operations at the Upper and Lower Works ceased, with the exception of the refinery. Demolition began immediately. The Anaconda refinery continued to operate until 1903, when Amalgamated closed it and began shipping converter copper from the Washoe works to the trust's giant new refinery at Perth Amboy, New Jersey, and to the Boston and Montana refinery at Great Falls, which Amalgamated had acquired. By 1908 all that remained of the Old Works were a few dwellings at Carroll (company housing built near the Lower Works), some offices, a storehouse, and the refinery and silver mill. Soon they were demolished, too, with only the foundations left standing at the Old Works (fig. 12.6).[19]

The combined facilities of the Upper and Lower Works at Anaconda had given Daly the largest nonferrous metallurgical plant in the world. In 1902 the honor moved to the Washoe smelter.[20] Considering the scale of operations (fig. 12.7), surprisingly little is left of these giant industrial plants, yet much evidence of their presence remains on the Anaconda landscape. The town itself still has many businesses whose names refer to its identity as a smelter city. Complexes of buildings that housed industrial operations ancillary to the ACM's smelters are still prominent in the valley: AFFCO is a thriving foundry and steel fabricating business occupying the nineteenth- and early twentieth-century plant of the foundry department of the ACM on the east end of town; the Rarus Railway utilizes the nineteenth- and early twentieth-century roundhouse and shops complex of the BA&P on the west end of town. BA&P tracks still pass through Anaconda, and the tracks, scale house, and

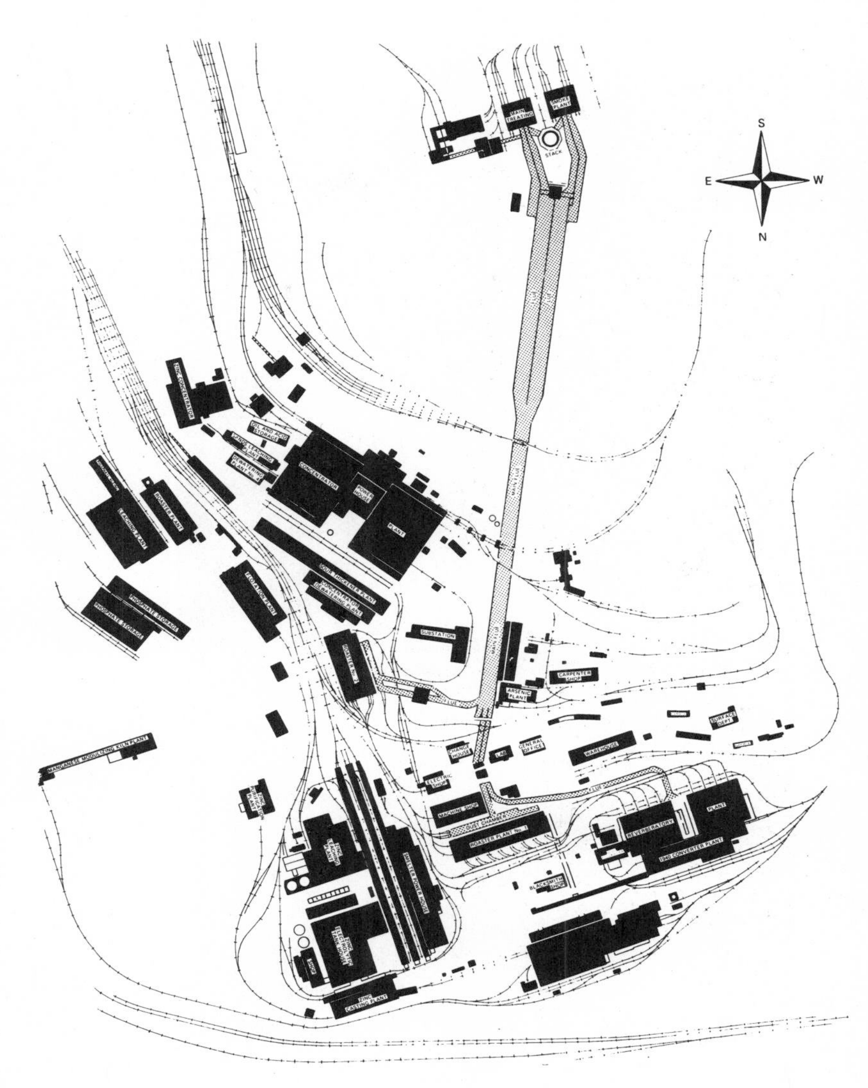

Figure 12.7. Site plan of the Washoe smelter. This illustration shows the scale of the ACM's smelter operations. The entire complex (with the exception of the stack, located upper right) was demolished in the mid-1980s. (Courtesy Montana Bureau of Mines and Geology)

other buildings are still in place at the East Anaconda Yard at the foot of Smelter Hill, where long trains of ore cars were broken into shorter lengths to be pulled up the steep grade to the smelter.

The most remarkable features of Anaconda's human landscape, however, are those surviving the demolition of the smelters (Atlantic Richfield, the oil company, acquired the ACM in 1976 and demolished the Washoe Smelter in the early 1980s). Adjacent to the Old Works and the Washoe smelter sites are giant piles of black slag, the by-product of the reverberatory and blast furnaces. Near these slag piles and extending out into the Deer Lodge Valley to the northeast are vast tailings piles, remnants of the concentration process. Averaging fifty to seventy-five feet in depth, these tailings cover about thirty-six hundred acres (almost six square miles). Also surviving are features associated with the treatment of the gaseous byproducts of smelting. In addition to the sulfur dioxide given off by roasting, smelting, and converting copper ores, smoke from the Anaconda smelters contained arsenic and particulates consisting of other heavy metals.

Smoke pollution from the smelters was a constant source of irritation for Anaconda residents and ranchers in the Deer Lodge Valley and, therefore, a steady source of litigation for the ACM.[21] The ACM tried early to abate the smoke pollution problem by carrying the smoke farther aloft so that winds would disperse it over a greater area. This led to the construction of stacks on the hills adjacent to the Upper and Lower Works, with flues connecting the smelters to the stacks. The foundations of these flues are prominent on the hillsides where the Old Works were located. More noteworthy is the giant stack that still survives atop the hill overlooking the Washoe smelter. Built in 1919, the brick structure stands 585 feet tall and is the tallest freestanding masonry structure in the world. The flue leading from the smelter to the stack and the Cottrell treaters built at the base of the stack to remove particulates from the smoke have all been demolished, but the stack itself has been made a state monument (fig. 12.8).

Visiting Anaconda today it is hard to grasp the full extent of its historic identity as an urban industrial city, and the same may be said of Butte. Before about 1900, the mines on the Butte Hill were owned and operated by a number of relatively large companies. William A. Clark, a Deer Lodge banker who invested in Butte mining properties and came to be Daly's chief industrial and political rival, controlled the Moulton Mining and Milling Company, the Butte Reduction Works, as well as at least ten valuable mines, including the Original and the Steward. Marcus Daly, in partnership with Hearst, Haggin, and Tevis, operated the Anaconda Copper Mining Company, which owned the Anaconda, St. Lawrence, and other mines as well as the great smelters at Anaconda. New York and Boston interests, such as the Lewishon Brothers, owned the Leonard, Colusa, Mountain View, Pennsylvania, Badger State, and other major Butte mines, the Boston and Montana and the Butte and Boston smelters in Butte, and the new Boston and Montana smelter and refinery in Great Falls. F. Augustus Heinze, along with his brothers, formed the Montana Ore Purchasing Company and operated the Rarus and other successful mines. In the fabled War of the Copper Kings, these companies, especially those of Clark, Daly, and Heinze, struggled for control of the Butte Hill. Amalgamated and the ACM eventually brought all these properties into a single corporate system of truly monumental and national stature. These companies integrated the actual mining operations on the Butte Hill as well.

The consolidation of the mines at Butte and their integration into the national industrial economy are depicted by several features on the landscape, the most striking of which are the thirteen surviving steel headframes on the Butte Hill, each straddling a vertical mine shaft (fig. 12.9). Adjacent to the headframe, each mine had a hoist house containing a hoisting engine. The hoisting engine drew in or let out cable slung over sheave wheels at the top of the headframe and extending down the shaft to pull ore from the mine or to lower men and materials into the mine. Early western mines followed eastern practice in using wooden headframes. Wood was convenient for local companies because timber could be cut and milled locally and the headframes could be erected using local carpenters' skills. At the very end of the nineteenth century, however, a new material—steel, with its greater strength and permanence—took the place of

Figure 12.8. The Washoe stack. Now a state monument, the stack is the only surviving structure on the grounds of the Washoe smelter. At 585 feet, the stack is the tallest freestanding masonry structure in the world. (Photo by author)

Figure 12.9. Surviving steel headframes on the Butte Hill. Five of Butte's thirteen surviving headframes are visible in this view, including *(left to right):* the Diamond, the Steward, the two headframes at the Kelley, and the Original. Dwellings in Butte's Centerville neighborhood are on the far left; St. Mary's Roman Catholic Church is on the far right. (Photo by author)

wood for headframes, drawing the Butte mines further into the national economy as technologies changed. Steel companies in the East and the Great Lakes region fabricated truss members for the headframes. Bridge-building companies, also from outside the region, received contracts to erect the headframes in Butte. Among the earliest steel headframes built in Butte were those erected by the Gillette-Herzog Manufacturing Company of Minneapolis in 1898. Three of them survive: the Steward, the Original, and the Diamond, the oldest.[22]

Only one mine from the historic period of underground mining in Butte—the Anselmo—has a virtually complete complement of ancillary structures, including the hoist house, auxiliary hoist house, change house, carpenter shop, mines offices, idler towers, warehouse, and various sheds (figs. 12.10, 12.11). Of the other twelve steel headframes surviving on the Butte Hill, some, such as the Diamond, stand devoid of any associated structures or, like the Travonia, retain only their attached ore bins. The Belmont Steward, Original, Badger State, and Mountain Consolidated still have their associated hoist houses. The integration of operations on the Butte Hill is depicted also in vent housings over some of the shafts (all the underground workings were interconnected for ventilation purposes) and in the tracks of the BA&P connecting the mines to the smelter in Anaconda. A subtle reminder of the technological system in place at Butte is the array of compressed-air pipes snaking across the Butte Hill, connecting mines to centralized compressors (fig. 12.12). Many of these compressed-air pipes stem from the electrification of the Butte Hill over a period of years around the turn of the twentieth century and serve as evidence of the complexity and reach of Montana's copper industry during that period.

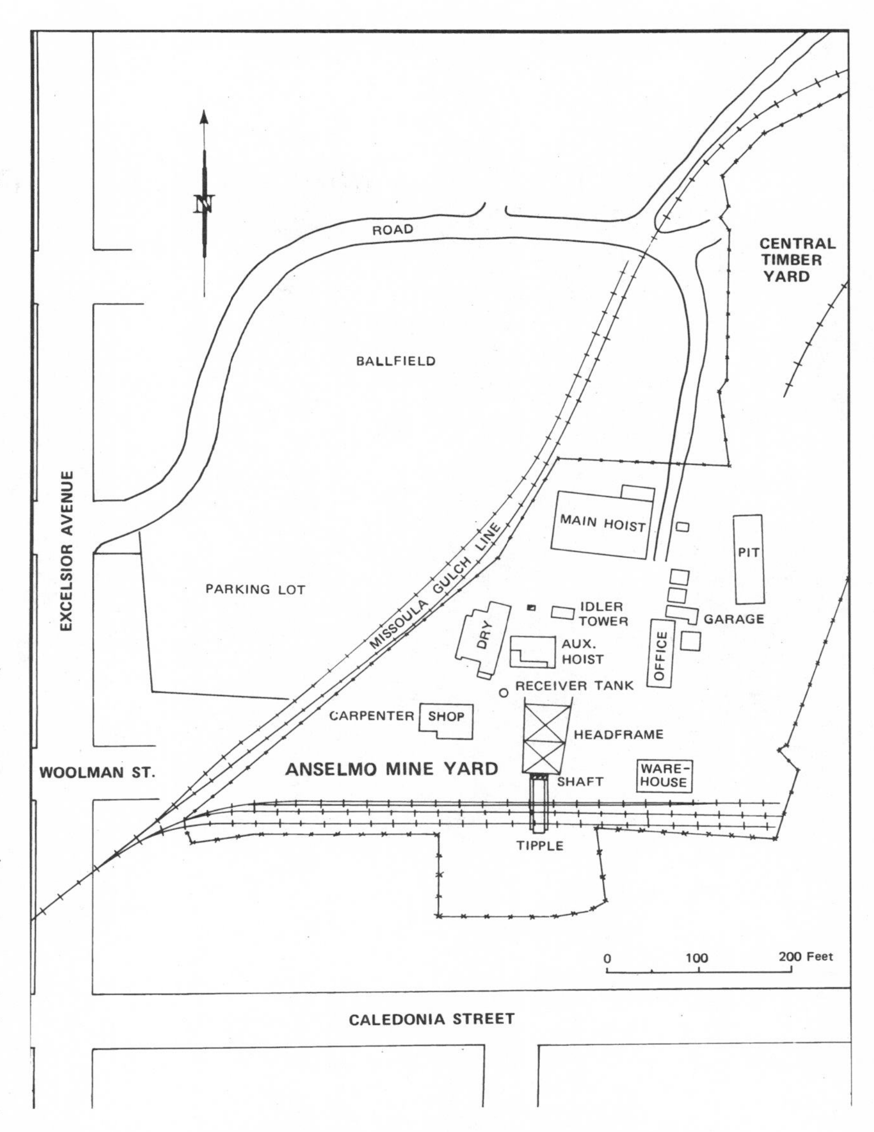

Figure 12.10. Site Plan of the Anselmo mineyard. The site plan shows the arrangement of buildings and structures, the rail spur linking the mine to the BA&P's Missoula Gulch Line (by which ore cars were hauled to the smelter at Anaconda), and the Anselmo's general proximity to the neighborhood on Butte's West Side. The pipeline supplying compressed air to the Anselmo runs parallel to the Missoula Gulch Line. (Courtesy Montana Bureau of Mines and Geology)

Although the advent of electrical power and the rising demand for copper wire provided the basis for Butte's copper-mining industry, early mining in Butte, as elsewhere in the West, did not have ready access to electric power for lighting, drilling, ventilating, tramming, hoisting, pumping, and other operations central to mining. Mine owners relied on candles or oil for lighting and on human, animal, and steam power for the other operations. Miners drilled rock underground using sledge hammers, and men, horses, and mules moved ore in cars both on surface and below ground. Each mine

Figure 12.11. Anselmo mineyard. The only intact mineyard from Butte's historic period, the Anselmo consists of a headframe over the mineshaft *(right)*, idler towers (the other two truss structures), and several buildings, including *(left to right):* the main hoist house, the dry (or change) house, the auxiliary hoist house (behind the dry), and the carpenter shop. Not visible in this view are the warehouse, mine office, and garages. A tipple, for sorting ore and waste from the mine and loading them into railroad cars, is attached to the right side of the headframe. (Photo by author)

typically had its own coal-fired steam plant to provide power for the other operations. The first electric lights at a Butte mine went into service at the Alice Mill in 1881.[23] Although electric power was used in the Rocky Mountain region for such heavy operations as hoisting as early as 1888,[24] Butte companies did not use electricity—other than for tramming on surface and for lighting—before the turn of the century. The first major mining-related use of electricity in Montana was actually for metallurgical purposes at the electrolytic refineries at Anaconda and Great Falls.

Despite the absence of electricity in the mines, Butte miners extracted vast quantities of ore from underground using hand drills and hammers. Miners working in the stopes (the large underground cavities opened in the process of mining a vein of ore) bored holes in the rock into which they could place explosives. After evacuating the work area and setting off the charge, miners waited for the dust to clear and then moved back to load the broken rock into ore cars (an undertaking called mucking). Then the ore cars were moved to the shaft (a process called tramming), often with the aid of mules. At the shaft, workers loaded the ore into skips to be hoisted to the surface. Not all the rock moved from underground was ore. In the process of sinking shafts and driving drifts and crosscuts (horizontal workings parallel and perpendicular to the vein, respectively), miners bored through large quantities of rock containing no valuable mineral deposits. Such rock was kept separate from the ore. On the surface, ore was transported to the mill for concentrating while the waste rock was dumped near the shaft. Numerous waste dumps punctuate the Butte Hill, some near the structural remains of the surface works at mines, others merely articulating where a mine was once in operation.

Figure 12.12. Hoist house at the Anselmo mine. This view shows the compressed-air line that supplied the Anselmo and other mineyards from a central compressor plant. Because the Anselmo hoist was powered by electricity, compressed air at this mineyard was used only to power the rock drills used by miners underground. (Photo by author)

After 1900 mining companies began to use electricity to drive air compressors for rock drills (the largest single source of demand for electricity), to drive underground water pumps, and for underground and surface tramming. The companies also began to ventilate the mines, which grew hotter as the shafts were driven deeper, and became dustier and more unhealthy as natural ventilation grew less effective at depths below two thousand feet.[25] Although electricity was available in the mines for lighting in the late nineteenth century, it did not completely replace the open flame until

Figure 12.13. Rainbow Falls Dam. The timber-crib, rock-filled dam sits atop Rainbow Falls. The steel-truss bridge crossing the Missouri River in the background was built by the Great Northern Railroad at the turn of the century for a rail line that linked Butte with Lake Superior. (Courtesy Montana Power Company)

the 1930s. Electric lights were used underground only to illuminate shafts and drifts. Butte miners relied on candles for light in the stopes until about 1912 when the carbide lamp was introduced. Battery-powered miner's lamps replaced the carbide lamp in the 1930s.[26]

Beginning in 1908, the ACM began to investigate the possibility of converting from steam to electricity to drive its mine hoists because Montana's mountain-fed rivers made relatively inexpensive hydroelectric power available. The great depth and number of the ACM mines, the volume of ore hoisted, and the irregularity of the actual hoisting at each mine, however, could create technical problems if the ACM used electric motors to directly drive the hoists. If two or more hoists started at once, the controls and switching gear of the period could not readily handle the resulting large peaks in electrical demand. The ACM decided instead to use electric motors to drive air compressors on a continuous basis, to store compressed air in a series of receivers, and to connect the mine hoists to the centralized compressed air system. This meant that the company needed only to modify, rather than replace, its existing steam-powered hoist engines so they could be driven by compressed air.[27]

This centralized compressed-air system went into operation in 1912. With that development, electricity to drive air compressors for hoisting and drilling consumed two-thirds of the nearly twenty-five thousand kilowatts used in Butte for mining. The other major demand for electricity by the copper industry then at Butte, Anaconda, and Great Falls was for milling, smelting, and refining, which consumed nearly as much as the mines at Butte. The electrical consumption by the ACM in Montana in 1912 totaled about forty-two thousand kilowatts.[28] Together with other industrial uses, this represented over 95 percent of the Montana Power Company's load in Montana, a remarkable figure for a state not known for its industrial character.[29]

Figure 12.14. Rainbow Falls powerhouse. Built in 1910 to generate electricity for the ACM smelters at Great Falls and Anaconda and the mines at Butte, the powerhouse still houses its original turbines and generators and serves as the Montana Power Company's control center for the five hydroelectric generating stations along the Great Falls of the Missouri. (Photo by author)

To provide a reliable and inexpensive source of power for the new hoisting system and the expanded use of compressed air drills, ACM president John D. Ryan began negotiating with James J. Hill in 1908 for the purchase of the Great Falls Water Power and Townsite Company. At the same time, Ryan set his engineers to work designing a new hydroelectric facility at Rainbow Falls (figs. 12.13, 12.14). Power from two of the generators was transmitted to the Boston and Montana smelter at Great Falls. The power from the other four generators was stepped up to 102,000 volts and transmitted 130 miles to Butte and Anaconda over lines carried by steel transmission towers (fig. 12.15). This transmission system, constructed at the same time as the Rainbow Falls plant, was one of the earliest in the United States to operate at over 100 kilovolts. The Rainbow plant and transmission system began operating in 1910.[30] The plant was designed, and continues to serve, as the central control station

Figure 12.15. Steel transmission towers from 1910. Nearly all the transmission towers along the 130 miles between Great Falls and Butte, such as these in Elk Park east of the Continental Divide near Butte, are intact. Although they now serve the Montana Power Company's general statewide grid, they were originally built specifically to supply electricity to the ACM's mines and smelter. They represent the extensive area embraced by the copper industry centered in Butte. (Photo by author)

Figure 12.16. Steward mine. The Steward headframe (1898) is one of the oldest in Butte. The hoist house on the left still houses the original steam-powered hoist, which merely had to be converted for use with compressed air when the ACM systematized its Butte Hill hoisting operations in 1912. (Photo by author)

for all the hydroelectric plants along the Great Falls of the Missouri. The transmission towers linking Rainbow Falls with Butte and Anaconda still stride through Butte and across the state's more remote landscape, suggesting the reach of mining activities in Butte and the technological system that Ryan created.[31]

With the consolidation of its Butte holdings, the ACM Company centralized the various activities historically performed by individual mines or companies. Consolidation affected all aspects of the mining process. For the first time, the ACM created a geology department to examine the district as a whole and make recommendations for future development. The ACM produced mine timbers at a central framing plant at Rocker (about five miles west of Butte), although individual mines still maintained framing shops for special timbers. Most of the thirty shafts operated by the ACM were connected on the twenty-eight-hundred-foot level to facilitate drainage and removal of mine water through a centralized pumping station.[32] Compressed air was delivered to the various mines for hoisting and drilling through twelve- and sixteen-inch pipes connected to large compressor plants at the High Ore, the Leonard, and the Bell mines. The ACM constructed central heating plants to serve the entire hill, and the company centralized shops for boilermakers, machinists, and blacksmiths, although most of the larger mines still maintained their own blacksmith shops.

But the history of Butte and Anaconda is much more than the history of several large companies. The dangers and hardships associated with mining and smelting led to the birth of a powerful labor movement in the area. Butte's Miners Union, founded in 1878, became Local No. 1 of the Western Federation of Miners. In 1906 Local No. 1 sent the largest of the delegations to Chicago for the founding convention of the Industrial Workers of the World (IWW). In the nineteenth century, Butte unions fairly easily achieved their demands as mining companies competed for scarce labor. But when Amalgamated consolidated its operations, workers lost leverage, leading to bitter and often violent struggles between unions and the ACM during the World War I era.[33] Although the foundation wall of the dynamited Miners Union Hall (destroyed during labor unrest in 1914) is still visible, Butte industrial structures remain the most vivid monuments to Butte's labor history.

Copper sustained Butte's growth into a heterogeneous, cosmopolitan, and urban island in the midst of ranchland and wilderness. During World War I, Butte boasted a population of nearly eighty thousand inhabitants from all regions of the United States and all corners of the globe, making it one of the largest cities in the Northwest. Early skilled miners were Cornish, although the Butte mines and Anaconda smelters also attracted many Irish, who soon became the cities' dominant ethnic group. Of all U.S. cities in 1900, Butte was the most heavily populated by Irish immigrants and their children (26 percent of Butte's population).[34] The late nineteenth and early twentieth centuries meant an influx of others as well: Italians,

Serbs, Croats, French Canadians, Finns, Scandinavians, Jews, Lebanese, Chinese, Mexicans, Austrians, Germans, Swiss, and African-Americans. By 1910 70 percent of Butte's population was either foreign born or born of foreign parents. Yet Butte's diverse cultural heritage is not evident in its residential, commercial, and institutional architecture. Such buildings reflect prevailing national fashions and are similar to those found in most American industrial communities. To understand what drew the many immigrants to Butte and Anaconda, we must once again look to the headframes and the other reminders of Montana's historic copper industry (fig. 12.16).

Montana has an industrial history and an industrial landscape. The ACM operations at Anaconda and Butte gave wealth to those who controlled the corporation's industrial system and provided livelihoods to thousands of families who worked it. The ACM operations also forged the Montana landscape into a technological system linking the destinies of people as far away as Great Falls with the mines in Butte, and linking the destiny of Montana with the evolution of the national industrial economy. Despite the fact that the copper industry in Butte is now limited to an open-pit mine and a nearby concentrator, elements on the Montana landscape still embody that earlier technological system. Viewed through eyes accustomed to seeing the influence of such systems, the landscape of the Montana copper industry exhibits the process by which the expanding national economy claimed much of the American West.[35]

Notes

I conducted some of the research that supports this essay while working with Renewable Technologies, a historic preservation consulting firm based in Butte. Mark Fiege, Mary McCormick, and Brian Shovers also worked on those research projects. I acknowledge the contributions of those individuals and thank them for the exchange of ideas that contributed to this article. The editor of this volume and Christa Wilmanns-Wells offered useful editorial suggestions. Responsibility for any errors in this essay, however, remains with me.

1. Hughes, *American Genesis: A Century of Invention and Technological Enthusiasm* (New York: Viking, 1989), 3–4. In his earlier *Networks of Power: Electrification in Western Society, 1880–1930* (Baltimore: Johns Hopkins University Press, 1983), Hughes offers a model for examining and beginning to understand modern technological systems. He demonstrates his method by examining the historical development of electrical utility systems. By looking at such aspects of technological systems as invention, innovation, development, reverse salients, technology transfer, and technological momentum, he is able to articulate important differences in the ways a seemingly singular technology—the system of electrical generation, transmission, and distribution—evolved in three Western nations (United States, Great Britain, and Germany). In *American Genesis,* Hughes uses the same concepts to present a more general picture of large-scale technological systems in the United States, suggesting that such systems, coupled with America's ability to generate them, are an important and per-

haps centrally defining characteristic of the nation. In the light of Hughes's argument, it would not be surprising to find that U.S. system-builders shaped Montana's copper industry as a large-scale technological system and that the industrial landscape exhibits characteristics of such a system.

2. Larry Lankton, *Cradle to Grave: Life, Work, and Death at the Lake Superior Copper Mines* (New York: Oxford University Press, 1991), 8–9.

3. For a good overall history of Butte's beginnings, including its mining origins, see Michael P. Malone, *The Battle for Butte: Mining and Politics on the Northern Frontier, 1864–1906* (Seattle: University of Washington Press, 1981).

4. William B. Daly, "Evolution of the Mining Practice at Butte," *Engineering and Mining Journal* 128 (24 August 1929): 280.

5. U.S. Geological Survey, "Butte Mining District," 1904 map, Montana Bureau of Mines and Geology, Butte.

6. Richard P. Rothwell, ed., *The Mineral Industry: Its Statistics, Technology, and Trade in the United States and Other Countries from the Earliest Times to the End of 1892,* vols. 1, 2 (New York: Scientific Publishing, 1893-94), 109, 241; Otis E. Young Jr., "The American Copper Frontier, 1640–1893," *The Speculator: A Journal of Butte and Southwest Montana History* 1 (summer 1984), 7.

7. For a good general description of the prelude to Daly's decision to build his smelter at Anaconda, see Malone, *Battle for Butte,* 15–33.

8. *Anaconda Weekly Review,* 10 May 1884; Malone, *Battle for Butte,* 30; Jess Monk, "Chronological History of the Old Reduction Works," manuscript (1958) in Anaconda Copper Mining Company subject files, box 62A, folder 17, p. 2, Montana Historical Society Archives, Helena; E. P. Mathewson, "The Story of the Smelters," in *The City of Anaconda: Its First Twenty-Five Years, 1883–1908* (Anaconda: Standard Publishing, 1908), 23.

9. Not content to have simply founded a smelter city, Daly decided to enter Anaconda into the electoral contest for Montana's capital city shortly after statehood in 1889. Anaconda lost the election to Helena, the former territorial capital, in a bitterly fought statewide campaign. The battle was part of a much larger political feud between Daly and his fellow Butte copper baron, William A. Clark, who supported Helena. The Clark-Daly feud spread throughout electoral contests in the state and tarnished Montana's political reputation with corruption for years to come. For a good general treatment of the war of the copper kings, see Malone, *Battle for Butte,* 30, 80–130.

10. Mathewson, "The Story of the Smelters," 23.

11. Ibid., 23–25; Monk, "Chronological History," 3; Peters, *Modern Copper Smelting* (New York: Scientific Publishing, 1895), 528.

12. Mathewson, "The Story of the Smelters," 25; Monk, "Chronological History," 5–6; Titus Ulke, *Modern Electrolytic Copper Refining* (New York: John Wiley and Sons, 1907), 2.

13. Frederick Laist, "History of Smelting in Montana, 1879–1933," in *Transactions of the American Institute of Mining and Metallurgical Engineers,* (New York: A.I.M.E., 1933), 106:23–87, hereinafter cited as *Transactions* with date, vol., and page numbers.

14. C. H. Repath, "The Mechanical Engineer: A Factor in Modern Mining, Milling, and Smelting—Illustrations Shown at Copper Mining and Reduction Works, Butte, Mon." *Mines and Minerals* 23 (November 1902): 173.

15. General overviews of railroads in Montana's history may be found in Michael Malone and Richard Roeder, *Montana: A History of Two Centuries* (Seattle: University of Washington Press, 1976), 129–40; and Rex Myers, "The Butte Rail Connection: Mining and Transportation, 1880–1890" *The Speculator: A Journal of Butte and Southwest Montana History* 1 (summer 1984): 30–37. Marcus Daly to J. B Haggin, 21 July 1890, Dispute with Montana Union Railway and Union Pacific Railroad, Correspondence, 1889–90, in Anaconda Copper Mining Company subject files, folder 12, box 63, Montana Historical Society Archives, Helena.

16. Articles of Incorporation for the Anaconda Mining Company (1891) and the Anaconda Copper Mining Company (1895) on file at the Montana Secretary of State's Office, Helena; Monk, "Chronological History," 4, 6.

17. Malone describes this consolidation in *The Battle for Butte,* 131–58.

18. Monk, "Chronological History," 7; L. S. Austin, "The Washoe Plant of the A.C.M. Co. in 1905," *Transactions* (1906), 37:266, 307. Alfred D. Chandler Jr. in *Strategy and Structure: Chapters in the History of the Industrial Enterprise* (Cambridge: MIT Press, 1962) credits Henry Clay Frick of Carnegie Steel with organizing that giant metallurgical enterprise into departments functionally arranged under a central-

ized structure and with providing the model followed by other basic industries in the early twentieth century (285).

19. Mathewson, "The Story of the Smelters," 25; Monk, "Chronological History," 8.

20. Peters, *Modern Copper Smelting*, 528; H. O. Hoffman, "Notes on the Metallurgy of Copper in Montana," *Transactions* (1904), 32:259-70; Ulke, *Modern Electrolytic Copper Refining*, 2; Anaconda Copper Mining Company, *A Brief Description of the Washoe Smelter* (Anaconda: Standard Publishing, 1907), 9, 10, 23.

21. The problems associated with smoke pollution from copper smelting at Butte and Anaconda are analyzed in Don McMillan, "A History of the Struggle to Abate Air Pollution from Copper Smelters of the Far West, 1885–1953," (Ph.D. diss., University of Montana, Missoula, 1973). On litigation against the ACM's Anaconda works, see Gordon Morris Bakken, "Was There Arsenic in the Air? Anaconda Versus the Farmers of Deer Lodge Valley," *Montana: The Magazine of Western History* 41 (summer 1991): 30–41.

22. Fredric L. Quivik, "Montana's Minneapolis Bridge Builders," *IA: The Journal of the Society for Industrial Archeology* 10 (1984): 42; Milo S. Ketchum, *The Design of Mine Structures* (New York: McGraw-Hill, 1912), 121, 368. Ketchum reports that the first steel headframe in the Butte district, that at the Boston and Montana's West Colusa mine built by Pittsburgh-based Jones and Laughlin in 1897, was built of members of relatively thin section, leading to excessive vibration. The 1898 structures built for the ACM by Minneapolis-based Gillette-Herzog, which survive to this day, were built of thicker members. The Milwaukee Bridge Company also built early headframes in Butte.

23. *Butte Miner*, 1 March 1881, cited in *Hard-Rock Epic: Western Miners and the Industrial Revolution, 1860–1910*, by Mark Wyman (Berkeley: University of California Press, 1979), 103.

24. Irving Hale, "Electric Mining in the Rocky Mountain Region," *Transactions* (1897), 26:409–12.

25. John Gillie, "Use of Electricity in Butte," *Transactions* (1914), 46:818.

26. Brian Lee Shovers, "Miners, Managers, and Machines: Industrial Accidents and Occupational Disease in the Butte Underground, 1880–1920" (master's thesis, Montana State University, Bozeman, 1987), 21, 34.

27. Bruno V. Nordberg, "The Compressed Air System of the Anaconda Copper Mining Co., Butte, Montana," *Transactions* (1914), 46:826–41; Thomas T. Read, "Compressed-Air Hoisting At Butte," *Mining and Scientific Press*, 105 (2 November 1912): 554-56.

28. Gillie, "Use of Electricity in Butte," 818–19; Gillie does not explicitly state whether his figures are for the ACM only or for all mining operations in Butte, but his narrative seems to imply that they are for all of Butte.

29. In 1915, 96.5 percent of Montana Power's electricity was consumed by industrial customers, according to Max Hebgen in "The System of the Montana Power Company," *Electrical World* 65 (12 June 1915): 1,536. Hughes, in *Networks of Power*, lists transmission systems in the United States that exceeded one hundred thousand volts (282–83). They all linked generating stations with cities with greater populations than Butte. Presumably the loads in those cities consisted of greater percentages of residential and commercial customers.

30. Carrie Johnson, "Electrical Power and John D. Ryan," *Montana: The Magazine of Western History* 38 (autumn 1988): 28–29; Max Hebgen, "The Great Falls Hydroelectric Power Plant," *Cassier's Magazine*, August 1911, 273-88.

31. Fredric L. Quivik, "Early Steel Transmission Towers and Energy for Montana's Copper Industry," *Montana: The Magazine of Western History* 38 (autumn 1988): 67–69.

32. William B. Daly, "Evolution of Mining Practice at Butte," *Engineering and Mining Journal* 128 (24 August 1929): 281.

33. The most comprehensive treatment of Butte's labor history is Jerry W. Calvert, *The Gibraltar: Socialism and Labor in Butte, Montana, 1895–1920* (Helena: Historical Society Press, 1988).

34. David M. Emmons, *The Butte Irish: Class and Ethnicity in an American Mining Town, 1875–1925* (Urbana: University of Illinois Press, 1989), 13.

35. The driving role of capitalism in shaping the development of the American West and the importance of industrialization to shaping the mining landscape are the subjects of two books published after this essay was written: William R. Robbins, *Colony & Empire: The Capitalist Transformation of the American West* (Lawrence: University Press of Kansas, 1994); Richard V. Francaviglia, *Hard Places: Reading the Landscape of America's Historic Mining Districts* (Iowa City: University of Iowa Press, 1991).

CHAPTER THIRTEEN

American Modernism in the West

Hoover Dam

RICHARD GUY WILSON

To many Americans and foreign observers during the 1930s and 1940s the massive concrete, multipurpose dam became one of the great symbols of American modernism. In ways both explicable and inexplicable the imagination of millions was caught by the great dams that arose: Hoover in the Southwest, Shasta in Northern California, Grand Coulee and Bonneville in the Northwest, and the Tennessee Valley Authority dams in the Southeast. Families would be loaded in cars and driven for hundreds of miles to see these great dams, both under construction and upon completion. In a ritual that continues today, people toured and contemplated these massive structures that man had built in out of the way places. So popular did Hoover Dam become that beginning in 1934 the Union Pacific Railroad offered special excursions to view its construction, and then the completed edifice.[1] Constructed in the West by the Bureau of Reclamation and the Army Corps of Engineers, and in the East by the TVA, these dams were products of endless political negotiations and bureaucratic maneuvering. The great dams and many smaller ones transformed vast areas of the continent, tamed rivers and prevented floods, provided new water transportation routes, stored water for irrigation and drinking, created new agricultural land, generated electricity for industry and home, and substantially changed the living standards of millions of Americans. Dams helped to bring new industry and commerce to once forsaken areas and provided, through their large reservoirs, major recreation centers. In the case of southern Nevada, the abundance of cheap electricity at Hoover Dam allowed the development of that air-conditioned mecca, Las Vegas. The political, economic, and social backgrounds and consequences of these dams has been thoroughly investigated. But as works of architecture and as symbols of American modernism they are just beginning to receive scholarly attention.[2]

At the time of construction, especially in the 1930s, large multipurpose concrete dams and earth-fill dams were widely regarded as prime symbols of American ingenuity, prowess, and modernity. A photograph by Margaret Bourke-White of spillway gate construction at the Fort Peck Dam in Montana graced the first cover of *Life Magazine* in 1936. Dams caught the American imagination because they represented work for a depression-affected economy and the benevolent aspects of government planning. The dams suggested that humans could alter and control their environment; they also signified the coming of age of a new source of power—hydroelectricity.[3] Yet the dams were more than functional structures; they were symbols that observers struggled to understand. In 1935, as construction neared completion, journalist Theodore White stood on the rim of the Black Canyon and pondered Hoover Dam: "It is a beautiful tantalizing thing. It is complex. It has a meaning, not to be grasped in weeks, or perhaps years. It is subtle, sometimes cruelly obvious."[4]

White's attempt to understand Hoover Dam echoed Henry Adams's effort three decades earlier to understand what Adams considered to be the prime symbol of the twentieth century, the dynamo, "a symbol of infinity." Adams tried to understand the dynamo, but ultimately concluded that it was "silent and infinite." White reached a similar conclusion about Hoover Dam as he watched the sun go down over its wall: "I stay on, fascinated. I stare at the thing trying to comprehend it, to fix it forever in mind's eye. I have been inspired and provoked in the weeks I have tried to know it. And now, the minds that invented it, the bodies that are building it, the complexity and spirit of it, the love of it which men feel—all, all of it bewilders me."[5]

Of the several large and impressive concrete dams of the 1930s, the first and the most famous is Hoover Dam, constructed between 1931 and 1936 on the Colorado River between Arizona and Nevada. (Begun as Hoover Dam, the name was changed to Boulder Dam in 1933 when Roosevelt entered the White House; the name was changed back to Hoover Dam in 1947 under a Republican Congress.[6]) Still one of the largest dams, the impact of Hoover Dam is overpowering. A massive wall of concrete—a large, seemingly plastic concave mass wedged between two nearly sheer canyon walls—holds back Lake Mead and 12 trillion gallons, or 28,537,000 acre-feet, of water that stretches for 115 miles up the Colorado River. A great functional structure resulting from the precise calculations of engineers, the dam is also a superbly designed and conscious work of architecture that takes advantage of every possibility to make a statement. It is one of the great designs of the 1930s, a true architectural landmark that also spurred many of the public works programs of the Great Depression. The full story of Hoover Dam involves many thousands of individuals and many years of evolving ideas and political decisions. Hoover Dam—like all dams—can be considered from the standpoint of its function, its construction and engineering, and its architectural design. It may also be understood as a symbol. Hoover Dam is a modern work of architecture that contains several key themes of modernism: efficiency, the utilization of advanced technology, the use of abstract and ahistorical images, and the emphasis on beneficial results. As a self-consciously modern structure the dam illuminates some of the themes of and myths about American modernism.[7]

Hoover Dam is located in what still must be considered one of the most inhospitable parts of the globe. Sited in the Black Canyon area of the Colorado River between Nevada and Arizona, its surroundings have not changed much. Desert sand and rocky outcroppings predominate. The little vegetation consists of greasewood and sage brush. Rattlesnakes coexist with ground animals. In the late 1920s, when the decision was made to locate the dam at Black Canyon, the nearest town was Las Vegas, 30 miles away. Then a ramshackle community, Las Vegas served primarily as a refueling junction for the Union Pacific Railroad. The nearest electric power source was in San Bernardino, California, 222 miles across the desert. Housing for the five-thousand-person work force, plus dependents, was nonexistent. The result was the construction of Boulder City, a model town for six thousand laid out by the government and located about 8 miles from the damsite.[8]

The reason for locating the dam at such a site was the necessity of controlling the Colorado River, which drains rivers of seven western states. Every year, despite levees and canals, the Colorado River would overflow its banks, sometimes causing severe damage as with the overflow of 1905–7 that created the Salton Sea and the 1916 inundation of the Yuma Valley. Flooding would occur in late spring or early summer; yet by late summer, fall, and winter, when the Imperial, Coachella, and Yuma valleys needed water, the Colorado River was merely a trickle. A controlled river could also serve as a transportation link for these areas of the Southwest. Finally, the expanding population of Southern California—Los Angeles in particular—badly needed water to survive.[9]

Plans for harnessing the Colorado River received major impetus with the establishment in 1902 of the Reclamation Service (later renamed the Bureau of Reclamation) under President Theodore Roosevelt. Charged with developing agricultural land in the West, the Reclamation Service focused on the Colorado River, and by the early 1920s its geologists and engineers had concluded that the Black Canyon area was the best site for the first major dam on the Colorado. Other smaller dams—the Parker, the Davis, and the Imperial—would follow in a few years. Political squabbles among the neighboring western states over water rights continued through the 1920s. But by late 1928 Congress passed a bill authorizing the dam, and President Calvin Coolidge signed it into law on 21 December. Construction of the dam might have languished for several years except that Herbert Hoover, a professional engineer who had been Secretary of Commerce under Coolidge and had strongly supported the idea of a dam, now occupied the White House. By 1930 President Hoover could foresee the general outlines of depression and unemployment. Consequently, in 1930 a large appropriations bill was pushed through Congress for the dam's construction and preliminary site work by the government. Designs and specifications were hurriedly drawn up by December 1930; in March 1931 bids were opened for construction.[10]

The intention was to construct a large concrete dam at Black Canyon that would be capable of containing in reservoir about 30 million acre-feet of water, the equivalent of two years of normal Colorado River flow. The engineering design of the dam had begun back in the 1920s with site investigations and a series of test models. Gradually a consensus emerged among the Bureau of Reclamation's engineers that of the various possible dam types—including earth fill, rock fill, and straight gravity dams—a concrete, gravity-arch dam would be best. Since concrete works better under compression than in tension, a wedge-shaped form had to be devised that was thicker at the bottom than at the top and was convex on the reservoir side so that the stress, or weight and pressure, of the water held behind the dam would be carried by an arch to the abutting canyon walls and downward to the canyon floor. Between 1928 and 1931 extensive tests of models were carried out at the Denver laboratories of the Reclamation Bureau. These tests revealed that increasing the thickness of the dam at the top would also increase the horizontal tension, an effect to be avoided. Tests were also conducted on other parts of the dam's design to obtain the best profile for maximum velocity and minimum turbulence. This technical engineering design, which opened to bids in December 1930 and then was modified and finally approved by the Colorado River Board on 19 November 1932, called for a massive concrete structure rising 726.4 feet from bedrock with a base thickness of 660 feet and a crest thickness of 45 feet, wide enough for four lanes of vehicular traffic and pedestrians. The crest length of 1,244 feet is nearly a quarter mile long, while the arch on axis has a radius of 500 feet (figs. 13.1, 13.2).

Construction of such a large dam—at the time the largest ever attempted—staggered the imagination. It involved diverting the Colorado River through tunnels drilled in the solid rock walls of the canyon, building temporary cofferdams to block the river, excavating the site, and then building the dam and power plant. This process translated into drilling four diversion tunnels fifty-six feet in diameter and three miles in length, excavation of more than 5.5 million cubic yards of rock and gravel, and the placement of about 5 million barrels of concrete. Two concrete batch plants were brought in along with eight steam locomotives. The concrete presented special difficulties. If it was simply poured and left to harden naturally, it would have taken about a century to cool, and the shrinkage would have cracked the dam and left it unusable. The solution was to circulate refrigerated water through tubing placed in the wet concrete, which cooled each pour in seventy-two hours. Grouting was then pressure-injected into the space resulting from the contraction. The concrete was poured in blocks measuring five feet thick and between twenty-five and sixty feet square. Poured in successive vertical layers, or columns, the blocks were notched on

Figure 13.1. Hoover Dam, downstream face with water overflow test.
(Photo by Ben Glaha, 11 September 1936; courtesy U.S. Bureau of Reclamation)

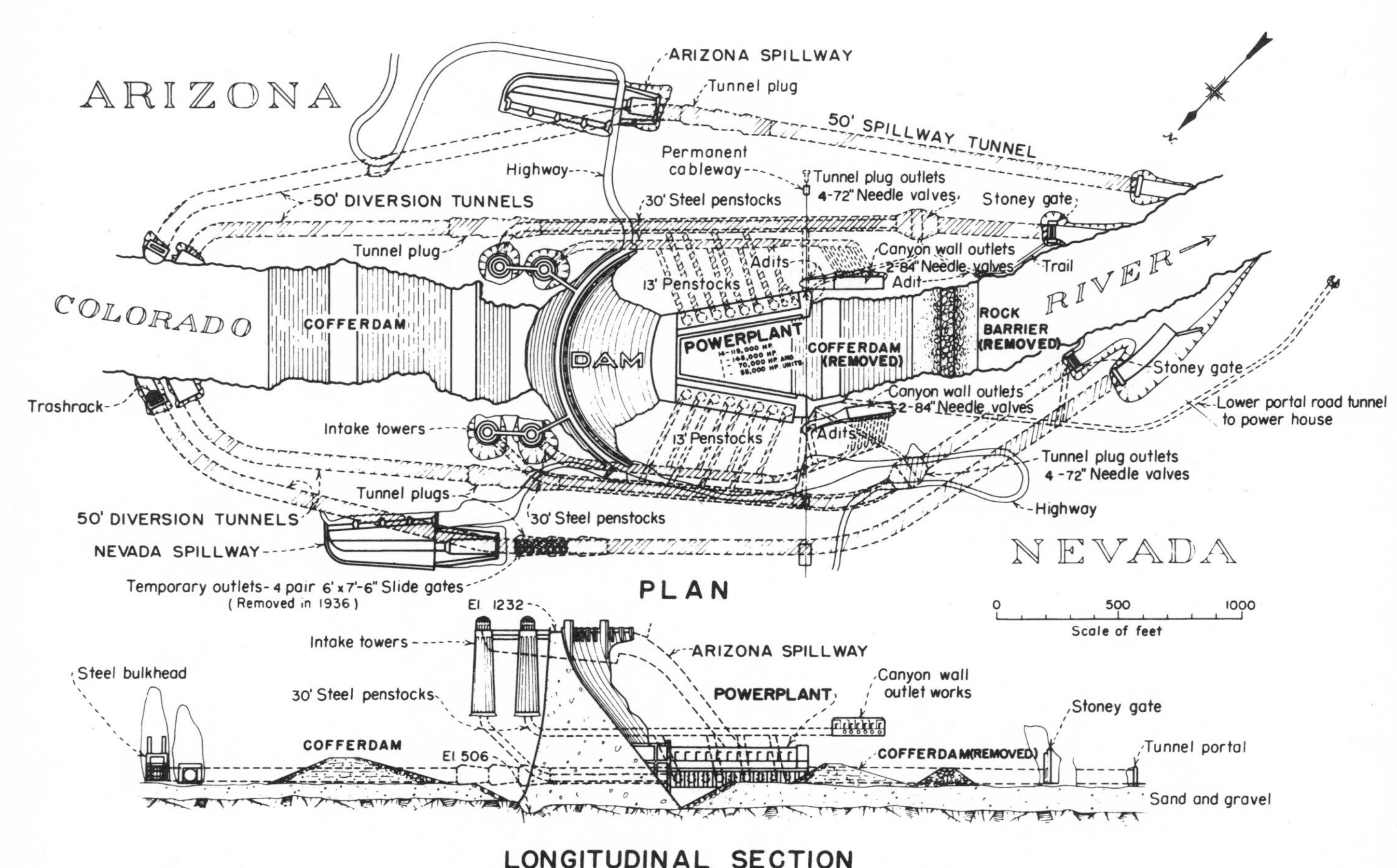

Figure 13.2. Hoover Dam, plan and section. (Courtesy U.S. Bureau of Reclamation)

their sides so they could be keyed to adjoining blocks. A monolithic concrete mass resulted. A "zipper," or eight-foot slot, for the refrigeration pipes remained at the center of the dam as construction climbed upward. This was the last column to be poured. The concrete, composed of cement, water, and aggregate, was rigidly controlled. The often-told tale of workers buried in the concrete during construction is apocryphal; the tolerances of the concrete could never stand such a messy water-filled object.[11]

Fundamental to any work of architecture is the process of construction, the putting together of various materials to build the design. While in most considerations of architecture this process is ignored, some reference must be made to the actual construction of Hoover Dam. Initially the government estimated the dam would take seven years to construct; it was finished in five years. The dam's builders were a consortium of contractors known as Six Companies Inc., consisting of the Utah Construction Company, the Pacific Bridge Company, the MacDonald and Kahn Company, the Morrison-Knudsen Company, the J. F. Shea Company, and the combined W. A. Bechtel and Henry J. Kaiser companies. The general superintendent for the Six Companies was a Morrison-Knudsen construction engineer formerly with the Bureau of Reclamation, Frank T. Crowe, who had supervised several earlier large dam construction jobs in the West. A legendary figure in his own right, Crowe was known as a man of action who wasted little time on paperwork and knew intimately the job of every one of the five thousand men under his direction.[12]

The size and scale of the undertaking, along with the human effort involved in the project, quickly assumed heroic dimensions. It was a major organizational undertaking to supervise at the height of construction several thousand men crammed into a canyon of less than forty-five hundred square feet. Men and equipment working on top of each other in the narrow gorge made the construction of the dam one of the great attractions of the day. Initially the insurance companies for the job estimated that over two hundred men would lose their lives in the first year of construction. Realizing this would be unacceptable, the government and Six Companies worked to improve the working and living conditions; the official toll for the entire project was ninety-six job-related deaths. However this does not take into account the sometimes incapacitating injuries (and later deaths) along with the deaths of dependents. Labor problems plagued the project throughout, especially concerns over working conditions and wages. A strike in August 1931 resulted in improved working and living conditions. Certainly the circumstances of working on the dam were daunting: summer temperatures at the canyon rim could hit 126 degrees Fahrenheit and over 140 degrees in the bottom of the gorge and in the diversion tunnels. Strong winter winds could come at any time and cause temperatures to plummet below zero. The Colorado River, always dangerous, was a constant worry as it tried to break through the temporary cofferdams and flood the entire project. The heroic qualities of the "construction stiff," as the press termed itinerant workers on the project, were played up by writers. One journalist for the *New York Times Magazine,* reflecting on the use of machines, regarded construction at the dam as "Pioneering of the Machine Age."[13]

The actual building of the dam reenforced the heroic dimensions of the project. Black-and-white photographs record some of the story, though the most memorable aspects of construction were captured through the motion picture footage shot by Bureau of Reclamation photographer Ben Glaha. Construction went on twenty-four hours a day, every day of the year. At night the site was brilliantly lit and seemed to some observers like a movie set. There were large machines, some of them new to construction sites: 250-horsepower Mack trucks with sixteen-yard dump bodies; dinosaurlike cranes, shovels, and draglines; Caterpillar tractors; "Jumbo"

Figure 13.3. Hoover Dam, highliners at work on canyon wall. (Photo by Ben Glaha, 10 April 1933; courtesy U.S. Bureau of Reclamation)

drilling rigs; and the cableways carrying men and equipment back and forth and up and down the canyon. While it seemed as if a new race of mechanical giants were inhabiting the earth, a choreographed dance step appeared to control the actions of many of the workers as they swung down the canyon walls with jack hammers and crow bars to scale away loose rock (fig. 13.3). Hand signals would direct the descent of the eight-yard Crowe concrete buckets until, when finally in place, buckets would open at the bottom and concrete would rush out to be tamped and vibrated into place (fig. 13.4). The result, caught in photographs, were concrete cliffs, entirely abstract in their distance from both a human scale and a functional dimension (fig. 13.5). They were pieces of a larger whole, possessing an eternal beauty and finality all their own. These unfinished forms were one level of the aesthetic of large dams.[14]

The technical design of the dam was largely the work of the Denver office of the Bureau of Reclamation. The individual responsible for the conception of the project in 1902 and for directing the early investigations was Arthur Powell Davis, a nephew of the first explorer of the Colorado River, John Wesley Powell. Davis was an engineer and a director of the Reclamation Service in the 1910s and 1920s. Although he left the agency in 1923, his ideas formed the basis of the design. Elwood Mead, the commissioner of reclamation during most of the construction period and for whom Lake Mead—the reservoir—was named, approved the plans. To assign actual responsibility for the technical design to one individual is pointless, however. The chief engineer was Raymond F. Walter, and the chief designing engineer was John L. Savage. Walker R. Young served as the Boulder Canyon project office construction engineer and worked closely with Frank Crowe. These individuals, in turn, supervised a staff of over a hundred engineers who also had a hand in the technical design.[15]

Technical design for an engineer meant essentially working out plans so a structure could be built. Visual considerations did enter into engineering design, but the primary purpose was not to express beauty or abstract aesthetics. Rather, it was to create a functional structure. Some modern architectural theorists of the 1920s and 1930s, such as Le Corbusier, found great beauty in the designs of engineers, and certainly much of the power of Hoover Dam form comes from engineering calculations and design. But in addition to the great concrete wedge, such features as the crest, the towers, the bridges, the spillway gates, the power house, and the ornamentation and color of the dam resulted from self-conscious aesthetic decisions.[16]

Figure 13.4. Hoover Dam, placing concrete in column forms. (Photo by Ben Glaha, 26 June 1933; courtesy U.S. Bureau of Reclamation)

The design of these features, which added considerably to the dam's appearance and symbolic power, was largely the work of the project's architectural consultant, Gordon B. Kaufmann. Kaufmann came into the project through the back door; he was initially selected by the Bureau of Reclamation to design three permanent buildings for Boulder City in early 1931. His designs for the administration, post office, dormitory, and guest house buildings were in the Spanish style, at which he was adept.[17] Kaufmann had no prior experience as a dam architect, but during the design of these buildings he must have looked at the plans for the dam and made suggestions that led to his appointment as architectural consultant. Up to 1931 Kaufmann had been a traditionalist in architectural design; he was known as an accomplished residential designer in Southern California where he worked especially in the Spanish Colonial idiom. But Kaufmann was ready to change in 1931 and embrace some aspects of the new modernism.[18]

Gordon Kaufmann (1888–1949) was born in London of a Scottish mother and German father. He attended the London Polytechnic and Royal College of Art before being apprenticed to a London architect. Apparently he went to Germany to work for a short time in an architect's office before immigrating to Canada, where he worked for three years. In 1913, because of his wife's poor health, he migrated to

Figure 13.5. Hoover Dam, construction of dam and intake towers. (Photo by Ben Glaha, 4 October 1934; courtesy U.S. Bureau of Reclamation)

Southern California. By 1916 he was associated with Reginald Johnson and Roland E. Coate, suave designers in the Spanish Colonial Revival. Kaufmann struck out on his own in 1924 and designed a series of hotels and houses that, while reflecting the "period" styles, were extremely simplified. By the early 1930s his work was beginning to show some Art Deco mannerisms. His Los Angeles Times Building was under design in 1930 and after going through a Mediterranean phase was redesigned in 1932–33 with a setback, plastic profile, and strip pier buttresses (fig. 13.6). Harry Chandler, the owner of the *Los Angeles Times,* was a powerful proponent of water for Southern California and may have helped Kaufmann obtain the Boulder City commissions. Other work by Kaufmann through this period and later in the 1930s showed an increasing simplification of design and adoption of modern stylistic images, while still retaining vestiges of ornament and plastic modeling.[19]

The choice of Kaufmann as the architectural consultant was in retrospect excellent. He was willing to conform to the dictates of the technical design. As he wrote, the dam was the "result of pure engineering" and his "architecture followed the structural design, and it was considered as a complementary treatment rather than a dominant phase of the whole design." He was accustomed to molding broad plastic surfaces. In a sense this was his approach to the various appurtenances of the dam, integrating them into the whole and emphasizing the plastic qualities of concrete. As Kaufmann explained in an article: "There was never any desire or attempt to create an architectural effect or style, but rather to take each problem and integrate it to the whole in order to secure a system of plain surfaces relieved by shadows here and there where the plan or requirements suggested." Kaufmann, in other words, was not a radical modernist subscribing to the dictates of the International style (as it was christened in February 1932), but he obviously knew enough about modernism to clean up the engineers' *retardataire* design.[20]

Figure 13.6. Los Angeles Times Building, Los Angeles; Gordon B. Kaufmann, designer, 1935. (Photo ca. 1984; courtesy Los Angeles Times)

Kaufmann drew on several modernist sources for inspiration. Los Angeles had some of the country's most avant-garde architects, led by R. M. Schindler and Richard Neutra. Neutra had in fact worked for Kaufmann briefly in 1925. By the early 1930s several of the leading American architectural journals were showing with great regularity modern architecture, both European and American. Kaufmann's work at Hoover Dam reflected other modernist sources as well. Dams had appeared in Tony Garnier's *Une Cité Industrielle* (1901–17) and in the 1912–16 drawings of Italian Futurist Antonio Sant' Elia. Garnier's dam appeared in a distant panoramic view as a large cliff-like concrete structure with predominant vertical buttresses molded into the dam face and with a power house standing at the bottom. Because no details were shown, the overall impression was of a large monolithic concrete mass. Sant' Elia had projected several central power stations that bore similarities to dams. But Sant' Elia's drawings generally lacked a context and sense of how the buildings were supposed to function. His drawings glorified the mechanical parts as abstract objects; their stepped-back and molded characters perhaps influenced modernist massing of conventions of the 1920s and 1930s.[21] While it is uncertain whether Kaufmann knew of the dams of Garnier or San' Elia, he certainly knew the work of the architectural illustrator Hugh Ferriss. Many of Ferriss's drawings in his popular book *The Metropolis of Tomorrow* projected immense building forms, plastically molded, with predominant vertical and horizontal setbacks. His charcoal drawings emphasized light and shadow, and represented a distinctly modern approach.[22] Finally, it can hardly be coincidental that Hoover Dam resembled a science fiction movie set. The emphasis Kaufmann placed upon drawing visitors' attention to such machinery as the turbines and on lighting the dam at night recalled Fritz Lang's expressionist movie *Metropolis.* As with Garnier and Sant' Elia, Fritz Lang's connection and possible influence on Kaufmann is circumstantial. But Kaufmann did have ties to Hollywood, where he designed some buildings for various show business personalities.[23] Since he also had spent time in Germany, he was probably aware of the Deutsche Werkbund's attempt to reconcile art and industry. The historian Walter Creese has speculated that foreign born and trained architects such as Kaufmann were more alert to the possibilities of an American art coming out of engineering. Kaufmann's work at Hoover Dam, as well as the dam itself, surpasses any of the various Futurist–Expressionist–Art Deco influences that might be cited, yet they do exist in the background.[24]

Exactly why the Bureau of Reclamation hired an architect is apparent from the drawings the bureau submitted to contractors for bids in December 1930 (fig. 13.7). On the crest of the dam, the balustrade and access towers appeared as attachments to the dam face with little attempt at integration. Two towers were topped by enormous eagles that also appeared in the pediments of the powerhouse below. Aside from these pediments and the flagpole, the powerhouse resembled a boring windowed factory. A variation on the factory fenestration and pediment even carried over to the awkwardly shaped outlet houses perched on the canyon walls.[25]

By November 1932 Kaufmann made the recommendations that resulted in a preliminary sketch published in January 1933 (fig. 13.8). While some adjustments would continue to be made in the design of the dam, especially in the powerhouse, the direction of Kaufmann's work was apparent (13.9). He simplified and modernized the various parts of the dam. On the crest, the overhanging balcony and four unequal towers gave way to a series of observation niches and towers that rise from the wall and continue upward unimpeded. The emphasis, according to Kaufmann, was on "an orderly series of small vertical shadows punctuated by the larger shadows of the elevator and utility towers." He treated these extrusions as continuations of the

Figure 13.7. Hoover Dam, artist's conception of dam, power plant, and Arizona outlet works, as designed by Bureau of Reclamation engineers, 1930. (Courtesy U.S. Bureau of Reclamation)

dam face, not as separate moldings. The four large towers have cutback corners and tops reminiscent of the set-back Los Angeles Times Building, but were treated much more simply. The two outer towers were for utilities and public restrooms, while the two inner towers acted as public entrances to the dam; from them, elevators descended inside the concrete to the internal galleries and powerhouse. Appropriately, these inner entrance towers contained the only ornament on the dam—two large cast-concrete panels by sculptor Oskar J. W. Hansen (13.10). These panels depicted such subjects as flood control, irrigation, power, and the history of the area. Their low-relief, semiclassical, cubist style typified Art Deco sculpture.[26]

The four large intake towers that provide water to the turbines were purposely placed in a symmetrical position even though the site dictated asymmetrical placement. Anchored to bedrock about 250 feet above the original river bed, the towers stand 395 feet tall—the equivalent of a thirty-three-story building. The engineers'

Figure 13.8. Hoover Dam, Gordon B. Kaufmann's conception of dam, power plant, and Arizona outlet works as approved, 19 November 1932. (From *Reclamation Era,* January 1933, cover; courtesy U.S. Bureau of Reclamation)

original design for the control house on top of each tower resembled crenelation, with the piers, or fins, creating a crown of thorns. As actually built following Kaufmann's suggestions, the control house appears as a cap on the tower with vertical buttresses terminating in a green-tinted concrete roof. Kaufmann, moreover, placed a light globe atop each tower so that at night the illumination of the interior of the house and the lighted globe conveyed an almost supernatural effect, as if some hidden dynamo was pulsating energy (fig. 13.11).[27] The spillways located on either side of the dam were intended for controlling the reservoir level, especially during the flood seasons. Kaufmann again had a hand in their redesign. Originally the bureau's engineers had projected a large overhead gate for each side. When they realized that this might be inadequate, they continued extensive model studies. The final design was for a series of four rolling drum gates for each side separated by substantial concrete piers that were carefully studied in profile to provide the smoothest flow of water. Their streamlined shape—consisting of a series of rounded forms built upon each other—conveyed a nautical feeling. The design of the spillways was abstract and modern, with the Art Deco stylisms receding in the face of the powerful masses of the concrete forms. On the Arizona side the topography made it necessary to construct a bridge over the spillway (fig. 13.12). The design resulted from engineering and especially architectural considerations. As the bureau's report circumspectly noted, "the design of the bridge was governed to a considerable extent by architectural considerations, in order to provide a structure in harmony with the general massiveness of the dam and spillways. Consequently, some of its members are of greater size than actually required for utility."[28]

The powerhouse at the base of the dam that contained the turbines was also substantially modified by Kaufmann. He noted that while "engineering principles" determined the overall size, shape, and plan of the powerhouse, his role was to mold

Figure 13.9. Hoover Dam, downstream face and powerhouse as completed. (Photo by E. E. Hertzog, 6 May 1977; courtesy U.S. Bureau of Reclamation)

the facades into a more harmonious statement. Taking the predetermined column spacing of the structure as a given, Kaufmann created recessed vertical fenestration panels in between the columns. Horizontally placed wood formwork (two-by-six-foot lagging) was used on the exterior walls to align them with the horizontal layering of the concrete work of the dam face. Along the front of the powerhouse on either side, Kaufmann arranged smaller boxlike switch houses with horizontal aluminum fins across their tops that contrasted with the predominant verticalism of the powerhouse. By placing transformers on the exterior in full view, Kaufmann glorified the technological nature of the project.[29]

The outlet, or valve, houses located on the canyon walls and intended for overflow were also substantially modified from their earlier pedestrian mien. The bureau's report noted that "architectural considerations suggested an appearance of stability and security, and a color in harmony with the surroundings." The result was a denser

Figure 13.10. Hoover Dam, Nevada entrance tower with sculpture by Oskar J. W. Hansen. (Photo by Ben Glaha, 11 April 1938; courtesy U.S. Bureau of Reclamation)

structure with fewer openings, especially openings containing references to traditional fenestration. Five vertical windows and six circular ports for water discharge were the basic features, while the form itself had horizontal grooves at the corners and a battered base. Kaufmann explained that the horizontal grooves gave "a feeling of stability—as if they served to hold the structure against the sheer wall of the canyon."[30]

Kaufmann also had some impact on the final color of the dam. During the curing and cooling of the concrete when all surfaces had to be kept moist—generally by continuous spraying—it was noticed that the concrete became colored. Reddish and brownish stains developed that came from the iron oxide in both the water and the pipes used for the curing. As a consequence, Kaufmann attempted to graduate the depth of color on the dam's face, the powerhouses, and the valve houses. The valve houses were cured to a warm dark red at the base and a lighter red at the top. On the dam Kaufmann tried to graduate the color from the bottom to the top, though as the report stated, "the results . . . were not entirely satisfactory." Subsequent aging and weathering obliterated most of the color graduation and the dam now—more than fifty years later—is a light tan in color.[31]

Kaufmann's imprint is also obvious on the dam's interior. From the beginning it was assumed the structure would be a great publicity bonus for the Bureau of Reclamation and would attract visitors. Kaufmann recommended that the bureau engage Denver artist Allen True to act as color consultant for portions of the interior. True found the task conducive to furthering modernist aesthetics and declared: "it no longer suffices that a hydroelectric plant which serves millions of people be encased in a mere building—its housing must express through architectural planning the new understanding of functional form and satisfy in every respect the pride and esthetic joy that man finds in his accomplishments." Largely due to True's efforts, the four towers on the crest included small, yet elaborate, lobbies with floors of

Figure 13.11. Hoover Dam intake towers at night, and Lake Mead. (Photo by Cliff Segerblom, 17 May 1940; courtesy U.S. Bureau of Reclamation)

highly polished dark green-and-black terrazzo encased in walls of dark green-and-black marble with white stucco and aluminum ceilings and trim. Since the elevator towers served as public entrances, their bronze doors opened onto terrazzo decorative panels set in the floor. True based his design of these panels on decorative motifs of Southwest Indians and extended these patterns in the floors and around drains of the tunnels down in the dam through which visitors moved to view the turbine galleries and powerhouse (fig. 13.13). True's patterns came from Pima baskets, Ácoma bowls, and Navajo sand paintings. While acknowledging their apparent primitiveness, True claimed that many of the patterns were also strikingly modern and appropriate for the dam. The swirling central motif, he claimed, "will reveal its striking similarity to what might be termed an engineer's basic diagram of a generator or turbine, with valves, gates, and suggestion of centrifugal motion."[32]

The visitor coming to the dam would enter the elevator lobby, drop some 528

Figure 13.12. Hoover Dam, Arizona spillway. (Photo by G. Lawrence Ullom, 8 March 1936; courtesy U.S. Bureau of Reclamation)

feet in the elevator within the dam, walk through a gleaming white interior tunnel lined with glazed brick, stand on a floor patterned with True's Indian designs, and finally arrive at the platform for viewing the turbines. In the color scheme for the powerhouse interior, True selected ten colors that had "Indian characteristics" but were "made as brilliant as possible." The result was a striking interior set against repetitive concrete piers. Huge turbine galleries gleamed with the generators in their deep red casings and aluminum trim and piping. Overhead cranes painted a jade green along with vermilion, blue, and yellow valves, gray control panels with switches and dials in full view offered a far more dramatic setting than even Fritz Lang could have conceived.[33]

The physical fact of the dam, coupled with the act of construction, would seem testimony enough of the project's significance, but Americans have often wanted their achievements, whether small or large, to be seen in a cosmological light. Hoover

Figure 13.12. Hoover Dam, Arizona spillway. (Photo by G. Lawrence Ullom, 8 March 1936; courtesy U.S. Bureau of Reclamation)

Dam was no different. Under the guidance of Kaufmann, a competition was held for a monument to accompany the dam. The result was the commissioning of Norwegian-born Oskar J. W. Hansen. Hansen, who contributed the low-relief plaques over the elevator towers, had also designed a memorial, placed on the rock canyon wall on the Arizona side, to the ninety-six workers who officially lost their lives during construction. Hansen's monument, located on the Nevada side was a grand affair (fig. 13.14). Hansen designed a base of polished black diorite for a 142-foot flagpole and two 30-foot-tall seated winged figures. These surrealistic apparitions underscored the unreality of a dam and lake in the middle of a hostile desert. Made of bronze, the figures' wings and arms were molded into a single unit similar to the unity Kaufmann achieved between the crest towers and the dam face. Hansen claimed that the figures symbolized the universal aspirations of mankind and the achievement of Americans. More specifically, he intended their stoic visages "with the look of eagles" to represent those who settled the West. To further underscore the universality of the dam, Hansen embedded in the floor of the monument the Great Seal of the United States, signs of the zodiac, and a large star map indicating such important historical dates as the construction of the pyramids and the birth of Christ, along with the precise astronomical time of the dam's dedication on 30 September 1935, at 8 hours, 56 minutes, and 2.25 seconds in the evening. With constellations, stars, and planets placed in an intersecting pattern of circles, triangles, and straight lines similar to that used by the Russian Constructivists of the 1920s, Hansen, in effect, froze the entire universe at this one point in time. Looking at his creation, Hansen forecast that "in remote ages to come, intelligent people may view the star map out of which rises the monument at Boulder Dam and from it learn . . . the astronomical time of the dam's dedication."[34]

On 29 May 1935 the last bucket of concrete was placed in the dam, and on 30 September Pres. Franklin Delano Roosevelt dedicated the dam. In February, water had already begun to be impounded in Lake Mead and in October the first electric power surged over 266 miles of transmission lines to Los Angeles, where a major celebration was held. The impact of the dam on the Southwest would be tremendous, for in a very real sense it allowed Southern California and Los Angeles to continue to develop. Furthermore, the dam led to the growth of southern Nevada and Las Vegas as recreation spots, and permitted the continued agricultural development of the great food-producing valleys of California and Arizona. So great was the power potential of Hoover Dam that not until 1961, twenty-six years later, was the last hydroelectric generator placed in service. Not until then had the energy demand risen enough to consume all the dam's output. If, when the dam was completed in 1935, all the generating units had been placed in service, their combined horsepower would have equalled one-eighth of all the horsepower available in the United States for generating electricity.[35]

Hoover Dam was the first of the great American dams of the 1930s and 1940s and in a sense a prototype for the transformation of great areas of the American West and the Tennessee Valley Authority in the Southeast. For Gordon Kaufmann his success on the Colorado River led to an extensive career as an architectural consultant on dams. He advised Roland Wank, the chief architect of the TVA, on Norris and Wheeler dams; his interest in patterned concrete and the treatment of large masses is apparent throughout TVA. Back out West Kaufmann advised on the design of Parker Dam (1931–38), down the Colorado River from Hoover Dam; Grand Coulee Dam (1933–41), on the Columbia River in Washington; Shasta Dam (1938–45), in Northern California; and several smaller dams. Although the story of the design and construction of these and other great western dams (that is, Bonneville, Fort Peck, and so on) awaits further study, their relation to western modernism is worthy of comment.

Figure 13.14. Hoover Dam, *Winged Figures of the Republic* by Oskar J. W. Hansen, Hoover Dam dedication monument. (Photo by R. C. Middleton, September 1959; courtesy U.S. Bureau of Reclamation)

The study of modernism in the American West has been largely focused on California and on the design of individual buildings. While there have been a few excursions to Arizona and Frank Lloyd Wright, or the presence of the Prairie School elsewhere, and a few other designers in other states, the presence of these larger complexes that combined engineering and architecture has been scarcely acknowledged. With the exception of the Golden Gate Bridge and a few poetic acknowledgements of the Los Angeles Freeway, the possibility that the West might have a different design agenda has seldom been commented on.[36] How different the West is from the East Coast or the Midwest (or indeed other areas such as Canada) might be more an issue of degree than diametrical opposition, but it does seem that the vastness, varying topography, relative newness, and lack of settlement of the West called for a type of design that combined engineering and architecture. Large scale and functionality are two of the elements, but they receive their meaning through the confrontation of the man made with the natural, and how the two coexist. Fundamental to this confrontation is the actual process of construction, the effort by individuals and their machines to tame the landscape and build. Geography is altered in the West, and the design becomes a new geological feature.

Architects are always caught up in matters of style or appearances, and certainly Gordon Kaufmann was no different. His designs passed through the common stylistic vocabularies of the time, and they can be identified. But Kaufmann's work at Hoover Dam also belies one of the myths of modern architecture, as proposed by Le Corbusier and others, that the great functional structures were simply the work of engineers.[37] Kaufmann—an architect—converted the dam's banal, warmed-over classicism created by the engineers into a vibrant symbol of modernity. His modernist vocabulary not only respected the engineers' technological demands but enhanced them. The crest and intake towers have the setbacks of Art Deco skyscrapers. The spillways are streamlined with their rounded forms and thin incised "speed whisker" lines near the top of each pier. Far down at the dam's base the powerhouse—with its vertical fenestration, horizontal layering of form work, and gleaming aluminum and stainless steel transformers—captures the spirit of high technology and the inherent beauty of machines. In each case the different style fits the particular activity as well as the overall form.

All of these elements—the setting, the engineering, the construction, and the architecture—contribute to the impact of the dam as a physical entity that captures the imagination (fig. 13.15). One approach to the edifice is across the harsh desert, then down a winding canyon until around a corner there appears the massive, smooth cliff, a concave wedge of concrete—the machine hand of man—pushing apart the rough walls of Black Canyon and holding back trillions of gallons of water. Behind the dam a glistening miragelike lake of deep blue stretches out into the far distance (fig. 13.16). Alternatively, the dam can be approached at night with the vast wall brilliantly lit. From the inky depths of Lake Mead the intake towers emerge, glowing with messages of energy and light. Hoover Dam is one of the few structures built in scale with the vast landscapes of the West. It exerts control over that landscape, both through size and design.

Equally impressive is the interior: the public lobbies of black, green, bronze, and aluminum; the hygienically white tunnels; Allen True's angular and circular Indian patterns set into the floors; and, finally, the great turbine chambers on either side of the powerhouse. The reiterated piers of the galleries and the humming turbines encased in their smooth and glistening jackets recall Henry Adams's confrontation with the dynamo; "he began to feel the forty-foot dynamo as a moral force, much as the early Christians felt the Cross. The planet itself seemed less impressive, in its old-fashioned deliberate, annual or daily revolution, than this huge wheel, revolv-

Figure 13.15. Hoover Dam, Nevada spillway. (Photo by Cliff Segerblom, 18 August 1941; courtesy U.S. Bureau of Reclamation)

ing within arm's-length at some vertiginous speed. . . . Before the end, one began to pray to it." Artists like Charles Sheeler, Hugh Ferriss, Ben Glaha, and Cliff Segerblom tried to capture the dam's force in paint, charcoal, and photographs. Writers from J. B. Priestley to Theodore White and Joan Didion have speculated on its moving power. For them, Hoover Dam represented a new modern world of special beauty that was simultaneously "strange and uncomfortable." In 1937 Priestly saw in the dam

> that world we catch a glimpse of in one of the later sequences of Wells's film, "Things to Come," a world of giant machines and titanic communal enterprises. Here in this Western American wilderness, the new man, the man of the future has done something, and what he has

Figure 13.16. Hoover Dam, aerial view with Lake Mead. (Photo by E. E. Hertzog; courtesy U.S. Bureau of Reclamation)

> done takes your breath away. When you look down at that vast smooth wall, at its towers of concrete, its power stations, at the new lakes and cataracts it has created, and you see the men who have made it all moving far below like ants or swinging perilously in midair as if they were little spiders, and you note the majestic order and rhythm of the work, you are visited by emotions that are hard to describe, if only because some of them are as new as the great Dam itself.[38]

Ultimately Hoover Dam, like all great works of art and all important symbols, transcends description and interpretation. It is more than what can be written or expressed. As a work of art it tugs at the base of emotion, offers new experiences, and opens a new reality. Hoover Dam is one of the great architectural landmarks not just of the West, or modernism, or of America, but of the ages.

Notes

The original version of this article appeared as "Machine-Age Iconography in the American West: The Design of Hoover Dam" in *Pacific Historical Review* 54 (November 1985): 463–93. Portions of it have been rewritten and brought up to date for this publication. Some of the original research for this essay was done under a National Endowment for the Humanities grant to the Brooklyn Museum for an exhibition titled "The Machine Age in America, 1918–1941," which was seen in 1987–89 in Brooklyn, Pittsburgh, Los Angeles, and Atlanta. For research assistance I thank Virginia Fenton of Boulder City, Nevada; Julian Rhinehart, Public Affairs Officer, Lower Colorado Regional Office, Bureau of Reclamation, Boulder City, Nevada, and his staff; and the staff of the Engineering and Research Center, Bureau of Reclamation, Denver, Colorado.

1. "See Boulder Dam," advertisement, *Fortune,* November 1934, 42; Union Pacific Railroad Timetable, 1 February 1935, 27. By late 1933 the first souvenir booklet had appeared: *View-Book of the Boulder [Hoover] Dam "World's Biggest Job"* (Los Angles, 1933). It cost twenty-five cents. Exactly when the Union Pacific stopped promoting tours to Hoover Dam is unclear; promotional materials exist from the early 1950s.

2. The extensive political and reclamation history is cited in notes below. On scholarly attention to the design of dams, see Carl Condit, *American Building Art: The Twentieth Century* (New York: Oxford University Press, 1961), 219–73; and Marian Moffett and Lawrence Wodehouse, *Built for the People of the United States: Fifty Years of TVA Architecture* (Knoxville: Art and Architecture College, University of Tennessee, 1983). The latter contains essays by William Jordy and Walter Creese. See also Walter L. Creese, *TVA's Public Planning: The Vision, The Reality* (Knoxville: University of Tennessee Press, 1990). Two other considerations of Hoover Dam are Richard Guy Wilson, "Massive Deco Monument," *Architecture* 72 (December 1983): 45–47, which contains a preliminary assessment of the visual character of the dam, and Wilson, Dianne Pilgrim, and Dickran Tashjian, *The Machine Age in America: 1918–1941* (New York: Abrahms, 1987), 111–22.

3. Critical views of these accomplishments are Donald Worster, *Rivers of Empire* (New York: Pantheon Books, 1986), and Marc Reisner, *Cadillac Desert* (New York: Viking, 1986).

4. Theodore White, "Building the Big Dam," *Harper's,* June 1935, 120. Selected commentary includes "Power and Industry," *Progressive Architecture* 32 (November 1951): 56–62; "The Dam," *Fortune,* September 1933, 74–88; "Remaking the World," *Collier's,* 16 March 1935, 60; "Boulder Dam: Engineering Triumph," *Literary Digest,* 17 October 1935, 19–20; Mildred Adams, "Taming the Untamable at Boulder Dam," *New York Times Magazine,* 24 February 1935, 5, 19; editorial, *New York Times,* 7 December 1935, p. 16; "Portfolio of Public Works," *Architectural Record* 77 (June 1935): 340–41; "Undertakings without Precedent," *Engineering News-Record,* 29 November 1934, 675–77; Walter K. M. Slavif, "Monuments to the Living," *Reclamation Era,* February 1940, 42–43. On the TVA, see, for example, "Tennessee Valley Authority," *Architectural Forum* 71 (August 1939): 73–114; Talbot Faulkner Hamlin, "Architecture of the TVA," *Pencil Points* 20 (November 1939): 720–31; *Life,* 23 November 1936, front cover.

5. Henry Adams, *The Education of Henry Adams* (1918; reprint, New York: Random House, 1931), 380; White, "Building the Big Dam," 121.

6. On the political issue of the dam's name, see Harold L. Ickes, *The Secret Diary of Harold L. Ickes,* vol. 1 (New York: Simon and Schuster, 1953), 37–38.

7. Determining the size and relative ranking of dams is tricky, because they can be classified in many ways. At the time of its completion in 1936 Hoover Dam was the tallest dam in the world, had the greatest power capacity, and the largest reservoir. Today it has been surpassed in all categories. For the general history of dams, see Norman Smith, *A History of Dams* (Secaucus, N.J.: Citadel Press, 1971); Allen H. Cullen, *Rivers in Harness: The Story of Dams* (Philadelphia: Chilton, 1962); Julian Hinds, "Continuous Development of Dams Since 1840," paper no. 2605, and K. B. Keener, "Dams Then and Now," paper no. 2606, both in *Transactions of the American Society of Civil Engineers* 101 (1953): 489–535. See also T. W. Mermel, *Register of Dams in the United States* (New York: McGraw Hill, 1958).

The best survey of Hoover Dam is Joseph E. Stevens, *Hoover Dam: An American Adventure* (Norman: University of Oklahoma Press, 1988). Between 1938 and 1950 the Bureau of Reclamation issued a series of bulletins recording some of the dam's history, design, and technical features, which have provided information for this study. See U.S. Bureau of Reclamation, *Boulder Canyon Project, Final Reports,* 7 parts, (Boulder City, Nev.; Washington, D.C.; and Denver, Colo.: U.S. Department of the Interior, 1938–50). The bureau's magazine, *Reclamation Era,* provides information for the 1930s. See also T. H. Watkins, "Conquest of the Colorado," *Idaho Yesterdays* 6 (April 1969): 4–9, 48, 60. Participants' viewpoints and local history can be found in Dennis McBride, *In the Beginning . . .* (Boulder City, Nev.: Boulder City Chamber of Commerce, 1981); Marion V. Allen, *Hoover Dam and Boulder City* (Redding, Calif.: C. P. Printing and Publishing, 1983); Angela Brooker and Dennis McBride, *Boulder City: Passages in Time* (Boulder City, Nev.: Boulder City Public Library, 1981); and William J. Williams, "The Town . . . That Built . . . the Dam," *Reclamation Era,* spring–summer 1981, 1–10. Because of charges that there was excessive overtime, the Six Companies commissioned George A. Pettitt to write *So Boulder Dam Was Built* (Berkeley: Six Companies, 1935), which contains valuable information on construction. A short popular history is U.S. Department of the Interior, Bureau of Reclamation, *The Story of Hoover Dam* (Washington, D.C.: Government Printing Office, 1976). The Bechtel Company has produced a video, *The Taming of Black Canyon* (San Francisco: Bechtel, [ca. 1979]). Another film is the Bureau of Reclamation's *Story of Hoover Dam* (Washington D.C.: U.S. Department of the Interior, Bureau of Reclamation, 1960). On the political context, see Alfred R. Golze, *Reclamation in the United States* (Caldwell, Idaho: Caxton Printers, 1961); Paul L. Kleinsorge, *The Boulder Canyon Project: Historical and Economic Aspects* (Palo Alto: Stanford University Press, 1941); Norris Hundley Jr., *Water and the West: The Colorado River Compact and the Politics of Water in the American West* (Berkeley: University of California Press, 1974); Hundley, *Dividing the Waters: A Century of Controversy between the United States and Mexico* (Ph.D. diss., UCLA, 1966), University Microfilms International, Ann Arbor, Mich.; Linda J. Lear, "The Boulder Canyon Project: A Re-examination of Federal Resource Management," *Materials and Society* 7 (1983): 329–37; Lear, "Boulder Dam: A Crossroad in National Resource Policy," *Journal of the West* (forthcoming); and Remi Nadeau, *The Water Seekers* (Garden City, N.Y.: Doubleday, 1950). From a popular point of view, Hoover Dam has been considered by David O. Woodbury, *The Colorado Conquest* (New York: Dodd Mead, 1941); and Frank Waters, *The Colorado* (New York: Editions for the Armed Services, 1946). Among other places, archival materials are located at the Bureau of Reclamation offices in Denver and Boulder City, the Boulder City Public Library, and the University of Nevada, Las Vegas.

8. S. R. De Boer, a city planner, laid out the town of Boulder City in 1930–31. See S. R. De Boer, "The Plan of Boulder City," *Architectural Record* 73 (March 1933): 154–58. See also "Government Plans Model Town at Boulder City, Nevada," *New Reclamation Era,* February 1931, 28–30, 41; and "Boulder City—Government's Model Town to Rise on the Nevada Desert," *American City,* March 1931, 16–19. In execution, De Boer's plans were significantly modified. See Imre Sutton, "Geographical Aspects of Construction Planning: Hoover Dam Revisited," *Journal of the West* 7 (1968): 301–44.

9. U.S. Bureau of Reclamation, *Final Reports, Part 1—Introductory, Bulletin 1, General History and Description of Project* (Boulder City, Nev.: U.S. Department of the Interior, 1948), 22–42.

10. William E. Warne, *The Bureau of Reclamation* (New York: Praeger, 1973) provides a general history of the reclamation program; U.S. Bureau of Reclamation, *Final Reports, Part 1—Introductory,* 52, 54–56.

11. This tale has become folklore in the West. I remember hearing it as a child in Los Angeles, and guides today at the dam repeat the tale. While many individuals did lose their lives, none were buried and remained in the concrete.

12. A popular history of the construction companies is Neill C. Wilson and Frank J. Taylor, *The Earth Changers* (New York: Doubleday, 1957). Some history can also be found in Paul D. Nations, ed., *River Tamers* (Boise, Idaho: Morrison-Knudsen, 1947); "50 Years of Construction Progress," *Em-Kayan* 21 (1962): 1–36; "'The Earth Movers': The Epic of the Six Companies of the West," *Fortune,* August 1943, 99–107, 210–14; and "Memoir No. (1818) Francis Trenholm Crowe, Hon. M. ASCE," *Transac-*

tions of the American Society of Civil Engineers 111 (June 1946): 1–7.

13. Guy Louis Rocha, "The IWW and the Boulder Canyon Project: The Final Death Throes of American Syndicalism," *Nevada Historical Society Quarterly* 21 (1978): 2–24; Edmund Wilson, "Hoover Dam," *New Republic,* 2 September 1931, 66–69; "Open Shop at Boulder Dam," *New Republic,* 24 June 1931, 147–48; Elwood Mead, "Boulder Dam," *New Republic,* 26 August 1931, 48; "Engineers-Contractors Committee Finds Hoover Dam Conditions Satisfactory," *Reclamation Era,* February 1932, 32; and Pettitt, *So Boulder Dam Was Built,* 38–39. See also Roosevelt Fitzgerald, "Blacks and the Boulder Dam Project," *Nevada Historical Society Quarterly* 24 (1981): 255–60; "The Dam," *Fortune,* September 1933, 75; Duncan Aikman, "New Pioneers in the Old West's Deserts," *New York Times Magazine,* 26 October 1930, 7.

14. William H. Gater, comp., *Hoover Dam including the Story of the Turbulent Colorado River* (Los Angeles: Nevada Publications, 1932), 14. There were numerous photographers associated with the project, but Ben (Bernard D.) Glaha (1899–1971) stands out as the best. See Ben Glaha, "Boulder Dam: The Photography of Engineering Works," *U.S. Camera,* January–February 1939, 18–23, 78–79; "Glaha Complimented," *Reclamation Era,* July 1935, 152; "Photographs Exhibited," *Reclamation Era,* August 1935, 168, and September 1935, 185; and Willard Van Dyke, "The Work of Ben Glaha," *Camera Craft,* April 1935, 166–72. Glaha's work was exhibited nationwide in 1935 and praised by several individuals, including Ansel Adams. In 1938 Cliff (Clifford) Segerblom (b. 1917) became the official bureau photographer for the dam and is responsible for the excellent photographs of the test of the spillways and valve outlet houses. Interview with Cliff Segerblom, 15 May 1984. See also, Richard Guy Wilson, "Dams: Photographs from the Depression," *Modulus, The University of Virginia Architectural Review* 17 (1984): 34–43.

15. "The Dam," *Fortune,* September 1933, 75.

16. Le Corbusier, *Towards a New Architecture* (1927; reprint, New York: Praeger, 1963), 33.

17. "Designs for Government Buildings at Boulder City Approved," *Southwest Builder and Contractor,* 29 May 1931; see also *Southwest Builder and Contractor,* 22 May, 14 August, 21 August, 1931. Kaufmann's designs also appeared in "Buildings Approved for Construction at Boulder City . . ." *Reclamation Era* May 1931, 105 and back cover.

18. For information on Kaufmann see Jay Belloli, ed., *A Partnership in the California Style: Gordon B. Kaufmann, Reginald Johnson, and Roland Coate* (Claremont, Calif.: Galleries of Pomona at Scripps College, 1992), which contains essays by Jan Muntz, Stefanos Polyzoides, and Richard Guy Wilson; Alson Clark, "The 'Californian' Architecture of Gordon B. Kaufmann," *Society of Architectural Historians, Southern California Chapter Review* 1 (summer 1982): 1–8; Joseph Giovannini, "Gordon Kaufmann" in *Caltech 1910–1950: An Urban Architecture for Southern California* (Pasadena: California Institute of Technology, Baxter Art Gallery, 1983); "Gordon B. Kaufmann: Obituary," *Southwest Builder and Contractor,* 4 March 1949, 7; *Los Angeles Times,* 2 March 1949, pt. 2, p. 1; and Harris C. Allen, "It Can Happen Here: A Classical Scholar Learns a Modern Language," *Architect and Engineer* 129 (May 1937): 13–34. Additional biographical information on Kaufmann can be found in his application for a fellowship from the American Institute of Architects in the AIA Archives, Washington, D.C.

19. In particular in California are the San Pedro High School (1935–35); the Federal Building, Long Beach (1932); the Royal Laundry, Pasadena (1927, 1935); the ALCOA Building, Vernon (1938); and in Utah the Salisbury Building, Salt Lake City (1936).

20. Gordon B. Kaufmann, "The Architecture of Boulder Dam," *Architectural Concrete* 2, no. 3 (1936): 3. See also Wesley R. Nelson, "Ornamental Features of Boulder Dam," *Compressed Air Magazine* 43 (June 1938): 5,615–20.

21. Henry-Russell Hitchcock and Philip Johnson, *The International Style: Architecture Since 1922* (New York: W. W. Norton, 1932); see also Richard Guy Wilson, "International Style: The MoMA Exhibition," *Progressive Architecture* 62 (February 1982): 92–105; Thomas S. Hines, *Richard Neutra and the Search for Modern Architecture* (New York: Oxford University Press, 1982), 59. Two principal journals were *Architectural Record* and *Architectural Forum,* both of which converted from rather staid conservative magazines in 1928 and 1929 and began actively supporting modernism, though it should be noted there was no general agreement on what was modern. *American Archi-*

tect—the oldest U.S. architectural magazine, founded in 1876—was slower to change, but was showing some modern work by 1930. *Pencil Points* remained very conservative. An aggressive display and argument about modernism—both American and European—can be found in the *AIA Journal* from the mid-1920s.

Both Garnier and Sant' Elia had made minor appearances in books by such American authors as Henry-Russell Hitchcock, *Modern Architecture* (New York: Payson and Clarke, 1929), 146, 171, 199. Garnier's work was published in *Une Cité Industrielle* (Paris, 1917). See also Dora Wiebenson, *Tony Garnier and the Cité Industrielle* (New York: Braziller, 1969). Futurist paintings were displayed at the San Francisco Panama-Pacific International Exposition in September 1915. However, Sant' Elia was evidently not shown. See Anne d'Haroncourt, *Futurism and the International Avant-Garde* (Philadelphia: Philadelphia Museum of Art, 1981). For a record of Sant' Elia's exhibitions and bibliography, see Luciano Caramel and Albert Longatti, *Antonio Sant' Elia* (Como, Italy: L'Ente, 1962).

22. Hugh Ferriss, *The Metropolis of Tomorrow* (New York: Washburn, 1929). See also Jean Ferriss Leich, *Architectural Visions: The Drawings of Hugh Ferriss* (New York: Whitney Library of Design, 1980). Ferriss published a drawing of Hoover Dam in Hugh Ferriss, *Power in Buildings* (New York: Columbia University Press, 1953), plate 49.

23. *Metropolis* was filmed in Germany in 1925–26 and released in 1927. It was shown in the United States and widely reviewed in 1927. Lang came to Hollywood in 1934. See Frederick W. Ott, *The Films of Fritz Lang* (Secaucus, N.J.: Citadel Press, 1979), 123–41; and Lotte Eisner, *Fritz Lang* (New York: Oxford University Press, 1977).

24. Creese, *TVA's Public Planning,* 213.

25. *Hoover Dam, Power Plant and Appurtenant Works, Specifications, Schedule, and Drawings: Specifications No. 519* (Washington, D.C.: U.S. Department of the Interior, Bureau of Reclamation, 1930).

26. "Report of the Colorado River Board," *Reclamation Era,* January 1933, 4; the revised design is shown on the cover. Kaufmann, "Architecture of Boulder Dam," 3.

27. U.S. Bureau of Reclamation, *Final Reports, Part 1—Introductory,* 78.

28. U.S. Bureau of Reclamation, *Final Reports, Part 6—Hydraulic Investigation, Bulletin 1, Model Studies of Spillways* (Denver: U.S. Department of the Interior, 1938); U.S. Bureau of Reclamation, *Final Reports, Part 4—Design and Construction, Bulletin 3, Diversion, Outlet, and Spillway Structures* (Denver: U.S. Department of the Interior, 1947), 318–21.

29. Kaufmann, "Architecture of Boulder Dam," 3.

30. U.S. Bureau of Reclamation, *Final Reports, Part 4—Design and Construction, Bulletin 3,* 202; Kaufmann, "Architecture of Boulder Dam," 4.

31. U.S. Bureau of Reclamation, *Final Reports, Part 4—Design and Construction, Bulletin 4, Concrete Manufacture, Handling, and Control* (Denver: U.S. Department of the Interior, 1947), 171. See also Kaufmann, "Architecture of Boulder Dam," 4; and U.S. Bureau of Reclamation, *Final Reports, Part 4—Design and Construction, Bulletin 3,* 202.

32. Allen True, "Color and Decoration at the Boulder Power Plant," *Reclamation Era,* January 1936, 12–13.

33. True, "The Planned Use of Color at the Boulder Dam Power Plant, *Reclamation Era,* February 1936, 48.

34. Oskar Hansen, "The Sculptures at Boulder Dam—Part 1: With the Look of Eagles," *Reclamation Era,* February 1942, 32; Hansen, "The Sculptures at Boulder Dam—Part 2: Split Second Petrified in the Face of the Universal Clock," *Reclamation Era,* March 1942, 57. These two articles by Hansen are reprinted in a pamphlet, *Sculptures at Hoover Dam* (Washington, D.C.: Government Printing Office, 1968).

35. "Boulder Dam: Engineering Triumph," *Literary Digest,* 17 October 1935, 19.

36. Specifically might be noted, John van der Zee, *The Gate: The True Story of the Design and Construction of the Golden Gate Bridge* (New York: Simon and Schuster, 1986); Reyner Banham, *Los Angeles: The Architecture of the Four Ecologies* (London: Allen Lane, 1971); and David Brodsly, *L.A. Freeway: An Appreciative Essay* (Berkeley: University of California Press, 1981).

37. Le Corbusier, *Towards a New Architecture,* 33, 42; Erich Mendelsohn, *Amerika: Bilderbuck Eines Architekten* (Berlin: R. Mosse, 1926).

38. Adams, *The Education,* 380; "Power: A Portfolio by Charles Sheeler," *Fortune,* December 1940, 73–83. On Ferriss, see note 22; on Glaha and Segerblom, see note 14. See also

Stanley Wood, "Boulder Dam, Portfolio of Watercolors," *Fortune,* May 1934, 92–100; William Woollett's lithograph of the dam under construction in *California Arts and Architecture* 47 (January 1935): front cover; and *Pencil Points* 19 (July 1938): 421. Woollett did a number of lithographs on the dam (Woollett to author, 15 July 1984); see Woollett, *Hoover Dam, Drawings, Etchings, Lithographs* (Los Angeles: Hennessey and Ingalls, 1986). White, "Building the Big Dam"; Joan Didion, "A Piece of Work for Now and Doomsday," *Life,* 13 March 1970, 25, reprinted with changes in *The White Album* (New York: Simon and Schuster, 1979), 198–201; J. B. Priestly, "Arizona Desert," *Harper's Monthly Magazine,* March 1937, 365.

Contributors

ANNE BLOOMFIELD is a consultant in the architectural history of northern California and a commissioner on San Francisco's Landmarks Preservation Advisory Board. After graduation with honors from Swarthmore College, teaching, and raising a family, she came to architectural history by way of seeking to preserve her own neighborhood. The article reprinted here marked the beginnings of her third career and of the scholarly reputation she now enjoys.

THOMAS CARTER is an associate proffessor at the University of Utah's Graduate School of Architecture. In 1990, he founded the Western Regional Architecture Program in an effort to stimulate scholarly interest in the vernacular architecture of the American West. The program sponsors an ongoing monograph series entitled *Building the West* and conducts an annual summer field school in architectural research and documentation.

PHILIP DOLE, a graduate of Harvard and Columbia, is professor of architecture emeritus at the University of Oregon and was the first director of the school's Historic Preservation program. Vernacular architecture is his research interest. He received an award in 1989 from the American Association for State and Local History for "leadership and development of the theory on historic pioneer architecture and settlement patterns in the Pacific Northwest." His essay "The Picket Fence at Home" is included in the catalogue the Princeton Architectural Press published for *Between Fences*, the 1996 exhibition at the National Building Museum.

KINGSTON HEATH holds a doctorate in American studies from Brown University. His dissertation, "Striving for Permanence on the Western Frontier: Vernacular Architecture as Cultural Informant in Southwest Montana," drew, in part, from fieldwork and documentary research undertaken as Montana's State Architectural Historian. Later, he taught architectural history and preservation at Montana State University. Currently, he is an assistant professor in the College of Architecture at the University of North Carolina at Charlotte and is writing a book on the cultural transformation of the three-decker flat in New Bedford, Massachusetts. It is entitled *The Patina of Place: The "Cultural Weathering" of a New England Industrial Landscape,* forthcoming from the University of Tennessee Press.

ALISON K. HOAGLAND is an assistant professor of history and historic preservation at Michigan Technological University. Previously, she was senior historian at the Historic American Buildings Survey of the National Park Service, which undertook documentation of historic Russian Orthodox churches in Alaska; this paper is an outgrowth of that project. Hoagland received her B.A. from Brown University and her M.A. from George Washington University, both in American studies.

RICHARD LONGSTRETH is professor of architectural history and director of the graduate program in historic preservation in the American studies department at George Washington University. His books *City Center to Regional Mall: Architecture, the Automobile, and Retailing in Los Angeles, 1920–1950* and *History on the Line: Testimony in the Cause of Preservation* were published by MIT Press and the National Park Service, respectively, in 1996. Previous books include *The Buildings of Main Street: A Guide to American Commercial Architecture* (1987), *On the Edge of the World: Four Architects in San Francisco at the Turn of the Century* (1983), and, as editor, *The Mall in Washington, 1791–1991* (1991). He has written chapters in a number of books and journals, including *JSAH, Winterthur Portfolio, Journal of Urban History, Harvard Architectural Review, Perspecta,* and *Historic Preservation Forum.* For over a decade he took a leading role in the initiatives to preserve and restore major examples of twentieth-century commercial architecture in the Washington area. He is currently working on a book on the department store in the U.S. during the mid-twentieth century.

BLANTON OWEN received an M.A. in folklore from Indiana University in 1977. He is self-employed and has explored the built environments of Nevada, Utah, Montana, Idaho, and California for more than a decade. He is currently completing *Things Great and Small: Northeastern Nevada's Ranch Architecture* for the University of Utah's Vernacular Architecture Program, to be published by Yale University Press. Owen holds a commercial pilot's license and flies his small plane to remote ranches, reservations, mining camps, and towns throughout the intermountain West.

Margaret Purser is an associate professor of anthropology at Sonoma State University in Rohnert Park, California. She received her Ph.D. in anthropology from the University of California, Berkeley, in 1987. As a historical archaeologist specializing in the expansion of industrial capitalism during the nineteenth century, she began to address the role of gender in the material culture of the industrializing West in her 1991 publication, "Several Paradise Ladies Are Visiting in Town: Gender Strategies in the Early Industrial West," *Historical Archaeology* 25, no. 4 (1991): 6–16. Her recent work has turned to defining a comparative study of historical material culture created in the postcolonial Pacific. She has conducted fieldwork in Nevada and California and is currently working on two projects, one in the Sacramento River delta of California, and one on the Pacific coast of Guatemala. Dr. Purser is also the director of Sonoma State University's Center for the Pan Pacific Exchange, an interdisciplinary institute set up to coordinate scholarly and educational exchange on Pacific-related issues.

Fredric L. Quivik is the founder of Renewable Technologies, Inc., a historic preservation consulting firm in Butte, Montana. He is currently on leave to pursue a Ph.D. in the history of technology from the University of Pennsylvania. Mr. Quivik now lives in Froid, Montana, where he works as a consultant historian and is writing his dissertation, an environmental history of copper smelting technologies in Montana, 1880–1920.

Freelance cultural historian Chris Wilson is the author of *The Myth of Santa Fe: Creating a Modern Regional Tradition* and co-author of *La Tierra Amarilla: Its History, Architecture, and Cultural Landscape.* He lives in Albuquerque, where he is adjunct professor at the University of New Mexico.

Richard Guy Wilson holds the Commonwealth Professor's Chair in Architectural History at the University of Virginia in Charlottesville, where he is also chair of the Department of Architectural History. His specialty is the architecture, design, and art of the nineteenth and twentieth centuries, both in America and abroad.

Christopher Yip was trained as an architect and architectural historian. His research interests include the study of Asian American environments, the building traditions of the Pacific islands, and colonial architecture in Asia. He has taught at the University of California, Berkeley, the University of Colorado, Boulder, the University of Hawaii at Manoa, and presently teaches at California Polytechnic State University, San Luis Obispo.

Credits

"False-Front Architecture on Montana's Urban Frontier," by Kingston Heath, is reprinted from *Perspectives in Vernacular Architecture, III,* edited by Thomas Carter and Bernard L. Herman, by permission of the University of Missouri Press. Copyright © by the Curators of the University of Missouri, 1989.

"Folk Design in Utah Architecture," by Thomas Carter, appeared in *Utah Folk Art: A Catalog of Material Culture* (Provo: Brigham Young University Press, 1980). Reprinted by permission.

"The Calef's Farm in Oregon: A Vermont Vernacular Comes West," by Philip Dole, was published under the title "The Calef Farm: Region and Style in Oregon" in the *Journal of the Society of Architectural Historians* 23, no. 4 (December 1964). Reprinted by permission.

"When a Room Is the Hall," by Chris Wilson, appeared in *MASS: Journal of the School of Architecture and Planning* (University of New Mexico), Summer 1984. Reprinted by permission.

"A Chinatown of Gold Mountain: The Chinese in Locke, California," by Christopher Yip, was published under the title "Time for Bitter Strength: The Chinese in Locke, California" in *Landscape* 22, no. 2 (Spring 1978). Reprinted by permission.

"The Real Estate Associates: A Land and Housing Developer of the 1870s in San Francisco," by Anne Bloomfield, was published in the *Journal of the Society of Architectural Historians* 37, no. 1 (March 1978). Reprinted by permission.

"American Modernism in the West: Hoover Dam," by Richard Guy Wilson, was published under the title "Machine-Age Iconography in the American West: The Design of Hoover Dam," in *Pacific Historical Review* 54, no. 4 (November 1985). Copyright © 1985 by the Pacific Coast Branch of the American Historical Association. Reprinted by permission.

Index

ACC. *See* Alaska Commercial Company
Ackerman Ranch, 95
ACM. *See* Anaconda Copper Mining Company
Adams, Ansel, 317*n*14
Adams, George, 251, 255
Adams, Henry: on Hoover Dam, 292, 312
Additions, 108, 184, 186, 192–93, 195; back-of-the-house, 188, 190
Adobe houses, 113, 117 (table), 123
AFFCO, 275, 277
AIA Journal, 318*n*21
Aladdin prefabricated houses, 188
Alaska Commercial Company (ACC), 133, 138, 139, 140; houses by, 134, 135 (photo), 136
Albright, Kenneth, 252
ALCOA Building, 317*n*19
Aleuts, 130, 147; houses for, 131–32, 134, 136, 140–41, 144–45; photo of, 137; Russian Orthodox church and, 129, 148–49
Alhambra Post Advocate, 258*n*3
Alice mine, 269, 278, 282
Alien Land Law (1913), 161, 170
Alleys, 181; photo of, 162, 163
Allred, James, House, photo of, 52
Alpha Beta Market, 246; photo of, 247
Alterations, 183; gender-based, 186–87
Amalgamated Copper Company, 275, 277, 279; unions and, 287
American Agriculturist, 88*n*17; on barns, 80
American Architect, 317–18*n*20
American Genesis (Hughes), 267
Americanization, xv, 134, 139
Anaconda, 268, 272, 273, 274; location of, 268 (map); map of, 273; refinery at, 283
Anaconda Copper Mining Company (ACM), 275–79, 286–88, 290*n*28; electricity for, 284, 285 (photo); headframes for, 290*n*22; smelter operation of, 277 (site plan), 278; unions and, 287
Anaconda Gold and Silver Mining Company, 275
Anaconda mine, 269, 278
Anaconda Mining Company, 275
Anaconda Townsite Company, 275
Anaconda Water Company, 275
Anselmo mineyard, headframe at, 280; photo of, 282, 283; site plan for, 281
Architectural Forum, 317*n*19
Architectural Record, 317*n*19
Architecture of Country Houses, The (Downing), 88*n*17
Aries, Phillipe, 121
Armitage, George, 82, 89*n*27; barn by, 77–78; house by, 65
Armitage barn/house, illustration of, 66
Army Corps of Engineers, 291
Arnold, Max, 241
Art Deco, 300, 302, 303, 304, 312
Ashlar walls, photo of, 48
Astor, John Jacob, 202, 225*n*8
Asymmetrical facades, 120–21, 123
Atlantic Richfield, ACM and, 278
Austin Company, commercial/industrial buildings by, 251

BA&P. *See* Butte, Anaconda & Pacific
Back yards, 182, 191
Bacon Hall, 227*n*36
Badger State mine, 278, 281
Bagardus, E. F., 239, 241
Bailyn, Bernard, 11; core-periphery theory of, 10
Baldwin, "Lucky," 227*n*36
Baldwin's Hotel and Theater, 214, 227*n*36
Balloon-frame construction, 31, 72, 74, 75, 88*nn*23, 24, 220; illustration of, 34; photo of, 36
Bank of California, 216, 227*n*36
Bannack, 30; description of, 23, 28-29, 35–36; photo of, 20, 28; population of, 21–22; sketch of, 24
Barabaras, 130–31, 133, 136; photo of, 131
Barns: hay storage, 105; photo of, 84
Barry, Edward, 215, 227*n*34
Bashford's, 205
Bates, William, 95
Bates cabin, 98, 100, 108; photo of, 93, 97
Bates Ranch, 95, 96
Bauman, Emil, 95, 96
Bauman, "Hoppy," 95, 96
Beall, Harry, 255
Beaver Head Mines, 23, 25
Beehive House, 47. *See also* Brigham Young
Bell mine, 287
Bering, Vitus, 129
Beverly Boulevard, photo of, 245
Beverly Hills Citizen, 258*n*3
Big Bear, 259*n*5
Billie Bird Markets, 246, 260*n*11
"Bird's Eye View of Las Vegas," 115
Bishop, Ellis, 241
Bitton, Davis, 58
Black Canyon, 293, 294, 312
Blacksmith shop, 102–3; floor plan of, 103
Blaisdell, Nathaniel: Saints Peter and Paul and, 142–43
Blanchard-Gallegos House, 125; floor plan of, 126; photo of, 126
Bloomfield, Anne, 14–15
Boathouse, 171
Bonneville Dam, 291, 310
Boomtowns, 28–29, 176
Borresen House, illustration of, 56
Boston and Montana Copper and Silver Mining Company, 276, 278–79, 285, 290*n*22; smelter/refinery, 277, 279
Boulder City, 293, 299–300
Boulder Dam. *See* Hoover Dam
Bourke-White, Margaret, 292
Bricking, 59*n*14; photo of, 48
Brohaska Opera House, 227*n*36
Bryant, Charles, 134, 136, 150*n*13; Aleuts and, 137
Bryant, W. R., 240
Buckingham, Anna Kemler, 197*n*1
Bugbee, S. C., 227*n*36
Building Department (T.R.E.A.), 213
Building investments, 246, 248
Bullock and Jones, 214
Bungalowcraft Company: drive-in markets by, 254; plan books by, 264*n*37
Bunkhouses, 106; floor plan of, 99, 106
Bureau of Land Management, 110*n*5
Bureau of Reclamation, 291, 302, 306; Hoover Dam and, 293, 294, 298, 299
Burnham, D. H.. and Company, 231
Burris, Nathan W.: planning by, 30
Burton, Sir Richard, 95
Burton and Company, 240
Buschlen, Charles, 255
Bush houses, 23
Butte, 268; cultural heritage of, 287–88; location of, 268 (map); mining in/near, 269, 271, 274
Butte, Anaconda and Pacific (BA&P), 273, 277, 281; incorporation of, 274–75; mining and, 271
Butte Hill, 278, 286; compressors on, 281; copper mining at, 267–68; headframes on, 280–81; photo of, 280
Byrnes House, 188; floor plan for, 186

Calef, Charles, 74
Calef, Cutting, 74
Calef, Elmer Norton, 63–65, 67–68, 70, 73, 76, 80, 84, 86; barn 76–79, 80–81, 88–89*n*25: barn raising by, 82–83, farm, 62, 64, 70–71, 85, 88*n*11, 89*n*44: house, 68, 69, 73–76, 83, 88*n*13
Calef, Ira, 68, 70, 84; barn, 76, 88–89*n*25; house, 68, 85, 86
Calef, John, 70
Calef, Martha Paine, 68
Calef, Mira: on yellow barn, 78

Calef, Otis, 74
Calef, Sarah Naomi Harlow, 67, 70
California Architect and Building Review, 221
California Constitution (1878), Chinese and, 156
California's Architectural Frontier (Kirker), 8, 226*n*13
Campbell, Robert, 71
Carbonari, 95, 96, 110*n*8
Carter, Thomas, 13
Cartwright and Huffman, drive-in markets and, 255
Case, Irving, 192
Cellars, 108, 190
Center-hall house, 60*n*26, 123, 125; impact of, 120–21
Centerville (Butte), photo of, 280
Central Park Homestead Association, 217
Centuries of Childhood, The (Aries), 121
Chandler, Harry: Kaufmann and, 300
Chapman, Charles, 240
Chapman Park Market, 240, 246, 251, 263*n*34; photo of, 253
Charcoal Burner's War (1879), 95, 110*n*8
"Cheap and Convenient Barns for New Countries" (*American Agriculturist*), 80
Chee Kung Tong, 165–66, 170
Cherkashenin, Ignatii, 131, 133
Chicken houses, 105, 191; floor plan of, 105
Chinatowns, 163, 168–69, 170; fires in, 160, 161, 162
Chinese: discrimination against, 155–57, 170; labor by, 167–69; professional employment for, 170; social groups for, 165–66
Chinese Consolidated Benevolent Association (Six Companies), 157
Chinese Exclusion Acts, 156, 170
Chungshanese, 160, 161, 166–69
Church of St. George the Great Martyr: belltower for, 145 (drawing); floor plan for, 145
Clark, William Andrews, 278, 289*n*9; Butte Hill and, 279
Clay Street, 205, 215
Cleaveland plan, 72
Clements, Stiles: drive-in markets and, 249, 250, 255
Clock Market, photo of, 256
Coachella Valley, flooding in, 293
Coate, Roland E., 300
Colorado River, 294, 310; flooding by, 293
Colorado River Board, Hoover Dam and, 294
Colorado Smelting and Mining Company, 278
Colorado Smelting Company, 269
Colusa mine, 278
Commercial buildings, 22, 31, 249; photo of, 238
Company towns, 272
Composition, 44, 51–54, 56–58
Compressors, 281, 284, 285, 287; electricity for, 283
Construction stiffs, 297
Constructivists, 310
Coolidge, Calvin: Hoover Dam and, 293
Copper mining, 269, 270, 274, 283; demand for, 281–82; immigrants and, 287–88; in Montana, 267–68, 271
Core-periphery model, 10–11, 13–14
Corrals, 99–100, 108; photo of, 99
Cottage Residences (Downing), 88*n*17
Cottrell treaters, 278
Country Club Plaza, 231
Cramer and Wise, 252
Crawforth, Charles, House, illustration of, 56
Creese, Walter: Kaufmann and, 302
Crenshaw Street, property values on, 243
Crisman, George, 34
Crisp House and Hotel, illustration of, 56
Crocker mansion, 217
Crowe, Frank T.: Hoover Dam and, 297, 298
Cultural identity, 5, 10, 29–30, 179
Curson, Samuel, 241
Curtis, J. M.: drive-in market and, 241
C. W. Wilson and Sons, 254

Daemon, Reinhardt, 227*n*36
Dai Loy Gambling Museum: elevation drawing of, 159; floor plan of, 158
Daily Evening Bulletin, 215; T.R.E.A. ads in, 221
Daly, Marcus, 269, 271–73, 277–79; ACM and, 275, 276; BA&P and, 274–75; Upper Works and, 274; War of the Copper Kings and, 289*n*9
D. A. MacDonald's Enterprise, 221
Damele, Benny, 95, 96, 109; bunkhouse by, 106; horsehair mecarty by, 91; photo of, 92
Damele, John, 95, 96
Damele, Peter, 95

Damele, Peter, Jr., 96
Davis, Arthur Powell: Hoover Dam and, 298
Davis, W. W. H., 115, 118
Davis and Cowell, 229*n*57
Davis Brothers, 229*n*57
Davis Dam, 293
Day, Delia Harlow, 71
Day work, 221, 229*n*57
de Baca House, Tafoya-C., 123–24; floor plan of, 124; photo of, 124
Decatur, Stephen: on Chinese, 155
Deckbar, H. C., 252
Decoration, 44, 47–49, 51
Deer Lodge Valley, 271, 278
DeLacy, Captain, 25
Department of Commerce, 139, 140
Deutsche Werkbund, Kaufmann and, 302
Diamond mine: headframe at, 280; photo of, 280
Didion, Joan, 313
Diffusion studies, vernacular architecture and, 5
Dishbrow, Frank, 239
Doe, B. and J.S., 221, 229n64
Dole, Philip, 13
Doorway, 1689 Sutter Street, photo of, 210
Dore, Maurice, 215, 216
Downing, Andrew Jackson, 71–72, 86, 87, 88*nn*17, 18
Drive-in markets, 231–57; designers of, 248–49; designs for, 250 (figure), 254–55, 262*n*30; development of, 241–42, 248, 257, 258*n*3; investing in, 244–45; owners of, 260*nn*11, 17
Dry Creek Ranch, 91, 96, 98; aerial view of, 93 (photo); entrance to, 93 (photo); main house at, 106, 107, 107 (photo), 108, 109; map of, 102; stable at, 92; working at, 94–95
Dry Creek Station, 91
Dry goods stores, 231
Duboce Park, 219
Dugouts, 23, 106
Dunraven, Earl of: on Virginia City, 21
Dunvian Saloon-Billiard Hall, 39*n*10
Duplexes, 246, 248
Dwight, Timothy, 85

East Anaconda Yard, 278
Eckert, Robert, 255
Economy: barn by, 80, 82; barn floor plan by, 82
Eddy, Link: horsehair mecarty by, 91; photo of, 92
Edgerton, Governor, 34
Edgerton, Martha, 34
Edgerton, Mary: on Bannack, 35; on saloons, 27; 1848 and 1836 Pine Street, photo of, 220
Electricity, 283–84, 285, 292, 302, 290*n*29
El Gringo (Davis), 115
Elliott, Cassandra, 192
Elliott, Henry Wood, 134, 136–37
Elliott, James, 192
Emerson, Ralph Waldo: on Chinese, 155
Emilio, Luis: T.R.E.A. and, 223
Entrance tower, photo of, 306
Ephraim, photo of, 46
Exclusion Acts, 156, 170
Expressionism, 302

False fronts, 22, 28, 37–38; commercial, 31; illustrations of, 26, 32–33; photo of, 37
Farquharson, David, 204, 213–14, 217, 227*n*36
Favor, Sarah, 217
Federal Building, 317*n*19
Federal style, 48, 51
Ferriss, Hugh, 302, 313
FHA, standards by, 127
Fields, Marshall, 231
Fife, Austin, 59*n*17; on Mormon houses, 47
1501 South Pacific Avenue, photo of, 120
1513 Golden Gate Avenue, photo of, 214
Fillmore and Cottage Row, 205
Fillmore Street, 205, 215
Finlay, François, 38*n*2
Fisk, James L., 28
Flewelling, Ralph: work of, 250–51
Floor plans, schematics of, 179
Folk architecture, 51; Hispanic, 127; Mormon, 45, 50 (illustration), 57–58; Spanish-Mexican, 113. *See also* Vernacular architecture
Folk builders, 43, 44, 52–54, 125
Folk Housing in Middle Virginia (Glassie), 121
Folk housing, 44, 52–54; in Utah, 41–42, 43
Folland, Walter, 252
Food stores, 237; chain, 238–39, 245; design of, 255
Ford, Silas P., 213; T.R.E.A. and, 220
Forges, stone-and-brick, 102

Fort Marcy, 119, 121
Fort Peck Dam, 292, 310
Fort Union, 119
Foundry Department (ACM), photo of, 275
Frame houses, 182, 204
Freeman, B. H., 215
Freemont-Gastenaga House, 188; floor plan for, 184
Frick, Henry Clay, 290*n*18
Frontier, as process, 6, 8–9
Front rooms, 177, 194–95
Futurism, 302
F. W. Woolworth, 246

Gable and Wyant, 251
Gable-ended log store/house, 25, 26, 29, 39*n*7; illustration of, 26, 30
Gagnon mine, 278
Gallatin City, 30
Gambling houses, 28, 163, 166
Ganns, Jack, 39*n*9
Garden, wilderness and, 45
Gardner House, photo of, 55
Garnier, Tony, 318*n*21; Hoover Dam and, 301, 302
Garrard, Lewis, 118
Gaynor, John P., 227*n*36
Gendered architecture, 173–97
Gender roles, 180–81, 196; spatial organization and, 173–75, 184, 186, 188
Gerrard, J. A., 246
Gillette-Herzog Manufacturing Company, headframes by, 280, 290*n*22
"Gilmer Map of Santa Fe" (1846), 115
Glaha, Ben (Bernard D.), 317*n*14; Hoover Dam and, 313; photo by, 295, 298, 299, 300, 306; work of, 297–98
Glassie, Henry, 59*n*, 121; map by, 4
Glendale News-Press, 258*n*3
Goddard, George H., 202
Gogerty, H. L., 251
Gold Rush, Chinese and, 156–57, 160
Gompers, Samuel: anti-Asian activism of, 156
Gonyeau, John B.: T.R.E.A. and, 220, 223
Goodrich, Bill, 39*n*9
Goodrich's saloon, 29
Gordon, George, 202
Goss, Peter, 59*n*; on Utah styles, 48–49
Gothic Revival, 29, 48, 51, 65, 77, 88*n*17; vernacular expressions of, 70–73
Grand Army of the Republic hall, 216
Grand Coulee Dam, 291, 310
Grand Hotel, 227*n*36
Granite, photo of, 37
Grasshopper Creek, 25; mining along, 38*n*2; settlement along, 23–24
Great Basin, 92, 94
Great Falls, 288; refinery at, 283
Great Falls Water Power and Townsite Company, 285
Great Northern Railway: Daly and, 274; mining and, 270, 271
Greek Revival, 29, 48, 51, 65, 217
Greeley, Horace, xiv
Griffith, G., 217, 229*n*57
Griffith, Raymond: drive-in market and, 241
Gruen, Victor, 232, 258*n*2
Guangdong, 158, 160

Haddad, Alexander, 260*n*11; drive-in markets and, 248, 261*n*17
Haggin, James Ben Ali, 275, 278; ACM and, 276; Daly and, 271
Hakkas, 157
Hale, William: T.R.E.A. and, 223
Hallways, 121
Halsey, Charles: T.R.E.A. and, 223
Hansen, Oskar J. W., 303, 306, 311; Hoover Dam and, 309–10
Hanson, Ackerson and Co., 221, 229*n*64
Harlow, Andrew Jackson, 71
Harlow, Mahlon, 64, 65, 71, 82
Harpending, Asbury, 216
Harrington, Frank, 252
Harris, J. Robert, 252
Harvey, James R., 192
Hastings, H. C., 203
Hattem, I. M., 239, 261*n*17
Hattem's markets, 242, 246, 252
Hay derricks, 105; drawing of, 105
Hayes, Thomas, 202
Hayes Park Pavilion, 202, 216
Hayes Tract, 202
Headframes, 279–81, 290*n*22; photo of, 280, 282, 286
Hearst, George, 275, 278; Daly and, 271
Heath, Kingston, 13
Hegedohm, Walter, 252
Heinke and Pillot, 259*n*5
Heinze, F. Augustus: Butte Hill and, 279

Helgoth, Henry, 207, 229*nn*57, 64
Hickison, John, 95, 96
Hickison, Matt, 96
Highliners, photo of, 298
High Ore mine, 287
Hill, James J., 285; Daly and, 274
Hinkel, Henry T., 205
Hispanics, adobe houses and, 113
Historians and the American West (Malone), 9
Hoagland, Alison, 14
Hoist houses, 284, 285; photo of, 282, 283, 286
Holladay, Robert: sketch by, 24
Hollis, William, 215, 227*n*34; illustration of, 218; T.R.E.A. and, 217–18, 219, 222, 229*n*64
Hollywood Daily Citizen, 258*n*3
Homestead associations, 204
Hooley, Richard M., 227*n*36
Hooley's Opera House, 227*n*36
Hoover, Herbert: Hoover Dam and, 293
Hoover Dam, 291–314, 314–15*n*7; conception of, 304 (reproduction); construction of, 294, 296–300, 299 (photo), 300 (photo); illustration of, 303; photo of, 295, 305, 306, 307, 308, 309, 311, 313, 314; plan and section of, 296 (reproduction); power potential of, 310; promotion of, 314*n*1; symbolism of, 292–93, 313–14
Hopkins mansion, 217
Horsehair mecarty, 94; photo of, 92
Howard, William, 202
HUD, standards by, 127
Hudson Bay Company, *piece sur piece* construction by, 31
Hughes, Thomas, 267, 288–89*n*1
Hui (rotating credit system), use of, 161–62
Humboldt County, Euro-American immigrants in, 175
Hunters Point, 217
Hunting in the Yellowstone (Dunraven), quote from, 21
Huntington and Hopkins, 229*n*57
Huntington Park Signal, 258*n*3
Hyde, Orson, House, illustration of, 56
Hydroelectricity, 284, 285, 292, 306

Iconostas, 133, 143; photo of, 144, 146
Icons, 133, 138
Immigrants, 156–57, 175, 177, 287–88
Imperial Dam, 293
Imperial Valley, flooding in, 293
"Improvements in Progress" (*California Architect and Building Review*), 221
Indian houses, 96, 98
Industrialism, 180
Industrial Workers of the World (IWW), 287
Inglewood Daily News, 258*n*3
Installment Homestead Union, 224
Installment plan, 221, 222
Intake towers, 303–4; photo of, 307
International style, 301
Investment Securities Company, 241
Italianate, 211, 226*n*13
IWW. *See* Industrial Workers of the World
Izba, 133

Jackson, J. B.: on Hispanic houses, 116, 118
Jessie Street, 209, 222
J. F. Shea Company, Hoover Dam and, 297
John Kentfield and Co., 221
Johnson, Cary, 240
Johnson, Elmer, 240
Johnson, Reginald, 300
Johnston and Mooser, 204
Jones, Clyde, 255
J. R. Kelly and Company, 229*n*57
Judd, Thomas, House, photo of, 54
Julanita Romero de Baca House, 119; floor plan of, 119; photo of, 119

Kaiser, Henry J., and Company, Hoover Dam and, 297
Kaufmann, Gordon B., 310, 312, 317*n*17; Boulder City and, 299–300; on engineering principles, 304–5; Hoover Dam and, 300–303, 305, 306, 309
Kearney, Denis, 222; T.R.E.A. and, 223
Kellet, Samuel, 229*n*57
Kelley mine, photo of, 280
Kelly, Arthur, 251
Kemler, Catherine, 197*n*1
Kemler, Johanna, 197*n*1
Kesseler, J. and F., 229*n*57
Ketchum, Morris, 232, 258*n*2
Key Street, 164; photo of, 171
King, Elliot, 83
King Kullen, 259*n*5
Kirker, Harold, 8, 204, 226*n*13
Kitchens, 192, 197; organization of, 186, 188; women's roles and, 195

Klepetko, Frank, 276
Kong Chow, 157

Labeau's Jewelry, photo of, 36
Laclede Hotel, 39*n*10
Ladies Home Companion, 197
Lake Mead, 292, 298, 312; photo of, 307, 314
Lane and Pullen, 229*n*57
Lang, Fritz, 229*n*57, 308; Kaufmann and, 302
Lankton, Larry, 267
Las Gorras Blancas, 121
Last Best Place, xiv
Laundry, 173, 190; photo of, 174
Lawrence, D. H., 86
Lawson, G. K., 229*n*57
Lebedev-Lastochkin Fur Company, 129
Le Corbusier, 299, 312
Leess, Samuel, 240
Leess Drive-In Market, 251; photo of, 253
Leimert Company, 261*n*13; drive-in markets and, 241
Leimert Park, 261*n*13
Leonard mine, 278, 287
Lestenkof, Innokenty, 138
"Let's Play Store" (*Saturday Evening Post*), quote from, 243–44
Levee Street, photo of, 154, 164
Lewishon Brothers, 278
Lexington Street, 209, 210
Life Magazine, 292
Limerick, Patricia: on Turner Thesis, 9
Linear circulation patterns, 125
Lintels, 106, 213
Lion House, 47. *See also* Brigham Young
Liotard family, photo of, 193
Loafing sheds, mud-and-willow, 100, 100 (photo), 101 (floor plan)
Local No. 1 (Western Federation of Miners), 287
Locke, George, 161, 165
Locke, California; Chinese in, 153, 169, 171; population of, 162–63; site plan for, 161 (drawing)
Lockeport, 161
Log-and-canvas structures, 28; illustration of, 26
Log walls, photo of, 48
Long Beach Press-Telegraph, 258*n*3
Longstreth, Richard, 14–15
Los Angeles Brick Company, 241
Los Angeles Electric Railroad, 252
Los Angeles Investment Company, residential development by, 254
Los Angeles Times, 258*n*3, 260*n*11, 300
Los Angeles Times Building, 300, 303; photo of, 301
Lower Works, 272, 273, 274, 276, 277, 278
Lyceum Theater, 227*n*36

McCray, Louis, 242; Toluca Lake Park and, 239–40
MacDonald, D. A., 215, 227*n*34
MacDonald and Kahn Company, Hoover Dam and, 297
McGee, Sarah, 74
McIntyre, William J., 137
McKenzie, Rosa, 241
McKinley, James: drive-in market and, 241
McPhee, John: on Great Basin, 92, 94
Machado, L. D., 255
Mac Marr food store, photo of, 238
Magee, Thomas, 218, 229*n*64
Maguire, Thomas, 227*n*36
Main house (Dry Creek Ranch), 106, 108, 109; floor plan of, 107; photo of, 107
Main Street (Bannack), 37–38; photo of, 28; signage along, 35
Main Street (Locke), 162, 163, 164; elevation drawing for, 165, 168; photo of, 154
Main Street (Paradise Valley), photo of, 177
Mallon, John, 229*n*57
Malone, Michael: on regional history, 9
Manuel Romero House, 115–16, 118–19; floor plan of, 116
Market Street, 202, 216, 219
Market Street Railway, 202
Marston, Van Pelt, and Mayberry, 251; drive-in markets and, 250
Martin, Harly, 255
Mary Pickford Company, 241
Mason House, photo of, 53
Mead, Ellwood: Hoover Dam and, 298
Meat vs. Rice, American Manhood against Asiatic Coolieism (Gompers), 156
Mechanics Real Estate Association, 224
Meinig, Donald: on folk colonization, 5–6
Melovidov, Alexandra, 136
Meredith, Emily: Murphy wagons and, 23
Mesa-Vernon Market, 255; floor plan for, 235; photo of, 256

Metropolis (movie), 302
Metropolis of Tomorrow, The (Ferriss), 302
Meyer, Daniel, 216
Meyer-Echeverria House, 188; floor plan for, 184
Miller and Lux, 241
Mills Building, 216
Milwaukee Bridge Company, 290*n*22
Milwaukee Road, mining and, 270, 271
Miner's cabin, photo of, 25
Miners Union Hall, dynamiting of, 287
Mine timbers, 287
Ming Dynasty, 157
Miscegenation laws, Chinese and, 160, 170
Mission Addition, 205, 208, 219, 223
Mission Motor-In Market, 252
Mission, Valencia, Twentieth, Twenty-first Street block, 205, 209; map of, 209
Missoula Gulch Line (BA&P), 281
Modernism, 291, 293, 299, 311
Modernization, 6, 8, 119
Montana Ore Purchasing Company, 279
Montana Power Company, 284, 285, 286; electricity from, 290*n*29
Montana Union, 272; Daly and, 274
Montgomery Ward, 259*n*5
Morey-Liotard House, 181–82; additions to, 194; house plan for, 193
Morgan, Octavus: drive-in markets and, 249
Morgan, Walls, and Clements, 249–50; drive-in markets and, 248, 251
Morgan, Willard, 261*n*17
Mormon houses, 42, 43; types of, 50 (illustration)
Mormon landscapes, 45, 47, 58
Mormon society, 42–43, 109
Morris, William, 39*n*16
Morrison-Knudsen Company, Hoover Dam and, 297
Mortgages, 221, 222
Mother Goose Market, 239, 252
Moulton Mining and Reduction Works, 278
Mountain Consolidated mine, 281
Mountain View mine, 278
Mount Vernon Proprietors, 202, 225*n*8
Movement of ideas, map of, 4
Mud-and-willow construction, 96, 98, 101, 108, 110*n*10; photo of, 97
Mud houses, 96
Muller Brothers, 240
Murphy, Edward: drive-in markets and, 241
Murphy wagons, 23
Muybridge, Eadweard, 214

Nagel, Conrad: drive-in market and, 241
Nelson, Fernando: T.R.E.A. and, 224
Neoclassical style, 49, 53, 65, 82
Neutra, Richard, 251, 301; drive-in markets and, 248, 263*n*33
Nevada Bank, 216, 217
New Mexico Historic Building Inventory, 113
New Montgomery Street Real Estate Company, 216
Newsletter, 229*n*63; T.R.E.A. houses in, 221–22
New Western History, 8–9
New York State Dutch barn, 77
New York Times Magazine, on Hoover Dam, 297
Nichols, J. C.: retail architecture by, 231
Nimmons, George: Sears and, 231–32
929–45 Valencia Street, photo of, 207
Nixon, Richard, 156
Noble, Allen: vernacular architecture and, 17*n*3
Nomland, Kemper, 251
Norris Dam, 310
Norstrom and Anderson, taxpayer blocks and, 252
North American Commercial Company, 139, 140
Northern Pacific, 272; mining and, 270
Nuclei, Western, 7 (map)

"Old Fashioned New England Farmhouse, An" (Robinson), 84
Old Works, 277
O'Neal-Harvey House: house plan for, 189; modification of, 188, 190; photo of, 189
Original mine, 278, 281; headframe at, 280; photo of, 280
Outbuildings, 173, 182, 183, 188
Outhouses, 168, 182
Overland Stage and Mail Company, 91
Owen, Blanton, 14
Owen, John, 25
Owens, J. B., 229*n*57

Pacific Bridge Company, Hoover Dam and, 297
Paiutes, 176

Palace Hotel, 227*n*36
Palm Market, 242, 246, 255; photo of, 247
Panic of 1893, Butte and, 269
Paradise City: domestic architecture in, 178-179; failure of, 176
Paradise Valley, 174, 185, 191, 196–97; changes in, 180; developers in, 181; domestic architecture in, 175–76; houses in, 178, 180, 195; photo of, 177; plat map for, 182; residential property in, 183 (map); residents of, 179, 192
Parker Dam, 293, 310
Parkinson, Donald B., 251; drive-in markets and, 248, 249
Parkinson, John, 251; drive-in markets and, 248, 249
Parlors, 192, 193–94, 196, 197; importance of, 194–95
Pasadena Star-News, 258*n*3
Patent Brick Company, 229*n*57
Pattern books, 51, 213, 264*n*37
Paul I, Tsar, 130
Pearl River Delta, immigrants from, 156–57
Peckham, C. L.: drive-in market and, 241
Pellissier Building, photo of, 245
Pencil Points, 318*n*21
Pennsylvania mine, 278
Peters, A. V., 71, 72; house, 73, 74
Pickford, Mary, 241
Piece sur piece construction, 31; illustration of, 35; photo of, 35
Pioneer houses, 42
"Pioneering of the Machine Age" (*New York Times Magazine*), 297
Pioneer Milling Company, 39*n*8
Placitas, 115
Plasterers' strike (1877), 228*n*45
Platts, Jonathan, 54
Platts House, illustration of, 55
Plaza Market, 251; photo of, 252
Plazuelas, 115
Pletsch, Theodore, 251
Plumbing, indoor, 190, 197
Polack, J. S.: T.R.E.A. and, 229*n*64
Pony Express, 91, 100
Porches, 192, 197; adding, 190
Portals, 119
Post-and-beam structural system, 77
Post and lintel, 213
Powell, John Wesley, 298
Powerhouses, 306, 312; photo of, 285, 305
Powers, C. Waldo, 252
Prairie School, 311
Pribilof, Gerasim, 129
Pribilof Islands, 129, 144, 147; churches in, 138, 142; Department of Commerce and, 139; housing for, 130, 131–32; Russian-American Company in, 134; settlement history of, 148–49; Treasury Department and, 133, 134, 140
Priest, Alfred, 251
Priestley, J. B.: Hoover Dam and, 313–14
Private residences, 176
Prohibition Act (1919), 169
Promyshlenniki, 129
Property records, 195, 198*n*10, 239
Prostitution, 158, 164, 166
Pueblo Indians: adobe houses and, 113; architects/planners, 127
Pugin, A. W., 31
Purlins, 102, 103, 106, 108; drawing of, 81
Purser, Margaret: vernacular building process and, 14

Qing Dynasty, 157
Quivik, Fred, 15
Quonset huts, 92, 101, 105; photo of, 93

Rainbow Falls, 287; hydroelectricity at, 285
Rainbow Falls Dam, photo of, 284
Ralphs Grocery Company, 236, 255, 259*n*5
Ralston, William, 216
Ranch architecture, 91–109, 110*n*1
Rarus Railway, 274, 277, 279
Rasche, Frank, 255
Read-Case House, 188; additions to, 192–93; floor plan of, 185; photo of, 185
Real Estate Circular, 218, 221
Reclamation Service. *See* Bureau of Reclamation
Redman, Leonard, 260*n*11
Redpath, James C., 138
Regionalism, 9, 11, 13, 15; western, 7 (map)
Regionalism in America (Vance), 9
Remer, John A., 210, 214, 227–28*n*36, 228*n*38
Renaissance Revival, 29
Residential property, map of, 183
Residential structures, 178–79, 264*n*37
Resources of California, T.R.E.A. and, 218
Retail architecture, 231–57

Retaining wall, photo of, 220
Rice, Cindy: on Mormon houses, 43
Rice, Dave, 83
Riley, Lizzie, 190
Riley House, house plan for, 190
Ritchie, James, 192
Ritchie, Josephine, 192
Ritchie-Harvey House: additions to, 192; house plan for, 191; photo of, 191
Rivera-Huie House: floor plan of, 123; photo of, 122
Robert Campbell House, floor plan of, 72
Robinson, Solon, 83
Rockefeller, William, 275
Rocker, framing plant at, 287
Rogers, Henry H., 275
Rondel's Homesteads, 205
Roosevelt, Franklin Delano: Hoover Dam dedication and, 292, 310
Roosevelt, Theodore: Hoover Dam and, 293
Rotating credit system, use of, 161–62
Roundhouse (BA&P), photo of, 274
Roundtree Brothers, 224
Royal Laundry, 317*n*19
Ruby Valley, xv
Ruoff, Allen, 251
Ruskin, John, 31
Russian-American Fur Company, 130, 133, 134
Russian Orthodox church, 133; Aleuts and, 129, 148–49; churchyard of, 141 (photo); influence of, 131–32, 137–38; photo of, 148
Ryan, John D., 285, 287

Sacramento Courthouse, 227*n*36
Sacramento-San Joaquin Delta, Chinese settlement at, 153–55, 169
Safety Steel Products, 255
St. George Island, 130, 140, 147; Aleuts on, 138; church at, 133, 143–44; photo of, 139, 148; seal hunting at, 134
St. George Orthodox Church: iconostas at, 146 (photo); photo of, 146
St. Lawrence mine, 278
St. Mary's Roman Catholic Church, photo of, 280
St. Paul Island, 130, 147; church on, 132 (photo), 137 (photo), 138, 140–41, 144; drawing of, 132; houses on, 141 (photo); photo of, 131, 135; seal hunting at, 134
St. Paul Saloon, photo of, 27
Saints Peter and Paul Church, 133, 138, 142–43, 145; elevation drawing of, 143; floor plan of, 142; iconostas at, 144 (photo)
St. Vrain, Señora, 118
Salas, 115, 118, 125
Salisbury Building, 317*n*19
Saloon on the Rocky Mountain Mining Frontier, The (West), quote from, 28
Saloons, 27, 28, 29, 36, 39*n*8, 194; photo of, 27
San Carlos Street, 209, 210
Sanders, Wilbur Fisk: on Crisman store, 34
San Francisco: map of, 203, 206; number buildings erected in, 204 (figure); population of, 202
San Francisco Chronicle, T.R.E.A. ads in, 221, 221 (reproduction)
San Francisco Directory, 202, 203, 204, 213, 223, 227*n*34; on Hollis, 218; T.R.E.A. and, 214
San Francisco Examiner, T.R.E.A. ads in, 221
San Francisco House and Loan Association, 224
San Francisco Panama-Pacific International Exposition, 318*n*21
San Joaquin Delta, Chinese in, 169
San Pedro High School, 317*n*19
Sant' Elia, Antonio: Hoover Dam and, 301–2, 318*n*21
Santa Ana Daily Register, 258*n*3
Santa Fe Trail, 118
Santa Monica Boulevard, property values on, 243
Santa Monica Evening Outlook, 258*n*3
Saturday Evening Post, quote from, 243–44
Savage, John L.: Hoover Dam and, 298
Scherer, L. G., 251
Schindler, R. M., 301
Schumacher Home Builders, 254
Schuster Brothers, 229*n*57
Sears, Roebuck, 196, 231–32, 259*n*5
Second Empire, 48–49, 217
Security Building and Loan Association, 241
Segerblom, Cliff (Clifford), 313, 317*n*14
Sena-Silva House, floor plan of, 114
Settlement history/geography, 5–6
1712 and 1710 Bush Street, photo of, 212
Severence, J. Byron, 252, 255
Shannon and Luchs, 236
Shapiro, Herman, 240
Sharecropping, 167–69

Shasta Dam, 291, 310
Shayashnikoff, Paul, 138
Shayashnikov, Kassian, 131, 133, 138
Shed, photo of, 84
Shed-roofed stores, 26, 29; illustration of, 26; photo of, 27
Sheeler, Charles: Hoover Dam and, 313
Shipps, Jan, 59*n*
S. H. Kress, 246
Shopping centers, 232, 235, 236
Silver Bow Creek, 268–69, 271
Silver mining, 269, 270; foundation ruins/waste dumps from, 270 (photo)
Single-pen cabins, 24
Six Companies. *See* Chinese Consolidated Benevolent Association
Six Companies, Inc.: Hoover Dam and, 297, 316*n*7
Skinner, Cyrus, 39*n*9
Skinner Saloon, illustration of, 34
Smith, Joe Billy and Julia, xv
Smith, Louis, 240
Smith, Malcolm, 255
Snodgrass Slough, 165, 171
Sod-roof store/house, 29; photo of, 30
Southern Pacific Railroad, 252
South Gate Tribune, 258*n*3
South Hall, 227*n*36
South Park, 202
South Vermont Avenue: photo of, 238; property values on, 243
South Vernon Avenue, photo of, 237
Southwest Builder and Contractor, 258*n*3, 260*n*11, 262*nn*27, 28, 30
Southwest Wave, 258*n*3
Spanish Colonial Revival, 299, 300
Spanish-Mexican style, 113
Spanish-Pueblo style, 127
Spatial organization, 181, 191–92; gender roles and, 173–75, 184, 186, 188
Specialization, 121, 181, 191
Spencer, John H., 95
Spillways, 304, 312; photo of, 308
Spores, Jacob, farm/house, 65, 78; illustration of, 66
Spring City, houses in, 54, 56, 55 (illustration)
Stables, 92, 98–99, 101; floor plan of, 104; open-fronted, 100, 103, 104 (photo)
Standard Fire Brick Company, 275
Standard Oil Trust, 275
Stanford mansion, 217
Stanton, Gary: on collateral connections, 11
Steiner, Emil, 95
Stevens, Jimmy, 63, 71
Stevenson Street, 209, 210, 222
Steward mine, 278, 281; headframe at, 280; photo of, 280, 286
Stewart, A. T.: dry goods by, 231
Stiff, Frank, 252
Stock Exchange, 216
Stone houses, 106, 109; floor plan of, 107; photo of, 42
Summerson, Sir John: on T.R.E.A., 211
Sunset-Western Market, 239, 246, 251; photo of, 242
Sun Yat-sen, 167
Supermarkets, 235, 236
Sutton, Milton, 252
Sutton, William, 215
Swasey, McNeal, 252
Sweeny and Vance, 229*n*57
Swenson, C. S., 215
Symmetrical facades, 121, 123; internal-external, 56–57
Sze Yup, 160

Taiping Rebellion, 157
Taxpayer blocks, 237–39, 249–50, 252; photo of, 237
Taylor, John: on houses, 58
Taylor, N. C., 74
Taylor Grazing Act (1934), 110*n*5
Taylor-Riley House, floor plan for, 188
Technological systems, 268, 287, 288
Ted R. Cooper Company, 254
Tenant farmers, Chinese, 167–69
Tennessee Valley Authority (TVA), 291, 310
Territorial Style, 125
Tevis, Lloyd, 275, 278; Daly and, 271
The Real Estate Associates (T.R.E.A.), 201, 205, 208–11, 215, 216, 224; assets of, 223; construction standards of, 220; financial structure of, 218–19; houses by, 226*n*16; incorporation of, 214, 223; installment plan by, 221, 222; sales by, 207; standard plan by, 212–13; stockholders of, 223; suppliers for, 221
The Real Estate Associates Building, 214, 217, 223, 228*n*45; illustration of, 215; photo of, 200

"Things to Come" (Wells), 313
Thomas, George M., 252
324 Perez Road, photo of, 122
330–42 Lexington Street, photo of, 208
Three Bar Ranch, 96
Tie girt, drawing of, 81
Tin roofing, 106
Tocqueville, Alexis de, 45
Toluca Lake Park, 239–40
Toluca Market, 240, 242, 246
Tract houses, 125, 127, 202, 240, 254
Transmission towers, 287; photo of, 286
Travonia mine, 281
T.R.E.A. *See* The Real Estate Associates
Treasury Department, 133, 134, 136, 140; Aleuts and, 136; in Pribilofs, 133, 134, 140
Triad Society, 157, 165–66, 167
True, Allen: art of, 306–7, 308, 312
Tucker, J. W., 204
Tuckerville, 204
Turbine galleries, 308, 312; photo of, 309
Turner, Frederick Jackson, 9; frontier thesis of, 6, 8
Tuttle Manufacturing and Supply Company, 275; photo of, 275
TVA. *See* Tennessee Valley Authority
Twentieth Street, 209
Twenty-first Street, 209; drawing of, 213
230 Montgomery Street, 217; illustration of, 215
2209 Jackson, 205
2315–19 Webster Street, photo of, 210
2373 California Street, photo of, 212
2564 Sacramento Street, photo of, 216

Ugaldea House, 188; house plan for, 187; photo of, 187
Unalaska, 130, 133
Underwood, Gilbert Stanley, 251
Une Cité Industrielle (Garnier), 301
Uniform Building Code, standards by, 127
Union Pacific Railroad, 291, 293; Hoover Dam and, 314*n*1; mining and, 270–71
Unions, miners, 287
U.S. Forest Service, 110*n*5
U.S. Mint, 217, 219
Union Square Theater, 227*n*36
Upper Works, 272, 276, 277; closing of, 274; ruins of, 276 (photo)
Urbanization, 38, 180, 239
Utah and Northern Railroad, 270, 272
Utah Construction Company, Hoover Dam and, 297
Utilities, installation of, 125

Vacant lots, 201–2
Valencia Street, 209, 222
Valve houses, 306
Vance, Rupert, 9
Van Ness, T. C., 202
Van Nuys News, 258*n*3
Vegetable gardens, photo of, 166
Venice Evening Vanguard, 258*n*3
Vernacular architecture, 3–4, 11, 94; diffusion studies and, 5; discovery of, xiii–xiv, 13; westernness of, 14. *See also* Folk architecture
Victorian period, 49, 51, 179
Village and Farm Cottages (Cleaveland and Backus), 71–72
Virginia City, 21, 30
Voght, Eugene, 252
Voll vs. Hollis, 218, 223
Von's Grocery, 246; photo of, 247
Voznesenskii, I. G., 133

W. A. Bechtel Company, Hoover Dam and, 297, 316*n*7
Wade's Opera House, 227*n*36
Wah-to-Yah and the Taos Trail (Garrard), 118
Walker, Albert: drive-in markets and, 249
Walker and Eisen, drive-in markets and, 248
Walker Brothers, silver mining by, 269
Wallerstein, Immanuel: modern world system and, 10
Walnut Grove Chinatown, 160, 162; burning of, 161; school at, 163
Walter, Raymond F.: Hoover Dam and, 298
Walter H. Leimert Company, 240
Wanamaker, John, 231
Wank, Roland, 310
Warm Springs Valley, 271, 276
War of the Copper Kings, 279, 289*n*9
Washington Street, property values on, 243
Washoe smelter, 273, 277, 278; construction of, 276; site plan of, 277
Washoe stack, photo of, 279
Webb, Walter Prescott, 9
Weber, David: provincialism and, 15
Webster, Frank, 252

Webster, H. Sage, 252, 254
West: image of, xiv–xv; as cultural region, 12 (map)
West, Elliott: on Bannack, 35–36; on saloons, 28
West, Robert, 115
West Anaconda Yards (BA&P), photo of, 274
West Colusa mine, 290*n*22
Western Addition, 204, 205, 219, 224
Western Avenue, 241; property values on, 243
Western Federation of Miners, 287
Weyl, Carl Jules, 251
W. H. Abrams and Brothers' Sash and Door Factory, 83
Wheeler Dam, 310
White, John, 38*n*2
White, Richard, 9
White, Theodore, 292, 313
White Caps, 121
White House (Salt Lake City), photo of, 49
Wholey, Bill, 96; bunkhouse by, 106
Wickiups, 23
Wilderness, garden and, 45
Willamette Farmer, 67
Willard Creek, 38*n*2
Willow houses, 96
Wilshire and Harvard Market, photo of, 234
Wilshire at Fourteenth Drive-In Market, photo of, 233
Wilshire Boulevard: photo of, 245; property values on, 243
Wilshire Professional Building, photo of, 245
Wilson, Chris, 14
Wilson, Richard Guy, 15
Winburn, David: on Mormon houses, 43
Winged Figures of the Republic (Hansen), photo of, 311
Withey, Henry, 251
Woestman, Karl, 240
Wood, Robert E.: Sears, Roebuck and, 231
Woollett, William: lithograph by, 319*n*38
Workingmen's Party, 222, 223, 229*n*57
Worster, Donald, 13; on regional history, 9
Wright, Frank Lloyd, 251, 311

Yankee Flat, 39*n*9
Yankee traders, Chinese and, 155–56
Yip, Christopher, 14
Young, Brigham, 58; on beautiful houses, 45, 48; residences of, 47, 49 (photo)
Young, Walker R., 67, 298
Young, Mrs. Walker R., 67
Yturbide, Juan "John," 95
Yuma Valley, flooding in, 293

Zaguan, 116
Zelayeta, Jose, 95
Zimmerman, A. C., 251
Zoning, 244